DAVID BRI

best walks
of the
DRAKENSBERG

IN ASSOCIATION WITH **Getaway**

This edition published in 2003 by Struik Publishers
(a division of New Holland Publishing (South Africa) (Pty) Ltd)

London • Cape Town • Sydney • Auckland

80 McKenzie Street
Cape Town, 8001
South Africa

www.struik.co.za

New Holland Publishing is a member of the Johnnic Publishing Group

First published in 1988
3 5 7 9 10 8 6 4

Second edition published in 1995
3 5 7 9 10 8 6 4

Third edition published in 2003
1 3 5 7 9 10 8 6 4 2

ISBN: 1 86872 780 7

Copyright © 1988, 1995, 2003 in published edition: Struik Publishers
Copyright © 1988, 1995, 2003 in text: David Bristow
Copyright © 2003 in photographs: David Bristow
with exception of the following:
David Rogers: front cover; Karl Beath: pages 182–183;
Cathy Lanz: pages 169, 201 (bottom), 202 (bottom), 203;
Greig Stewart: pages 50, 201 top, 205–207 (all)
CLB/Struik Image Library: page 36

Copyright © 1988, 1995, 2003 in maps: David Bristow
Copyright © 1988, 1995, 2003 in illustrations: Felicity Harris
Copyright © 2003 in illustration, pages 220–221: Tod Collins
Copyright © 2003 in illustrations, pages 224–227: Reg Pearse
(artwork by Muriel Zonneveld)

Publishing Manager: Dominique le Roux
Managing Editor: Lesley Hay-Whitton
Design Director: Janice Evans
Designer: Illana Fridkin
Editor: Amanda Chapman
Maps by Philippa Scott and Anne Westoby
Maps updated by Illana Fridkin
Proofreader: Inge du Plessis
Indexer: Mary Lennox

Reproduction by Hirt & Carter (Cape) Pty Ltd
Printed and bound in Hong Kong by
Sing Cheong Printing Company Limited

All rights reserved. No part of this publication may be reproduced, stored in a retrieval system or transmitted, in any form or by any means, electronic, mechanical, photocopying or otherwise, without the prior written permission of the publishers and copyright holders.

The Publishers invite any comments or suggestions for future editions.
Please write to: The Editor, *Best Walks of the Drakensberg*
Struik Publishers, PO Box 1144, Cape Town 8000

Log on to our photographic website
www.imagesofafrica.co.za for an African experience.

The first version of this book, *Drakensberg Walks*, appeared around the time my first son, Daniel, did. Its companion, *Western Cape Walks*, was conceived and delivered at much the same time as my daughter Isabella. *Best Walks of the Drakensberg* was laboured over while my last born, Ben (2), stayed at home to look after his mom. In the hope that he might use it one day, or perhaps be inspired by it to become a lover of the Drakensberg, this book is dedicated foremost to him. Secondly, it is dedicated to two great, indefatigable mountaineers, father Reg and son Malcolm Pearse. Between them they walked these mountains flat and produced the definitive books on the Berg which inspired their own generations and ones after, including mine, to become true believers.

David Bristow

acknowledgements

One of the most satisfying things about working on a book such as this is the many hikers, mountaineers and conservationists whom I met personally or made contact with. For the checking and updating of my previous book I cajoled a fairly large number of people, and I fear there were times when I might have made a nuisance of myself – but rather that than have you wandering aimlessly round Lesotho.

For this I'd like to thank especially chief conservator for the northern Berg, Rob Faure, and Oscar Mthimkhulu at Royal Natal National Park; Meridy Pfotenhauer of Bergwatch for the Mnweni area; Alan Howell at Monk's Cowl; Raymond Zikhali at Injisuthi; Peter Chadwick and Alfred Sigubudu at Giant's Castle; Eduard Goosen at Lotheni; Steven Richard at Vergelegen; Charl Brummer at Kamberg; Chris Wex and John Crowson at Cobham; and Henry Hibbett at Garden Castle/Bushman's Nek.

Many people also helped me with accommodation, including Brett Dungan (MD of Planet Hotels) at **Cayley Lodge**, Isaac Motlaung at **Witzieshoek Mountain Resort**, Peter Chadwick at **Giant's Castle**, Jonathan Aldous at **Sani Top Chalet**, and Brad Weston and Anton Zunckel at **Bushman's Nek Hotel**. My special thanks to the rock art guides – Absolom Zondo in Didima Gorge, Promise Mncube at Kamberg and Florian Xaba at Cobham.

My own 'grand traverse' of the high Berg (I made it from Witzieshoek to Sani Top before the winter blizzards drove me down) was made possible by the people who helped with food drops: the very helpful people at Central Drakensberg Information based at Thokoziswa, especially Anna Dlujoleck; and at the Sani Saunter information office Lungi Mtolo for her impressive efficiency; again Meridy Pfotenhauer at Mnweni, as well as guides Caiphus Mthabela and Mkhonjiswa Mtolo; at Cathedral Peak Hotel, general manager John Turner, and guide Wiseman Mdluli who hauled our supplies up Organ Pipes Pass; and, at Injisuthi, Klaus Piprek and two Ezemvelo KwaZulu-Natal Wildlife (EKZNW) rangers for going the extra 20 miles, carrying our food up Leslie's Pass when the appointed guides chickened out – for this I cannot thank them enough. And Basotho guide Adolf and his ponies Cheeva and Toby who helped us lug our gear from Sani Top to Giant's Pass.

For general help and information Tom Wimber of White Cottage Books in Underberg; Underberg vet Tod Collins for the use of his excellent cross-section of the southern Berg, as well as information on peak names and details of the passes; for the sketch diagram of the northern Berg, Malcolm Pearse and Muriel Zonneveld; Midlands farmer Greig Stewart for information especially on the passes; and the many hikers over the years who have offered suggestions or corrections. Adrian Bailey with whom I shared a tent, good whisky and many fine moments on our 'grand traverse'. Photographers are good people to hike with, because they think more than they talk. My assistant at *Getaway*, Margy Beves-Gibson, who beat my wayward prose into better shape. And at Struik Publishers I have to thank the real workers: Dominique le Roux, Lesley Hay-Whitton, Illana Fridkin and Amanda Chapman.

And, finally, to all the men and women of EKZNW, as well as everyone else who helps to conserve uKhahlamba-Drakensberg – we salute you.

contents

INTRODUCTION	8
NATURAL HISTORY	18
ROCK ART	30
DRAKENSBERG MAP	34
THE AMPHITHEATRE (AM)	36
Mont-aux-Sources via the Chain Ladders (AM1)	38
Thukela Gorge (AM2)	40
Gudu Bush and Falls (AM3)	42
Plowman's Kop and spa pools (AM4)	43
Devil's Hoek Valley (AM5)	44
Vemvaan Valley (AM6)	46
Sigubudu Ridge to Surprise Ridge (AM7)	46
Surprise Ridge and Cannibal Cave (AM8)	48
Lion Buttress (AM9)	57
Fairy Glen (AM10)	59
The Grotto (AM11)	60
Rugged Glen to Mahai (AM12)	61
MNWENI (MN)	63
Mnweni Pass (MN1)	65
Rockeries Pass (MN2)	68
Waterfall Cave and Ntonjelana Pass (MN3)	70
Fangs Pass (MN4)	72
Icidi Pass (MN5)	73
Ifidi Pass (MN6)	75
Contour Path: Mnweni to Cathedral (MN7)	76
CATHEDRAL PEAK (CP)	79
Cathedral Peak (CP1)	82
Mlambonja Pass to Twins Cave (CP2)	84
Mlambonja Valley (CP3)	86
Oqalweni Valley Walk (CP4)	87
Oqalweni Circuit (CP5)	88
Sherman's Cave and Ganapu Ridge (CP6)	90

Rainbow Gorge (CP7)	91
Masongwana Gorge (CP8)	92
Didima Gorge (CP9)	93
Mushroom Rock and Tarn Hill (CP10)	95
Tryme Hill and waterfalls (CP11)	96
Tseketseke Hut (CP12)	97
Blue Pool and Nyosi Grotto (CP13)	98
Two Passes (CP14)	99
Contour Path: Cathedral Peak to Didima Valley (CP15)	102

MONK'S COWL/NKOSANA (MC) — **104**

Fern Forest (MC1)	107
Barry's Grave and Grotto (MC2)	108
Steilberg and Van Damm's Cascade (MC3)	109
Stable Cave (MC4)	110
The Sphinx and Crystal Falls (MC5)	111
Zulu Cave (MC6)	113
Monk's Cowl Cave (MC7)	114
Valley of Pools (MC8)	116
Champagne Castle via Gray's Pass (MC9)	117
Champagne Castle via Ship's Prow Pass (MC10)	120
Contour Path: Monk's Cowl to upper Didima Valley (MC11)	130

INJISUTHI (IN) — **134**

Van Heynigen's Pass to View Site (IN1)	137
Wonder Valley Cave (IN2)	138
Poacher's Stream (IN3)	138
Battle Cave (IN4)	140
Lower Injisuthi Cave (IN5)	141
Grindstone Caves (IN6)	142
Grindstone Caves and Marble Baths (IN7)	143
Contour Path to Monk's Cowl (IN8)	145
Contour Path: Centenary to Bannerman Hut (IN9)	146
Tree Fern Cave (IN10)	148
Leslie's Pass (IN11)	149

GIANT'S CASTLE (GC) — **152**

Main Caves (GC1)	154
Forest and River Walk (GC2)	155
Grysbok Bush (GC3)	157
Meander Hut (GC4)	158
Giant's Hut (GC5)	159
Bannerman Hut (GC6)	160

Two Huts via Contour Path (GC7)	162
Lotheni via Contour Path (GC8)	163
Bannerman Pass (GC9)	165
Langalibalele Pass (GC10)	166
Giant's Pass (GC11)	167

MKHOMAZI (MK) — 169

Contour Path: Lotheni to Sani Pass (MK1)	172
Game Pass Shelter (MK2)	175
Cypress Cave and Sinclair's Shelter (MK3)	176
McKenzie's Cave (MK4)	185
Yellowwood Cave (MK5)	186
Ash Cave (MK6)	187
Hlathimba Pass and Redi Peak (MK7)	188
Ngaqamadola Passes (MK8)	189
Mkhomazi–Nhlangeni Pass (MK9)	191
Sani Pass	192

MZIMKHULU (MZ) — 193

Giant's Cup Trail (MZ1)	195
Gxalingenwa River Trail (MZ2)	199
Ngenwa River round-trip (MZ3)	200
Pholela Cave and Amakehla Pass (MZ4)	209
The Hike of Many Caves (MZ5)	211
The Lake District (MZ6)	212
Mzimkhulu Pass (MZ7)	213
Sleeping Beauty Cave (MZ8)	214
Mashai Pass and Rhino Peak (MZ9)	215
Bushman's Cave and Pass (MZ10)	216
Sehlaba Thebe Caves Traverse (MZ11)	218

THE HIKING PASSES	220
THE HIGHEST PEAKS/'KULUS'	228
HELPFUL WORDS	230
USEFUL CONTACTS	231
BOOK LIST AND EXTRA READING	235
INDEX	237

introduction

'Go out alone on the hills and listen.
You will hear much . . . Alone amidst nature,
a man learns to be one with all and all with one.'

I first read these words by the great mountaineer Frank Smythe in *A Camera in Quathalmaba*, Malcolm Pearse's classic photographic work – to my mind the best photographic book yet published in this country (the 'Ansel Adams' of South Africa if you prefer). They gripped my attention, because they expressed exactly why I became a mountaineer, a concept I found so hard to explain to others. It's why I still love to climb and roam the hills, mostly on my own – to listen. Sometimes I believe it is the voice of God that comes to me on the wind or in a gale; yet I am not otherwise a religious person.

The mountains are my church, nature my religion and, although I have tramped up and over mountains from the bottom of South America to the Himalayas, the Drakensberg remains the cathedral I most cherish. A lot of the appeal lies in the almost uncountable array of the rock paintings to be found here, the deeply spiritual message these 'images of power' convey, as well as the legacy of the Bushmen that I can only dream of, and mourn.

The Drakensberg is a wild and wonderful place, sometimes brilliant in colour and form and utterly beguiling; at other times hard, harsh and unforgiving. From the time I first laid eyes on the tall spires and crumbling towers of the upper ramparts they have reminded me of Europe's sublime Gothic churches, and patently not me alone for names like Cathedral Peak, Mbundini Abbey, the Bell, Organ Pipes, Monk's Cowl, Twelve Apostles and similar names are testimony to their lofty character.

From Mount Olympus to Everest, Kilimanjaro to Denali, Mount Kalais to Fujiyama, great mountains have long been associated with major religions; of 'getting closer to one's god'. The Drakensberg is no exception, except here it is a more ancient religion – the animistic beliefs of hunter-gatherers, as depicted by their shamans while in induced trances and painted on the walls of innumerable caves and overhangs. These rock art images have only recently been appreciated to have a deeply spiritual nature: they have been variously called the world's greatest outdoor church, and the world's finest outdoor art collection. What a detailed study of the many cave paintings reveals, whatever you might make of their meaning, is just how fine the artwork is. But more of this in a following chapter (see page 30).

No-one who has hiked in the Berg, or scaled its awesome precipices, can fail to be moved by these ancient mountains. The mists that swirl around massive spires, storm clouds which mass over the high buttresses and lightning which slams into the basalt cliffs, or the burst of sunlight that paints the crags and cloud bottoms with soft colours, mountain birds which soar effortlessly across the intimidating faces, or a blush of colour where an orchid or everlasting bursts through snow: every image, every moment, is super-charged, leaving an indelible impression in our minds, and draws us back forever. Even old hikers who are no longer able to tackle the daunting passes say they relive them clearly in their mind's eye.

THEN & NOW

Since I produced the first version of this book, *Drakensberg Walks*, in 1988, much has changed there. True, much has remained the same: the wild, windswept summit ridges and vales, the secret Little Berg gorges, streams and forests, although the Escarpment itself is retreating at a rate of about one centimetre every decade. The Bushman paintings that are such a quintessential part of the Berg have changed little (although in some cases not little enough) in the intervening decade and a half.

Also little changed is the lifestyle of the hardy Basotho herders who brave fearful summer storms and freezing winter blizzards as they tend their flocks of sheep, herds of cattle and semi-wild horses. Surprising indeed in our fast-changing world. And the significance of this for the survival of another 'tribe' of hardy 'mountaineers' is perhaps imperceptible to the casual hiker here, but cannot be overstated.

In *Barrier of Spears* Reg Pearse recounts the episode of capturing in 1961 the first photographs in Africa of the lammergeier. (By then it had been captured on film only twice before, in the Himalayas in 1942 and Spain in 1959.) It's a wonderful story, which I will not recount other than to say that, but for one brief sighting, no-one knew if any still survived. It took three years and careful detective work to locate a nest in the Mokhotlong region.

In the 1970s it was estimated there were some 200 breeding pairs remaining in southern Africa (Lesotho). In 1987 I saw the lammergeier just three times during a three-month stay in the Berg. Then two feeding stations were started, one in Giant's Castle and another at Witzieshoek, and I'm convinced this has made all the difference. During the high traverse which I undertook in autumn 2002, I saw them virtually every day for two months.

The bearded vulture (*Gypaetus barbatus*), or lammergeier (from the German words for lamb and vulture), is neither a vulture nor a lamb catcher. It's an evolutionary cross between the eagles and vultures, a most majestic creature that is perhaps the definitive mountain dweller (for it is a supremely adapted high-altitude creature), but it has been heavily persecuted. *Gypaetus* loves bone marrow: it is such a specialist feeder that without bones it cannot survive. And for this it needs carcasses left long enough for only the bones to remain. These conditions are found only where traditional pastoralists remain in mountain areas, and the only place in southern Africa where these occur is Lesotho. In pre-industrial times the lammergeier was found from the Cape Peninsula, up the mountains of East Africa to Ethiopia and Morocco, then from Spain, right across Europe to the Himalayas and the higher ranges of China. Today it is found only in beleaguered colonies scattered along its former range.

A major change in the area is that, where before it was a patchwork of private land, wilderness areas, forestry reserves, and nature and game reserves, today nearly the entire KwaZulu-Natal Drakensberg is contained within the uKhahlamba-Drakensberg Park and all controlled by the provincial parks board (Ezemvelo KwaZulu-Natal Wildlife, which I think we can get away with calling EKZNW). Centralised conservation has also allowed for it to be declared a World Heritage Site – one of only 23 such sites in the world that combine great natural beauty and cultural significance. The cultural component is due to the 230 000 hectares of protected area containing some 40 000 Bushman painted images in about 500 known locations within the park.

The next 'great leap forward' in land status will be the creation of the Drakensberg-Maloti Transfrontier Conservation Area (these areas are also known as 'peace parks'). It's a grand plan, with no clearer focus than raising lots of foreign aid and investment to improve the region's infrastructure for tourism development and poverty relief (access roads, aerial cableways up the Berg, fancy hotels on the summit plateau, ski lodges and the like – brace yourself for the era of globalised tourism).

Within the park, camping regulations have changed somewhat: whereas previously you could walk and camp anywhere in accordance with the rules of wilderness areas, now you cannot. For example, in the Cathedral area, there are around 40 designated camp sites and 15 caves, which have to be booked and paid for, as well as two huts (Old Lookout and Tseketseke). In Royal Natal National Park (which is not, in fact, a national park) you cannot camp at all except in the main Mahai caravan/camp site. In Giant's Castle area (the former game reserve) you can camp anywhere beyond a five-hour hike from Giant's Camp. You may not camp near the two huts, which have to be booked. You can also book Spare Rib Cave and the two huts on the Contour Path.

All huts and caves must be booked through the EKZNW head office in Pietermaritzburg (see page 231), while camp sites can be booked when you enter a hiking area. Summit caves are open to all comers including Basotho herders, dagga smugglers, stock-theft patrols and ice rats.

Also remember, if you are going on an overnight hike, you *must* complete the **mountain register**. This is as important as a pilot filing a flight plan. In the event of misfortune, the register should provide the necessary information to effect a rescue. Where there is no register (for example, if you set off from Sani Top which has no official hiking control), at least leave details of your group, colour of tents and hiking itinerary at the lodge.

KITTING UP

A final change that needs to be noted is the change in **hiking and camping equipment** over the years. In the 1980s I carried a state-of-the-art Backpacker Kestrel tent (which I still use on occasion), wore Lubbe Trailbuster car-tyre soled kudu-skin boots, hiked in jeans and T-shirts, over which I piled various cotton or woollen shirts and jerseys, and whatever rain coat I had at the time. Then I bought my first Gore-Tex jacket, in the days when the South African rand was worth two pounds.

But I sweat a lot and on the summit I used to freeze in cold weather, wondering how other people coped. It was around this time I discovered the pleasure of, and necessity for, a proper expedition down sleeping bag and was able to afford one. Since then, just about everything has changed, even the down sleeping bags which are now made locally, with their modern shower-proof and non-rip materials.

If you're going to hike in the Berg, and until you know the area so well you know where every cave is located, you will need a **tent**. The less said about tents used in days gone by the better (up Everest with canvas and wooden poles!). Lightweight dome tents were made by North Face (USA) and Mountain Dome (UK), using aluminium poles and rip-stop nylon fly sheets. After that came the local Backpacker Kestrel, which was lighter than any of the others, but still the basic A-shape.

I now own four tents, but the ones I use most are the two Sunseeker Iso Domes with Kevlar poles, one two-man and the other three-man. For high quality value-for-money, you will struggle to find better tents to withstand the most savage storm.

A fact that took around two decades to sink into my stubborn head (stubbornness in a mountaineer is a virtue) was that cotton sucks. Literally – it absorbs sweat and rain, and in cold conditions this can be a killer or at least make you very miserable.

Modern hiking **clothing** is made from such high-tech creations as Gore-Tex (imported) or Ventex (locally manufactured) outer rain-proof fabrics, Polartec and Polarfleece insulating materials and the khaki-type K-Way Release 2000 (a Cape Union Mart patent) hiking garments. What all these materials have in common is that they wick moisture from the inside out. That means they keep you relatively dry ('relatively' being the crucial term) and warm. Everything I wear for hiking these days, barring underpants and socks, is made from these materials, and I only wish I could have discovered – or afforded – them earlier.

Avoid cotton **socks**. Woollen socks have never really been bettered; not until now that is. I've usually used nylon inners, such as tennis socks, rather than thin little office socks. For outers I used woollen socks for decades, but am now a true convert to modern combination socks. They are thick, elasticised and don't fluff up in lumps and then pull off in chunks like so many other kinds of hiking socks. There are shortish, relatively thin ones that can be used with light boots or trainers, or as inner socks if your proper hiking boots allow. Falke TK2 hiking or slightly thicker TK4 trekking socks are a marvel of modern sock technology. They are a combination of polypropylene and wool, with padded soles, negligible toe seams and shaped left and right socks.

Two kinds of outer socks from Cape Mohair in Plettenberg Bay that match the Falke socks are a mohair-synthetic fibre mix called Trailmaster or Skimaster and the K-Way Snow Peak (polypropylene, wool and lycra mix). Wearing a combination of these socks is not quite like walking on clouds, but it's the closest you'll get.

Some people have a fetish for **boots**. I'm one of them and have a mean collection. I also have a leather fetish: I once tried artificial-fabric boots, but now use them only for mountain biking or as cross-trainers. Over the years I've gone from 'Wuppertals' (the car-tyre kind David Kramer wears), to Stellenbosch-made Lubbe Trailbusters (they were great in the 80s, got awkward and banana-shaped in the 90s, but are again among the best medium-priced boots available), then to some serious Austrian Dachsteins for high altitude climbing, came a bit down to earth with a pair of fabulous M Gordon & Sons thin, double-layered boots, and now swear by my expensive Italian La Sportiva Tibets. With each pair the price of course went up (nowadays the Dachsteins would set you back plenty). La Sportivas combine the strength of a proper mountaineering boot with the lightness and slipper-like comfort (no blisters, ever) of a synthetic boot. But they are not cheap (about R1 500 at the time of writing).

For people who prefer the synthetic look (or feel), Hi-tec is the yardstick and has various models from which to choose and there's a factory shop in Durban that's worth a visit.

Sleeping bags come with all manner of inner and outer characteristics. Basically though there are just two types: down and hollowfibre (or similar synthetic filling). Down will keep you warmer, but synthetic fillings will retain some measure of warmth when wet, which down will not. For summer hiking it matters little, but one that zips open all the way is a boon. You can double up in winter by adding a Polartec inner sheet, but if you're going to the top of the Berg in winter nothing short of a full down expedition bag will do. Just remember, when a bag stipulates that it is rated to 0 or −10°C, it does not mean you will be warm and cosy at that temperature, just that you will survive. That's a fairly basic and important difference. Of course a down expedition bag will cost you plenty, but that's just the way it is.

While sleeping bags have changed little since Scott went walkabout in the Antarctic, not so **backpacks**. My first pack was a canvas Bergens with leather hip belt and steel A-frame. For a long time I preferred an external-frame pack, so I could attach tents, sleeping bags and the like on the outside. However, in recent years internal-frame packs have become so advanced you should not consider anything else. Backpacker is the local hero in this field, and I have two. However, each person's shape is unique and fitting a pack is like fitting a boot: you have to get the one that fits you best. Always try it with a lot of weight, and walk around a bit with it on. Packs these days are quite complex and can be adjusted to any size person – ask to see how, and try adjusting all the straps at various settings till you find the one that feels just right. After five days on the trot lugging 20 kilograms, you'll be glad you did.

In the beginning (about 20 years ago that is) there was only one good local manufacturer, mainly of tents and packs. Today there are a number of really world-class local acts, producing or importing just about everything you need for hiking. Cape Union Mart carries stocks of nearly all types of clothing and equipment, local and some imported, although most of its clothing ranges are made in South Africa. Cape Storm makes quality mountaineering clothes and sleeping bags, and First Ascent has a smaller but equally good range. And Backpacker is still equipping the next generation of Everest hopefuls and Drakensberg faithfuls. So buy local; you can hardly afford not to any more.

HIKING GRADES

I've never been big on **grading hikes**, although some people seem determined to make a science of the subject. The length and steepness of a path are only two of several factors that apply, some others being how strong and fit you are, the weather, your hiking group and the pace you set, how often you stop, the weight of your pack, comfort of your boots and, believe it or not, your state of mind. A, B, C ... are rock climbing grades bestowed by the climbing community. A to D are non-technical. The letters correspond to a parallel numeric system, where E=14, 15 and 16, F=17, 18 and 19 and so on.

I am firmly against the need to measure and quantify everything; I like to go with the flow, let my mind wander, taking pleasure as I go in discovering new things, and so not become frantic to have the whole experience packaged, labelled and measured out in centimetres and grams before I set off. But then I'm just like that – I believe if you're not lost at least

SIMPLE GRADING SYSTEM

Easy: a short hike, with no very long or steep sections, from two to four hours' duration and two to 10 kilometres long (but remember these are mountains, even the 'foothills');
Moderate: this may be short and sharp, or longer than 10 kilometres, but never strenuous;
Strenuous: this is usually a full day's outing, but has no sustained ascents. Generally, a hike of this grade would be between 14 and 20 kilometres;
Severe: this would be a fairly long and very steep, or very long and fairly steep, hike. There will almost certainly be some sustained ascending and descending in one day, or a two- or three-day hike into the Little Berg (say, up Didima Gorge);
Extreme: this will invariably entail a slog up one of the passes to the top of the Escarpment. Not all trips to the summit are equal, but very few can be done in one day from the starting point except by the mentally challenged.

some of the time you can't be having fun. All distances and durations given are for a return trip, or a round-trip, but either way from start to finish. A general rule-of-thumb to calculate hiking speed is that a moderately fit person, walking on not-too-steep a path and carrying a reasonably loaded pack will cover around three kilometres in an hour. Make that two kilometres per hour for climbing the Little Berg, and just one kilometre per hour when tackling a pass to the top (when your pack will also be heavier). This does not take into account any stops.

FINDING YOUR WAY

The scope of this guide is limited to the main KwaZulu-Natal Escarpment, from the Amphitheatre in the north to Bushman's Nek and Sehlaba Thebe in the south. With one exception, the Giant's Cup Hiking Trail, all the walks described are my own creation. I have tried to include all the popular walks and overnight hikes, as well as some challenging options that are not obvious or commonly walked. The thing is, you can walk wherever you choose, and are not restricted to my given paths.

I cannot pretend to know the Drakensberg as well as some people for whom these mountains are their hiking backyard; therefore it's inevitable that there will be omissions. Over the years numerous people have corresponded with me, offering corrections and suggestions, and I thank them for this. If you have any information that might improve a future edition of the book, please contact me through the publisher.

When I first started hiking in the Berg I used the sketch **maps** found in various books of the time. In the mid-1970s Peter Slingsby produced his now-famous set of three double-sided maps to the northern, central and southern Berg (I still have two copies of each). One major omission on these maps is that they give virtually no detail of the Lesotho side of the watershed. But as Peter told me, 'we weren't very friendly with Lesotho back then'. Another drawback is that the location of caves was often a little arbitrary: in the Berg everything is (as my hiking partner Adrian would say) 'Very Big' – a few extra contours on the map can add an hour or two to your hike. These maps are like gold (since they are no longer in print), and represent a monumental cartographical effort.

However, at the time of writing this book EKZNW was preparing a **new set of maps** for the uKhahlamba-Drakensberg Park area, including up to 50 per cent of the map area devoted to the 'other side' of the watershed. This is incredibly useful for anyone hiking on the summit where paths are usually vague or non-existent, and for the increasingly popular pastime of doing a traverse along the top of the Berg. These will undoubtedly become the new standard hiking references.

One thing about them that needs pointing out though is that they show only those caves that are now officially sanctioned for overnighting (as well as those caves, with rock art, that are protected and can be visited only with a guide). This is a very small percentage of the total, but it is perhaps a necessary measure for restricting damage to the invaluable rock art of the area. On the other hand, it excludes information that could be useful in an emergency. There's always a chance that you could 're-discover' a cave!

Unfortunately not all the new maps were available before my deadline for this book, so I could not make reference to them all. Maybe in the next edition. One thing that I need to say about them, though, is how very, very fine they are. If Slingsby's maps elevated hiking maps to new heights, the new generation of EKZNW maps 1 to 6 represents another quantum leap in quality and information. Unfortunately they have not been printed on coated paper and so will have a limited life span. However, they do have a **global positioning system** (GPS) grid superimposed on the 1 km by 1 km (2 cm x 2 cm) topographical grid, as well as notes on how to use a GPS.

On hearing that I was preparing a new version of this book, a number of hikers asked if I was going to hike with a global positioning system (GPS), and give location points for places such as peaks, passes and caves. Originally I had planned to and, although I did hike with a GPS, after careful thought I have decided not to give the readings. The reasons for this are complex, but I will try to justify them in terms of my own wilderness ethics. I believe part of the hiking experience should be about finding your way, and yourself, in the wilderness. The uKhahlamba-Drakensberg Park, and especially the summit, is one of our last remaining true hiking wildernesses. The GPS is a very sophisticated navigational instrument, triangulating off a number of satellites to give you your position (and time, date, altitude and more) to within a few square metres. I would hate to see hikers walking through the mountains, GPSs in hand, watching their route being plotted on a screen between way points instead of looking at and interpreting the landscape through their own instincts and their map.

I have no problem with hikers using GPSs, but they should find the places themselves and then plot the position, on a map, for future use. But I'm just an old-fashioned guy.

Similarly with **cellphones**, to which I have an old-fashioned attitude. I think in the event of an emergency they are wonderful tools, but one person's emergency is another person's phoning to wish a friend 'happy birthday'. I think if I were hiking in the Berg, and sleeping in a cave, and I heard someone's cellphone ringing, I would be sorely tempted to throw the thing over the Escarpment. When, oh when, will cellphone users realise they can *switch the thing off* and look at or listen to messages in private? And, if you have to make a call while hiking, slink off somewhere where no-one else can hear you. There is reception along the summit in most places where you have a long line of sight towards the towns on the N3 freeway, or to most hotels. However, it seems that signals for MTN and Vodacom alternate every 10 or so kilometres (Cell C was not operational at the time of my field work).

ABBREVIATIONS

KZN: KwaZulu-Natal
EKZNW: Ezemvelo KwaZulu-Natal Wildlife (provincial park authority)
RNNP: Royal Natal National Park
U-D Park: uKhahlamba-Drakensberg Park
MCSA: Mountain Club of South Africa
GPS: global positioning system
mya: million years ago

PLACE NAMES

At the time *Drakensberg Walks* was being researched in 1987, there was a move to change the anglicised spelling of Zulu place names to a more correct Zulu spelling: Tugela became Thukela; Injasuti became eNjesuthi (I see the latest spelling for the old 'Injasuti' is Injisuthi!) and so on. I tended to change some, but to retain the old spellings of the most familiar places. However, I'm sure most people will agree that it's now high time to throw out the old colonial ways and use only the corrected spellings for all place names – Zulu for Zulu names and the same for Sotho, Afrikaans and English names. I have done exactly that in this edition, but there might appear to be some contradictions where a place's name retains an old spelling, such as 'Umkomaas cottage' and 'Mkhomazi River'.

TRAIL FARE

I remember the first time I went hiking with real mountaineers. I took a length of boerewors and raw potatoes for supper. Imagine my horror when I discovered no fire was allowed and that each member of the group had his or her own pocket stove, one-person pot and even powdered food. Over the years I have refined my own hiking menu, and will give an idea of what I consider to be the full needs for a long hike. The over-riding principle, however, is that you carry light and walk easy. People have their own dietary requirements and preferences, but I suspect you'd go a long way to improve on this.

I'm not big on muesli for **breakfast** on short hikes, because then you usually need milk and sugar and it takes more kilojoules to chew the stuff than you gain from it. For hikes of no more than three days, I take pre-cut whole-grain bread and cheese. Together with coffee or hot chocolate, that's breakfast. On longer hikes I've re-discovered my taste for oats, in this case instant oats – simple to prepare and available in five flavours so you don't need sugar.

For this and drinks I carry a small plastic bottle in which to make powdered milk: pour in water, toss in the equivalent of a few tablespoons of milk powder, give it a good shake and you've got milk for a night and a morning.

In recent times I've simplified my **lunch** menu considerably. It used to be cucumber, salami, cheese wedges, Provita and often a fresh onion and maybe a tomato. These days it's biltong and chocolate. Add to this a small packet of peanuts and raisins and you have a scrumptious, high-calorie meal (the peanuts and raisins are by far the most calorie-packed food of all).

Dinner used to tax me the most, and other hikers I'm sure, and I experimented with every kind of pasta and sauce and tinned thing I could think of. Now simplicity is the key: one packet of two-minute noodles a person, toss in the spice packet supplied and add a few slices of chopped-up salami (or a small tin of tuna or pickled fish) for a dose of high-impact low-weight energy.

Added benefits of this menu are that it creates a minimum of mess to clean, and you use very little cooking fuel. One small 'pocket rocket' type of stove with one gas cylinder can last two people up to four or five days, including making four hot drinks a day.

Add a few tasty items for **sundowners** or **snacks** and you've got all you need for light but tasty hiking fare. I go for French pork pâté (which is available quite widely in small, easy-to-open tins), French cheese blocks in four flavours, on Provitas, and whisky to toast the setting sun. Or one 250- or 500-millilitre box of red wine (from Woolworths or Pick 'n Pay) a day on shorter hikes. You can be even more adventurous, with various pâtés and meat spreads, tins of smoked oysters, exotic cheeses, imported chocolates – whatever you fancy. Just keep it small, tasty and light.

Try to decant everything you've got into zip-lock plastic bags, small plastic jars (I keep a load of old plastic peanut butter jars for hiking) or plastic containers.

For long hikes where you have to carry extra water, a two-litre plastic cold drink bottle works very well. All drinks not bought in boxes should be decanted into aluminium or plastic bottles (for example, whisky in a 500-millilitre plastic bottle does the trick nicely). And remember, you are not allowed to light fires anywhere in the uKhahlamba-Drakensberg Park.

DOS & DON'TS

I was brought up in the old school of **mountaineering ethics** and, add to this my academic grounding in things environmental, I have a strong ecological bias. Not only do I not leave anything behind, but I spend a lot of time picking up other hikers' sweet wrappers and worse.

When it comes to **washing**, try not to let any soap, shampoo or other detergent enter a natural water body. Mountain streams and vleis have extremely sensitive ecosystems and the inflow of any strong nutrient or pollution can do untold, albeit short-term, harm. Rather wash and rinse off on the ground alongside the water so the detergent is filtered out.

For me, one of the pleasures of going to the **toilet** in the wilds is the view. I find two rocks which make a corner and then I have a comfortable seat (some people can squat, but I can't; also, finding a natural seat allows you just to pull your trousers down, not right off!). Some people advocate carrying a trowel and burying everything; others advocate burning the paper only. What I do is scrape out a hollow and bury my deposit with soil or a small rock, and burn the toilet paper. The secret here is not to roll or bunch up the paper, but concertina it, so that it burns easily. And don't forget the view.

GRAND EXPECTATIONS

The appendices contain some tables that you might enjoy and find useful – places to stay and contacts, good references, the highest peaks of the Drakensberg, and some useful Zulu and Sotho phrases to help you get around.

But the part of this new book that I like most is the passes of the High Berg from Mont-aux-Sources to Bushman's Nek. They are presented in three side elevations of the entire KZN Drakensberg, south to north (or left to right as you look at them), with brief descriptions. These are meant as tempting bait, to catch your interest and then reel you in slowly, so that you start contemplating your own 'grand traverse' – whether it's a five-day round-trip or the full expedition (like Tom Wimber's: he walked from Mont-aux-Sources to Xalanga Peak in the north-eastern Eastern Cape – an amazing 549 kilometres as opposed to the more or less 270-odd of the 'standard' KZN traverse).

Hiking in the Berg is about the freedom of a wilderness experience, not about 'how much' or 'how far'. Just go out there and enjoy the mountains like a Bushman. Then you'll discover why the Drakensberg is a cathedral of the senses.

KEY TO COLOUR MAPS
- Park boundaries
- Roads – minor and major
- Rivers with falls
- Contour lines (not to scale)
- Hiking path with junction – minor and major
- •2212 Peak beacons and spot heights
- Caves
- Hotel and entry point (permit required)
- Camp site and caravan park
- Ezemvelo KwaZulu-Natal Wildlife
- Hut
- Natural forest
- Plantation
- Game fence

KEY TO BLACK AND WHITE MAPS
- – – – Hiking route
- ——— Major road
- – – ··· Possible detour/other hike
- ☒ Visitors' Centre/Start
- • 3 299 Mountain peak altitude
- Cave
- Chain ladder
- Bridge
- Forested area
- Plantation
- Waterfall
- Dam
- Game fence
- Hotel
- Ezemvelo KwaZulu-Natal Wildlife
- Official camp site
- Unofficial camp site – NO FIRES
- Caravan park
- Hut

natural history

HISTORICAL GEOLOGY AND TOPOGRAPHY

The geological composition of the Drakensberg is fairly simple to comprehend – it's the vast time scale that's difficult to grasp. The Escarpment and high peaks are the capping atop numerous horizontal layers of the Karoo Supergroup of rocks which cover some two-thirds of South Africa, much like the icing on a tiered wedding cake. (Another geological point you need to understand, and which geologists are slow to point out, is that the period when a layer of minerals was deposited will not be the same as the one when a certain landform, comprising those sediments, was formed.)

The Karoo Period began about 250 million years ago (the earth is about four and a half billion years old) when the present continents of Africa, South America, Australia and Antarctica, as well as Madagascar and parts of the Middle East and India formed one supercontinent that has been named Gondwanaland.

Around this time present-day southern Africa was covered by a vast sheet of ice. When this continental glacier melted, it left behind a sludge of eroded material which solidified into the Dwyka Group lying in a basin that stretched from the south-western Cape to Mpumalanga and into Zimbabwe. This is the oldest and deepest layer of the Karoo Supergroup. The basin started off as an immense inland sea, and, as it filled up with further deposits and dried, the Ecca Group, containing vast forests of primitive trees, was laid down as mainly shales (these are the deposits which now yield our coal). Then came the Beaufort Group, largest and deepest of all, comprising mudstones, sandstones and shales. Over the tens of millions years of the Beaufort Period conditions varied greatly but that era was characterised by swampy landscapes where the first amphibians crawled out of the Triassic seas to colonise the emerging land masses. They in turn evolved into mammal-like reptiles and later the earliest mammals.

After about 30 million years of watery conditions the Karoo Basin filled up, with sediments which in time became rocks, and dried out, lakes becoming swamps and dry plains and then the wind-swept deserts of the Stormberg Group. It is the rocks of the Stormberg Group that make up the Drakensberg. The first, or lowest, layer is the Molteno Beds comprising mainly blue-grey sandstones which form ledges and terraces at the base of the Little Berg. Plant fossils are abundant, but no animal remains have been found. The Red Beds form the second layer, with their typical red to purple mudstones and shales, which form the steep grassy slopes of the mid-Little Berg. These rocks are seldom exposed in today's landscape, but the increased aridity which caused their deposition is thought to have brought about the slow demise of the mammal-like reptiles of the Karoo dynasty (not to be confused with the dinosaurs of the later Jurassic Period). Large, dinosaur-type fossils are abundant in this layer. The large-grained, yellowish Cave Sandstone (or Clarens) layer appears to be largely aeolian (wind deposited). These rocks are extremely soft and erosive, which accounts for the cliffs that define the Little Berg, and the many caves and overhangs found in this very visible band of rock. Fossils are rare, mainly reptiles and fish. Towards the end of the Cave Sandstone time, Gondwanaland began to heave and buckle and split apart. What followed was a long

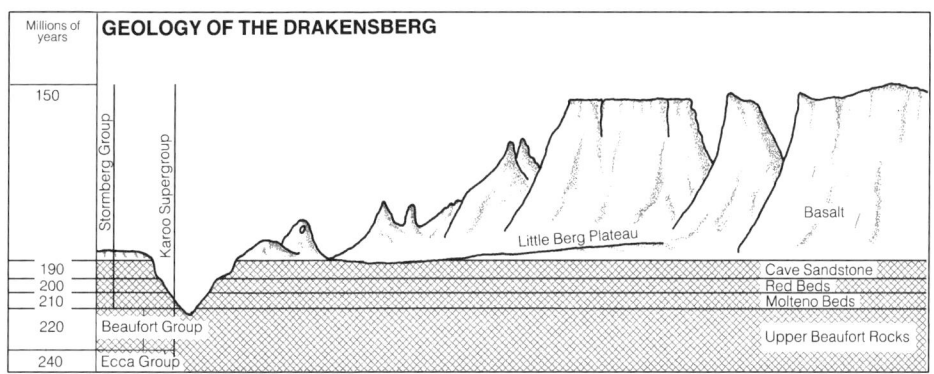

period of fireworks: about 190 million years ago the land opened in huge cracks and fiery lava poured out to cover most of what today is KwaZulu-Natal, Lesotho and the Free State. When solidified they formed the relatively soft, aerated basalt 'icing' on our mountain cake. With the break-up of Gondwanaland, continental uplifting and the climatic influence of the sea initiated a cycle of erosion which continues today.

What we see from below as the Drakensberg Mountains is really a giant step that is being continuously worn back by water and gravity. It is a mountain range that has no 'other side'; beyond our line of vision lies the mountain stronghold of Lesotho, the country which reputedly has the highest low point in the world.

When the last of the basalt covering has been chiselled away (at a rate of about one centimetre a decade) the soft sandstones and shales will soon be planed away by river erosion. During this time the climate will change, and so will the plants and animals. Then the area will likely look much as it did before the Stormberg period began – but just what creatures will inhabit the area is beyond our ken.

CLIMATE

Climate is the average weather pattern of a place recorded for several decades. Weather, on the other hand, which is the daily state of the atmosphere, is what most concerns hikers. We could say the Berg is in a summer rainfall area, but for a hiker this would be pretty misleading, if true. Unlike much of South Africa with its very mild climate, the Berg has four distinct seasons: summers are warm and experience fearsome thunderstorms, and possibly snow; autumns are cool, and are characterised by lots of low cloud and heavy mist above – and probably some snow; winters are cold, windy, dry, and you can expect snow – and gales; springs experience all of the above. An important factor determining the weather is synoptic conditions, or the relative positions of high- and low-pressure cells across the sub-continent, and the winds they produce. During summer there is usually a low-pressure system over the interior, with a high-pressure cell over the Indian Ocean. Wind tends to flow from high to low pressure, in this case bringing with it lots of rain from the moisture picked up over the warm sea. As this moist air reaches the Drakensberg it rises, cools and condenses to form dramatic storm clouds in the afternoon.

During winter this pattern is reversed: there is a high-pressure system over the interior, while low-pressure cells (cold fronts, or temperate cyclones) move across the country from the south-west. We've become quite familiar with these from television weather broadcasts.

Temperate cyclones are masses of warm and cold air which revolve around one another, and one can actually see the cold front and the warm one. The cold front is usually heralded by a hot berg wind, as well as very high, streaky cirrus clouds (those 'horses' tails'), and then progressively lower and thicker ones. When the low, dark ones (nimbo stratus) arrive, so does the cold front which can bring rain, hail, sleet or snow, or any combination.

An anomaly of winter in KZN is the occurrence of high temperatures which prevail when strong westerly winds course over the Escarpment, warming up as they descend and sweep to the coast. In the mountains, even as late as October, it can gust and be as hot as 40°C. Also in October, supposedly lush springtime, it can still be tinder-dry and dreary. Whatever time of year you go hiking in the Berg, it is essential that you go prepared for all seasons.

Climate and weather are the muscles behind the tools that shape the landscape. Although water is the main agent which shapes the land, the force at work here is gravity. Also, water can never erode rock: it is the particles in the water that do the work. What water does is carry the eroded material (often topsoil) away. A lightning bolt cracking into the basalt cliffs has a more visible effect than the ongoing but virtually undetectable water erosion.

Often permafrost is the cause of the terrace-like erosion of steep hillsides at higher altitudes: on cold nights moisture in the topsoil freezes and this literally lifts the top few centimetres of ground. When it thaws, the soil drops back and 'steps down'. Overgrazing greatly accelerates this process.

VEGETATION

The flora of the Drakensberg is broadly described as being Afro-montane in the Little Berg foothills and Afro-alpine on the summit. On a local scale the vegetation is affected mainly by altitude (height) and attitude (angle to the sun). With altitude it is not only the low winter temperatures but also the greater temperature range that cause the consequent stresses on the things living there. With regard to attitude, north-facing slopes are hotter than south-facing ones, and also experience high evaporation. Therefore on north-facing slopes of the Little Berg you'll find open grass with scattered protea bushes while on the south-facing slopes there's usually forest or dense bush. On the summit things are much the same, but here marshes are prevalent and affect vegetation more.

There are three major vegetation zones, each with a number of characteristic species and/or plant communities (some though are common to more than one). The montane belt includes both the grasslands *(Protea savanna)* and temperate (yellowwood) forests of the lower slopes and gorges.

The main trees growing in the grasslands are the Highveld protea *(Protea caffra)* and the silver-leafed protea *(Protea roupelliae)* with its reddish flower heads. A smaller shrub is *Protea subvestita* which has dense, vertical branches and yellowish flowers. In rocky areas, mainly valleys, you'll find the small, rounded tree with its diagnostic large, round leaves that bursts into a riot of scarlet decorations in summer; this is the KZN bottlebrush, *(Greyia sutherlandii)*.

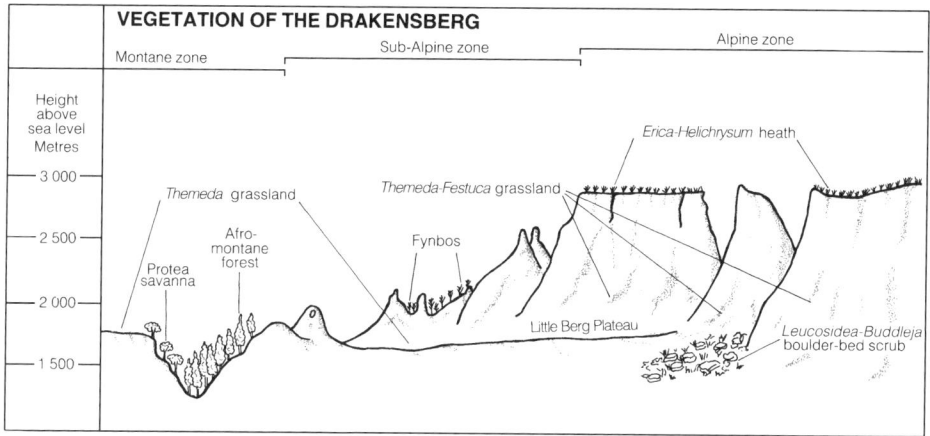

The main grasses here (and indeed pretty much throughout eastern South Africa) are the red oat grass *(Themeda triandra)* and tussock grass *(Festuca costata)*. The former is a sweet grass and excellent for grazing while the latter is sour and poor for grazing. For hikers the most important grasses are the *steekgrasse* of the *Aristida* genus (especially the ones whose seed pods work their way into your socks and drive you mad). In moist areas the diversity of species increases, and tree ferns *(Alsophila dregei)* and Berg cycads *(Encephalartos ghellinckii)* are found along stream banks or in marshy areas.

The forests are characterised by two species of yellowwood: the real yellowwood *(Podocarpus latifolius)* and the larger Outeniqua yellowwood *(Podocarpus falcatus)* with its spiky-looking, shorter leaves. Other common trees of the forests read like nature's picnic basket: wild pear, wild peach, African holly, assegai wood, forest olive or ironwood, white stinkwood *(Celtis africana)* ... the list goes on, but it is harder learning to identify trees than birds – it's not a hobby but a calling. On the forest margins and along river banks the four most common species are easier to identify: ouhout *(Leucosidea sericea)* (the Zulu *intshishi*)

Highveld protea
(Protea caffra)

Silver-leafed protea
(Protea roupelliae)

KwaZulu-Natal bottlebrush
(Greyia sutherlandii)

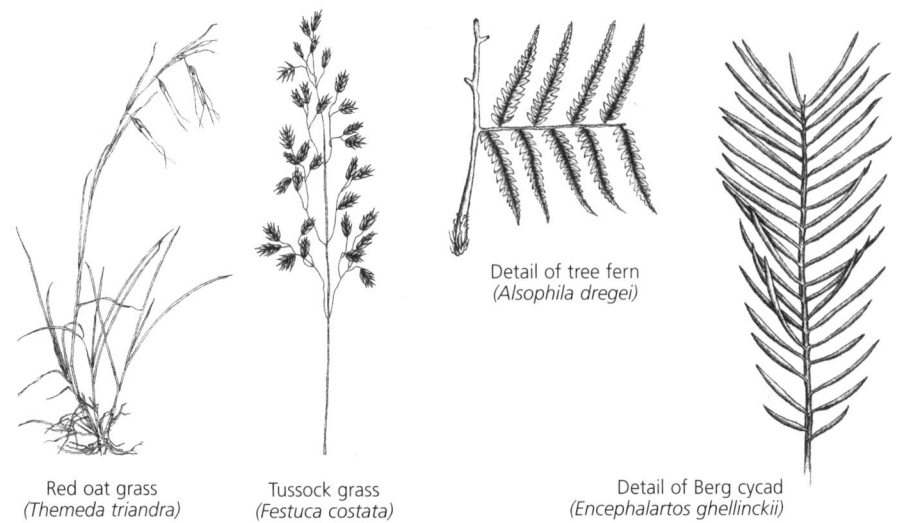

Red oat grass
(Themeda triandra)

Tussock grass
(Festuca costata)

Detail of tree fern
(Alsophila dregei)

Detail of Berg cycad
(Encephalartos ghellinckii)

with its dark, shaggy bark and small serrated silvery leaves, mountain taaibos or nana-berry (*Rhus dentata*) with its tri-foliate leaves, sagewood (*Buddleja salviifolia*) with its woolly, droopy leaves, and the common spikethorn (*Maytenus heterophylla*) with, yes, long thorny spikes.

The sub-alpine belt extends from near the top of the forest zone, coinciding with the tops of the Little Berg gorges, to the base of the Escarpment cliffs, including the Little Berg plateaux. There are fewer species here, mainly open *Themeda* grassland with *Leucosidea–Buddleja* scrub along the rivers and in rocky areas. *Protea dracomontana* is a small protea bush that grows, sometimes in quite dense patches, on top of the Little Berg. *Protea nubigena* ('in the clouds') is represented by one known community within the Royal Natal National Park. Small *Rhus* bushes are also found near streams.

Many bulbous plants, mainly watsonias and irises, burst into flower every spring, while in late summer the delicate ground orchids show themselves, and then later still the bright yellow dollars and tiny pink thimbles of the everlastings. Higher up the dominant grass is sour *Festuca* tussock with less sour *Themeda* oat. Sour grasses survive the harsh winter conditions by withdrawing their nutrients into their roots, hence the word 'sour' to describe their poor nutritional value. There are species of 'spear grasses' that hikers in this zone will come to know, namely *Heteropogon contortus* and the giant variety *Trachypogon spicatus*. Flowers that grow mainly along the bases of the cliffs are the crinkly pink Guernsey lily (*Nerine sarniensis*), and the little blue bonnets of *Wahlenbergia undulata*.

In the summit alpine zone there are no trees or anything growing taller than one metre. Tussocky grasses, low heaths and small everlastings are what you will find. These plants, of which the genus *Helichrysum* is dominant, are important in Zulu and Xhosa lore, harbouring the power of the 'shades' (dead ancestors) whose spirits are released through the burning or boiling of the flowers. This is done when a child is born, when seeking guidance or when something needs to be blessed. In marshy areas in summer you will see irises, orchids and

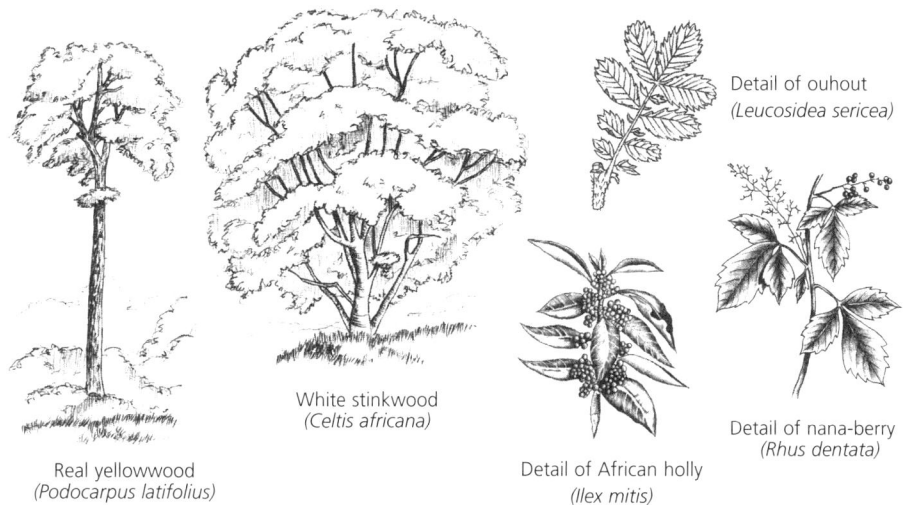

Real yellowwood
(Podocarpus latifolius)

White stinkwood
(Celtis africana)

Detail of African holly
(Ilex mitis)

Detail of ouhout
(Leucosidea sericea)

Detail of nana-berry
(Rhus dentata)

red-hot pokers in their hundreds of thousands. Sparse grass cover is provided by *Danthonia distica*, *Festuca caprina*, *Poa binata*, caterpillar grass *Harpechloa flax* and June grass *Koeleria cristata*, which offer frugal grazing to the herds of sheep, cattle, goats and horses of the hardy Basotho herders.

The mountain ranges of East Africa are like ecological islands in a sea of grassland or savanna (grassland with scattered trees). They are connected by a common thread of species and communities, both Afro-montane and Afro-alpine. As the climate of Africa has warmed and dried over the past 10 million years or so, the mountain flora has ebbed and flowed like a vegetable tide up and down the mountains and into the surrounding sea of savanna. Around 15 million years ago (mya) the whole continent was covered in tropical forest; by 2.5 mya this had shrunk to 50 per cent and it is less than 5 per cent now.

We are currently in a warming cycle, where even the glaciers on top of Kilimanjaro, Mount Kenya and the Ruwenzoris are retreating, and are expected to disappear within a hundred years. The montane and alpine vegetation is confined to only the highest peaks, stretching from Ethiopia all the way to Table Mountain. But, whereas in East Africa the plants are huge because of extremely high rainfall and a year-round growing season near the equator, further south they get progressively smaller: everlastings and lobelias, which in the Drakensberg are less than half a metre tall, reach five metres high on Kilimanjaro, Mount Kenya and the like! Also, in the tropics there are only a handful of fynbos species, while in the Western Cape there are thousands, so many in fact that the south-western Cape is the tiniest but richest of only seven floral kingdoms covering the whole world.

It's an interesting phenomenon that has allowed these plants to migrate along the African mountain archipelago (one species, *Protea caffra*, is found all the way from the Eastern Cape to Ethiopia). Near the equator the peaks rise up to 5 000 and even 6 000 metres, but as you travel south they get progressively lower until in the Cape they are right down at sea level. The combined effects of lowering altitude and increasing latitude create similar growing conditions. The genus protea is a defining plant type of the Afro-montane belt, as are the yellowwoods in the forests. The Afro-alpine zone is characterised by an *Erica–Helichrysum* community, whether on top of the Drakensberg or the Simian Mountains near the horn of Africa. How *Protea nubigena* came to exist on just one high ridge of the Little Berg is a question you can ponder, but it's got to do with the 'ebb and flow' scenario. We can assume its days in the wild are numbered. Likewise, why the Cape has thousands of fynbos species and Kilimanjaro only a handful, has to do with the ecological concept of niches: Kilimanjaro has but three, whereas every little pocket of every mountain range in the Western Cape has its own microclimate. (It all gets quite complicated, but if you'd like to pursue the subject check the book list on pages 235 and 236.)

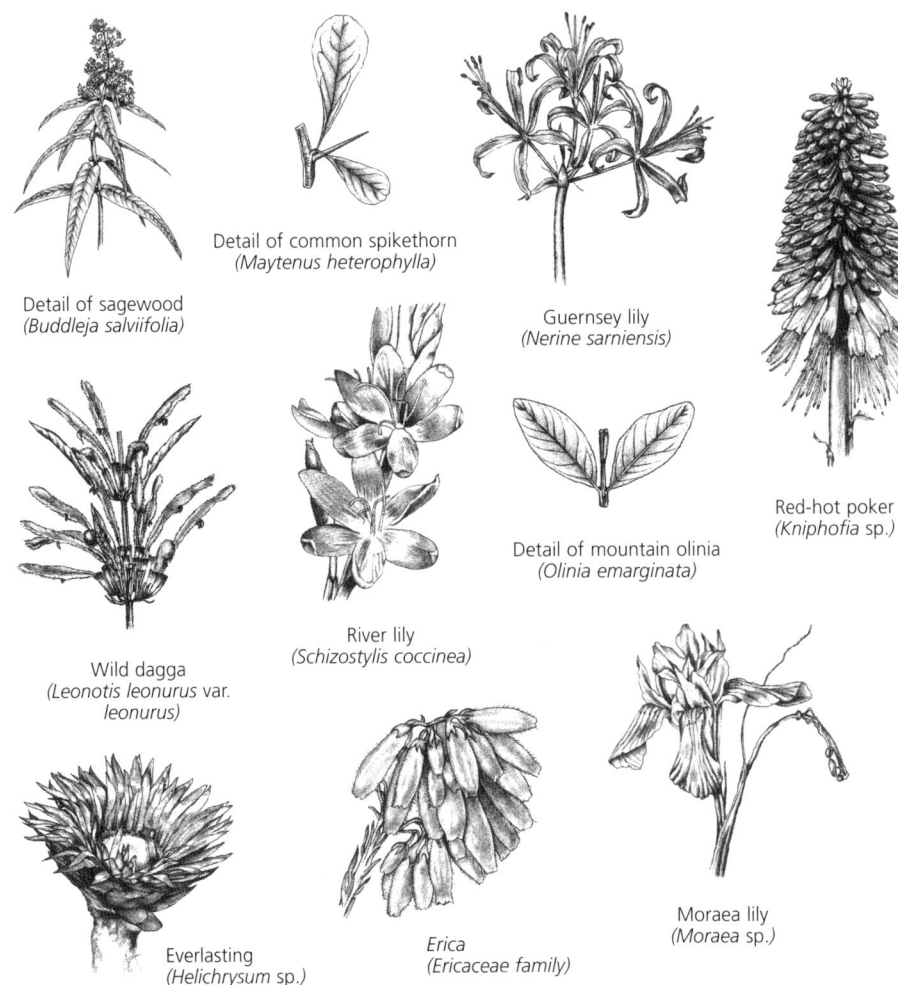

Detail of sagewood
(*Buddleja salviifolia*)

Detail of common spikethorn
(*Maytenus heterophylla*)

Guernsey lily
(*Nerine sarniensis*)

Detail of mountain olinia
(*Olinia emarginata*)

Red-hot poker
(*Kniphofia* sp.)

Wild dagga
(*Leonotis leonurus* var. *leonurus*)

River lily
(*Schizostylis coccinea*)

Everlasting
(*Helichrysum* sp.)

Erica
(Ericaceae family)

Moraea lily
(*Moraea* sp.)

In the Drakensberg (as indeed most of the rest of Africa) there is one more force which plays a major role in shaping the area's vegetation. And that is fire. It's a natural force and the open grasslands and savanna have adapted over millions of years to cope with random, sporadic fires. Many have fire-resistant bark, or rootstocks that re-coppice after severe burns, or even seeds that germinate only after they have been scorched by flame and smoke. That's all natural, but then along comes 'man' who starts burning the veld far too often and upsets the whole balance.

Burnt too often, some species just cannot cope and slowly they disappear from the scene. Others take their place. Things are never the same. The whole Drakensberg is protected, not so much for the animals, or even the Bushman art, as for the vegetation. It's the main catchment area for a dry country, and the plants determine how much and how good the water is that flows down from the mountains. So park managers do rotational burns of the veld, supposedly to keep it young and healthy – but not all ecologists agree with the practice.

I have long been intrigued by the use of indigenous plants for food and medicine, but must confess I have been too timid to try unless I have been shown something. However, I have had the fortune to meet the 'white witch of the Magaliesberg', Margaret Roberts, who has been an inspiration to learn. If you'd like to follow this path, get hold of her books which are mines of information about the uses of many local plants. For instance, the humble agapanthus has magical properties, and its leaves can be used as a poultice for tired feet. Jelly made from aloe leaves relieve stings, burns and blisters, and the pulp is applied to snakebites. So be brave, and give it a go.

ANIMALS

The first animals of the Drakensberg were mammal-like reptiles, creatures that predated the true dinosaurs by tens of millions of years, like the massive, lumbering *Melanosaurus* or the fleet-footed sharp-toothed *Massospondylus* found in the Red Bed deposits. Often when I'm driving across the Karoo and day-dreaming I fancy there's a six-metre-tall *Massospondylus* reared up on its hind legs and then belting along the veld next to the car. Imagine coming across one in a forest of the Little Berg! Increasingly dry conditions drove these animals away, but dassie-size primitive mammals survived, probably because they were burrowing animals, and dassies are the evolutionary result of their tenacity.

Some of these creatures did leave their footprints for us to see, near Leribe in Lesotho and Giant's Castle reserve. More important, they left their skeletons in the soft Stormberg rocks. Geologist and conservationist Gideon Groenewald has made a profession out of finding them and conducting 'dinosaur tours' in the Golden Gate area.

Mountains are by their nature highly stressed environments and any organisms that exist in them have to become specially adapted. Jackals and baboons do it by being supremely versatile and opportunistic feeders. Reptiles beat the harsh winter by going underground and hibernating. Others, such as the lammergeier and grey rhebuck are specifically adapted physiologically and are highly specialised feeders. The problem with this group is: squeeze their habitat (overgrazing, hunting, fencing) and they have nowhere else to go.

Some animals, such as baboons, jackals and grey rhebuck, are found at all altitudes in the Berg, and it's a thrilling wilderness feeling when you're wakened by the cry of a jackal in the

Bushbuck *(Tragelaphus scriptus)*

Oribi *(Ourebia ourebi)*

morning in a valley on the summit. Others have more specific habitat preferences. For example, lammergeiers nest in and cruise only above the highest crags and summit plateaux, dropping down to the Little Berg to look for carcasses.

Eland tend to stick to the grassy plateaux of the Little Berg, descending to the outer reaches of the foothills along the river valleys in winter, where they browse on *Buddleja* leaves. Oribi are synonymous with tall grassland where they will lie hidden till you are almost on top of them before they break cover in sometimes startling fashion.

Mountain reedbuck *(Redunca fulvorufula)*

Bushbuck – as their name implies – stick to the dense riverine bush and forest. You would expect klipspringer to be fairly conspicuous in the sub-alpine and alpine zones, but in my experience they are scarce.

Who knows what animals might have roamed the Berg summit in days gone by, but today the most frequently seen (in areas where herders don't live permanently) are grey rhebuck. I've watched them doing territorial battle. Two males will dash about the hillsides and valleys at top speed, covering up to five kilometres in the 10 minutes or so it has taken me to get my breath back after cresting a steep ridge. Truly humbling athleticism – and on top of it they never seem to have to look where they're going over the broken ground.

Most guide books will tell you that leopards occur in the Berg, and they certainly did once, but I've yet to see any sign of them, or hear of anyone else who has. What I have seen is the scat of large cats, or cat-like things. Big enough for a small leopard, but more likely a caracal or a serval. You'll see plenty of small cat scat – mongooses, genets, African wild cat, African weasels

Grey rhebuck *(Pelea capreolus)*

Klipspringer
(Oreotragus oreotragus)

and zorillas (striped polecat). Along the rivers there are plenty of scattered remains of crab shells, a sign that otters are about, as well as the large and somewhat scruffy water mongoose.

We all have our phobias, and most hikers seem to have an irrational fear of snakes. The thing with snakes, as indeed just about all animals, is that they're far more scared of big lumbering you than you are of them. The chances of seeing a snake are really very small. The chances of seeing a poisonous snake remote, and the chances of being bitten by one are microscopic. Sure, they are there (and I seem to come across far, far more than my share) but wear a decent pair of boots and you reduce the chances of a bite to close to zero. But still people do get bitten. A famous story is that of university student mountaineer Ian Muller, recounted in more than one of Reg Pearse's books. Apparently Muller was terrified of snakes. One evening in 1955 he was hiking near Cathkin and was bitten on the wrist. A dark and stormy night followed, and in the morning one of the party set out for help, as the man's condition had become critical. He died early that morning, well before help arrived.

Another incident involved an acquaintance of mine who was in a high side valley of the Mnweni Cutback. He was nipped on a finger by a baby berg adder one afternoon and soon thereafter started experiencing motor difficulties (lame muscles and laboured breathing). It too was a stormy day and his partner put him in a sleeping bag, in their small tent set on a steep grassy bank, and set off for help. It came in the form of a helicopter the next morning. But the mountains were clouded in. On the chopper's last possible run a small hole opened in the cloud and, miraculously, the tiny orange tent could be seen through it. The victim spent a week in hospital and some two months passed before his facial muscles regained tone.

Treatment for snake bite is controversial, but the golden rule is to do nothing – especially if you are not sure what to do, or what species of snake is involved. If possible one person should go for help. Then treat the victim symptomatically, which means addressing problems, like difficult breathing, loss of sight or the use of a limb, as they occur. Mainly, you must keep the victim alive and breathing and reduce shock as best you can. Keep them warm and hydrated, but never with alcohol. If you decide to carry anti-venom serum, consider taking anti-histamine and cortisone as a general treatment for all types of poisonous bite (to stem the body's reaction). Only administer a serum if you are certain of the species and you know which serum to use. For example: adders are usually haemotoxic, in that the venom works slowly on the blood and body tissue. Cobras and mambas (not found in the Berg) are neurotoxic in that the poison affects the nervous system and within a few hours prevents the muscles working properly (hindered breathing is the the most serious consequence). Unlike their relatives, berg adders have a prevalence of neurotoxins – give a person with a berg adder bite a dose of haemotoxin serum and he gets a double whammy of poison. Avoid all tourniquets, as they just speed up tissue damage, and forget about cutting wounds and sucking: all you do is give the victim an extra wound.

Puff adder
(Bitis arietans)

Spitting cobra or rinkhals
(Hemachatus haemachatus)

Electric shock to the site of the bite seems to be extremely effective, but who carries a car battery in their pack, let alone a set of jumper leads?

One of the most likely snake mishaps to terminate a holiday is a bite from a puff adder – sluggish beasts that don't like moving off sunny paths, or being trodden on. A bite from one of these chaps is very serious. The bite victim needs to get medical attention, but you do have some time – more than many people would think: a minimum of several hours and often as much as 24 hours before serious effects take hold, depending on the variables. If you're deep in the Berg, you will somehow have to get the patient out of there with the least possible physical stress. Stress causes the toxins to flow more quickly through the body, speeding up the toxic effects especially in the case of a cobra or berg adder bite. The latter is not potentially lethal but can quickly render the victim immobile. If you cannot get the victim to help, you will have to go and fetch it. Another is a rinkhals encounter. This is one of the spitting cobras and you are more likely to be spat at than bitten. If you do get venom in your eyes, wash them out with water (urine or any liquid will do if you can't get water soon). If it's a bite, get help as fast as you can.

But forget about the things that grovel on the ground and lift your eyes to the heavens, from whence cometh the most beautiful sights of the mountains – the birds. I have given some details of the lammergeier in the preceding pages, but you have to see these great birds in flight to appreciate them. While juveniles have dark, mottled plumage, adults have almost black wings and tails, with striking golden brown bodies. If you see one up close the face is remarkable too: pale gold with a bright red ring around the eyes and a black mask, with the tell-tale 'beard' feathers hanging down from a stout, curved beak. Legend has it that the Greek poet Aeschylus died when a lammergeier dropped a tortoise, to try to crack it open, and it landed on the unfortunate man's head. The birds have favourite rocks called ossiaries (place of bones) which they use for dropping bones onto, to break open to get at the marrow. In the

Bible the birds are referred to as ossifrages (bone-eaters). Some bird books say the golden body colour of adults comes from rubbing against their sandstone roosts, but I cannot believe this. The colour is just too uniform, and many of them roost on basalt ledges anyway.

When in flight the diagnostic features (apart from very large size and colouring) are fast, falcon-like flight and a diamond-shaped tail. The more common Cape vulture has a stumpy, fan-shaped tail. But don't ignore the vultures, for they are masters of the air, catching thermals with an aerial efficiency that makes every paraglider pilot drool with envy. The black eagle, with its distinctive white back cross is, however, the definitive bird of the southern African mountains, being found just about wherever there are crags and dassies, its principle food. In fact the distributions of these two species overlap almost exactly. If you go down the raptor hierarchy, the next most impressive bird is the jackal buzzard, so named because of its jackal-like cry, usually issued while the bird is circling high up in the sky. Thereafter come the falcons, mainly the swift and handsome lanner, and then the hawks – African goshawk, marsh harriers and black sparrowhawk particularly. I've been lucky to see wattled cranes in the moist grasslands of Mkhomazi, bald ibises on the Little Berg of Giant's Castle, as well as marsh owls on the summit.

Grey-winged francolins, which local people variously call 'partridges' and 'pheasants', are pretty common throughout the grasslands. About half their size is the shy common quail which bursts up almost at your feet in a whirr of wings and 'skree' alarm call, only to disappear into cover a short way off. Possibly the most conspicuous grassland bird is the orange-throated longclaw, a pipit-like species that favours tufty grass areas; it scratches around on the ground for insects, uses tufts as a perch to look around, and when alarmed first crouches then flies off with a flap-glide-flap pattern. Rockjumpers are often mistaken for robins, but are more robust and often found rock hopping right on the summit.

rock art

Who made the thousands of rock paintings that can be found in innumerable caves and overhangs in the Drakensberg (and thousands more throughout southern Africa)? When were they painted? And why?

Most of us think we know the answer to the first question at least: obviously, it was the Bushmen, or San as they are also sometimes called. In truth we know so little about these 'first people' that we're not even sure what to call them. They were tragically misunderstood, driven off the land they once roamed freely, enslaved and shot out to the last person before we took the time to ask them who they were – let alone what they thought about things. The tiny fragments of their history which remain are just sad tatters flapping in the winds of time.

We can tell some of these paintings must have been done between the 1840s and 1890s, since they show men on horseback, horses, cattle and sheep, and in one or two places covered wagons with teams of oxen. But what about the rest? Dating them is fraught with problems, since by taking samples you destroy the fragile and already widely vandalised works. Also carbon, the element most commonly used for archaeological dating, is found in such minute quantities in the pigments that it has not yet been successfully used. From other archaeological evidence it has been estimated that the oldest may be around 35 000 years old, maybe more. They come to us from a time that dates so far back it lies beyond anything we know of human culture on this planet. Often, at first glance, they look quite crude. However, if you visualise the works as they were in their prime you suddenly realise that even the oldest paintings reveal an artistic ability and an understanding of human and animal physiology and behaviour that has never been bettered.

Given this knowledge, it is hard indeed to understand how anyone could wish to vandalise them – pouring water on the images, or cold drink, or rubbing them with half oranges to make the colours 'stand out', or shooting at them, scribbling over them with charcoal or stones, even crudely chiselling pieces off and ruining metres-long friezes. But people have done, and still do, all these things. Some damage is done inevitably by inquisitive and naughty children. However, something that has recently come to light is that sangomas sometimes steal into the caves to take scrapings of the pigments, to be used in strong muti. The irony is that these Zulu healers understand the spiritual power of the Bushman images better than anyone, and should behave better. Already probably less than 10 per cent of the original works remain in anything like recognisable condition. How do you stop this kind of destruction? It's hard, but we have to try, especially when we get round to answering the final question of why they were painted, and the significance of this massive outdoor art gallery becomes clearer.

There has never been any doubt that Bushmen did the cave paintings ... well that's not strictly true. Various researchers have in the past tried to attribute them to Bantu, Mediterranean and even Phoenicean peoples, but we can disregard all that. In fact, one of the last Bushmen known to have lived in the Drakensberg was shot (Bushmen were seen as vermin and had a price on their heads) in what a few years later became Giant's Castle Game Reserve. Around his waist he wore a leather thong from which hung small antelope horns that carried the pigments used for painting. We now know he would have been a shaman, for it was only they who did the paintings ... but we'll get to the 'why' a bit later. At first white settlers thought the paintings were crude if curious renditions of 'a day in the life of a Bushman' sort of thing. Hunters and wild animals were seemingly randomly rendered and often one on top of another, with inexplicable lines and dots and strange things that were of little interest to the viewers. The first attempts at any real understanding of the paintings (and this came from attempts to understand cave paintings in Europe), suggested the idea of 'sympathetic magic' – the images were an attempt to capture the spirit of an animal to ensure a successful hunt. This theory held sway until fairly recently, along with the theory that cave paintings are just crude renditions of everyday scenes.

But not everyone was convinced, and ever since the first European contact with the hunter-gatherers there were people who were convinced the paintings went to the core of Bushman culture. Just how right they were was given scientific credibility only recently through the work of South African archaeologists, especially those at the University of the Witwatersrand's Rock Art Unit.

The first major piece in the jigsaw was historical record, what little there was. Most important was the findings of George Stow, Wilhelm Bleek and Bleek's sister-in-law, Lucy Lloyd, who made it their lifetimes' works recording the stories of the Bushmen as told to them by Bushman prisoners in Cape Town's terrible Breakwater Prison (in the present-day V&A Waterfront). Bleek and Lloyd took down some 12 000 pages of verbatim dictation. The first breakthrough was when Bleek heard the interpretation of paintings as given to a Natal magistrate Joseph Orpen by a Bushman guide Qing during the Langalibalele rebellion. When the Bleek treasure trove was rediscovered and, through a stroke of academic inspiration, compared with the cave paintings of the Drakensberg, a door on the Bushmen's secret world suddenly opened to rigorous scientific analysis for the first time.

There is a lovely road that runs from Bushman's River into the hills. These hills are grass covered and rolling and they are lovely beyond any singing of it.... The road I speak of runs to Kamberg reserve, and not Ixopo as in Alan Paton's original version of *Cry the Beloved Country*. Mine is a little-used dirt road, but it is well worth the taking for it will lead you to what is arguably the most important rock art site in the world – Game Pass. Not only are many of the paintings here in near pristine condition, and of exceptionally high quality, but there is one particular frieze, the study of which helped to place the central pieces of the rock art jigsaw puzzle.

It was named the Rosetta Stone by Professor David Lewis-Williams as a sort of in-joke (and with reference to the nearby settlement of Rosetta); the name refers to the more famous Rosetta Stone that unlocked the meaning of Egyptian hieroglyphs. The main image is of an eland in red and white, its head held low and hooves crossed, with hairs standing up along its neck, back, dewlap and belly. Standing behind it is a human-like figure holding onto the eland's tail. This figure has an antelope-like head (a therianthrope, or shaman in trance state that has taken on the power of an animal) and its feet are crossed, except that they are hooves just like the eland's.

Looking at this image, and with Qing's words in mind about men figures with antelope heads, a penny dropped: 'They were men who had died and now lived in the rivers, and were spoilt ...'. To the Bushmen, a dance-induced trance and death were one and the same experience, so this painting is like an after-death experience conveyed in the world of the living. The eland in the painting is clearly dying, and, when the full meaning of the words 'died', 'river' and 'spoilt' came to be understood, it became apparent that there was a spiritual link between man and beast, between the painter and the supernatural world, that went much deeper than anyone had yet realised.

The truth that emerged here and everywhere else was that these paintings were painted by Bushman shamans after participating in an hallucinatory trance dance. They are reflections of what the trance had revealed to the shaman, who in turn conveyed the vision for his people to share and unwittingly to the world thereafter. The paintings have thus been called 'images of power'. In this context we need to re-evaluate these caves as holy places, as the churches of the Bushmen who until modern times were thought, in the words of a missionary and historian respectively, to have 'no religion, no laws ... a soul debased and completely bound down and clogged by his animal nature' and 'it was for the world's good that they should make way for a higher race'. Even our great 'holist' Jan Smuts considered the Bushmen to be no more than 'mentally stunted desert animals'.

Of course any artistically acute person looking at the images would have grasped something intrinsically sophisticated in them: they are incredibly fine renderings of humans and animals, often in motion, that could have been done only by true artists. That alone should have alerted arrogant critics to something a little deeper going on, but, alas, all that is past and now the best we can do is protect them. Luckily this is possible in the Drakensberg with a unified park under strong conservation authority. Unfortunately, it also means that the majority of caves with paintings in them are no longer accessible to the public. Only some can be visited and then only with a local guide accredited by Amafa, the KZN heritage authority.

The best such site, and one of the easiest to walk to, is Game Pass Shelter. The bonus here is that Kamberg reserve has a spanking new interpretive centre where for a very modest sum you can watch a 20-minute video on the Bushmen and their art, as well as take a guided walk to the cave. And it's always such a pleasure to stay at the EKZNW rest camps such as Kamberg, especially if you like throwing flies into trout-filled dams (there are several in the reserve), or just going walkabout in the Berg.

It is way beyond the scope of this book to get into a deep interpretation of the art, but the keys to it can be gained by considering just a few almost universal, archetypal images. The most important ones to get a handle on are scenes indicating dying, which for the Bushman is synonymous with going into a trance. Once 'dead' (also variously conveyed as 'going underwater' or 'flying') the shaman assumes the character of an animal, which will often also be depicted as dying. The most common symbol for this dying is lines of blood streaming from the nose. Animals, mainly eland – the greatest of all creatures in Bushman mythology – man–animal therioanthropes, and even such creatures as snakes (in Giant's Castle main caves) with bleeding noses are to be seen in most panels (although sometimes you have to look carefully to make out the marks). Water scenes, including fish, denote 'going underwater' and are not to be taken literally.

In their book *Images of Power* (Struik) David Lewis-Williams and Thomas Dowson make the point that rock art images should be understood as metaphors: just as a Bushman would be puzzled by our saying 'it's raining cats and dogs' so should we be viewing their painted language. Another symbol of dying is flying, and in the Drakensberg there are a number of strange antelope-like creatures with long, trailing wings. These are antelope spirits flying in a trance state. There are two fairly good examples in Junction Cave.

The next symbols to be discussed are lines or patterns of dots, which initially were considered graffiti, but mostly just confused people. But they too have 'power'. Firstly, areas of dot patterns are called entoptic phenomena and they are widely found in Aboriginal art in Australia. Their meaning was discovered only through the research (if you can call it that) of Timothy Leary in the USA when he experimented with LSD and other drugs in the 1960s. These dot patterns are strongly associated with hallucinatory states, and this is the crux of the Bushman trance: it was an hallucinatory state in which the senses were both heightened and mixed, very similar to an LSD experience.

Lines and lines of dots that seem to connect unrelated things are 'power lines'. There are many battle scenes to be found, most famously those in Battle Cave in the Injisuthi Valley. Close analysis reveals that the fight does not take place in the physical realm, but in the supernatural, and the lines of potency coming from an arrow tip, pointed finger or wherever (call them magic spells if you like) are what the battle is about.

In fact all scenes which appear to depict everyday scenes need to be studied carefully to grasp their true meaning. For example in Junction Cave above the Didima/Mhlawazini confluence there is a well-argued painting that appears to show a group of Bushmen crossing a bridge. But the women on the left clapping suggest it's a painting of a trance dance, as does the figure that seems to have fallen off the bridge. He's also clapping – a shaman that's fallen into a trance. There are often symbols to be found in these scenes that are clues to their true nature, such as fly whisks and other 'sceptres' which were used only in rituals such as trance dances. Unfortunately, they are now hard to see on the faded, flaking cave walls and so often escape the viewers' attention.

If you'd like to pursue this subject, you should read at least one of the books listed on pages 235 and 236. In areas where guides are available (the cost varies considerably so ask a conservator at the local office), the paintings are there for any hiker to visit and they represent one of the greatest collections of religious art in the world. They are our very own mediaeval cathedrals, and, if you wouldn't miss a visit to Chartres or Rheims on a trip through the French countryside, why should you miss this?

OVERLEAF: *A map of the Drakensberg area*

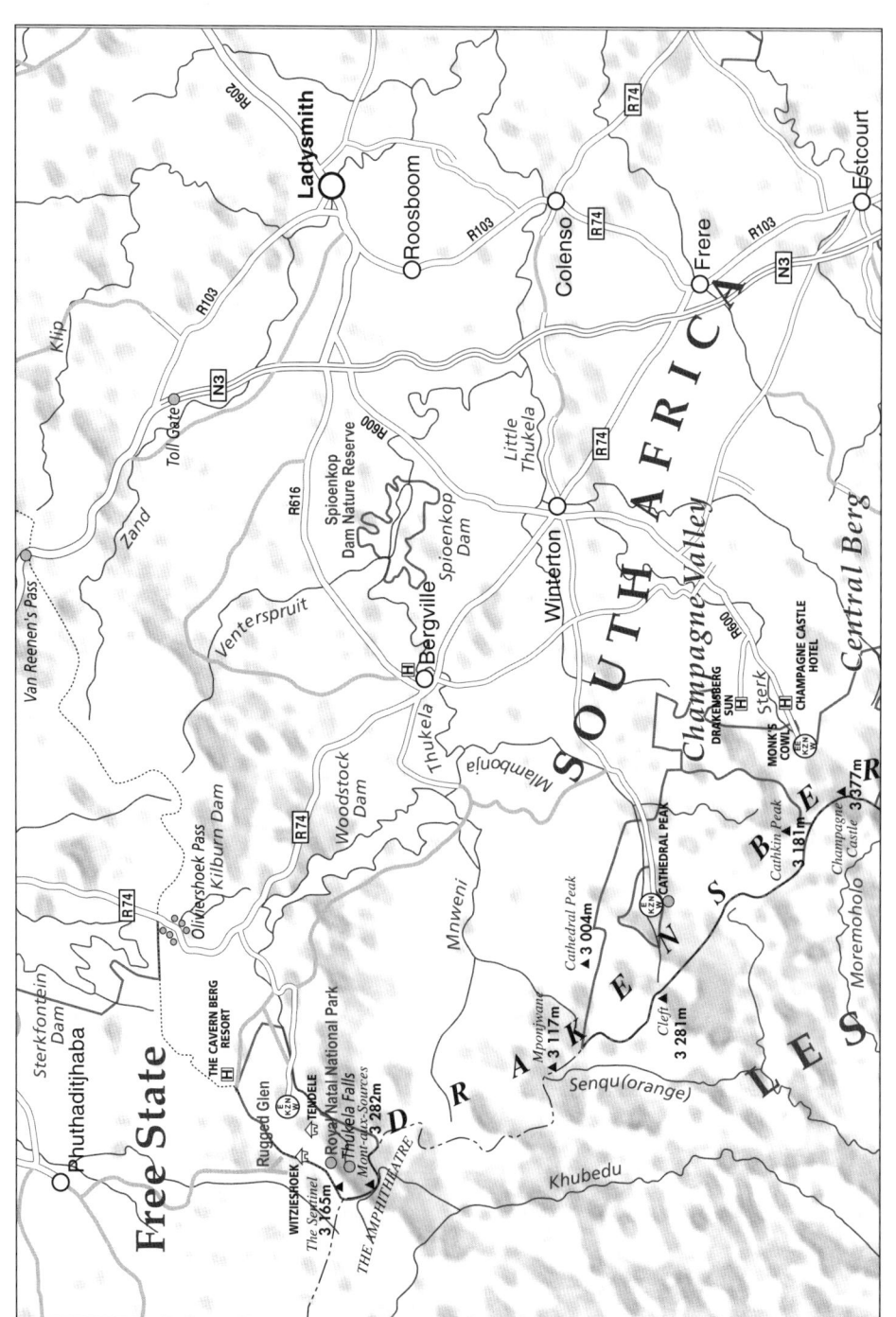

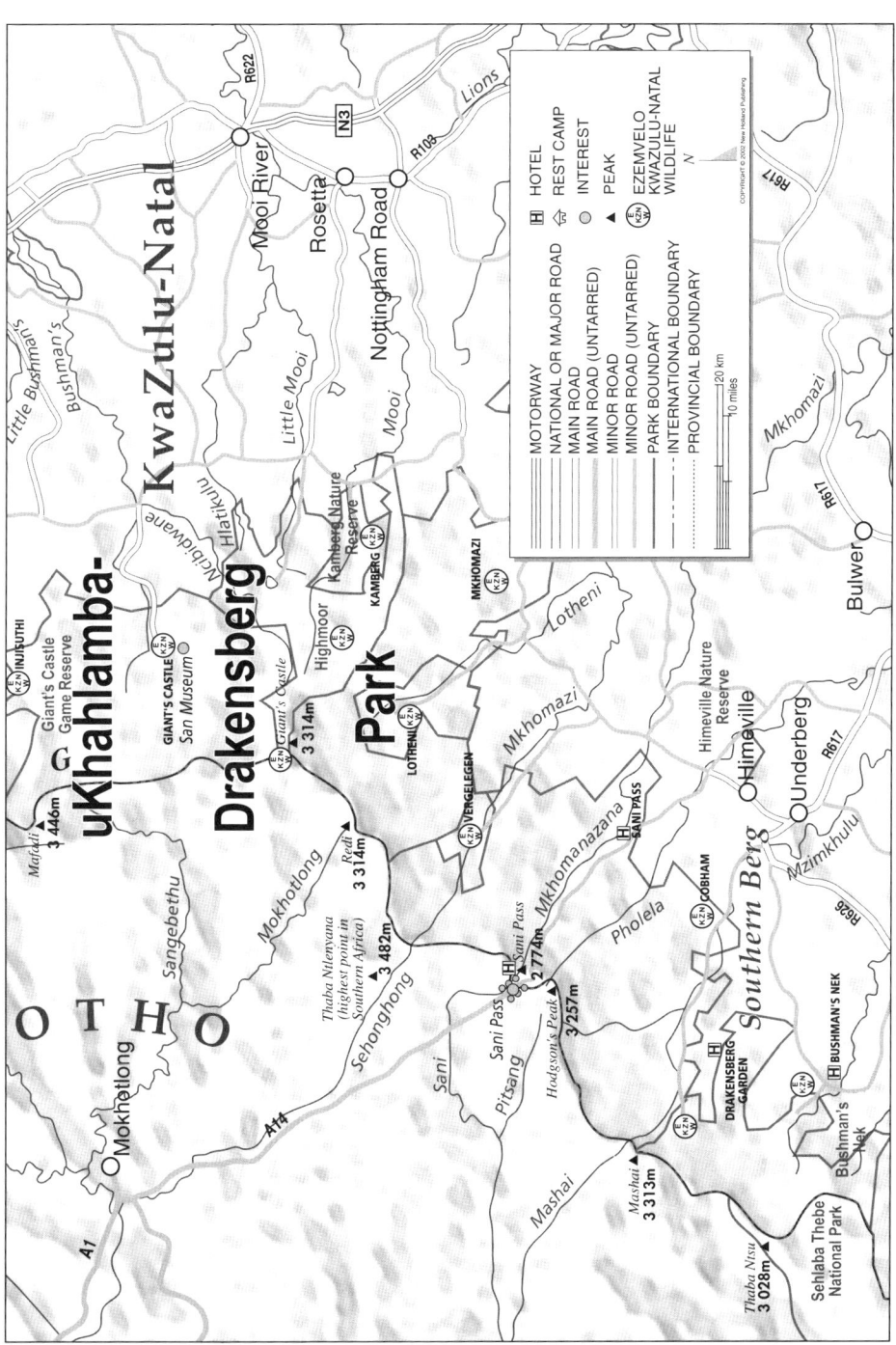

the amphitheatre

I've walked the Berg from one end to the other, top and bottom, and I've climbed all the highest peaks in Africa, and still – every time I see it – the view from the top of the Amphitheatre takes my breath away. There are other parts of the Berg that are wilder, or better for hiking, but no other area compares with the majesty of this natural wonder. It's a five-kilometre wall of basalt, rising about one kilometre from its base. Near its western 'book end' the Sentinel, the Thukela headwaters form the world's fourth highest waterfall, whose total drop is 614 metres before it tumbles through the Little Berg and reaches the Thukela Gorge. For the record the top three are Angel Falls in Venezuela (979 metres), Yosemite Falls in the USA (739 metres) and Mardalsfossen South in Norway (655 metres).

Part of the aesthetic power of the Amphitheatre is its near-perfect symmetry, boxed in at one end by the Sentinel and by the Eastern Buttress at the other. About two and a half kilometres inland (south) of the falls, the land rises up to Mont-aux-Sources (3 282 metres). It was named by two French missionaries Arbousset and Dumas, who claimed to have trekked with Basotho guides and ponies the entire length of the mountains. But their description of things on the summit does not tie in well with reality, especially their supposed layout of the four rivers, including the Senqu (Orange), which were believed to rise there. The rivers that do rise on Mont-aux-Sources are the Thukela, Khubedu, Bilanjil (small tributary that joins the Thukela in the gorge below) and a minor tributary of the Namahadi. Arbousset and Dumas also claimed Mont-aux-Sources was the highest peak along the watershed, something that many people still believe. In fact it is the 18th highest 'kulu' but only the 26th highest point along the watershed. Derived from the Zulu word khulu meaning 'big' the term has been coined to refer to free-standing peaks (see table of 'kulus', pages 228–229). And the

the amphitheatre

Senqu rises on the Ncedamabutho headland just behind Ledger's Cave in the Mnweni area, not here. Although there were various attempts at climbing the Berg by early die-hards such as the Stocker brothers as far back as the 1860s, once the Natal Mountain Club was formed, it was the Amphitheatre which beckoned the members. One reason for this was the existence of the Rydal Mount Hotel, originally the farmhouse of Herbert Smith who opened it to guests in 1890. But its heyday was from around 1910 when it was taken over by a crazy Irishman, Tom Casement, himself a climber. The hotel became the first real home to mountaineers not only in the Drakensberg but in the whole of South Africa. Parties would set out from the hotel, near Witzieshoek, by wagon or on horseback and head into the Namahadi Pass, about one and a half kilometres west of the present-day Chain Ladders.

As the Rydal Mount declined another legend was born when, in the late 1920s, Otto Zunckel and his son Walter took over a hostel in the Natal National Park and developed it into one of the Berg's renowned resorts. It was Otto who erected the now famous chain ladders to the top of the Amphitheatre. The Natal National Park (a wishful misnomer which survives), on the east side of the Sentinel ridge from Witzieshoek, was proclaimed in the upper Thukela Valley in 1916 but received its 'royal' qualifier only after the visit of the British royal family in 1947.

The people of Qwa-Qwa and Witzieshoek were originally Basothos granted land by President Petrus Brand of the Orange Free State. The Free State Government built a road to Witzieshoek in the 1920s, and in the 1970s extended it up the Sentinel spur to Basotho Gate (the old Gordon's Pass), and finally along the bridle trail cut by Walter Coventry in 1919, past the Witches to the car park below the Sentinel. The original idea was for the Lesotho Government to build a road to meet it. In the 1940s their chief Wessels Mota built a cluster of huts for use by mountaineers. Later this little resort, the highest in the country (at one time managed by Anton Zunckel, grandson of Otto), was incorporated into the Qwa-Qwa homeland and run by the 'Bantu administration'. Now, however, Witzieshoek Mountain Resort is managed and owned by the local community and it's a fine place to spend a night before starting a trip into the Berg. The hotel has a 'vulture restaurant' which attracts lammergeiers.

Down below is a group of hotels, the most impressive of which is the Tendele self-catering hutted camp in Royal Natal National Park (RNNP); it has the best views in the country. Also in the park is the old Royal Natal Hotel but at the time of writing it was not open; the plan is to refurbish – maybe even rebuild – it, and have it privately run. It started life as a hostel on the farm Goodoo, owned by Walter Coventry and run by Mr FC Williams. When the area was turned into a reserve, in 1916, the hostel was enlarged as the National Park Hotel (Natal then, as now, believed it was an independent state). When you went out hiking in those days, you'd round a corner on the path and find the guides from the hotel had laid out a white cloth on which was steaming porridge, smoking bacon and eggs and a pot of coffee boiling away invitingly.

When the hotel burned down in 1941 the Zunckels (the father was a stonemason) set about rebuilding a larger establishment. After the Zunckels left the place its fortunes waxed and waned, and its future is still a little uncertain. Whatever lies ahead, many old mountaineers pray that Otto Zunckel's fine stone walls will be preserved. He also built the stone house and trading post at the top of Oliviershoek, now the Caterpillar and Catfish Cookhouse, as well as the Drakensberg Inn in Bergville. One of the last remaining family hotels in the Berg is the Cavern Berg (and arguably the last with old-style values and prices), owned by the Carte family and situated over Surprise Ridge, the northern boundary of the park. Apart from the hotel's obvious attractions a prime site is the enormous Cannibal Cave nearby. Guided walks and horse-rides are offered. There is the weekend-getaway lodge of Montusi near Cavern Berg (also in the Carte family), while on the way to Oliviershoek Pass you'll find Orion Mont-aux-Sources Hotel, Alpine Heath, Hlalanathi chalet and caravan park, Sungubala bush-style camp, Little Switzerland, and the aforementioned 'cookhouse'. And then there is Mahai, which must be the most beautifully located camp site in the world.

MONT-AUX-SOURCES VIA THE CHAIN LADDERS — HIKE AM1

Route: From the Sentinel car park to the Thukela headwaters (or from Mahai/RNNP)
Distance: 10 to 12 km (variation 26 km)
Duration: 6 hours (variation 2 days)
Grade: Severe (variation extreme)
General: This is, by far, the easiest way to the top of the Berg, and consequently the most popular. It gives you access to one of the grandest places in the world, and certainly the most spectacular view sites in southern Africa. Just don't try this walk without being fully prepared for a mountaineering experience: storms can arrive without warning at any time of the year, and from time to time unprepared hikers have lost their lives. I've seen people up there with little more than a T-shirt to wear. In a blizzard you will get lost, and so have to hunker down where you are. You can turn this walk into a superb two-day outing, sleeping near the edge of the Thukela Falls and experiencing the glory of sunrise over the Amphitheatre. Also, it can be hiked from RNNP below, via Mahai Pass and Basotho Gate. This variation is a long and tough hike, much neglected these days, but one of the classic Drakensberg hikes. Just remember to practise eco-friendly ablutions, and take precautions against thievery (don't leave your boots outside your tent), which is prevalent here especially over holidays.

It's a 7-km dirt road from Witzieshoek resort to the Sentinel car park, where there is a guard house and gate. Here you have to fill in the mountain register and pay an entrance fee (less for day visits and more for overnight or longer hikes). The path starts off on the contour and climbs gently towards the Witches. The original path kept along this side, but a newly upgraded path swings away to the right and new zigzags have been cut to avoid erosion. Various hiking clubs, whose plaques can be seen along the route, maintain them. Do not take any short cuts, for two reasons: short cuts are never easier and they cause erosion.

The zigzags themselves take you up to the base of the Sentinel. The north face was first climbed in 1959 by Angus and Pam Leppan. The summit was first reached via the western rock bands in 1910 by W Wybergh and N McLeod, in what was then considered a mountaineering

the amphitheatre

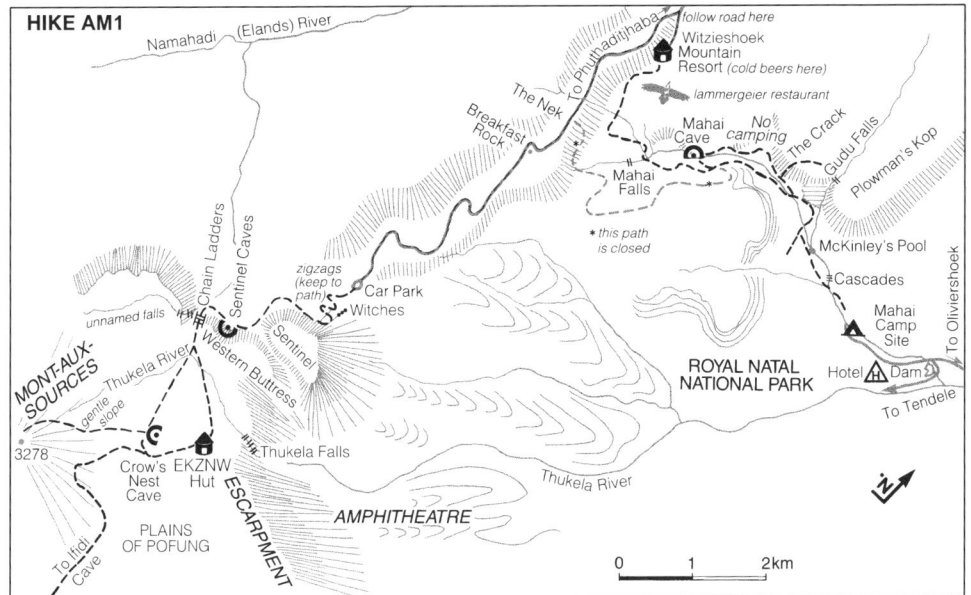

odyssey but is now regarded as a mere D-grade rock scramble requiring a rope over just one short section on the first rock band.

From the top of the zigzags the path veers off to the right (west) and climbs gently across the Western Buttress. There are magnificent views here of the Sentinel and Witches, the Malutis to the west and Witzieshoek's high plateaus to the north. In autumn the path is lined with yellow everlastings and the crinkly red blooms of Guernsey lilies, *Nerine sarniensis*. Where these lilies got their common name is worth noting: in 1659 a ship returning from the East past the Cape was wrecked off Guernsey. Its hold was full of bulbs which washed ashore and took root, and the plant was thought by early taxonomists to be native to the islands. Only when Kew Gardens' Francis Masson came collecting at the Cape was their true origin discovered – but how they came to be cultivated in Japan for centuries remains a mystery.

The 200-rung chain ladders (actually there are four ladders in total, two new ones having been added alongside the older ones so faster climbers can overtake those who 'freeze' on them) are reached after 3 km and a bit. The original ladders were commissioned in 1930 by the provincial administration and installed, according to Anton Zunckel, by his prolific grandfather. It was also Otto Zunckel who built the mountain hut on the Plain of Pofung as the top of the Amphitheatre is called by the Basotho. Originally it was equipped with tables and chairs, beds with mattresses, a stove and fireplace and open to all mountaineers, but over time it was ransacked and fell into total disrepair. It has been repaired but is now an EKZNW guard hut. The path from the ladders leads to the hut, and there's a turnoff to the edge of the Thukela Falls just before (1.5 km from the Chain Ladders).

The lip of the falls is situated close to the Sentinel gully, from where it's another 4 km to the far, eastern side of the Amphitheatre, which involves some ridge climbing. Just inland of Ribbon Falls (3 km on from the Thukela Falls) there is a stone kraal to give one tent shelter in a storm, or place to bed down under the stars. Another 3.5 km will take you to the top of Ifidi Pass, where an overhang forms the partial shelter of so-called Ifidi Cave. It's an easy day trip from the Sentinel car park. Plan to camp up here if you want the whole *enchilada*, as an exploration of the Amphitheatre would take most of a day. In about 1886 (a year before the Voortrekkers arrived in the area) this awesome formation was known as the Saddleback, or Horseshoe, gaining its current name only around 1900.

When you camp in the upper Thukela Basin (Plain of Pofung) take extreme care regarding ablutions and hygiene. Do not litter – anything, even food scraps (especially food scraps). Keep all soaps and shampoo out of natural water by washing a little way away. Bury all your bodily wastes and burn the paper (more of this in the 'Hygiene tips' box on page 87).

A variation of this hike is to start at RNNP/Mahai camp site and proceed up the right-hand bank of the Mahai River, past the trout hatchery and Queen's Causeway, and cross the stream after several hundred metres. The path goes quite steeply past Lookout Rock, veers back down to the river and crosses it to Gudu Bush about 2 km from the start. From here it continues parallel to the right-hand bank of the Mahai River, not too steeply under the sandstone cliffs of The Crack, crosses some side streams, and then rejoins the river just past Mahai Cave. Hikers are not allowed to camp out anywhere in the park so you can't make use of this cave. The path crosses the river and heads slightly uphill but more on the contour following a long spur. However, after about 300 m there is a junction where you have to turn sharp right (there are some old paths coming up from Tranquillity Pools in the river below which also join this section of the path). The path goes to The Nek, which lies on Coventry's bridle path, but it is closed at the top so you have to proceed to Basotho Gate/Witzieshoek.

Your route now winds up the 'inside' slope of the spur, rising gradually, and regains the river just above Mahai Falls (actually twin falls that join at the bottom but have one name). About 500 m above the falls (directly ahead and above is The Nek), the path veers off to the right and heads gently up to Basotho Gate and Witzieshoek Mountain Resort on the Sentinel Ridge. If you wish to carry on to the Sentinel car park, don't follow the paved road towards Phuthaditjhaba but take a short cut (this one is permissible) over the ridge to meet the gravel road.

THUKELA GORGE — HIKE AM2

Route: Thukela Gorge from car park just below Tendele camp
Distance: 14 km
Duration: 5 to 6 hours
Grade: Moderate to strenuous
General: Short of hiking to the top of the Amphitheatre, this is the most spectacular walk in the park, and one of the finest of all Berg walking experiences. Because of its relative shortness and ease, it is a popular hike. Added to these factors is the variation in vegetation, scenery and topography as the path passes through protea grassland, forest and finally the exciting gorge itself – only then is the real jewel of this hike revealed for the more intrepid souls who venture as far as their courage takes them....

the amphitheatre 41

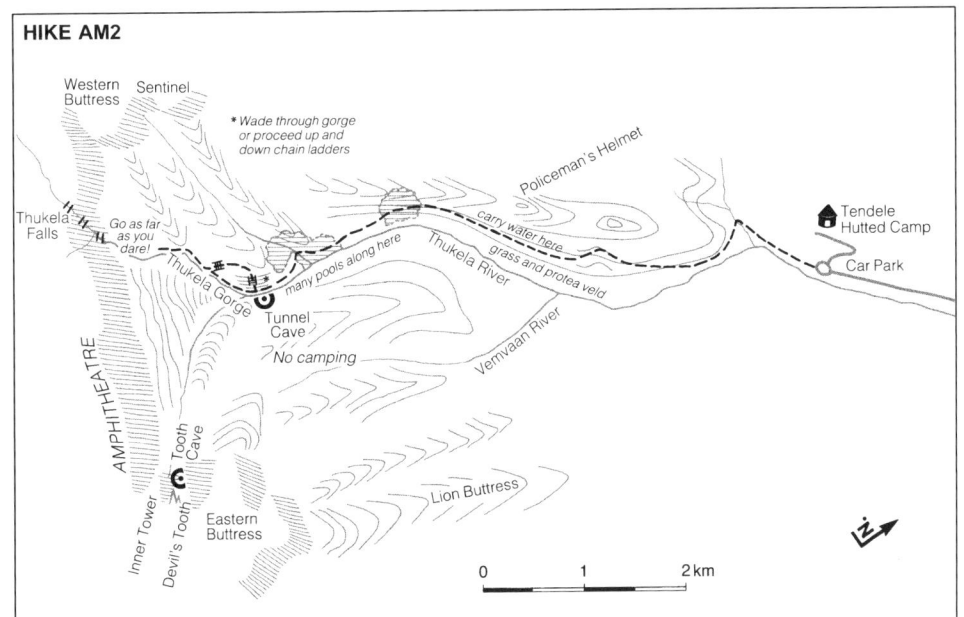

HIKE AM2

The path begins at the gravel car park: start from the visitors' centre, round the little dam and head for 2.5 km to the car park (the road continues up to Tendele). Park here and put on your boots: note the river braiding along the first sections, where deposition of a high-energy river (from its drop over the Escarpment and its funnelling through the gorge) has caused the small boulders to form braided channels. This is best seen in the drier seasons and slightly downstream of the start to the hike.

The path is easy to follow as it skirts the main valley. However, it does veer slowly away from the main channel to go a short way up the Vemvaan/Devil's Hoek Valley before turning off to the left and crossing the Vemvaan River after a kilometre. Along this stretch you are in protea veld where it gets surprisingly warm in summer, so carry water, even though you are following a river. The proteas will be either *Protea roupelliae*, identified by its hairy, silvery leaves and reddish flowers, or *Protea caffra*, with its larger, more waxy blue-grey leaves and whitish flowers. The silver-leafed protea is named after author and artist Arabella Roupell who published a flower book in the 1840s. It was once thought to be a distinct species, *Protea multibracteata*, but is now known to be the same one that occurs all the way up the Mpumalanga highlands from the Eastern Cape. It is similar in appearance to the famous waboom *Protea nitida* of the Western Cape. The grass habitat is called Highveld suurveld and consists mainly of communities of *Themeda–Festuca*.

In the days before farms and fences animals would feed high up in the foothills in summer, and then retreat to the pastures of sweeter thornveld in winter when the montane grasses became brittle and unpalatable to most grazers. This poses a major problem in the Berg, where those lowveld pastures are now located outside the park, as it severely restricts game numbers and variety in the park. Speaking of farms, this area was first surveyed in 1884 and many of the names in the RNNP are the names of the original farms – Dooley, Goodoo (Gudu), Vemvaan,

Devil's Hoek, Diamond, Basotho Pass and The Pastures. For about the next 2.5 km the path meanders along the cooler slope below the Policeman's Helmet, crossing a few side streams and passing through three small but delicious forest patches; the third is just over 300 m long, so provides a wonderful forest diversion.

These forests are part of the temperate Afro-montane biome and, depending on your terms of reference, are called (after the two dominant yellowwood species) yellowwood, temperate or Afro-montane forests. Yellowwoods, mountain hard pear and white pear, African holly, Cape beech, cabbage trees, stinkwoods, ironwoods (forest olive), ash, assegai and rooiels are the most important of the large forest trees you'll see here, while monkey ropes (*Secamone*) and beard lichens (*Usnea*) hang from their boughs.

A variety of ferns and flowering herbs grows among the forest litter and along the stream banks, most notably little white or pale blue *Streptocarpus* trumpets which so love the green gloom and silence deep in the forests. Along the stream banks you should look out for a variety of lily-like flowering bulbs, the star of which is the scarlet river lily, *Schizostylis coccinea*.

The main gorge is reached, usually after a crossing or two and some boulder hopping, at the confluence of the Thukela and Eastern Buttress gully: there is no need to mention pools as they are so numerous you can take your pick. From here you gain dramatic views up the gully to the Devil's Tooth and Inner and Outer Towers of the Eastern Buttress. Until 1950 the Tooth was deemed unclimbable, but most mountaineers are a headstrong lot and in that year E Scholes, D Bell and P Campbell formed the 'summit team' in the first successful assault on what is still considered one of the Berg's toughest rock challenges.

A short climb with a ladder at the top allows you to avoid wading through the gorge: this may be essential in wet weather when the gorge can become a death trap. This point is a good lunch stop, but if you decide to head back from here you'll miss the best part of the hike. A trip up the gorge is highly recommended in clear weather especially – if you're hiking in boots consider carrying trainers for this part as you will get your feet wet.

Near the end there is a slightly tricky but not difficult pool section to negotiate, and once you are through that the tunnel opens out at the base of the Amphitheatre where you will be quite gobsmacked by the enclosing basalt walls, echoing with booming silence. You can boulder hop and scramble from here for a few hundred metres further up the Thukela's course, as time and conditions allow. I would pace the trip to lunch in this bowl, where the scale of the place is a humbling experience, surrounded as you are by one of the greatest natural formations in Africa and beyond. And, another boon, you are unlikely to see other people.

GUDU BUSH AND FALLS — HIKE AM3

Route: Mahai camp site up the Mahai River to Gudu Falls
Distance: 4.6 km
Duration: 1.5 hours
Grade: Easy
General: A walk through diverse habitats and scenery, with some steep climbing (and sliding sometimes) and a cold invigorating swim at the end in a large pool at the base of the falls.

the amphitheatre 43

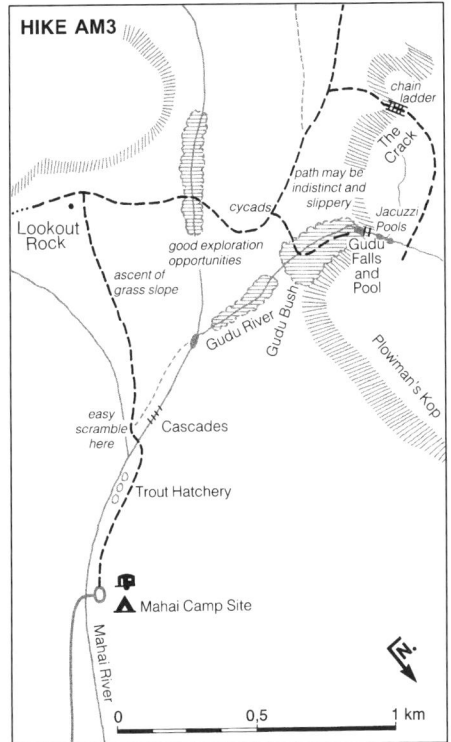

From Mahai camp site, follow the path up the Mahai River past the trout hatchery and then cross at the Queen's Causeway and continue past the Cascades – since this is a short walk it's a nice detour finding your way to the river and enjoying the spot where the river tumbles over the giant sandstone staircase. In late winter or early spring the tree fuchsias (*Halleria lucida*) should be glowing bright red with the tubular flowers that cluster on the stems; *lucida* means 'bright' or 'glowing' in Latin. The Zulu name *uTshwala-bezinyoni* means 'beer for the birds'.

Get back onto the path on the left-hand side of the river and proceed up the slight spur towards Lookout Rock (don't take the lesser path to the right about 150 m above the Cascades as this is a cul-de-sac to McKinley's Pool). The path climbs above Lookout Rock (on the left) and then veers to the right where a fork goes off to the left. About 300 m from Lookout Rock the path crosses Mahai River and carries on, more or less on the contour, around a shoulder and into a second river where you meet Gudu Bush. Along the route you should see quite diverse grass and vlei vegetation, including bracken, tree ferns and cycads, and veld flowers varying with the seasons.

A path, not shown on Slingsby's map, enters the forest and then turns left up the right-hand bank of the stream. The path ends on a bank above a large pool, surrounded by blocks of stone, into which the slender Gudu Falls drop. Due to a quirk of nature (or perhaps physics if you prefer), falling water cools so the pool is icy cold – in fact shocking as you enter, like Clifton in midsummer. But then that's the Berg for you, and it would be bad form not to take the plunge once you've reached it.

PLOWMAN'S KOP AND SPA POOL   HIKE AM4

Route: From Mahai camp site up Plowman's Kop and down the Mud Slide
Distance: 7 km
Duration: 2 to 3 hours
Grade: Moderate to strenuous
General: This is a round-trip over the Little Berg at Plowman's Kop. If you enjoy luxuriating in nature then you might consider making this a half- or even full-day outing, taking in the pool at the base of Gudu Falls and then backtracking onto the Mahai River path to reach The Crack.

44 the amphitheatre

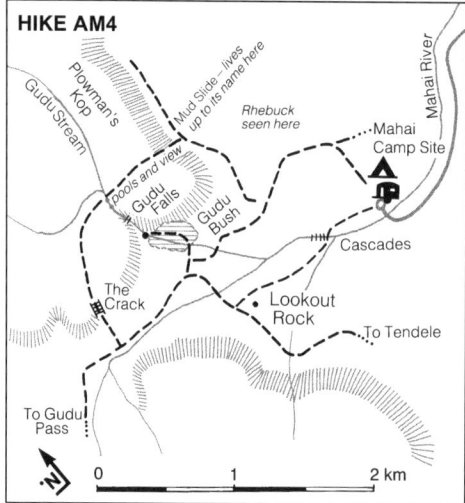

For the first 2 km this follows the Gudu Bush route, up past Lookout Rock and across the Mahai River to the edge of Gudu Bush. However, instead of entering the bush here you bear left and make your way along the slope of Plowman's Kop and parallel to and above the Mahai River for about another 700 m.

At this point you should see a lesser path leading up towards the cliffs of the Little Berg, and into The Crack. The way is quite clear, as is the break in the rock band. Scramble up through The Crack, using the chain ladder to get through the only potentially tricky section (although numbskulls might prefer to tackle the obstacle sans ladder).

Once on top of the cliff line, head for the high ground to your right, making for where Gudu Stream plunges over the edge. A series of natural 'Jacuzzi-style' pools lies in a shallow cutaway, connected by 'bum slides' – except that these pools have only the cold-water jet working! Around a corner is the lip of the falls, with views of the Amphitheatre and Mahai Valley neatly framed by the side of the rock channel.

Continue for about 400 m along Plowman's Kop in a line from where you first met the stream. Here you'll reach the edge of the Little Berg at the Mud Slide. This gully is the only way down here and it certainly lives up to its name (I always expect the park authorities to close it). At the bottom of the slide turn right for 800 m, then left for another 800 m where you cross an intermittent stream and the path veers down its left-hand bank towards Mahai. Rhebuck are often seen in this area. From here the path veers downhill for about another 800 m to a junction where you turn right along a well-maintained path to Mahai camp site, itself about another 700 m along the contour.

DEVIL'S HOEK VALLEY   HIKE AM5

Route: Thukela River car park to Devil's Hoek Valley
Distance: 6 km
Duration: 2 hours
Grade: Moderate
General: This hike takes you into the dramatic, oft mist-shrouded valley of the devil (actually named after the original farm on which it lies). Where the formal path peters out, adventure begins.... This walk begins facing towards the Devil's Tooth and Eastern Buttress, and ends heading in the direction of the Sentinel and Western Buttress. Once the mist clears the heat in the valley might get to you. If so, take some time out to savour the coolth while it lasts, and the birdsong in the small forest patches.

the amphitheatre 45

From the RNNP visitors' centre either walk or drive the 2.5 km to the car park on the north-east bank of the Thukela. Follow the river as for the Thukela Gorge walk (AM1). After about 700 m the path veers up the Vemvaan/Devil's Hoek Valley – there is (or should be) a concrete direction marker here. At the confluence of these two tributaries to the Thukela, our path keeps to the right-hand bank of the right-hand fork of the Devil's Hoek River. Make sure not to take one of the paths up to Tendele hutted camp which lies just above us, even where our path seems to be leaving the river's course. More or less 1 km from the Vemvaan/Devil's Hoek confluence (the path is far from straight), as you approach the first of two forest patches, a path branches off to the left to cross the river and proceeds up the Vemvaan Valley.

Our route carries on into the 'bush' which is about 300 m in length, and 400 m after you exit the first one the path enters the second 'bush'. This bush is quite a large one, and somewhere within its rank gloom the path just, in a word, disappears. Now you're getting onto steep ground and the cautious hiker will take it as a cue to turn back. But great mountains were never conquered by the cautious, so do as your heart dictates. Chances are you'll take a wrong direction and follow a tributary right out of the forest, but what does that matter?

Please take note that the Devil's Hoek River provides drinking water for some park guests so swimming in this river is strictly forbidden (if you're really hot, splash yourself only).

This is quite a convoluted area of valleys and ridges, rising up to the base of the great Amphitheatre wall. It's amazing to think that, nearly 100 years ago, the resolute men and women of the Natal Mountain Club dared to conquer its awesome precipices.

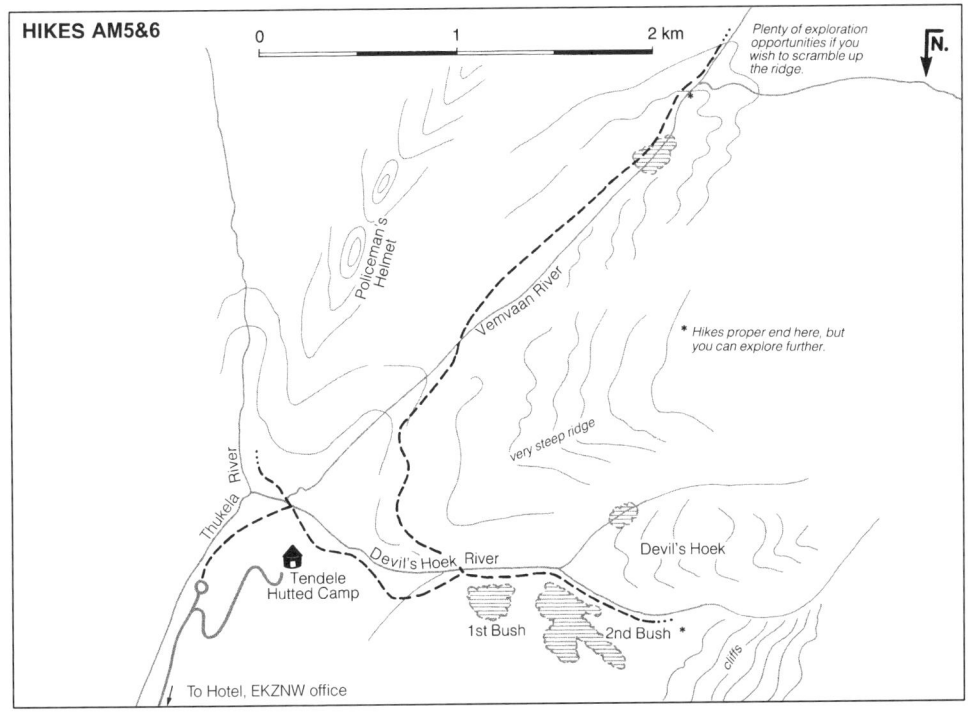

the amphitheatre

VEMVAAN VALLEY — HIKE AM6

Route: Thukela River car park up the Vemvaan Valley
Distance: 8 km
Duration: 3 hours
Grade: Moderate to strenuous
General: This valley walk is short and pretty easy, but 'pretty' is the operative word for obvious reasons. More energetic mountaineers can scramble up the ridges on either side: the Policeman's Helmet is especially rewarding for those with the mountaineer's curse (always one ridge further …), but you could start this one further down to make the going easier. The grade of the hike depends on how far you decide to go.

Start as for hikes AM1 and AM5, setting off from the Thukela River car park near Tendele and making your way through the protea veld to the Vemvaan/Devil's Hoek confluence (where the Thukela Gorge path takes a left branch to cross the stream). Continue up the Devil's Hoek Valley until just before the forest patch, where the Vemvaan path turns off to the left, goes uphill a short way and then crosses the Devil's Hoek River.

Now we're on new territory, but the path goes on an easy contour around a wide spur and into the Vemvaan River Valley just over 1 km from the Devil's Hoek crossing.

For about 1 km the path follows the left-hand stream bank, going quite steeply uphill towards a forest patch that lies just below the level of the cliffs on your left (this is the ridge of the Little Berg, at the end of which stands the Policeman's Helmet). Once in the forest the path reaches the river, follows it for about a hundred metres, exits the forest and vanishes into grassland on the side of the Policeman's Helmet ridge.

For fun you can make a sharp left turn to work your way onto the spine of the ridge and then go either up or down it. At the very upper end of this ridge are the three Witches who seem to have been torn away from the Sentinel.

Somewhere high above the Policeman's Helmet ridge grows the only known colony of perhaps the rarest and most threatened of all true proteas, *Protea nubigena* ('born of the clouds'), but you're unlikely to see them unless you're lucky enough to chance upon the small, leggy plants while they're flowering, in autumn. They're not much to look at, but they're a real botanical 'ooh-ah'.

SIGUBUDU RIDGE TO SURPRISE RIDGE — HIKE AM7

Route: A trip from the visitors' centre, via the Sigubudu Ridge to the park's north-eastern boundary
Distance: 12 km
Duration: 4 to 5 hours
Grade: Strenuous to severe
General: Make an early start if you want to see mountain reedbuck or grey rhebuck. Even though they have enjoyed nearly a century of protection here, to them you are a potential

and large predator. You might even see one of the last surviving blesbok in the park. Not all the paths in this area are distinct, so you might have to use your own judgement and general sense of orienteering if you want to get back to camp in time for tea.

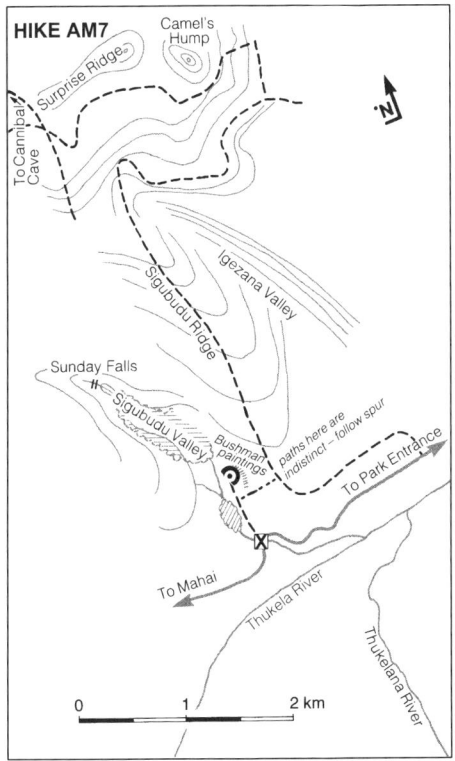

More or less midway between the visitors' centre and the guard's checkpoint the park road makes a big bend. On the cusp of this bend a path leads off to the left (going in the direction of the park entrance) to an overhang with some faded Bushman paintings – this is the route we take. Proceed, if you like, on to the cave at the base of the cliffs facing Sigubudu Stream, but our path turns off to the right a little way before the cliffs, making for the crest of the spur (Sigubudu Ridge). The path may be indistinct so follow your nose.

Once on the ridge a clear path runs all the way up for about 2.8 km, between two patches of forest, to the Igezana Stream. The path veers around to the right (east) to cross three branches of the upper stream. Here you are just several hundred metres shy of the Camel's Hump – but the path doesn't go that way; it wends its way further east as it goes to and around the next spur. What you should do is make for the hump along the line of least resistance (the normal procedure for getting across open ground in the Berg). Along the way you'll cross the contour path that runs all the way from Rugged Glen to the Mahai River.

The hump is situated on the park boundary on a side spur of Surprise Ridge. You can take the same route back, or take advantage of the network of paths in this area of the park, most prominent of all being the Rugged Glen/Mahai Valley contour path. Your choices are many: I would suggest that either you take the same route back, or you proceed for about 2.5 km westwards (the Amphitheatre on your left) where you can turn left onto the path that leads down past Sunday Falls and Fairy Glen and right back to the visitors' centre.

Bear in mind that this path does not go directly to the visitors' centre, but heads towards Mahai camp site, where you reach an intersection forcing you virtually to double back, cross two streams, head through a patch of bush and only then reach the centre.

Bushmen probably did not inhabit these ridges and valleys after the early 19th century – not because they lacked natural appeal but because of the Nguni invasions and tribal warfare that fomented around the rise of the Zulu people. Marauding Zulu impis laid waste the land and reduced the once peaceful pastoralists into cannibals. The Bushmen stood no chance.

48 the amphitheatre

SURPRISE RIDGE AND CANNIBAL CAVE — HIKE AM8

Route: Mahai camp site to Cannibal Caves and back
Distance: 14 to 16 km
Duration: 5 to 6 hours
Grade: Strenuous to severe
General: This hike more or less reverses a variation return journey of the Plowman's Kop hike (AM4), down from Surprise Ridge which forms the park boundary. The walk can be extended by following the contour path on the way back, westwards to the Mahai Valley and then back down to the camp site. The cave is on land owned by the Carte family, who own the Cavern Berg Hotel, but access is by right of way – just respect their rights and your privilege. This huge overhang is of historic interest, as will be alluded to below....

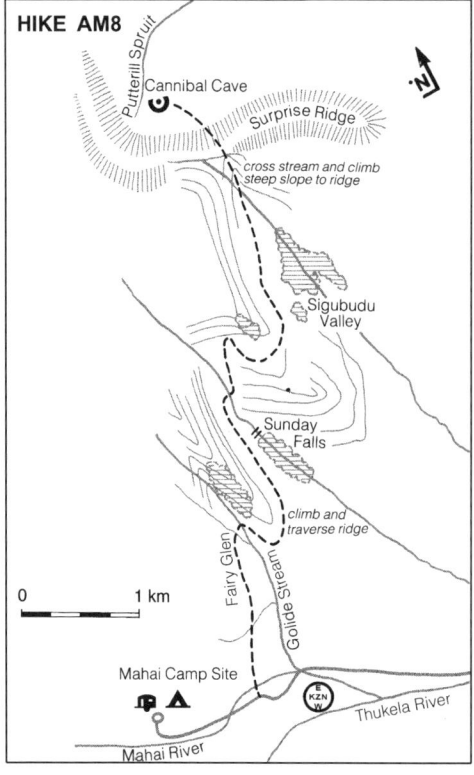

Our path to an uncertain fate at Cannibal Cave begins by reversing the first part of the Plowman's Kop walk (AM4), heading towards the Mud Slide. From Mahai camp site, take the path out of the 'back' (north) side of the camp site area, going on a gentle contour for about 700 m to a crossing, along the way crossing two small stream courses (ignore the side path up to the left, to Plowman's Kop). At the crossing, 100 m after the side junction, take the extreme left-hand path towards Fairy Glen, crossing a larger and a smaller stream before the path veers uphill into Golide Stream Valley.

Before reaching the Glen, however, take the side junction to the right to round a spur and proceed into the valley to the right, which climbs gently past Sunday Falls. About 1.2 km from the previous junction there is a turnoff to the right heading to the falls – well worth the 500-m return side trip.

The next 3 km is a delightful stroll which becomes nominally steep only as you approach Surprise Ridge. First you cross the Sunday Falls Stream, then you round a spur to enter the next valley to your right (north-east) and proceed on the contour into the Sigubudu Valley, and then up to a crossing with the contour path that runs from Rugged Glen to the Mahai River. Carry straight on here for 1 km, a little way further on crossing the park boundary and then keeping to the contour over Surprise Ridge to the cave. To your right you'll see the Camel's Hump (1 889 m); the large spur to your left is The Diamond,

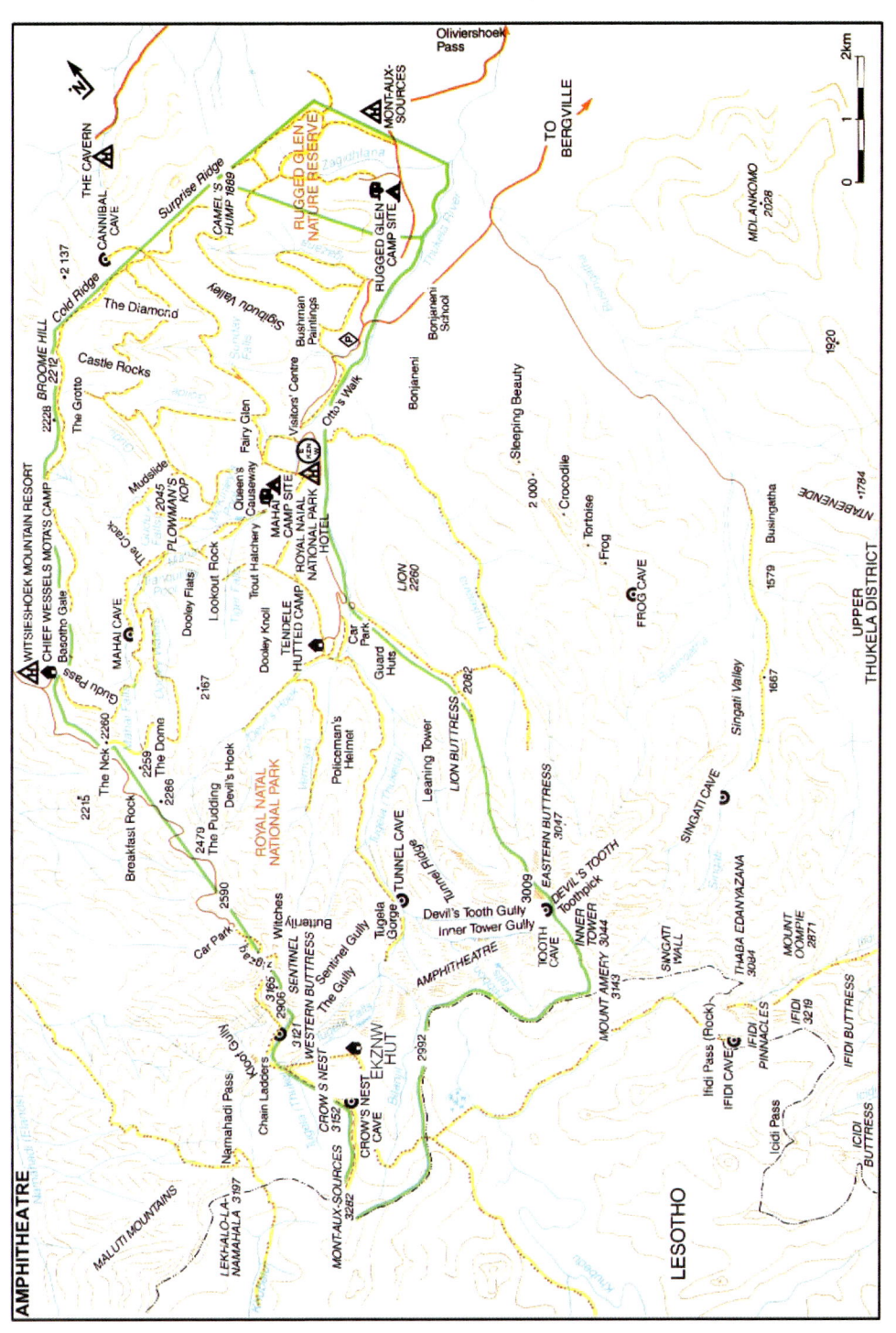

OPPOSITE: Looking through the gully between the Sentinel and Western Buttress; in summer fearsome storms brew around the ramparts of the dragon's lair.
ABOVE: A Zulu homestead in the Upper Thukela district, combining the old and new ways of building.
RIGHT: A hiker, laden for a long High Berg traverse, summits the upper of two sections of the Chain Ladders.

LEFT: Looking down into the Mnweni Cutback, at dawn.
TOP: The view from Ledger's Cave, looking out to a buttress that juts out from the Ncedamabutho headland.
ABOVE: Clusters of hailstones, the night after a thunderous storm.

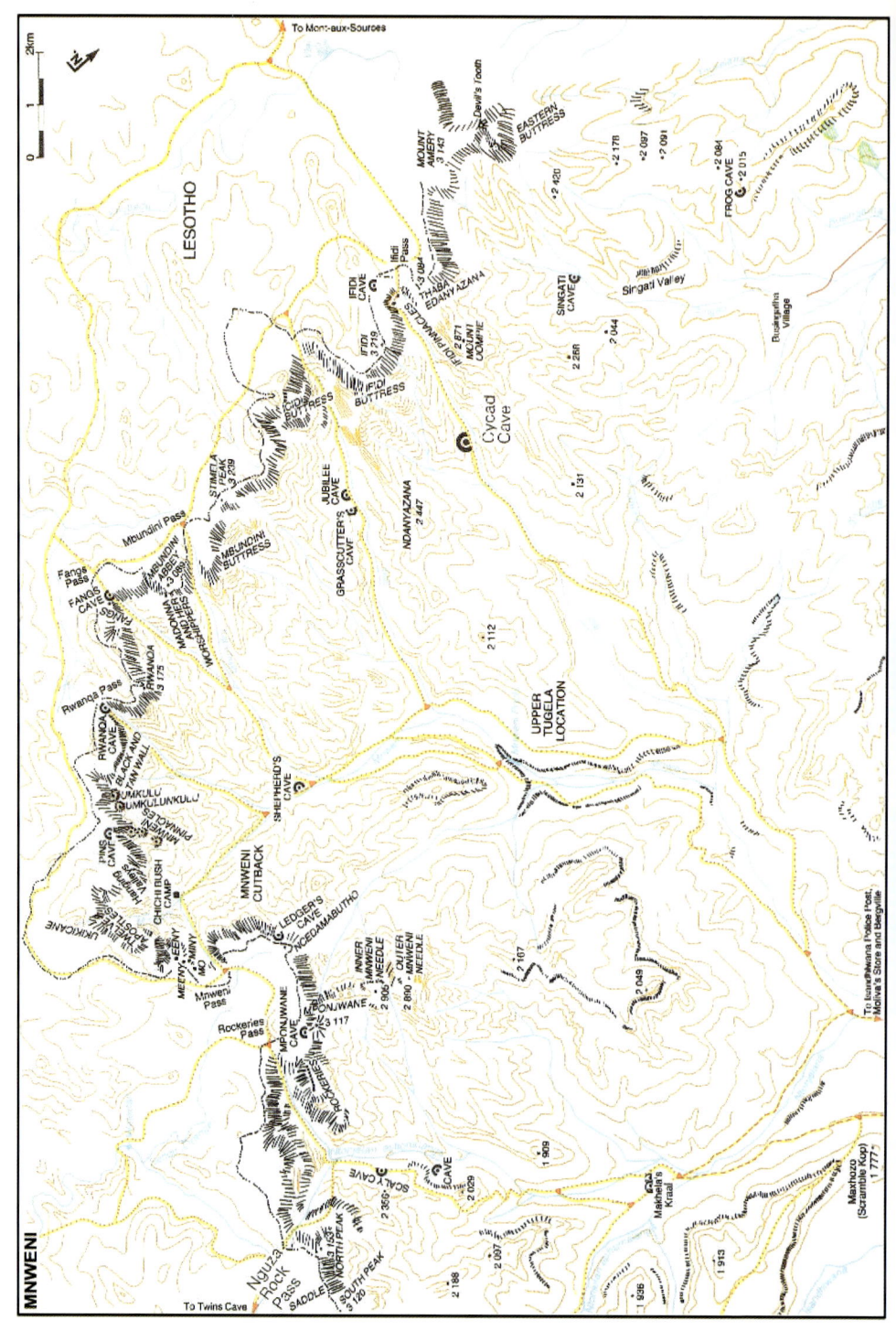

ABOVE: Two guides take shelter in Ledger's Cave after a wet night's ascent of Mnweni Pass. The Mnweni visitors' centre and trained guides are a welcome development of one of the less hiked but most spectacular (and toughest) parts of the Berg.

RIGHT: Red-hot pokers are common on the summit. This one grew close to the Ndumeni Caves, near where the summits of Organ Pipes and Thuthumi passes converge.

OVERLEAF: Mponjwane pinnacle stands proud from the Ncedamabutho promontory, where a hiker approaches the source of the Senqu, or Orange, to collect water for the walk to Ntonjelana Pass.

named after the original farm here. The 'cave' is really one huge overhang, partly shielded from below by some fair-sized trees.

Following the ravages of the impis of Shaka and other warlords, the whole Drakensberg area was decimated. This and subsequent upheavals which spread across much of southern Africa are often referred to as the Difaqane or Mfecane wars, but some historians dispute that there was one definite period of widespread warfare. Who knows? What we do know is that the tribes around the Drakensberg were displaced, one by the next, and that many of the surviving clans turned to cannibalism. One of these was led by a Chief Sidinane whose people occupied this cave. They would raid the lowlands and capture anyone they found alone or straggling behind a group fleeing from some or other terror. Victims were strung up alive from trees in the 'larder' to keep fresh. If passers-by were in short supply, they'd eat their own children and wives, it is recorded by white travellers and missionaries who passed through and actually visited the caves. Those images of missionaries in pots that made popular cartoons in Europe came from these parts and times.

To whet your appetite further, here's a quote from Reg Pearse's *Barrier of Spears*: 'People dared not move about except in large, armed parties, and preferably at night. Lonely strangers had hardly any chance at all. Victims would first be ham-strung and kept in the "pantry" until needed. Then they would be killed, often with a twist of the neck, cut up, skinned and roasted or grilled. After having devoured the flesh, they emptied the skull and made a cup of it. They melted the fat by the sun or the heat of a fire, and either drank it or anointed their hair with it.'

This occurred in the 1820s and 30s, and when the Voortrekkers reached KwaZulu-Natal they claimed they found no settlements from the mountains to the sea. An old man once told a historian that there was a path of white from Witzieshoek to Bushman's Nek 'and that mark was our bones'. So, Difaqane or no, those were rough times. The troubles, which reduced the population of the area from an estimated one million to around 5 000, started before Shaka's reign and appear to have been in the time of Dingiswayo and Matiwane, who started the first major war. One tribe pushed against another – Mthwethwe attacked Amangwane, who fled into the Drakensberg to displace the Amahlubi, who fled into the foothills and laid waste the Amazizi, who then turned on the Bushmen....

Once back at the contour path, you should consider turning right to head towards the Mahai Valley, rounding The Diamond, Castle Rocks and Plowman's Kop along the way. If you take this route, the total distance of the walk will be about 16 km.

LION BUTTRESS HIKE AM9

Route: Thukela River car park to Lion Buttress
Distance: 9 km
Duration: 3 to 4 hours
Grade: Strenuous to severe
General: This is a fairly steep but short hike, but since the Thukela forms the RNNP boundary most of it lies in what used to be known as 'Upper Tugela Bantu location' although the ridge itself now lies in the greater uKhahlamba-Drakensberg Park (U-D Park). Along the ridge you

58 the amphitheatre

gain views down into the Thukelana River Valley to your left and Singati Ridge beyond that, while to your right the upper Thukela Valley reveals itself. The Lion Ridge and Buttress lead directly up to the Outer Tower or Eastern Buttress of the Amphitheatre, so, although this is not an obvious walk, it is quite spectacular. There is no real end point to this hike, other than the main cliffs of the Drakensberg, and I have given the distance to a high point at about 2 500 m, which is the general altitude of the contour path that runs for much of the length of the range.

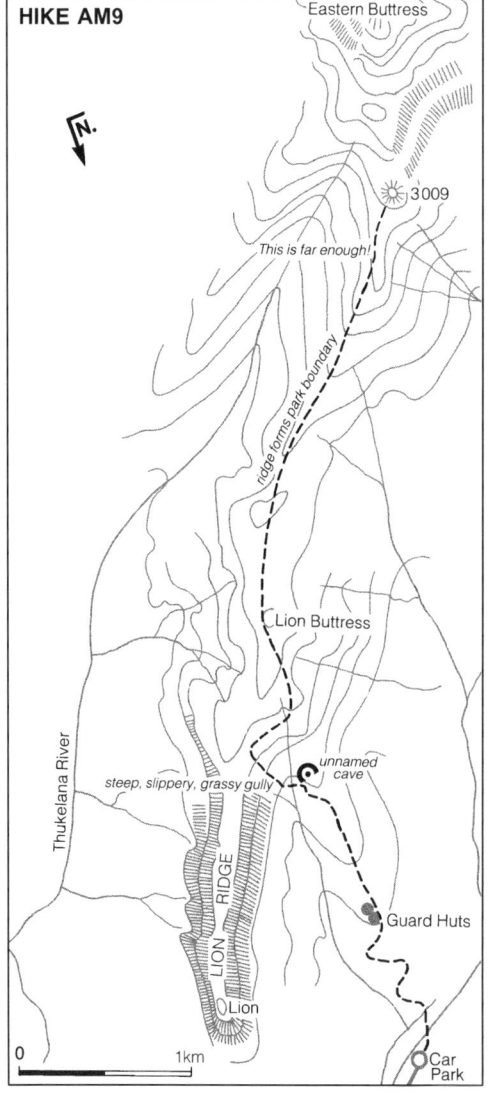

If you're staying at Tendele and have already done the obligatory Thukela Gorge walk, then you'll no doubt be looking at this ridge and wondering.... And yes, you can do it even though it lies outside the RNNP. Start at the car park next to the Thukela, and cross the river by going slightly upstream. The path, for which you have to look fairly carefully, winds its way up to the right of a side stream, moving up diagonally to the end of a line of cliffs on the other side of the stream, passing the huts of Lion Camp about 650 m above the Thukela (but longer by winding path). This guard post is on tribal land that has been ceded to the U-D Park, and is manned by RNNP personnel – all very confusing but of little concern to the hiker.

About 700 m above the guard post there's a cave near the end of the sandstone ridge, and since you're now outside the RNNP you are allowed to make camp here or anywhere else within the U-D Park.

From the level of the cliffs the path makes its way up a side shoulder, heading for the spine of the main ridge. Once on the crest of Lion Ridge, fine views open out on all sides: the Great Escarpment wall directly above, the entire bowl of the Amphitheatre to the north-west, and the pleats of the valleys to the south-east leading into the fields and villages of KwaZulu-Natal beyond. It's possible to continue for another 2 km or so up the ridge, but there is no specific end point. Just don't take unnecessary chances and do give heed to any inclement weather: you don't want to be trapped up here in a storm. There is an alternative walk, also outside the

RNNP, starting at the visitors' centre and behind the trout dam to cross the Tendele road and then the Thukela River. It then heads on a cattle path over the lower end of Lion Buttress and into the Thukelana River Valley. About 1 km from the Thukela it crosses the Thukelana (little Thukela) and proceeds up the left-hand bank for about another 5 km. It's a pleasant walk but it doesn't really go anywhere: return the same way.

If you've got one of Slingsby's maps of the northern Berg, and you really want to get away from the hustle and bustle of RNNP, it's a bit of a drive out of the park back towards Bergville (take the right-hand fork just outside the park, not the left-hand one which leads to Oliviershoek Pass) for about 3 km to a store at Busingatha village. Turn right here (about 200 m before a bridge) and proceed to the end of the road, a few hundred metres after crossing the Busingatha River (pay one of the villagers to look after your car – better still, give a rand or two and promise the rest of a tenner when you return and the car is safe).

Walk through Busingatha village on the path that leads up the Singati Valley (not to be confused with the Busingatha valley and ridge which lie across to your right). A little over 2 km from the end of the village the path climbs steeply for a short way, then heads diagonally to the right under a line of cliffs. About 3.5 km from the village it crosses a side stream, then another, and heads up a narrow gorge which lies in line with the Eastern Buttress and Devil's Tooth. This path ends at Singati Cave (facing north-west), which can sleep a large party. Enjoy the eventual solitude.

FAIRY GLEN — HIKE AM10

Route: From either Mahai camp site or the visitors' centre, into the Fairy Glen forest to a waterfall
Distance: About 5 km
Duration: An hour each way
Grade: Easy
General: This is a very fine short walk, suitable even for young children, in summer especially for it leads into the most gorgeous forest and then there's the sure attraction of a waterfall. How could anyone refuse? There is an alternative route to Sunday Falls halfway along the path to Fairy Glen (for a 6-km round-trip).

From both Mahai and the visitors' centre paths lead uphill to a crossing about midway between two streams that lie about 400 m apart (from either Mahai or the centre you will already have crossed two streams on the way: it's about 700 m from Mahai and the same from the centre, but on a winding path).

From Mahai turn left here, or right from the centre, onto a path that is marked Fairy Glen. This path heads gently into the Golide Valley, in which the Glen lies. From where a path leads off to the right to Sunday Falls the going gets a bit steeper as you follow Golide Stream up into the Fairy Glen forest. In the forest the path climbs a relatively steep slope before coming to an unmarked waterfall. This is an enchanting walk, where you lose all sense of the surroundings.

To make this a half-day outing, return down the Fairy Glen path but take the left-hand side junction to Sunday Falls – a different experience from that of Fairy Glen. The falls are 1.5 km along an easy path, making a 10-km round-trip.

60 the amphitheatre

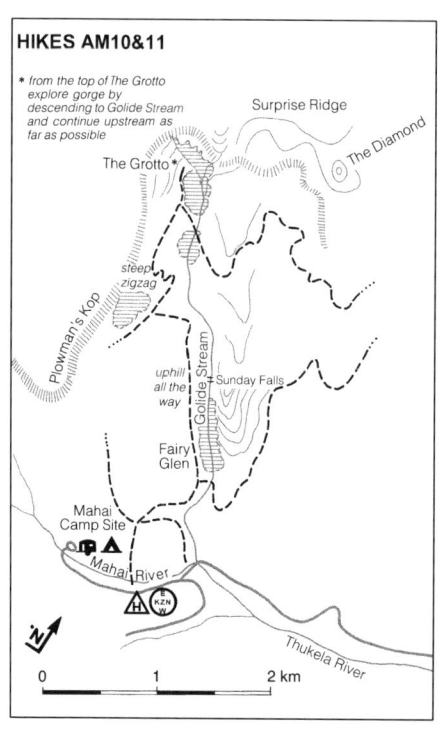

HIKES AM10 & 11

- from the top of The Grotto explore gorge by descending to Golide Stream and continue upstream as far as possible

SNAKE TIPS

- Snakes deserve consideration and conservation.
- They bite when there's no other survival option.
- Shock, not the venom itself, causes the most damage.
- If you're not absolutely sure of the type of snake – do nothing.
- Treat a berg adder bite with anti-venom serum and you only double the trouble.
- If bitten, stay calm and still to reduce blood flow and shock. Send for help.
- A rinkhals bite slowly decreases central nervous functioning.
- A puff adder bite affects local tissue but isn't immediately life-threatening.

THE GROTTO   HIKE AM11

Route: From either Mahai or the visitors' centre to the upper reaches of Golide Stream
Distance: About 9 km
Duration: 4 hours
Grade: Strenuous
General: This walk combines protea grassland, riverine and forest habitats with opportunities to explore around the top and above The Grotto. It takes in Fairy Glen along the way. The names alone are enticement enough.

For the first half the route is the same as for Fairy Glen (AM10 above), leading all the way to the Glen. And, since you're there, it would be a severe oversight not to stop at the waterfall within the forest glade. A 'glen' is a narrow, steep valley, but I imagine here it refers more to a forested valley, which does get narrow and steep in its upper reaches around the waterfall.

Once out of the forest the path continues for just over 1 km, after some zigzagging close to but above the stream, veering to the left away from Golide Stream to join the contour path from Mahai, where The Grotto is signposted. Follow the contour path for about 300 m on an easy gradient to a forest patch and some zigzags below the cliffs of Plowman's Kop, which you have to surmount (the switchbacks, not the koppie). From the top of the zigzags remain on the contour path for another 400 m back towards Golide, to where it swings to the right to cross the stream.

Here a path leads uphill to the left and after a short stretch of the calf muscles you enter the forest that encompasses The Grotto, which in fact consists of two connecting gorges cut through the sandstone cliff line, both worthy of exploration. The main path (if you can call it that for it peters out around here) keeps to the right – the main river course. You can also take a lesser path up the left-hand bank of the tributary that goes up to the left. But, as always, don't do anything foolish and never go up anything you can't easily reverse: it is far easier to climb up than to down-climb something, so make very sure before setting off to explore.

RUGGED GLEN TO MAHAI — HIKE AM12

Route: From Rugged Glen camp site to Mahai camp site, or vice versa
Distance: A one-way trip of 14 km
Duration: 5 to 6 hours
Grade: Strenuous to severe
General: Rugged Glen is a satellite of the RNNP, having been added well after the park was first proclaimed. It has its own camping facilities, as well as stables where guests can rest their feet and put the pressure on their rumps instead (i.e. go for a horse-ride). The park's main road connects the two camp sites, even though you have to go through the main gate to get there, allowing you to arrange transport from the end back to the beginning (or take the easier 6-km walk back along the road).

Starting at Rugged Glen, cross the road, proceed to the Zagidhlana Stream and head upstream in the direction of the Camel's Hump which lies at the eastern end of Surprise Ridge up ahead. The path crosses the stream four times, passing four forested side valleys before coming to a crossing about 2.4 km from the camp site. This section is moderately steep and sustained, but as long as you take it easy and pace yourself (never get to the point where you're gasping for breath, unless you're in training for a triathlon) you'll make it; whenever you feel the urge stop and enjoy the views.

At this point don't take the slip road to the left as we have to carry on ever upwards (we've veered well away from the stream and now the path begins to veer back). After crossing the upper reaches of the Zagidhlana a path joins from the right (coming up from a ranger's post) and here we begin a zigzag haul up towards the Camel's Hump. When slogging up slopes such as this one I always seem to end up reciting a poem by James Thurber as a sort of mantra:

The way is long and getting longer.
The road goes uphill all the way,
and even further.
I wish you luck. You'll need it.

And yes, our path does eventually slacken off and take a contour off to the left under the Hump (although a side path to the right goes all the way up the Hump – 1 889 m). We can now be said to be on a contour path all the way into the Mahai Valley, nearly 9 km onwards. However, like 'steep' and 'not far' round here the word 'contour' is something of a relative one. Spurs and river valleys get in the way and these

62 the amphitheatre

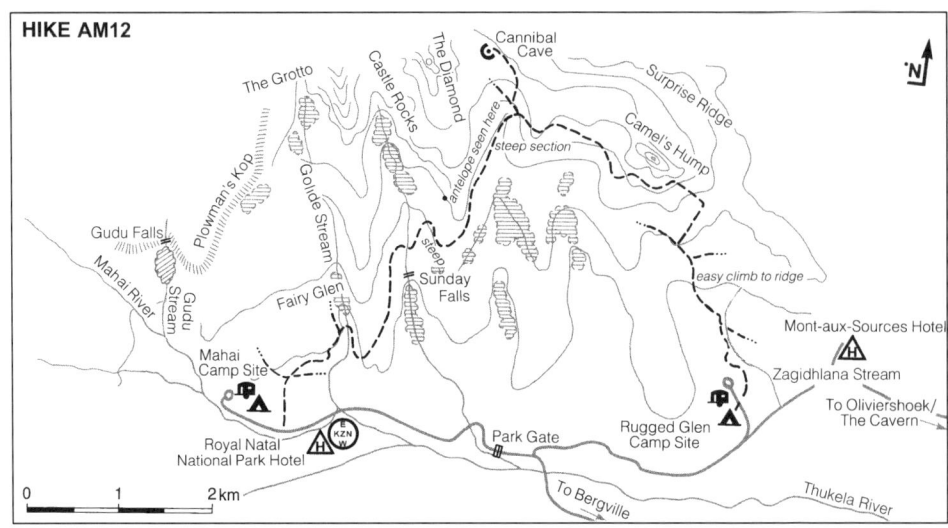

HIKE AM12

have to be gone round, over or through (down and up). On this route we have to round the Hump, another unnamed spur, The Diamond and Castle Rocks, crossing seven streams before we get to below Plowman's Kop. Oh yes, and there the small matter of a big switchback below Castle Rocks has to be 'negotiated' (climbed).

Once at Golide Stream (below The Grotto in the forest above you) there's a very short, easy climb out and then it's pretty much downhill all the way. First there are the zigzags, followed by a long, straight run (figuratively speaking) all the way below the cliffs of the Kop, past where the Mud Slide comes hurtling down, and so descending the main spur to a T-junction. There's a short cut here to the left and down to Mahai camp site. Otherwise turn right along an easy climb into Gudu Bush where you bear left to cross Gudu Stream and down and around to the Mahai River. In Gudu Bush you can proceed up the right-hand bank to the Gudu Falls, which is well worth the extra few hundred metres if you're not already pooped.

Once across the Mahai, the path descends away from the river to round Lookout Rock (keep left and don't take the right-hand fork to Tiger Falls) and then you're heading straight for home, or at least the end of this memorable and varied hike.

Note: There are any number of variations of hikes in RNNP that you can piece together with a good map, and not just accept what I say is or isn't a hike. There are also lots of shorter walks or strolls along any of the paths in the park – you don't have to do an 'official' walk to have a nice outing, just do whatever you want to. Some of these include the short and simple Otto's Walk that starts at the visitors' centre and goes down the left-hand bank of the Thukela for about 2 km: it may not seem grand – until you turn round and get one of the best views of the Amphitheatre to be had; real postcard stuff in the right light. Then there's the cave with faded Bushman paintings, reached by taking the path 1.4 km down from the visitors' centre, where the tar road makes a wide loop. The walk there is only about 300 m, and not too steep (though lounge lizards will tell me that these things are relative!). Whatever you do, remember that it's supposed to be fun. Since the park's drinking water is taken from the Mahai River, swimming (and the like) in it is not allowed.

mnweni

Sandwiched between the two popular hiking areas of Royal Natal National Park (RNNP) and Cathedral Peak is the wildest, most dramatic part of the Drakensberg – Mnweni. In *Barrier of Spears* Reg Pearse waxes so lyrical about this area there can be no doubt it was also his favourite hiking area, and few people knew and appreciated the Berg better than he. Mnweni is a place of streams and passes, rivalled only for these by the Lotheni/Mkhomazi area, but despite this Mnweni takes the prize for its daunting ruggedness and awesome beauty.

Other than perhaps spending a weekend – or a week – at Waterfall Cave in the Ntonjelan' ephumalanga valley (which was never a well-known outing and seems to have remained so), virtually all hikers come to Mnweni to get onto the summit, so to redress this the descriptions of the various easier passes form the bulk of this chapter. But in their haste to get to the top they miss many of Mnweni's most beautiful attractions – the rivers. And the fairest in the land of beauties is to be found on one of the most trodden paths – Mnweni Baths, found one kilometre upstream of the confluence of the Mnweni and Ifidi rivers. The baths are a series of cascades racing for about a hundred metres down a chute of polished sandstone, forming lovely pools at each level along the way.

I suppose the real reason few hikers linger in the lower valleys is that this is the only part of the Berg that does not fall into the uKhahlamba-Drakensberg Park (U-D Park). It was previously known as a 'Bantu location' and remains tribal land (probably because the land was too rugged to be claimed by white settler farmers). Although stunningly pretty in their own right, these valleys are choc-a-bloc now with kraals and fields. Until you get into the real foothills, you're likely to walk to the resounding call of 'sweets, sweets' and the pitter-patter of little children's feet. The people who live here are Amangwane and Amazizi, ancestors of once proud clans that fell victim to various pre-Zulu and Zulu impis and were left as scattered remnants in the high foothills. All hikes used to start at the Isandhlwana police post, as that was the only safe place to leave a car – this being a stronghold of dagga traders and cattle rustlers – and there did not used to be any visitor accommodation. However, with the help of Bergwatch, a community guiding centre has been opened. All hikes in the Mnweni area will leave from this centre, where an entrance fee will have to be paid (the money subsidising the guides) and the mountain register filled in. There is also rustic accommodation here. Guides are available for day and multi-day hikes as well as to show you the rock art sites of the area. The centre is located 100 m beyond the concrete causeway over the Ntonjelana (nTonyelane) River at its confluence with the Mnweni. This will also cut out the 'horrible' (to quote a Bergwatch member) six-kilometre slog up from the police post past Moliva's Store. I just hope they improve the road because the last time I drove it I had to enlist the help of several strong Zulu men to extricate my non-4x4 from the thick clay mud.

To get to Mnweni take the Rookdale turnoff at Bergville and then the P388 turnoff (the second turnoff to Woodstock Dam) onto a gravel road. Continue for a kilometre to a turnoff to the right (D13). From there it is nine kilometres to the police station (visible at the end of a gravel track on the right). Bypass this turnoff and continue for another six kilometres, past Moliva's Store, to the long concrete causeway which crosses the Ntonjelana River, and just beyond that lies the visitors' centre.

Once here, you've thankfully left most of humanity behind and are about to enter the realm of the mountains even though there are small kraals yet for some way up the Mnweni and Ifidi valleys. On the other hand, many of these are the traditional beehive huts or thatch and clay rondavels and the sense is of being in wildest Africa. Some scenes, especially at Hlongwane's and Makhela's kraals in the Ntonjelana Valley directly below the Saddle, make good photos.

There are so many rivers draining this heavily pleated land, but two that are often overlooked are the Ntonjelan' ephumalanga (of the rising sun – east) and the Ntonjelan' eshonalanga (of the setting sun – west). I've included a new walk up one of these valleys that is so straightforward and so rewarding it's amazing it's not better known: that up to Waterfall Cave. You'll see.

People often ask me about safety in the Berg, and although there were some incidents of robbery and even one of murder on the summit in this area in the late 1980s (not to mention a minor rebellion in the 1960s and full-scale war in the early 1800s), I have never felt personally threatened in any way. However, bad things can happen. One way of preventing them – and the more likely scenario of getting lost – is to contract one of the trained community guides who know the area and the language. On my traverse in 2002 I used the guides for a food drop, as well as to guide us in heavy mist from Mnweni to Cathedral, and can confirm they are top class. They can introduce you to places and shelters not known to outsiders.

The community guides, who can be contacted through the visitors' centre, form part of a long-term conservation and tourism initiative in the area, which was started in 1995 as a collaboration between the local community, Bergwatch and the Wildlife and Environment Society of Southern Africa (Wessa). Donga reclamation, which hikers will come across, is also part of this programme. The Rand Water-Mnweni Trust operates independently and also employs local people in donga rehabilitation.

The Mnweni area is the largest tribal tract in the Drakensberg, and it falls under amaNgwane Tribal Authority, the current chief being Inkosi Maswazi Hlongwane who lives in the Cathedral area. So remember that you are a visitor in their lands and at all times be courteous. Take some time to learn the few Zulu words and phrases found at the back of this book, and take note of the section on Zulu customs at the end of this chapter (see page 77), for they will stand you in good stead. Since this is a prime place for smugglers, you should not hike here in groups of fewer than three, and it is best to avoid sleeping near well-used passes or paths.

The earliest English name for the Mnweni Cutback/Rockeries area was Cathedral, and Mponjwane was the Cathedral, or Rockeries Tower. What is now called Cathedral Peak was called Mponjwane (the small horn on a heifer), or Zikhali's Horn after a local chief. But some map maker of the later 1800s got it all wrong and so it has remained. Mponjwane is one of the noblest of all peaks in the Drakensberg. The Zulu name for it is more appropriate – Nthabamabutho, meaning 'mountain of the warriors'. This far better suits so noble a mountain: with many name changes happening, now might be the time to rectify this one. It will undoubtedly offend some old-timer mountaineers, but it would be the right taxonomical thing.

'Politics' aside, for the mountaineer Mnweni offers the most exhilarating climbing in the Drakensberg, whether it's the mighty ramparts of Mponjwane, the solid rock of the Rockeries, or the even more exposed pinnacles and needles of Mbundini, it is this area more than any which exemplifies the name 'uKhahlamba' – the barrier of spears – and anyone who has hiked or climbed here would agree that a finer name would be hard to conceive.

As a final word before we set off hiking, with the exception of the last two walks described in this chapter, all hikes in Mnweni are passes routes that go to the Escarpment. All will therefore take three days or more, and even the last two will be at least two-day outings. So the duration given is conditional on what the rest of the hike entails and should not be seen as an isolated hike.

A warning: there are numerous river crossings in the following routes. This is a particularly well-watered area and in summer rains the rivers tumble furiously over steep ground. Lives have been lost in these rivers so, please, take extra care when crossing any flooded water course.

MNWENI PASS — HIKE MN1

Route: Departing from the Mnweni visitors' centre, up the Mnweni Valley and Mnweni Cutback topping out onto the Ncedamabutho headland
Distance: 21 km one way
Duration: 10 to 12 hours (2- or 3-day round-trip)
Grade: Extreme, very extreme
General: This is one of the longer, tougher passes to hike in the Berg, but amazingly it is fairly

popular. One reason is the pure grandeur of the place, as well as the beauty of the Mnweni Valley. Then there is the convenient location of Shepherd's Cave, 15.5 km away and just where the path starts its serious climbing into the Little Berg. If I had to choose just one hike that best showcased the Drakensberg's mighty appeal, it would have to be this one, or perhaps its twin, Rockeries Pass. Since most routes here will go up one and down the other, you're in for something awesome, so buckle up and take a deep breath. A round-trip up Mnweni and down Rockeries, or vice versa, should take four days, although it can be done on the trot in three.

You're going to want an early start, so I suggest overnighting at the visitors' centre (remember to fill in the mountain register because, if ever you need to be rescued, this is the most likely place to start looking – read about the incident in the section on snakes in the natural history chapter, page 27.

From the visitors' centre the path heads towards the Mnweni River (the right-hand fork), which it reaches after 1.5 km. But do not cross here, that path goes up towards Icidi/Ifidi; rather bear left up the left-hand river bank. Our path keeps away from the river and heads up the slopes on the left towards some kraals about 2.5 km away: at first this seems inexplicable, especially when you start climbing steeply up a twisting path, but to quote my hiking buddy Adrian, 'the path always knows best'. At one point you'll be at least 1 km away from and 200 m above the river, but don't panic. After about another 2 km from the start you round a large spur (the one coming down from the Outer Mnweni Needle) and look straight down to the Mnweni/Ifidi confluence. Amazing as it might at first seem, the Mnweni River here lies on a south-west/north-east axis and our path swings from north to south-east. The Mnweni Baths lie below you somewhere.

The path climbs and falls a few times along this section, sometimes as much as 120 m at a time. At one point it comes really close to the river, but with a steep drop-off. Then it heads well away from the river. At 10.5 km from the start the path splits.... But now I have to deviate to explain that this area is a criss-cross of cattle paths and it can be a challenge to keep on the right course. This is why you need to carry a good map, and have – or quickly develop one – a sense of mountain orienteering (what 'we' mountaineers call mountain sense). On the other hand, in all but closed-in weather it would be a challenge not to stick to the right course following the main Mnweni Valley. But to get back to our fork....

You have to turn sharp left here to climb about 100 m straight up the lower slopes of the Dassie (Mbazibalethe). This is the ridge that comes down from Ncedamabutho, with Mponjwane and the Needles to the left, divided by a deep valley. Now, if it hasn't hit you yet, you are getting yourself into serious mountains. Awesome. And yet for the next 4 km the path keeps as close to the 1 700-m contour as Thomas Bain could have engineered it – until you reach the Mnweni/Mbundini confluence.

The path crosses just below the confluence, then has to cross the Mbundini coming in from the right. I just love maps – you look at the small detail, not more than half a square centimetre and say, 'just cross the one river, then the other...'. Then you walk it and you realise that maps always lie. Adrian maintains that all maps of the Drakensberg should have a large, bold declaration on top stating: 'Every little detail on this map is huge'. But back to our walk.

You're now on the right-hand bank of the Mnweni, and the headland 100 m up on your right facing the river is important, for at the bottom of the rock band you'll find Shepherd's Cave. It's a medium sized shelter which can comfortably sleep around eight people. It's also a heavily used cave, so you should be prepared to share it with others. This is the meeting point of four passes (Mnweni, Rwanqa, Fangs and Mbundini), two of which are used by smugglers and traders. Your company could be colourful to say the least. This is the recommended overnight spot. Sleep well; you'll need it. There are other caves in the area which hikers use, such as Five Star Cave, but Berg aficionado Greig Stewart says there's also a great camp site among the trees and bushes near the Mnweni/Mbundini confluence.

(For an alternative description of how to get here, cross-reference this description with the first half of hike MN4, Fangs Pass, page 72. When describing things in the Berg you can write pages and pages on each leg of each hike, and still people will go missing, sometimes for years at a time and be found wandering around, bewildered, in Lesotho.)

About 600 m from Shepherd's Cave the path, now entering the sacred nave of the Mnweni Cutback and climbing steadily, crosses a side stream coming down from directly in front of the Black and Tan Wall. I say 'sacred' advisedly: somewhere up on the right is Mbundini Abbey and Madonna and her Worshippers, straight ahead are the Twelve Apostles, and way over to the left is the original Cathedral Peak (Mponjwane). You are in the heart of a natural Gothic cathedral, complete with spires, towers, fantastical gargoyles, flying buttresses and aerial colonnades. From the crossing it's a hard 2.5-km slog up the right-hand bank of the upper Mnweni, to reach 'Chichi' Bush Camp. This is a lazy anglicisation of the Zulu name for ouhout, *intshishi (Leucosidea sericea)*. This site was an oft-used overnight spot, but is less so nowadays. The supposed camp site is actually above where our path crosses the Mnweni to head up a side gully at a right angle to the main river. The going's been tough up to here, but from now it gets mercilessly steep. That's why all about you the mountainscapes are so sublime: you'll lift your sorry eyes and sweaty brow heavenwards to marvel at them: you are now in the cathedral's apse – the focal point of the Mnweni Cutback, where one would find the altar in a church and where the finest sculpture of our Gothic artist can be viewed.

What can I say about the pass that seems to rise into the sky towards the rock needles of Eeny, Meeny, Miny and Mo and then sneaks up a hellish gully to their left to reach the summit plateau at 2 910 m? The great landscape artist John Ruskin said 'Mountains are the beginning and end of all natural scenery'. Everywhere you look is breathtaking, if you have any breath left. In summer the summit is festooned with yellow everlastings while in winter the many streams falling over the cliffs turn the pass into a fairy-land of ice castles.

In ye olde days mountaineers tended to head for Mponjwane Cave, way up on the other (south) side of Ncedemabutho, a 2-km slog up from the top of the pass, because of the view I suppose. Or maybe they were just tougher and more senseless in those days. But I much prefer Ledger's Cave, tucked a little up and over the Escarpment, overlooking the Mnweni Valley and with as dramatic views as any. It's a little tricky locating the vague path over the lip to the cave, and not to be attempted in mist unless you know the way. It involves a short scramble down and to the left. For 'Kodak' sunrises, it's hard to beat. Alternatively you can camp in the bowl anywhere between the tops of Mnweni and Rockeries passes, which are separated by a 2.5-km-wide promontory. However, this area is the source of the Senqu (Orange) and becomes a veritable bogland in summer. The pinpoint source is a shallow vlei back from Ledger's Cave where the tip of Mponjwane is just visible.

68 mnweni

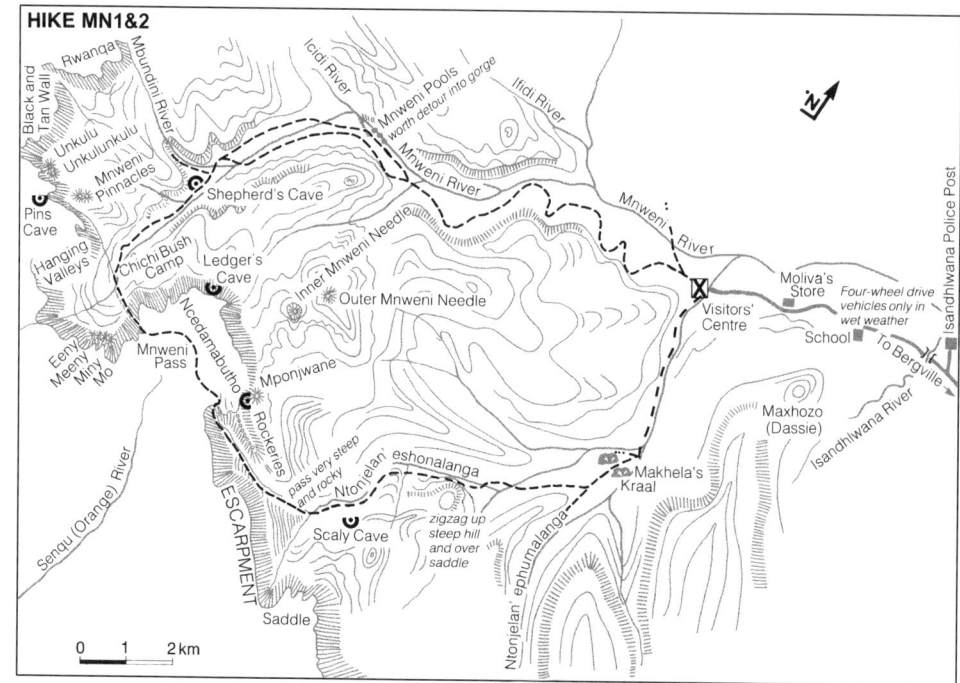

ROCKERIES PASS

HIKE MN2

Route: From the visitors' centre up the Ntonjelana Valley and behind the Rockeries
Distance: 17 km
Duration: 9 to 10 hours
Grade: Extreme
General: In *Barrier of Spears* Reg Pearse says this pass is little more than a 'wild jumble of rocks and stones, in places very steep'. He concludes the section saying it is little used 'these days' on account of its difficulty. Strange that, for it is now the favoured of the two passes going up to the Ncedamabutho (Mponjwane) headland, and both shorter and easier than Mnweni Pass. For sheer grandeur it's pretty much Mnweni's equal though, even if it lacks some of the more Gothic sculptures of the latter.

From the visitors' centre keep well left to head due south up the right-hand bank of the Ntonjelana River. The name of the river means 'oozing waters' and it could apply to the whole of this region. For the next 5 km the path rises only about 100 m, but it also comes back to the river only once on this stretch, after about 1.7 km. The conical hill on your left is Maxhozo or Scramble Kop, the very end of the main ridge coming down from the Cathedral range. This ridge is the southern boundary of the Mnweni area. Directly up ahead, looking over Makhela's Kraal, is the

Saddle with the North and South peaks creating an obvious landmark. At the 5-km mark, about 600 m below Makhela's Kraal, the Ntonjelan' ephumalanga and Ntonjelan' eshonalanga meet. Our path crosses Ntonjelana of the west and proceeds up the centre of the spur which comes down from the Saddle South Peak to Makhela's Kraal.

About 120 m above (and 1.5 km in distance) the Ntonjelana confluence, the path splits round the spur into the two Ntonjelana valleys. Our route is to the right, the eshonalanga. Below Makhela's Kraal an alternative path does lead from near the confluence up the eshonalanga, but then you'll miss the kraal (maybe this is the better option if you're not sure of your best Zulu manners). From the fork our path follows the contour along the South Peak ridge, as it makes diagonally for the river which is crossed after about 1.4 km, then climbs briefly and meets another path coming up the right-hand bank. We turn left and upriver here. Depending on how you're feeling at this stage, this is an option for an overnight stop, for you're only halfway and the hard half awaits you.

You'll be looking straight up the nose of the ridge coming down from the Saddle North Peak. After proceeding a short way up the bank to your right, the path crosses the river – on a hot day you might want to take a dip here because now the real work begins: you won't see the river again for the next 5.5 km, but instead have to carry your load up that ridge. For the first 240 m the path zigzags up the front of the spur, then moves across to the left-hand slope. Take heart, because the next 170 m is very steep and straight up, but take it slow and it won't hurt as much. In fact, so long as there is daylight you should make a point of taking all steep sections slowly. I know there is often the urge to push yourself when the going is hard, and of course you still have to displace your total mass however many metres upwards.

However, the speed at which you do it will determine how much you enjoy the gravity-defying act, or not. If you have to push time, rather do so on the less-steep sections.

Once you've crested the ridge and are going diagonally back towards the river, with the Rockeries dead ahead, it's almost flat for the next 1.5 km to Scaly Cave, which is usually the overnight stop of choice for ascents of Rockeries Pass. Water is a long way away, but there's no other suitable place to camp nearby. There are other caves on this route, but you've got to know how to find them, and they are heavily used by the local traffickers.

It's about 800 m along and 80 m up to the river, and this is the only tricky part of the pass, where you have to cross the stream coming down from Nguza Pass (a difficult rock climb) on the left. It's steep and difficult, but luckily short (Pearse's 'wild jumble of rocks and stones'). From where the Nguza Stream is crossed, there is still another 800-m stretch to climb, crossing many side streams up the left-hand bank of the river virtually to the top of the pass. There are some steep sections along the way, but the changing views as you proceed up behind the Rockeries are stunning. The fluted spires are named A to G, starting from the outside 'shoulder'.

Topping out on the Ncedamabutho headland, with Mponjwane Ntabamabutho over the high ground on your right, one path leads off to the left for 4 km to a waterfall on the Senqu, while another goes in a wide arc to your right to reach the top of Mnweni Pass, which actually lies straight ahead. If the weather's good it would be great to camp out in the open here, as water is abundant. However, there are two caves – Ledger's or Mponjwane. Both are found over the lip of the Escarpment: Ledger's about 2 km but with only a gentle climb to the north-east (its approach is marked by a cairn) and Mponjwane about half that distance but over steep ground to the sharp right (north).

WATERFALL CAVE AND NTONJELANA PASS　　　　　　　　　HIKE MN3

Route: From the visitors' centre up to Makhela's Kraal then up the Ntonjelan'ephumalanga Valley; the pass beyond that is an optional extra
Distance: 12 and 16.5 km respectively
Duration: 5 hours to the cave and another 3 up the pass
Grade: Severe to extreme
General: This is a walk that is seldom done but offers a wonderful Berg experience. The pass is an 'add-on' to the cave hike and although it is much overlooked by hikers it is one of the passes used by Basotho traders and their pack animals. If you've done Mlambonja Pass from Cathedral Peak, you might be surprised to discover this pass summits just 2 km to the north, which in my opinion is by far the nicer, if slightly longer, option.

The first 6.5 km of this hike are the same as for the previous route description (Rockeries Pass, MN2): from the visitors' centre up past Makhela's Kraal to the fork on the South Saddle ridge.

At the fork take the left-hand 'prong' which for 2.3 km goes gently down and then equally gently up along the right-hand side of the Ntonjelan' ephumalanga. It's a most pleasant stroll along the grassy spur, where innumerable streams create a scalloped, golden grass slope. But from here you have to haul yourself for the next 3 km to the cave.

The path continues along the right-hand side of the river, crossing even more side streams, some of them wooded and even forested. The Saddle South Peak looms up and seems to crowd the sky, standing sentry over this walk. Although the path gains 300 m in altitude over the next section, this is not really saying much for hiking in the Berg – sometimes you can gain 300 m in height over the same map distance.

The cave (also referred to as 'caves' in some older texts, in the tradition that any shelter was a 'cave') is not located on the path, but up a woody side gully. The way to find it is by cartographic backtracking ... I'll explain. From Makhela's Kraal the route climbs for 1 km before splitting to the left. For about 4.5 km from the split you reach a side stream every few 100 m. Then there's a gap for about 1 km where no side streams are encountered. The next side gully is ours. Here's a passage from Reg Pearse to help you get your bearings: 'A pleasant walk (directly down from Twins Cave) of an hour over gentle grass slopes brought me to the Caves.... They are in a lateral valley of the Ntonjelane, a tiny, wooded gorge, a truly lovely spot. The caves are high up in the gorge, very roomy, with a large waterfall flowing over at one end, right under the south face of South Saddle.' That should do it.

What I would do is what Reg Pearse did when first he found the cave, and stay put for three or four days. In spring when the sky-blue scilla lilies hang on the valley sides and the scarlet bottle-brush trees bloom, that's the time to lose yourself in this rumpled corduroy landscape of deep greens and blues. But some people will insist on setting off for the top, so goal-oriented have we become. For those who cannot stay in one place for long and just sit and stare, there's a lovely long pass waiting.

People say it's a really tough route, but it's very much on a par with Rockeries Pass which is a popular one. It's more that people who set off from remote Mnweni don't really want to go to Cathedral, since Ntonjelana tops out pretty close to the top of Mlambonja – then you've got the problem of starting in out-of-the-way

mnweni 71

HIKE MN3

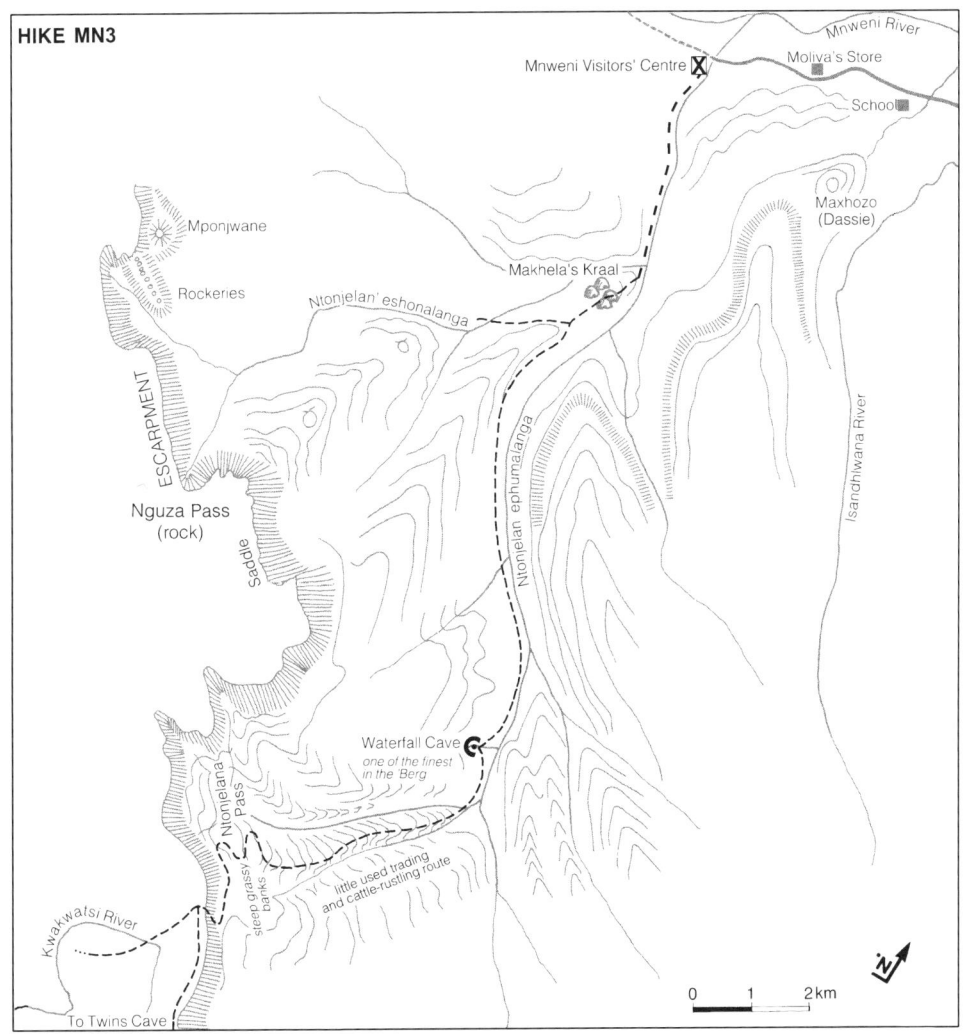

Mnweni and ending in the much more popular Cathedral area (if you descend Mlambonja Pass, hike CP2, page 84). Otherwise you could make a round-trip by linking this pass and Rockeries. It's a spectacular half-day hike between the two.

Since you're passing through a traditional Zulu kraal (one of the last genuine Zulu beehive *umuzi* and a major landmark for hikers), you might as well learn something about who's who and what's what in this neck of the woods (the following information was supplied by Meridy Pfotenhauer of Bergwatch). As already stated the amaNgwane *nkosi* of the area is Maswazi Hlongwane (there's a Hlongwane's Kraal just north of Makhela's). The area of the Mnweni Valley is called Mabhulesini; the Ntonjelana area is Khokhwane; the area bordering RNNP (Ifidi area) is inhabited by the amaZizi peoples and it's called Manzana; that bordering on Cathedral to the south is Ingoba.

FANGS PASS
HIKE MN4

Route: From the Mnweni visitors' centre up the Mnweni Valley to Shepherd's Cave and then up the side of Mbundini Valley into Fangs Pass
Distance: 22.5 km
Duration: 12 to 14 hours (2 days one way or 3-day round-trip)
Grade: Extreme
General: The first two-thirds of this hike is the same as that of Mnweni Pass (hike MN1, page 65), as far as Shepherd's Cave. Fangs Pass is just as spectacular an option as Mnweni, but a little longer (and not as steep).

Up to Shepherd's Cave follow hike MN1 (Mnweni Pass). Begin at the visitors' centre and follow the gravel road, which eventually becomes a wide path, for about 3 km. Then cut up a path to the left, which contours around kwaMfazi kraal. After several kilometres this path crosses the Nqeda Stream and runs up the slopes of the Dassie towards the last homestead (*umuzi*) belonging to a Mr Mlambo. Do not take a path down to the right, but continue up to bypass the homestead.

About 500 m from Mr Mlambo's home there's a cave in a small wood to the right of the path. It's used seasonally by Mr Mlambo for his stock but arrange through the centre to overnight here when it's not in use. If you do you should carry water from Nqeda Stream (use 2-litre plastic cold drink bottles).

Continue along the left-hand bank of the Mnweni on the slopes of the Dassie to where the path leads to a crossing of the river some 4 km further up the valley. The crossing is almost directly opposite the confluence of the Mnweni and Mbundini rivers, where a large grove of KwaZulu-Natal bottlebrushes is visible. After crossing head for the trees and angle left to find the path which runs up to the right-hand bank of the Mnweni. This is a good place to camp (as mentioned in hike MN1) if you have a tent. If not make for Shepherd's Cave by following the path from the crossing for about 500 m up the left-heading valley on the main Mnweni Pass path. A distinct path leads off this path to the right for about 50 m to the large shelter situated below a mushroom-shaped sandstone outcrop.

For hikers going up Fangs Pass there is an alternative: from the junction follow the left-hand bank up the Mbundini River for less than 500 m to Five Star Cave, comfortable for eight people. The shelter is to the left and some 20 m above the path.

The valley hereabouts is thickly matted with ouhout and mountain sage, and also occasional copses of bottlebrushes, while proteas grow among the grasses on the north-facing slopes above and below the sandstone cliffs. Fangs Pass consists of two sections: the first up the Mbundini River's left bank for 3 km, and then the second 4 km up Fangs Pass while the Mbundini Pass carries on up to the right after crossing the river. This means 7 km of hard work, which should take half a hiking day (5 to 6 hours). The whole way is up the left-hand bank of the Mbundini and, where that forks off to the right, up Fangs Stream.

As you make your way deeper into this narrow hanging valley you will start to make out the crumbling spikes and spires that make Mbundini one of the most photogenic of all passes. The freestanding Fangs themselves, as well as the Molar against the Escarpment, are certainly among the most prominent of the passes. In

mnweni

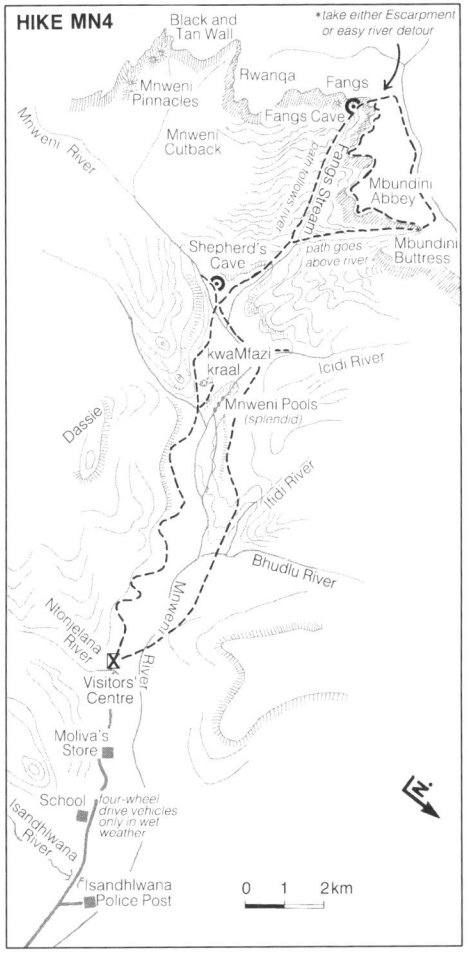

HIKE MN4

times past Mbundini Pass was a popular route, but I don't know of anyone who has ever used it.

About 100 m below the top of the pass the path comes to Fangs Cave, which is quite small and will sleep only four people comfortably. Alternatively carry on over the watershed and camp along a pretty stream 1 km into Lesotho. If you choose not to return the same way, then it's a good day's slog south, around the Mnweni Cutback to Mnweni or Rockeries passes, or about equidistant going northwards to the Amphitheatre. Ah, the choices.... (Note: the Mnweni Cutback is deceptive: you tend either to underestimate its scale and come out somewhere above the Hanging Valleys north of Mnweni Pass, or to overshoot it and end up somewhere deep in Lesotho. If you can see the terraced fields it's the latter; but if the ground suddenly drops away at your feet by about 1 000 m, it's the former.)

If the route you choose along the summit rounds the Mnweni Cutback, you are advised to keep the general line of the Escarpment and watershed always in view, and not to stray too far from it. The well-used paths and columnar cairns are invariably trade routes into Lesotho, and can be very misleading. If the Escarpment is shrouded in mist or cloud, you would do well to stay put or choose a different route, as it could be hazardous or exhausting to continue.

ICIDI PASS   HIKE MN5

Route: From the visitors' centre up the Mnweni and then the Icidi and Ifidi valleys respectively
Distance: 22 km
Duration: 10 to 11 hours
Grade: Extreme
General: Both these hikes (MN5 and MN6) are very long and lead to nowhere in particular. As far as I'm concerned they are good only for Berg sloggers who have tried everything else and are looking for new adventures – these two passes will certainly provide that. But that is also why I've decided to give only brief descriptions, together with their maps. My decision

was settled by the fact that both are fairly tricky near their tops: if you take the wrong fork up Icidi in summer you could be flushed out, while in winter you'll need crampons and ice axe; Ifidi requires some nerve-wracking scrambling on loose rock to get above the Ifidi Pinnacles. But, if you're still keen, here goes ...

Take the gravel road upstream from the visitors' centre, but, unlike all the previous Mnweni Valley hikes, after 1.5 km cross over to the right-hand bank. For the next 5 km the path veers right away from the river, past numerous kraals, at one point climbing about 160 m over 1.5 km. The path then reaches the Bhudlu (Ifidi) River 1 km upstream of its meeting with the Mnweni. Turn sharp left to cross the Bhudlu and head up a spur on the right-hand side of the Mnweni. After a steepish climb up about 200 m the path contours above the Mnweni until it reaches the Icidi River 7 km from the previous crossing.

Cross the Icidi and head up the left-hand bank for about 6 km, till you're two-thirds to the top of the pass. Here the path crosses over to the right-hand side, and 1 km further up crosses back again – only this time it's to a ridge that separates the two uppermost gullies. On the way you pass two very good caves, Grasscutters and Jubilee: the latter is situated close to the main path but up a side gully on the left about 4.5 km from the point where you first cross the Icidi, while the former is located a few hundred metres up a side gully to the left about 400 m below Jubilee.

There is some dispute as to exactly where the route goes: the Slingsby map shows a path going up the right-hand side of the middle ridge, although I have not used it. It is hellishly steep and should be avoided by anyone not comfortable with extreme exposure. Having looked down it, I would suggest anyone attempting it should carry a rope in case you find yourself on tricky ground.

Some hikers say you should use the left-hand boulder-choked gully and others the right-hand one where the stream flows. Problem is, in summer streams flow down both gullies, which freeze in winter and become nigh impassable to all but suitably equipped climbers.

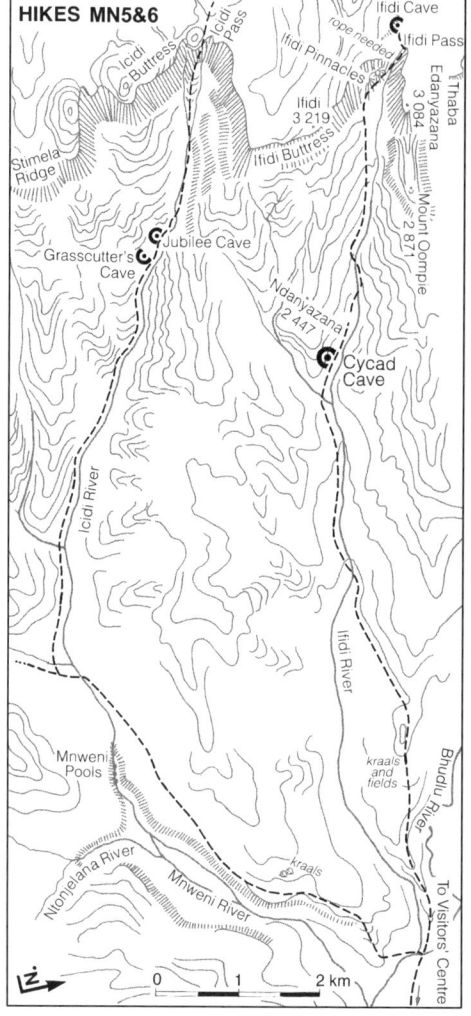

IFIDI PASS — HIKE MN6

Route: Starting at the visitors' centre, up the Mnweni, then the Bhudlu and the Ifidi rivers to the top of the Ifidi Pass
Distance: 21 km
Duration: 10 hours
Grade: Extreme
General: It's a whole lot easier to get to the top of Ifidi (and Icidi for that matter) Pass via the Chain Ladders and across the top of the Amphitheatre (see AM1). However, if it's the getting there that matters more than the end itself, as it would for a true mountaineer, go for it. Truth is, I've only ever gone down this pass, and I don't remember it being a particularly easy route.

From the visitors' centre take the track up the Mnweni Valley, as for hike MN5, and cross to the right-hand bank after 1.5 km. Over the next 5 km the path heads well away from the river, through a bunch of kraals, and when it returns to the river it will be the Bhudlu – a tributary of the Mnweni. Cross the Bhudlu and proceed up a short spur between the Bhudlu (on your right) and Ifidi (on your left) rivers. Paths lead off from here to various homesteads, but you need to bear slightly to the left and keep to the spur: the path does cross over from left to right of the main ridge, leading up through kraals that lie high above the Ifidi (which is down below to your left).

About 4 km after crossing the Bhudlu, our path takes a sharp left to contour for 2 km to the Ifidi River, dropping down a way at the river, which is then crossed (take care in wet weather as this can become a tricky crossing point). The path keeps to the left-hand bank for the next 2 km, beginning now to climb steadily but not too steeply. Here a side gully coming down from Icidi (to the left of Ifidi Buttress) is crossed, which leads into Ifidi Pass and up the left-hand bank. Now the real pass begins. There are some patches of bush in the pass, as well as many side streams. It's a long, 4-km slog up the pass, keeping mainly to the left-hand side of the gorge. At an altitude of about 2 200 m (about 1.25 km from the summit), the path reaches a particularly steep section, climbing 200 m up a tricky section where you might need to use grass handholds. The path then proceeds up the left-hand slope veering away from the river and up the side of a prominent spur. You follow this spur slope up towards the Ifidi Pinnacles, but about 200 m from the summit the path takes a sharp turn to the right, around a spur and then goes up a rocky gully to the top. You should consider carrying a rope for this final arduous section. Once you've recovered from the climb, you'll find the 'cave' overhang up on the ridge several hundred metres to the south, more or less above the Pinnacles.

There are other passes in the greater Mnweni area, such as Mbundini, Rwanqa, Nguza and the Saddle North Peak traverse, but, while some can be tackled by experienced mountaineers, others require technical climbing. Even Rwanqa, which is a proposition, entails ascending very steep grassy slopes. Add to this a heavy pack and you're courting danger. Some experienced mountaineers sometimes use them, but I do not believe hike descriptions are warranted. If you'd like to try them, I suggest you contact one of the hiking or mountaineering clubs from the 'Useful contacts' list on pages 231 and 232, and find out if they ever do these passes. However, mountaineering is not the business of this humble hiking guide.

CONTOUR PATH: MNWENI TO CATHEDRAL HIKE MN7

Route: Mnweni visitors' centre to Cathedral Peak EKZNW camp site
Distance: 28 km
Duration: 2 days (12 hours walking)
Grade: Severe
General: This route is not really part of the official Contour Path, which actually only starts on the southern slopes of Cathedral Peak above Sherman's Cave (the lower part of which is the route up Cathedral Peak from the hotel).

However, many hikers would like to see a proper contour path route established along the whole length of the uKhahlamba-Drakensberg Park, starting at Mahai camp site in Royal Natal National Park and ending at the Bushman's Nek EKZNW picnic site. What a great walk that would make, and it would certainly bring hikers to the Berg in bigger numbers and help the park pay its way. There was once an idea to create an Appalachian Trail-style hiking trail from Kosi Bay to the Cape Peninsula in sections, but en route the National Hiking Way lost steam. On the other hand we do now have over 300 hiking trails all over the country, but wouldn't it be great if EKZNW got their backs into a project like this, which would very quickly establish itself as Africa's premier hiking challenge (not that I'm in favour of competitive 'challenges', and mean this only in the sense that it would become a personal goal of every hiker). Much of the route already exists and it would not be a huge job to push the trail from end to end through each of the eight conservation regions. Hello EKZNW, anyone listening, over?

This route, as first described in *Drakensberg Walks*, used to start at the Isandhlwana police station, which was convenient because the path goes up Maxhozo (Scramble Kop), which is closer to the station than to the new visitors' centre. It's a 4-km walk or drive back down the road from the visitors' centre to the Maxhozo path which leads diagonally back up the koppie for 3 km. Below the conical peak of Maxhozo a side path to the left takes a sharp turn upwards to follow the main ridge of the spur, at the end of which is Maxhozo. Sorry, but this is our path. The next 400 m up is the hardest haul of this hike, so take it easy as the road is long (and getting longer ...).

For the next 5 km the path takes a very easy course along a plateau of the Little Berg, with the great ramparts of the Saddle to the right and Cathedral Peak rearing up ahead of you. The path rounds two spurs that come down from the Puddings at the end of the Cathedral range, bearing round to the left and still keeping on the contour. Then it descends easily down to the Isandhlwana River just above a patch of forest. This is a good place to take a long lunch break, as the next section requires some sustained ascending. You will have walked about 10 km from the Mnweni road, so you'll need the break.

Our intended overnight spot is as close to the halfway mark as the topography allows, on a nek below the Puddings spur and close to the head of the Isandhlwana River. It's only 3 km from the lunch spot, but since it involves a 320-m rise in altitude it will take about 2 hours. The path starts off crossing the Isandhlwana, rises gently to the right around the spur ahead with its rounded summit, climbs increasingly steeply across a stream gully and then to the left around another koppie before turning back towards Cathedral Peak, effectively completing a half-circle to the head of the river. Water is to be had close to the nek. The alternative is to continue for another 2 km, wending easily around the hill on your left, into a gully and more steeply down its left-hand bank, then over the open grass slope towards the Nxwaye River. About 60 m above and 200 m before the river is Sconqweni Cave, looking upriver directly towards Cathedral Peak.

From the cave the path crosses the river, climbs a short ridge and then contours to cross a second tributary. After a short contour the path climbs onto Ganapu Ridge to gain the Little Berg plateau for the last time, before heading towards and very steeply down Baboon Rock. Watch out for flying balls here, as the hotel's new 9-hole course is directly below. When you reach the tarred road below the hotel, you've still 4 km to go down to the EKZNW camp site (unless you have the means and taste for a celebratory stay in the hotel; I've done this more than once and, although the hotel now caters very much for the BMW-weekend set, it's still a great place to start or end a hike).

Only in the Mnweni area will you encounter traditional Zulu *umuzi*, or the extended family 'kraal' (The word 'kraal' is derived from the Afrikaans for 'barricade'). The most important home in the *umuzi* will be the grandmother's, or the great wife's, which would be the largest and face the kraal entrance. This building is known as *indlu yangenhla*, or the 'home of the ancestors'. The ancestors, called 'shades', play a critical and active role in Zulu life. Some of the customs you might wish to take note of before setting off into Mnweni tribal land are:

- Give and take only with the right hand, with the left hand held under the forearm to show it holds no weapon. You will notice all Zulus do this.
- Always sit on something, anything, never the bare ground.
- In a traditional building, men sit to the right and women to the left of the entrance.
- Never walk straight into a Zulu home or kraal, but await your welcome and possibly the *siyakuleka ikhaya* – 'greeting the home' praise and permission to enter.
- If you see a stone cairn (*isivane*) pick up a small stone, spit on it and add it to the heap to honour the shades (dead ancestors).

There are others, but these should do to show you at least take note of the basics of social etiquette, and the most basic knowledge of the language and customs will be greatly appreciated.

LOCAL NAMES WHICH DIFFER FROM THE MAPS

map name	local name
Dassie (stream)	Mbazibalethe
Ifidi (summit and pinnacles)	Bhedlana
Lower Ifidi (river)	Bhudlu
Bhudlu (river)	Kuze
Mnweni-Rockeries	Ncedamabutho 'place of the warriors'
Mponjwane	Ntabamabutho 'mountain of the warriors'
	Cathedral Peak
Mponjwane Cave area	Edlangeni
Scramble Kop	Maxhozo
Icidi (river)	Chakide
Mnweni Valley	kwaJele (Shepherd's Cave area)

78 mnweni

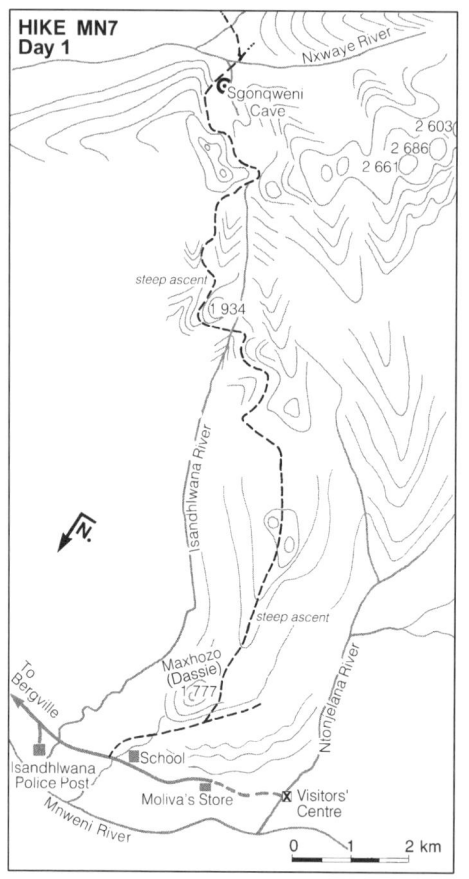

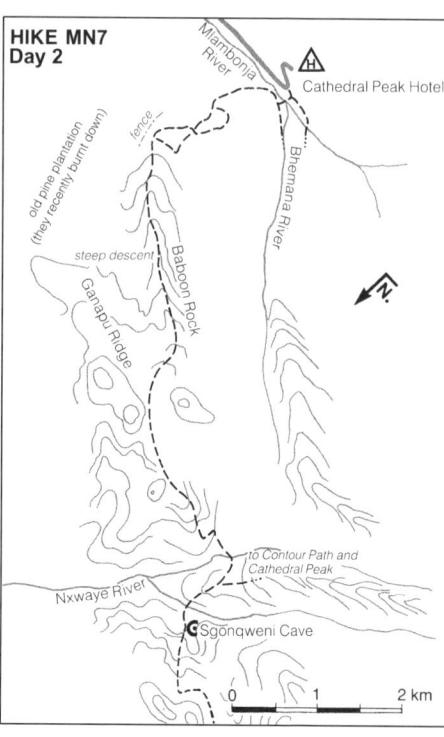

PHOTO TIPS

- 'Five kilometres of film' is what a colleague used to say was necessary before you could take good photos.
- The Drakensberg offers fantastic scenery and bewitching light.
- There's no substitute for a decent tripod, a good camera (and better lenses), quality film and practice.
- Serious photographers use slide film but most people prefer print film.
- You need a wide angle, medium focal length (around 50 mm) and a long lens (200 mm or more).
- Aperture rating makes a good lens: 2.8 is the best, up to 4.5 is okay, but 5.6 or more is for snap-shotters.
- Use a soft warming filter for most occasions, a circular polariser for harsh light and a graduated grey filter to make bright skies darker.

cathedral peak

It appears that the first English name given to Mponjwane was Cathedral Peak, and the Rockeries, which it stands over, was called the Cathedral. In Zulu the name for the Rockeries and Rockeries Tower is Ntabamabutho, the 'mountain of the warriors'. It seems that at some point a government cartographer got hold of a map from the 1800s that had the names of the peaks all mixed up, and decided they were the correct ones – and so it has remained. As late as 1948 official 1:250 000 topographical maps of the area have Rockeries Pass as Cathedral Pass, and the Rockeries as Cathedral.

The mountain we know as Cathedral Peak (3 004 metres) was the 'Mponjwane', with the Inner and Outer Horns standing on the Cathedral range between it and the main Escarpment. During the early 1800s it was renamed after a minor chief, Zikhali. He was the son of the bloodthirsty Chief Matiwane of the amaNgwane tribe who took advantage of the reign of Shaka to spread his own bloodshed in the Drakensberg. When Shaka sent impis to destroy him he fled to the Free State, but he was eventually killed by Dingane's soldiers. Dingane, Shaka's successor as King of the Zulu, allowed Zikhali to remain in the shadow of uKhahlamba, but when Dingane was assassinated Zikhali fled to Swaziland and took refuge with King Sobuza.

There he fell in love with Sobuza's daughter Nomlalazi and asked to marry her. Sobuza feared the alliance would provoke an attack by the Zulu so he plotted to have Zikhali secretly killed. Nomlalazi heard of this and warned Zikhali, who fled back to the Drakensberg. There he gathered together the remnants of the amaNgwane who had dispersed when Matiwane fled and abandoned them to the ravages of the Difaqane upheavals. Nomlalazi ran away and married Zikhali, so that today the people who live at the foot of Cathedral Peak can claim to be partly Swazi. The peak that loomed over the chief's kraal was renamed Zikhali's Horn.

80 cathedral peak

How much better it would be, I feel, if the original Zulu, Sotho and even Bushman names for the Drakensberg's peaks and rivers had been retained. They tend to be more musical and expressive of the character of the places, than some of the Euro-centric names like Sugar Loaf, Cockade, Plume and Windsor Castle! But the English names were given, I suppose, in the days of the British Empire, when things African were on the whole demeaned by white colonial society. There is a movement now to achieve an authentic Zulu spelling for names that were anglicised, as I have noted in the introduction (Umkomaas = Mkhomazi, Ndedema = Didima, Tugela = Thukela and so on). However, I believe we should go much further and trace the original names of places, as far back as we can. Failing that, we should consult local communities to find out what they call all the landscape features. In most cases those names will be found to be more historically correct, and often to refer to some inherent character of the place.

But back to the place we now call Cathedral. Up to 1910 the Mlambonja, Didima and eMhlawazini valleys and all the valleys lying between Cathedral and Cathkin peaks were little known to white settlers. At that time a government geological survey reported that the area was 'practically unknown and inaccessible'. Reg Pearse claimed that the oldest black people living in the area told him white people first came here in 1910. They would have been hunters and woodcutters. By 1918 eight farms had been established, but they were used only for summer grazing by farmers from elsewhere. Some of these names still survive on maps as bits of nostalgia – Solar Cliffs, Brotherton, Gewaagd, Tryme, Inhoek, Schaapkraal, Hopeton and Leafmore.

Early in the 20th century the Van der Riet family farmed near the top of Oliviershoek Pass. In 1937 the father Philip bought Inhoek and Schaapkraal farms from Ryk Isaak Buys of the Free State. The Van der Riets lived close to the Zunckels on top of Oliviershoek Pass, and the fact that they became the two great families of Drakensberg inn-keepers must be more than sheer co-incidence. Philip van der Riet's idea for the farms was to build a hotel, but it seems all he did was take his son Albert there on 'campin', fishin', huntin' trips'. In 1934 Albert, one of South Africa's greatest fresh- and salt-water fishermen, stocked the Mlambonja with brown trout taken from the Mooi River. In 1938 Albert chose the site on which Cathedral Peak Hotel was built, and what a site it is. Cathedral is a sub-range of the main Escarpment and, by choosing a site that looks up into the corner of these overwhelming ridges, Albert endowed the hotel with more panoramic grandeur than any other.

Only a wagon track ran up the Mlambonja Valley in those days, and everything one needed for the building had to be carried up from the railhead at Winterton. While the first stone buildings were being laid, the Second World War broke out. A young New Zealand bricklayer, who had been rejected for military service because of a heart condition, arrived seeking work. Skilled labour was hard to come by in those years, so Albert van der Riet took him on. The man's name was George Thompson and for many readers I need only say 'and the rest is history'. But, for newcomers to the Drakensberg and Berg folklore, I had better give a brief résumé of his life and 'works' in the Drakensberg: a full version would take the rest of the book.

From the moment he set his bags down at the new hotel site, Thompson spent every spare moment traversing the hill slopes and valleys of the area, even though he had never before so much as set foot on a mountain. But whatever heart condition had kept him out of the war seemed to hinder him not a bit, for he proved an indefatigable person and would easily climb several peaks in a day, eat a lusty dinner and dance into the night. The first real peak he climbed was the Pyramid, one of a twin of towers standing in the shadow of mighty Cleft Peak (3 281 metres) high up in the Tseketseke Valley. Pyramid is a scary D- and E-grade scramble of unnervingly steep grass slopes and friable basalt, and few climbers today would attempt it without a rope; George Thompson knew nothing of ropes at the time. In 1945 he decided that the adjoining twin, Column, would be a nice challenge and persuaded a young hotel guest to join him in the quest. At the base of the terrifying rock tower the younger man surrendered, so Thompson (in his mid-40s) pushed on alone. Today Column is graded a reasonable F3, or 18, but such grades are misleading in the Berg, where dizzying exposure and poor rock push the grade way upwards in terms of the commitment needed.

The climb up was tricky enough, along toenail traverses, around overhangs, even up chimneys ... but nothing compared with trying to down-climb the precipices. He got stuck on a narrow ledge with no way up, or down. Well, there was one way so he took it – he jumped. He hit a ledge three and a half metres below, too narrow to land on but enough to break his fall, grabbed a tuft of grass and managed to swing into a chimney below, where, by bracing his arms and legs against the walls, he was able to slow down enough to stop his fall by grabbing small bushes growing in the chimney.

That would put most people off ever touching vertical rock again, but not George. From this opening solo ascent of the Column, he went on to record opening ascents of numerous other hard Berg routes including Mponjwane and the Outer Mnweni Pinnacle. And then there was the time he was leading a route up Cathkin Peak. He found an old rope and began shinning up. Needless to say the frayed rope broke and George went plummeting. Concussed, and with a broken ankle, he resumed climbing and led his two companions to the summit. But then, for once in his remarkable life, he asked them to go for help. They arrived at Champagne Castle Hotel in the middle of the Christmas Eve festivities. A mounted party set out at first light and came upon Thompson, who had down-climbed Cathkin in the dark, crawling along the Contour Path on hands and knees.

Albert's son (Philip's grandson), the dapper William van der Riet, and his wife Belinda now run the hotel, and very successfully I can add. William too has a son, so who knows how long the Van der Riet tradition has yet to run. Competition is good, but I wonder what they think about the new EKZNW hotel going up down the valley, at the Didima junction? Guests will probably love it, but it does seem to overcrowd this once-quiet corner of the Berg where the Van der Riets ruled supreme. I suppose whoever chose the site for the new hotel (still under construction when this book went to print) tried to rival the spectacular views of the older hotel. While the architecture of the new Didima Hotel is fascinating, the buildings are strung out along a terrace above and in full view of the tarred road up the valley. Surely EKZNW had unlimited, and better, sites from which to choose. There is also an EKZNW camp site among the poplar trees near the guard office at Mike's Pass gate

82 cathedral peak

(where you have to pay your entrance fees), and several caves and 20 designated camp sites have been allocated for overnight hikers. The camp sites are open to all wilderness hikers, but caves have to be booked through a central reservations office. It's a pain – not like the old days when this was managed as a wilderness area and you could walk and camp anywhere, and even make fires – but times change, so there it is. You can contact one of the community guides through the EKZNW office.

CATHEDRAL PEAK   HIKE CP1

Route: From the Cathedral Peak car park at the boom, directly up Cathedral Peak and back
Distance: 19 km
Duration: 7 to 8 hours
Grade: Extreme
General: This is a great hike, especially as a testing one-day outing for anyone staying a while in the Cathedral area. For hotel guests it's a classic walk for which the hotel provides guides. If you're not staying *chez* Van der Riet, remember you start by traversing hotel property (and parking on their land), so especially during peak times take care not to make a nuisance of yourself at a very busy hotel. On the other hand, you might have to: the burgers served on the hotel terrace, with Cathedral Peak in the background, are world-class.

Although this hike affords you the chance to stand on top of one the Berg's more famous free-standing peaks, the path from Orange Peel Gap to the summit involves hairy scrambling and should not be attempted by anyone with a fear of heights or who is not hiking fit.

Park at the guard house, where there is parking provided by the hotel for non-guests. Where the tarred road makes a U-bend up to the hotel, take the path up the left-hand bank of the Mlambonja Valley through the riverine bush towards the trout hatchery. After 500 m cross the river and continue up the opposite bank, climbing for another 500 m to a side junction on the level to the right. But we, alas, must go ever upwards. There used to be a pine plantation but it burnt and has been cut down. Take the left-hand path here across a grassy area to the first band of sandstone cliffs.

The path is wide but eroded in places, so keep to the track and step over rather than on the erosion barriers, and they will last longer. On reaching the cliffs the path zigzags to the right of the main sandstone band, then contours for a short distance before ascending diagonally through the cliffs to the top of a gully. The slopes here are dotted with proteas, which provide the principle food for malachite sunbirds (metallic green with long, slender tails), and larger brown-and-yellow Guerney's sugarbirds with long flowing tails. The path crosses a small stream to emerge on top of a wide plateau, marking a dramatic change in both scenery and vegetation on top of the Little Berg. (At the base of the cliffs another path leads off to the right, along the contour into a wooded gorge where a delightful cascade runs into a pool surrounded by our forest familiars, and near the pool is the overhang known as Barker's Chalet.)

The Little Berg here gives hikers a sense of either freeness or agoraphobia as it sweeps past

cathedral peak 83

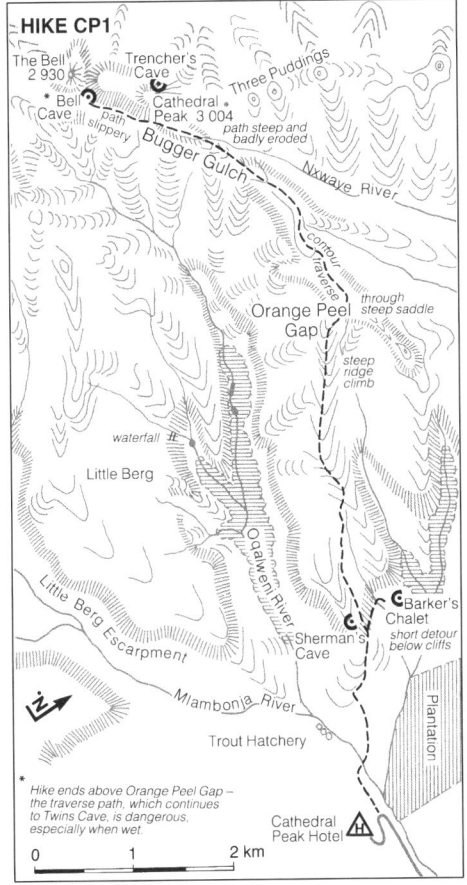

Intunja ('eye of the needle') to the hefty bulk of Cathkin. Grey-winged francolins (which people here prefer to call 'partridges' or 'quails') and common quails (the little fluff-balls) are flushed out virtually at your feet as you walk. With a frenzied squawking and thrumping of wings the francolins burst up and fly a hundred or more metres off before descending into the grass. The quails are pretty much silent and dart out of the grass and back in just as quickly, almost defying your vision. Hardly surprising that very little is known about these birds. My archetypal LBJs (little brown jobs), cisticolas, perch on tall grass stems or low bushes (could be fantailed, or cloud, or Ayre's, or wailing, or even desert LBJs). Halfway up this ridge, where clouds seem to have a permanent mooring, you'll find the beginning of the official Contour Path, leading off to the left above the convoluted ridges of Cathedral range and the bush line. I have not climbed this peak for some years, but I recall the last time I did so in autumn I encountered two very lazy puff adders lying in the path. They were so cold I could just ease them gently off the path with my hiking stick.

For the next 700 m the path heads up a steep gully followed by an even steeper ridge to the right before reaching an easy traverse for 2 km at around 2 400 m. (Halfway along here a minor path goes down a ridge to Sgonqweni Cave.) Now you begin the steep slog up to Orange Peel Gap, on a path that is very eroded; I named this section Desperation Gully. At the top of the gully you reach a shoulder that makes a good stop for a tea break, if the wind isn't howling. Then the path climbs the steep chute named Orange Peel Gap, which can be seen from the hotel.

Now you are on the level of the Bell contour traverse (which is a nasty bit of grovelling along very steep, treacherous slopes all along the range to Twins Cave, past Bell Cave, 7 km away). The path from the top of the gap to the summit of Cathedral Peak (3 004 m) rises 300 vertical metres on only 200 map metres, which should give an idea of its severity. The route is marked by cairns, and although no rope is required it is about a C-grade scramble and should be attempted only by competent hikers. Watch out for fickle weather because this ridge is very often in cloud – it's like a weather magnet. But of course the views are stupendous.

The peak was first climbed in 1917 by the prolific climbing partnership of D Bassett-Smith and R Kingdon. Both were schoolmasters from the UK, the former teaching at Maritzburg College and the latter at Hilton, and they were founding members of the Natal Mountain Club.

84 cathedral peak

MLAMBONJA PASS TO TWINS CAVE   HIKE CP2

Route: From the hotel or EKZNW camp site, up the Mlambonja River to the cave at the hinge of the Cathedral range and the Escarpment
Distance: 11 km one way
Duration: 6 to 8 hours
Grade: Extreme
General: This is one of the most popular routes to the summit of the Drakensberg, because of its easy access and shortness, but is by no means one of the easiest, the final sections being up very steep grassy slopes. However, anyone can do it given enough time. That last part really is unrelenting but, as my good old buddy Mao tse Tung would say, 'Every trek up the Drakensberg starts with a single step.' Just keep on putting one foot ahead of the other – even if it's two steps up, one step down – and you will get there. George Thompson would have no trouble leaving the hotel at dawn, stopping for lunch at the cave, then heading over to the Mnweni area to sleep in Mponjwane Cave the same night. But then there was only one George Thompson. One day Reg Pearse ended up sharing the cave with a man, and they chatted into the night. Pearse asked the then stranger if he'd done any climbing in the mountains, to which the over-modest reply was, 'Oh just a bit, not very much.' Only later did Pearse discover who his room-mate had been that night.

Before we set off hiking, a few points should be noted. The first is, this is a trip to nowhere and is really only part of what will inevitably be a longer round hike linking up to one of the other passes in the area, and usually that will be Rockeries Pass, which creates a three- or four-day round-trip. The name of the river, Mlambonja, means 'hungry dog, or dogs' and refers to the scarcity of game early Nguni hunters encountered. There's no reason why this large valley should have had less game than any other, other than that it had already been hunted out. Twins Cave is situated, like so many so-called summit caves, some way down from the summit ridge. It is very big, but has no water. There is a drip cave to the left as you face the Escarpment (south), but it's not infallible and you might have to head over into Lesotho to gather water in the Kwakwatsi River; it's a bit of a slog for tired hikers.

Final note: unless you start early you won't make this pass in one day so consider camping among the rocks and ouhout bushes where the Contour Path crosses the Mlambonja. Right, tighten boots, heft up your pack and tra-la tra-la it's to the Berg we go. If you're not staying there you can't park in the hotel's car park, even though that's where the path starts. Sometimes the hardest part of a hike is finding where the path starts, and this is no exception so ask at reception if you've been wandering around the hotel grounds with your large backpack for an hour or more. The wide track keeps well away from the river, going gently up through the rank grassland and away from the river (there are other paths, one up to Tryme Hill and another up to Mushroom Rock, but these get steep rather quickly so you'll soon know you've taken the wrong one).

After 2 km a path branches off to the left to Tarn Hill, but keep on straight ahead making an approach to the Mlambonja and crossing the Tseketseke Stream. Continue along the Mlambonja for 1.5 km, along a good, often

cathedral peak 85

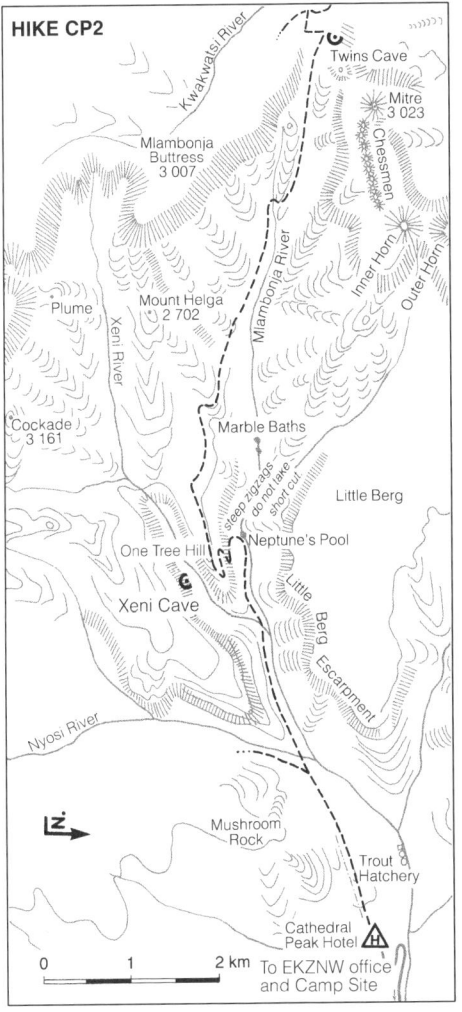

HIKE CP2

zigzag ascent of the Little Berg; this is One Tree Hill. When a sharp rocky ridge with protea trees is gained, this too must be climbed. Erosion has been caused here by people taking short cuts so don't (you recall what befalls you!). It's a hard 3-km slog up from the river to where our route meets the Contour Path, at 2 040 m.

Where you meet it the Contour Path rounds the lower spurs of Mount Helga, and here we must turn sharp right. For the first kilometre the going is pretty much flat, but for the next it climbs up the Mlambonja Valley to the river. This is a recommended stop for late starters, directly below the imposing bulk of Mlambonja Buttress.

Up to this point we're still on the Contour Path, which continues away to the right (east) to round the Inner Horn. But our path continues up the left bank of this valley, where it is quite bushy, and goes directly up this corner to its conclusion. It's a very steep haul, and for the first 1.5 km the path keeps close to the riverine bush, on the right-hand slope of a prominent ridge. Some small streams are crossed, and the ground can be boggy. Be careful where you place your feet because there are lots of holes between tufts and boulders, and higher up the scree is slippery. Under the Chessmen you start zigzagging up the grassy slopes to your left, and, although it's tough and sometimes unnerving work, when you look up you realise you are suddenly among the gargoyle sculptures of the Cathedral's roof and the flying buttresses of the nave.

Finally the path comes out on a narrow saddle that separates the Twins from the Escarpment and there you are greeted by the huge smiling grin of Twins Cave over to the right. To reach the top of the Escarpment, however, you have to cross the saddle and traverse around to the left (south) and climb about 120 m up a shallow gully. There is a sudden lip and from here you can look down into the Kwakwatsi River, which is about 1 km downhill.

shady path flanked by bottlebrushes and most beautiful blue scilla blooms in spring. At the Xeni Stream a path leads sharply up towards the cliffs above you on the left for 1 km to Xeni Cave. It's a great cave but don't try it in wet conditions as there's a traverse which gets tricky (and in fact someone has fallen there to his death). Cross the Xeni and soon our path, still following the Mlambonja's left bank, starts getting steep. About 700 m past the Xeni it begins a steep

86 cathedral peak

MLAMBONJA VALLEY HIKE CP3

Route: Cathedral Peak Hotel (lower car park) up the Mlambonja River to swimming pools
Distance: 3.5 to 12 km
Duration: 1 to 4 hours
Grade: Easy to moderate
General: The Mlambonja Pass route bypasses most of the charming lower river course, which makes a rewarding short outing especially if you're staying at the hotel. A number of paths can be taken to various scenic spots up the valley (you can even hire a horse at the hotel), which may be linked to make a 5-km hike. It's very easy to amble upstream on any path you find and make your own variation, but I'll describe three of my favourites. Take along binoculars and field guides as the area is rich in plant and bird-life.

Lower Valley round-trip: 3.5 km Begin at the U-bend at the bottom of the hotel driveway, and follow the path to the river through the riverine bush (ouhout, common spikethorn, mountain sage and mountain Rhus, or taaibos, predominate). Cross the river via the stepping stones, but be prepared to get your feet wet when the river is high. The path now makes its way through the tall reeds and grass, up a slope for some 500 m, and then finds its way along a side stream – the Bhemana. Cross this stream and head for 400 m along the contour to the junction with the Cathedral Peak path.

(When a river or stream is crossed there is nearly always a short, sometimes steep, climb out of the valley.)

Bear left and downhill to cross the Mlambonja about 600 m from the hotel driveway.

Neptune's Pool: 10 km The first 4 km or so of this walk follows the Mlambonja Pass route (CP2), but I suggest a variation that sticks closer to the Mlambonja River rather than heading up the slope behind the hotel: start off along the Cathedral Peak route from the end of the hotel's old bedroom wing, reaching the river after 1 km and crossing it. Climb a short way out of the valley and turn left, off the Cathedral Peak path, by keeping to the right-hand side of the river where the peak path goes to the right to head up a steep spur. The river banks are quite wooded, but you keep above and to the right for another 1 km before crossing to the left-hand side. Follow the left-hand bank – now on the Mlambonja Pass route – for 1 km to the Xeni Cave turnoff on the left (up a side valley towards the cliffs).

Don't take the cave path but cross the Xeni River and carry on up the river's steep left-hand side for another 750 m. Where the pass route turns sharply left to zigzag up the lower slopes of Mount Helga, keep on along the river course for another 500 m to the Pool. The path is not very distinct, but neither is it hard to find.

Marble Baths: 12 km From Neptune's Pool the valley opens out and Marble Baths is 1 km upstream, where the river has scoured out and polished the underlying sandstone to form smooth, marbled pools. For the adventurous there is a tributary halfway between Neptune's Pool and Marble Baths that heads off to the right. Follow the valley for 1.2 km to a waterfall. The first half of this detour is fairly easy going, but the final 500 m is steep and awkward. The area around Marble Baths is not often visited, so you might plan to make a whole day's outing of the hike, taking along a picnic.

cathedral peak 87

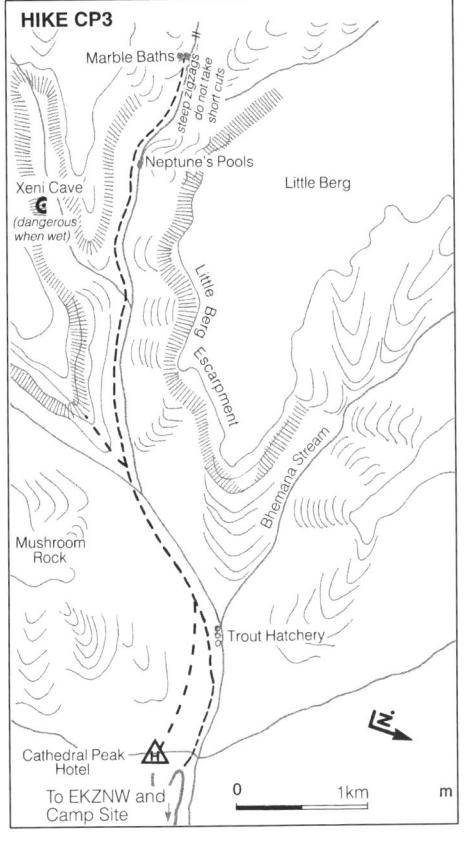

HYGIENE TIPS

- Your guiding hygiene ethic must be to leave no trace of where you've been.
- Wash (body and dishes) on the banks not in the streams.
- Let the sand filter the soap.
- Detergents are pollutants; they kill water bugs and microbes which keep mountain water so pure.
- For outdoor ablutions, a small trowel is useful to bury everything.
- Paper should be concertinaed so that it burns easily. Take matches with you.
- Always walk a good distance from where you're sleeping (don't do it 'on your doorstep').
- Find a nice view and two rocks to make a corner to sit on. Bury or cover everything afterwards.

OQALWENI VALLEY WALK   HIKE CP4

Route: Round-trip from Cathedral Peak Hotel via the Oqalweni Gorge
Distance: 5.5 km
Duration: 2 hours
Grade: Easy
General: The path to Oqalweni Gorge is not shown on Slingsby's map, but it is on the hotel's own hiking map, prepared by Reg Pearse way back when. This seldom used route is ideal for hikers who prefer secluded outings without having to mount a major expedition. This gorge is pretty spectacular, running directly up towards the Bell, between the lower ridges of the Outer Horn and Cathedral Peak. Cathedral Peak Hotel has been expanded from a cosy mountain resort to a bustling weekend getaway and tourist hotspot. It is less formal than in yesteryear and still welcomes hikers to the terrace and Harry's Bar (longs, please). The cheeseburger from the terrace menu is a feast to behold.

88 cathedral peak

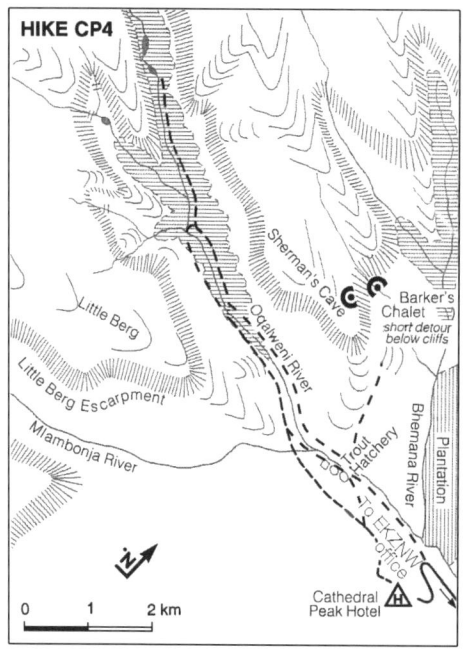

Begin either behind the hotel on the Mlambonja Pass (CP2) and then branch down towards the Mlambonja River after 200 m (hike CP3), or from the U-bend on the hotel driveway follow the left-hand bank of the river past the trout hatchery to the confluence of the Oqalweni 1.2 km upriver from the start. Cross the Mlambonja to proceed up the left-hand bank of the Oqalweni for a short distance, but where the pass route goes up to the left to begin climbing One Tree Hill, keep right to stay in the valley and head upstream to enter the forest.

About 1.5 km into the forest you'll come to a waterfall and pool. The path crosses the river here, returns along the opposite bank, passes close to a guard post and finally regains the Mlambonja River. Pass the trout hatchery and 700 m further downstream there's a crossing over a boulder causeway. Cross here and then continue along the jeep track to the hotel.

OQALWENI CIRCUIT   HIKE CP5

Route: Circular route from the hotel around the valley via a section of the Contour Path, taking in the lower sections of hikes CP1 and CP2
Distance: 16.5 km
Duration: 6 hours
Grade: Moderate, with some severity
General: This hike gives you a grand tour of the valley with even grander up-close views of the Cathedral range without your having to do any major climbing, although there almost certainly will be some pain and sweat in reaching the top of the Little Berg. The path travels through numerous micro-habitats, with a constantly changing panorama. Take all the field guides you can, your binoculars and your camera.

Start at the U-bend at the bottom of the hotel driveway, making for a crossing of the Mlambonja River about 200 m upstream (there's no real reason for going in this direction on this circular route, so feel free to go the other way if, like me, you don't like being told what to do). Keep left up a hill, crossing a grassy plain to the broken sandstone cliffs up ahead. The path zigzags up a steep section and through a rock band towards the right-hand side of a larger line of cliffs, into a gorge ... this is not our route: it is an interesting detour to Barker's Chalet shelter of about 500 m there and back. A little further along, about 750 m,

cathedral peak 89

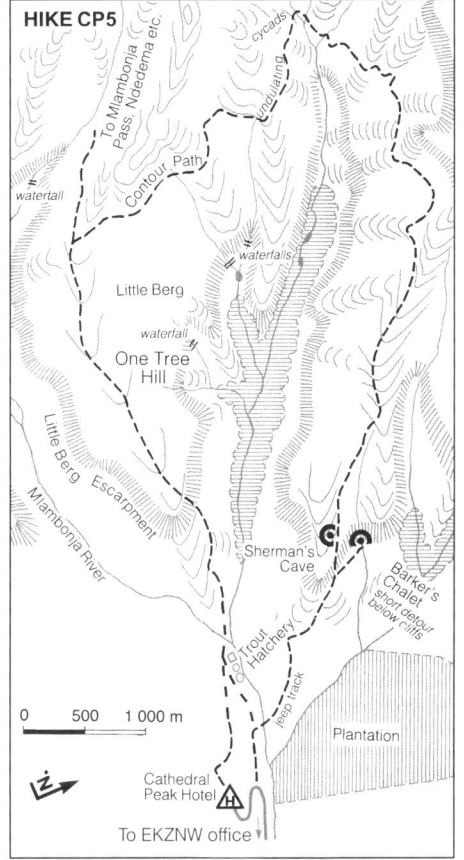

our path passes underneath Sherman's Cave. Keep going upwards to the head of the gorge, to where the path emerges onto a wide expanse of the Little Berg plateau. But the Little Berg is not just one flat plateau, as you are going to discover. This 'plateau' is really a sloping shoulder. Now you have to head steeply up, on the outside (right-hand side) of a ridge-like spur that is a continuation of the Orange Peel Gap ridge of Cathedral Peak itself. Below you to the left is the wooded valley of the Oqalweni, but it soon goes out of view as you heft your tired body up to the Contour Path.

At 2 100 m altitude you can gear down and breathe a sigh of relief, because here you meet the Contour Path. The next 3.5 km keeps more or less to that altitude, but with the usual ups and downs, ins and outs of side streams and gullies that make us so love the Contour Path (if you don't already know, you will learn to love and hate it; when your language becomes offensive to your hiking partners spare a thought for the early hikers who didn't have the convenience of this path – then you'll feel better).

Along this stretch you should encounter a fair number of the rare Berg cycad *Encephalartos ghellinckii* – if cycad thieves haven't stolen them all by now. Although the leaves of the genus are typically stiff and prickly, this species has very narrow leaves so that small ones might be mistaken for something else. Cycads have both male and female plants, harking back to the earliest time before flowering plants. Instead they have pineapple-like cones, the male's being greyish and the female's brown and slightly woolly. In Afrikaans they are known as 'broodbome' (bread trees), as Bushmen used to make a meal from the fermented trunk pith. However, the seeds are highly poisonous and Zulu herd boys are known to have died after eating them. About 20 species in South Africa and only a handful in tropical Africa represent this genus.

On crossing the head of the Oqalweni River you come to an old designated camp site, but since we're not camping it will make do as our lunch spot. A short climb up from the river leads to another 3.5 km along the Contour Path, which dips down to streams and climbs the opposite sides round bulges in the landscape. This brings you to the grassy spur above One Tree Hill, where you turn sharp left downhill. The path goes down moderately steeply for 2.5 km, before heading slightly to the left of the spur and steeply zigzagging down into the Mlambonja Valley for about 1.5 km. If you don't like steep descents, just be thankful you aren't going up with a heavy pack. When you reach the valley floor it's a 1.2-km trot back to the hotel.

90 Cathedral Peak

SHERMAN'S CAVE AND GANAPU RIDGE   HIKE CP6

Route: A circular route from the hotel, up one prominent Little Berg ridge and down another
Distance: 15 km
Duration: 6 hours
Grade: Strenuous
General: Once again you can do this hike in either direction as there is no real advantage to either. It starts at and returns to the hotel where the beers are cold and the tea is hot.

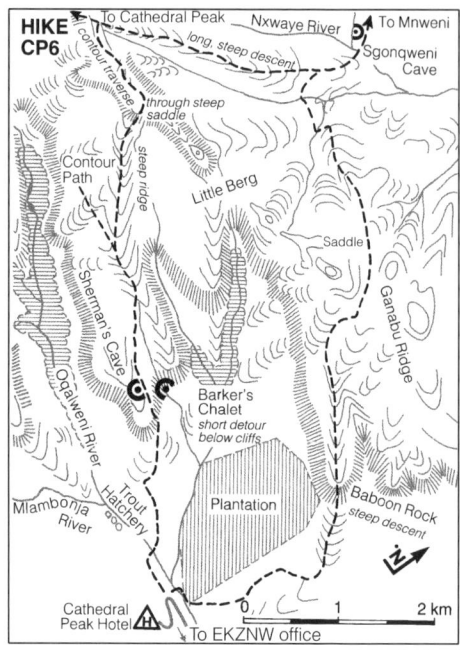

This route shares the first part with both hikes CP1 (Cathedral Peak) and CP5 (Oqalweni Circuit), up to the Contour Path so, in the interests of saving paper and my finger muscles, refer to them on pages 82 and 88. For the record, and to get your bearings, when sitting out on the hotel terrace Baboon Rock is the large sandstone promontory across the river, above and to the left of the golf course, on the lower slopes of which you can see the scarred area where a large pine plantation used to be.

On reaching the Contour Path at 2 100 m, where hike CP5 goes off to the left along the Contour Path into the Oqalweni Gorge, this path continues along hike CP1 up towards Orange Peel Gap. If you thought you'd done some climbing to get to this point, gird your loins because there's a 2-km descent awaiting you to the right – see that almost vertical drop 1 km straight ahead? Down it you must go, losing 300 m in height over 2 km.

Finally you reach the head of the Nxwaye River, where a lesser path heads at right angles to the right down a side spur. Continue down this path for 2.5 km to a side junction formed with the path coming over from Mnweni and going down to Cathedral – see hike MN7. (Not actually on the route but a pleasant diversion, Sgonqweni Cave is located over the ridge dividing the two upper tributaries of the Nxwaye, across the far stream and up a gully just 500 m from the junction.)

Although this is well over halfway in the hike, there isn't any other good place for a leisurely break, so this is the designated (by me) best lunch spot. Better yet, turn right at the junction and walk another 200 m – if you think you can – to the river and have lunch there. You'll find yourself in a wide bowl formed by the meeting of three upper tributaries of the Nxwaye. From the lunch stop you'll be looking along the path directly to the back side of Ganapu Ridge, which you have to climb, beginning with crossing the southernmost of the three streams (modern maps seem to have adopted the erroneous 'Ganabu' spelling for the ridge, but don't believe them). Over 2 km you gain about 160 m in height, but the angle is never punishing. This will bring you to a wide saddle where you look down along Baboon Rock into the Mlambonja Valley. The path heads for a short distance in the direction of the Escarpment, Cathkin Peak in the far distance, making its way onto and along the narrow spine of Baboon Rock.

At 5 km from the lunch spot the path takes a turn for the worse – curling down and round into a gully then onto the very steep nose of the rock before finding its way to a fence and past where the plantation used to be, and then following a somewhat circuitous route for the final 2 km to the Mlambonja River. Then it's time for tea or beer.

RAINBOW GORGE — HIKE CP7

Route: Up Ndumeni River Gorge
Distance: 11 km
Duration: 3 to 4 hours
Grade: Easy
General: This is a popular walk, and no wonder since it is one of the most beautiful in all the Drakensberg, and easy enough for even small children. It's also a photographer's delight, with the moving kaleidoscope of the stream, colourful fungi and leaf litter on the forest floor, rocks and intertwined roots, penumbral light through the forest canopy, and then the lace-like rainbows in the narrow gorge that give it its name. The path is easy to follow, but don't wear your best shoes, for at times you have to walk in the stream.

You can start this walk either at Cathedral Peak Hotel (and no doubt from the new Didima Hotel as well), or the guard house at the base of Mike's Pass which is supposed to be the point of entry for this area, or even from the top of Tryme Hill should you wish. This route starts at the old hotel, on the Ndumeni path, crossing a stream behind the hotel's parking area and turning sharp left. The river rises way up among the cliffs of the Castle Buttress near the Organ Pipes.

After 500 m you come to a fork, where you must turn left to skirt Tryme Hill, go through tall grass and across numerous streams for about 3 km, the path taking a wide arc into the eNdumeni Valley. Mike's Pass can be seen across the valley wending its brave way up through the cliffs opposite. The shiny little flying jewels that are collared sunbirds can sometimes be seen flitting round the proteas that grow between the isolated yellowwoods and other trees on the forest margin. Some of these trees are marked with their national tree list numbers, so don't forget to take a tree guide.

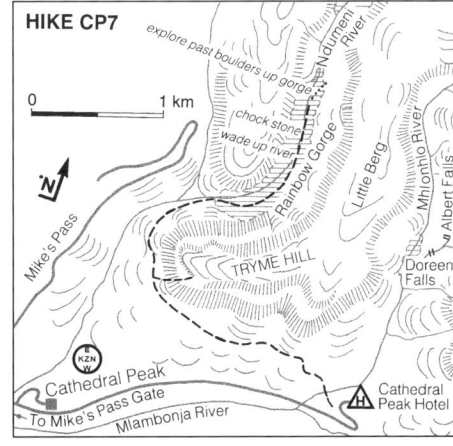

92 Cathedral Peak

The path comes upon an enchanting pool 1 km into the forest where a large moss-covered boulder forces the river to create two falls. From here on there are numerous stream crossings, each one marked by a line of stones – but they will be underwater and very slippery after rain. Once you enter the gorge, the path ends and you have to walk in the stream bed. This is where the sun creates, in the perpetual mist, a dazzling display of rainbows.

It's possible to walk to the top of the gorge, under a large chockstone wedged halfway up the vertical walls at one point (though earlier descriptions refer to two chockstones). Large boulders block the end of the gorge, but you can clamber over them and scramble up the slope diagonally to the right to the path on Tryme Hill and back to the hotel that way. If, however, you wish to return to the public camp site this will be a very long way round.

MASONGWANA GORGE   HIKE CP8

Route: From the Cathedral EKZNW office (or camp site) up the Masongwana Valley
Distance: 6 km
Duration: 2 hours
Grade: Easy
General: This gorge lies between the dinky Rainbow and spectacular Didima gorges in both geography and size. However, it is seldom visited by hikers because they don't realise they can go there. To get your bearings, it is the valley that lies just to the south-east of Mike's Pass. If you're looking for new places to walk in the area, this is a good one.

The hike starts up Mike's Pass for 1 km, taking the turnoff to the left to Cambalala House. This is the original Gewaagd farmhouse but is now a mountain club hut and not for public use.

The first owner of the farm was a Salmon Scholtz, but a few years later it was bought by Ryk Isaak Buys, a Free State farmer who by 1918 owned all eight farms in the upper Mlambonja Valley. JP Roux eventually bought the farm – and married one of Ryk Isaak's daughters.

In 1935 South Africa hosted a British Empire forestry conference, at which it was decided to research the effects of afforestation on the environment. In that year one research station was established in the winter rainfall area, one in Jonkershoek Valley near Stellenbosch, and one in the Drakensberg summer rainfall region, at Gewaagd. It remains an important conservation research station. The streams here have weirs for monitoring stream flow, even though the plantations are disappearing from the park, and rain gauges are to be seen all along the jeep tracks. The first forester here was AM (Mike) de Villiers and he had to have roads and bridges built. Mike's Pass is his claim to immortality.

From the club hut a track leads down into the Masongwana Gorge and thence a path goes upstream. It criss-crosses the river several times for 3 km to where the river divides into two. It's not possible to go all the way up the gorge as both forks are blocked by waterfalls, but you can explore up the left-hand one and then climb out via one of the side gullies. This will take you to a jeep track, one of the original tracks cut out from the top of Mike's Pass to reach numerous weir points. Turn right onto the jeep track and you will join the continuation of Mike's Pass on Arendsig plateau.

cathedral peak 93

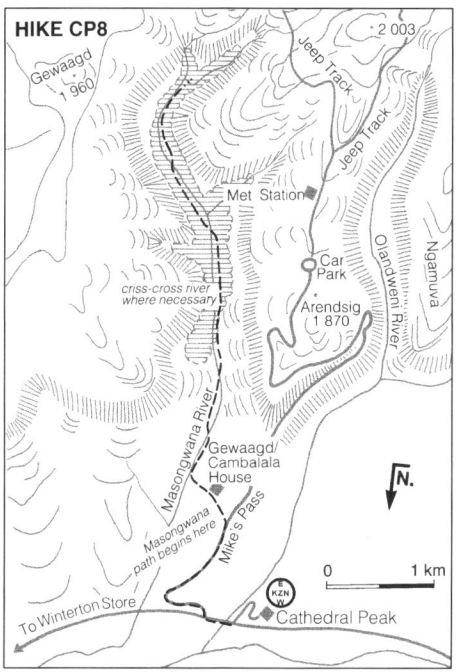

GPS TIPS

- A GPS will give you the date, time, co-ordinates and altitude of each important position.
- Set the position format to indicate degrees, minutes and decimal minutes (hddd0mm.mmmm) to read GPS grids in the new EKZNW hiking maps.
- Most GPSs are bought with the datum set at default WDS84. Reset it at Cape datum or your readings could be out.
- You can pre-programme in way points to show you the way.
- Switch on your GPS. Wait to pick up three satellite signals to triangulate your position.

DIDIMA GORGE   HIKE CP9

Route: From the old eMhlawazini (Brotherton) trading store, up the eMhlawazini Valley and the Didima Valley to the Contour Path
Distance: 32 km
Duration: 2 days (8 and 7 hours)
Grade: Strenuous
General: This gorge (previously Ndedema) was once called the Valley of the Bushmen, and Organ Pipes Pass above is one of several known as Bushman's Pass. I would love to see this old name reinstated, for two reasons. The first is that there is firm evidence that it was the very last stronghold of Bushman hunter-gatherers in the Drakensberg. In 1926 while out looking for stray cattle in the area, JS Lombard farming at Solar Cliffs came upon an enormous cave in a side valley of the eMhlawazini, partly hidden by bush and a waterfall. It was covered from one end to the other with exquisite paintings, including one large panel thick with eland. On a ledge he found a bow, 20 arrows, a blade with a leather handle, and a leather poison bag and poison spatula. But, there was also fresh bedding grass.

The other reason the name is appropriate is that there are something like 100 caves and overhangs with thousands of painted images, recorded in Harold Pager's labour of love *Ndedema*. Even if it wasn't the Bushman's last stronghold, it certainly was one of their special

94 cathedral peak

places. The air of sacredness still hangs over the Didima Valley, and I sense it whenever I venture there. I don't think it would surprise me if one day Bushmen, clad in animal skins carrying bow and arrows, stepped out from behind a rock.... You are prohibited from visiting any cave with paintings unless guided by an Amafa-registered guide (enquire at the EKZNW office).

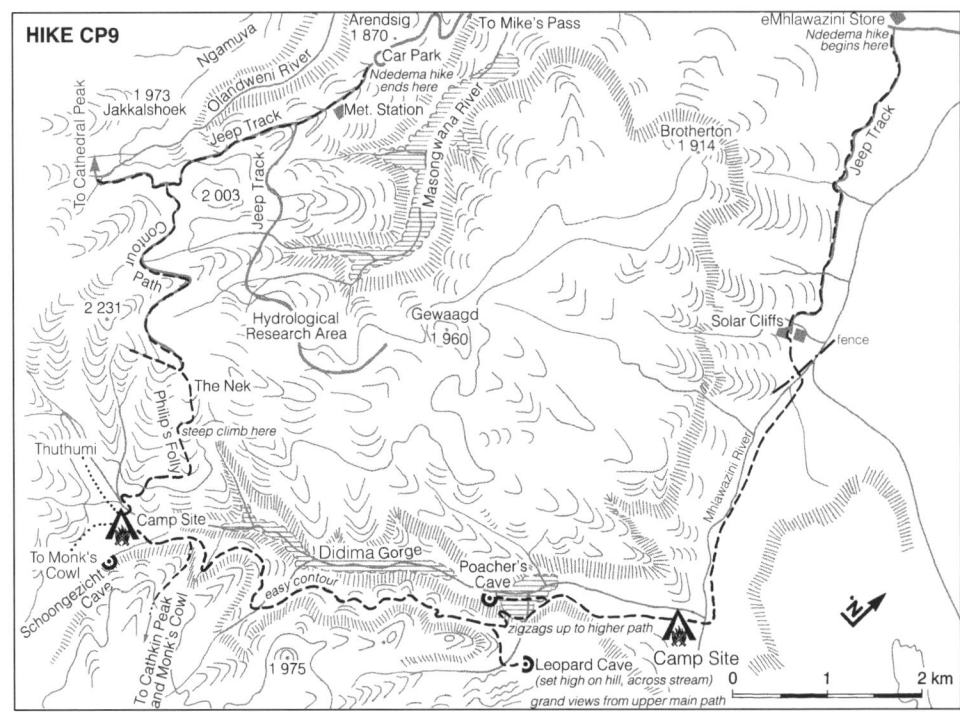

The one logistical problem is that all that is left of Brotherton Store (the starting point) is the pine trees (although I noticed someone building a spaza shop – an informal African shop – right next door). This means no free, safe parking for hikers heading up the eMhlawazini Valley.

Last time I was there I had to pay a local home-owner R20 to look after my car, plus R25 to get into the conservation area, and R150 for my guide (the minimum for 1 to 4 persons) to photograph rock art sites. Gulp! I'm not sure how the parking thing will be resolved, but you'll have to make a plan. Go through the gate where the store used to stand, along the jeep track that runs to Solar Cliffs, now a guard post. Where the track ducks and dives through the river valley, walking paths shorten the distance considerably (when in doubt stick to the right).

You'll see the gum trees at Solar Cliffs after about 3 km, and reach the river at 4 km from the start – from Solar Cliffs onwards you'll notice the paved stone path-making and erosion gabions. Go through a fence and cross the eMhlawazini, climbing above the river and then proceeding up the left-hand bank for 3 km, where the Didima Gorge forces its way into your consciousness (it's like that, those imposing headlands and the enticing gap). Here you cross the eMhlawazini again (might have to take off your boots) to a lovely camping spot within a grove of ouhout and wild willows, I think. The path goes through the camp site and heads for the left-hand side of the gorge through tall grass and bush.

After a gentle 1-km climb (ignore all half-baked paths up to the left) the path heads up a side gully of this Little Berg headland.

Two kilometres from the camp site, where one path goes up the valley to Poacher's Cave, our path takes the steeper option up through the sandstone terraces on the left. Somewhere along here there is a shady little grotto with a pool where you can take a dip on a hot day. And it does get hot in summer. Then it climbs up steeply to reach the semblance of a contour path off to the right (up the gorge).

For the next 5 km the path runs all along the top of Didima Gorge with views of Didima Buttress, Didima Dome and Little Saddle. Where you reach the head of the gorge the Contour Path proper heads off to the left towards Intunja (the peak with a hole through it) and Monk's Cowl eventually, but that's another hike description altogether (Contour Path, hike MC11, see page 130).

Keep right here and still head up the Didima River to an open area, which is the upper Didima camp site and our destination. It's the meeting place of three paths: Thuthumi Pass to the north-east (it comes out on Ndumeni Dome close to Organ Pipes Pass), the Contour Path crossing, and the path up the upper Didima Valley behind Eastman's Peak.

It's a wonderful spot decorated with tall daisy bushes in spring. For the record, Thuthumi is one of the Berg's easier passes but seldom used by hikers (which is a shame) because the start is so out of the way.

MUSHROOM ROCK AND TARN HILL — HIKE CP10

Route: From the hotel car park past Mushroom Rock to the Little Berg plateau at the tarn
Distance: 6 km
Duration: 3 hours
Grade: Moderate
General: This is a steep walk, but it's really short. It takes in two landmarks and offers lovely views of the Little Berg and Escarpment wall, especially at sunrise. Rise early and drag someone special with you (the hotel does have its own wedding chapel), then impress them by hauling a bottle of bubbly out of your day pack and pop the cork as the sun peeps over the horizon.

From the hotel car park take the path marked 'Mushroom Rock' which follows the right-hand bank of the Mhlonhlo River and then veers to the right after about 700 m up the steep grassy slope to the rock band. Mushroom Rock is a weathered feature of the Little Berg cliff line and you have to pass behind it. From the rock the path climbs for another 500 m before veering to the left and easing off on top of the Little Berg. From where the path eases off above Mushroom Rock it's another 1 km to the tarn. From there it's 750 m to the start of the jeep track, which joins and becomes the Contour Path 1.5 km further onwards and upwards.

Where the jeep track meets the Contour Path coming over from the Tseketseke Valley, the shortest way to the summit round here, by way of the Camel and Organ Pipes, commences.

96 cathedral peak

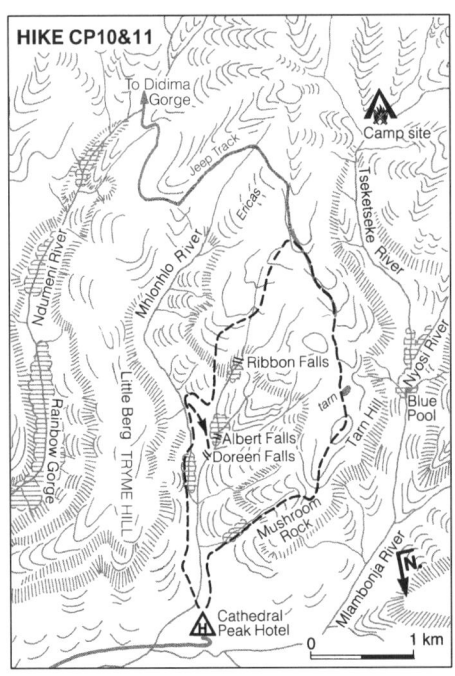

ETIQUETTE TIPS

- Respect others; go quietly.
- Don't throw rocks down the mountain.
- The Drakensberg protects the last viable populations of many flower species, so let them be.
- No fires are allowed anywhere.
- Don't leave old candle wax defacing caves.
- Never wash in any fresh water. Small fish, amphibians, insect larvae and micro-organisms are fragile.
- The least damaging place for human waste is in grassland areas away from caves, streams and forests.

TRYME HILL AND WATERFALLS   HIKE CP11

Route: From Cathedral Peak Hotel up the Mhlonhlo River past three waterfalls, up to the Contour Path and then over Tryme Hill back to the hotel
Distance: 12.5 km
Duration: 4 to 5 hours
Grade: Strenuous (or easy, but steep, to waterfalls)
General: This pleasant half-day outing to the top of the Little Berg brings you up close under the Organ Pipes and other big chunks of basalt on the mountains, but it also affords intimate meetings with cloistered falls. You don't have to do the whole route described here, though you might want to, but instead you could do just a 5-km round-trip to Doreen and Albert falls. These falls were named after the current hotel owner's parents for whom these were special places. Whether or not that is true, any lover of nature would be honoured to be immortalised in such a way.

You can start this walk at the boom in the hotel car park, heading for a junction on the slopes of Tryme Hill (from the boom keep right to head for the Mhlonhlo Valley and not up the hill).

Head first along the contour for 500 m and then go up the left-hand side of the valley for 1 km, to reach the river 1.5 km from the previous junction. Several paths lead off from here to the right to both Albert and Doreen falls. Cross the river and head diagonally up to the right away from the river, through the forest, to gain the crest of a ridge. Here the path veers to the left and climbs this ridge steeply for about 1 km, before lessening off the angle somewhat for another 1.2 km through rank grass to the Contour Path which is really a jeep track.

This is at the base of the Camel, up which you have to go for 500 m, turning left onto the Contour Path. When the angle of the ridge starts to make you nervous, take heart for the Contour Path then heads off to the left while the path upwards goes over the Camel to meet Organ Pipes Pass near the summit. Carry on along the Contour path for 2 km: this is really pleasant and easy walking, across the headwaters of the Mhlonhlo, and out along the southerly spur of the Camel (the spur up which you've come, and the one you now go down, are like two legs of a camel). Turn left to head down towards Tryme Hill – a prominence at the end of Little Berg, 3.5 km from the Contour Path turnoff. The path nips round the hill to the right and then descends steeply to the hotel.

Within sight of the end, you have to go either left-right, or right-left to get to your starting point. You can of course reverse the walk to visit the waterfalls near the end and have a picnic lunch beside the cool waters.

TSEKETSEKE HUT — HIKE CP12

Route: From Cathedral Peak Hotel up the Tseketseke Valley to the mountain hut
Distance: 19 km
Duration: 7 to 8 hours (preferably 2 days)
Grade: Strenuous to severe
General: This hike is one of those intravenous walks where over a shortish, almost direct route you get high really quickly; not so much in total altitude as in the feeling of being among the high peaks. In this case the impressive free-standing peaks of Pyramid (2 914 m) and Column (2 926 m) which rise up higher in the Tseketseke Pass, and the bonus of Cleft Peak looming over you. At one time Cleft Peak (3 281 m) was thought to be the highest in the Berg, so imposing is its bearing. This was one of the favourite playgrounds of George Thompson, whom we met in the introduction to the chapter.

Another great episode of early Berg mountaineering was the first climbing of Cleft Peak, by one of the boldest climbers, Brian Godbold. The 'bold' accreditation is for the feat, in 1936, of tempting fate and public opinion that anyone attempting to overnight on top of Cleft Peak in winter would die. He did it in July, in snow, with three friends and, although their food and boots froze, they returned ruddy and happy. Ten years later, in another cold July, he and two companions left their camp in the Mlambonja Valley and started up the cleft. They started climbing well before sunrise in just light clothing and tackies, going up the chimney. By sunset, having spent all day in the shade, they had to traverse out onto the right-hand face. By 20h30 they finally stood on top. Then they walked off down to Organ Pipes Pass and reached camp around 02h30 the next morning. Ah! What men were made of in those days (and women: one of the party was a Mrs Millard). Just look up at the peak and imagine setting off up its vertical face in tackies and with just a hemp rope for safety. Go on, I dare you!

98 cathedral peak

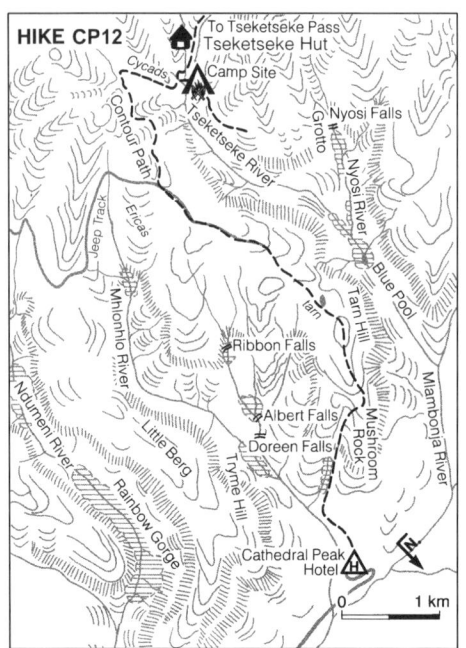

Oh all right, let's just walk up to near the base instead. You can take either the Mushroom Rock and Tarn Hill (CP10) or the Tryme Hill (CP11) paths from the hotel car park, as they are much the same. If you plan to overnight then I recommend Tryme Hill because it gives you the chance and the time, if waterfalls are your thing, to visit Albert and Doreen falls, as well as Ribbon. These are wonderful places. It's 5 km to where the waters meet at the base of a ridge at the foot of the Camel.

The path heads up the left-hand side of the Camel for about 500 m in distance (and 50 m in height) to meet the Contour Path. The Organ Pipes/Camel Pass carries on straight up, but we turn right along the Contour Path for 2 km, into and out of a deep stream gully, finally going steeply down an eroded path on a grassy spur into the Tseketseke Valley and to the camp site. The old mountain club hut can be seen a little way above the Contour Path, with its distinctive barrel-vaulted corrugated iron roof.

At the time of writing I was told by a senior conservator for the Northern Drakensberg that the hut was in poor condition and might well be removed. That is how I found it – not removed but in poor condition. However, a ranger at Cathedral Peak told me when I phoned that the hut was in fine nick and could be booked for overnight accommodation. It would be better to double check before you set out.

BLUE POOL AND NYOSI GROTTO   HIKE CP13

Route: Cathedral Peak Hotel over the base of Mushroom Rock and up the Nyosi Valley
Distance: 10 km
Duration: 3 to 4 hours
Grade: Easy
General: This is an undemanding walk from the hotel for a picnic and a swim. Stop at the Blue Pool on the Tseketseke River 3.5 km from the hotel, or venture another 1.5 km up a tributary (Nyosi) to a small waterfall.

Head off up the Mlambonja Pass path, from behind the hotel, next to but to the right of the Mushroom Rock path, heading over the rump of Mushroom Rock (parallel to the Mlambonja Valley, hike CP2). After 2 km our route deviates from the path where it reaches the Tseketseke River. The main Mlambonja Pass crosses the side river, but we head up its left-hand bank.

cathedral peak 99

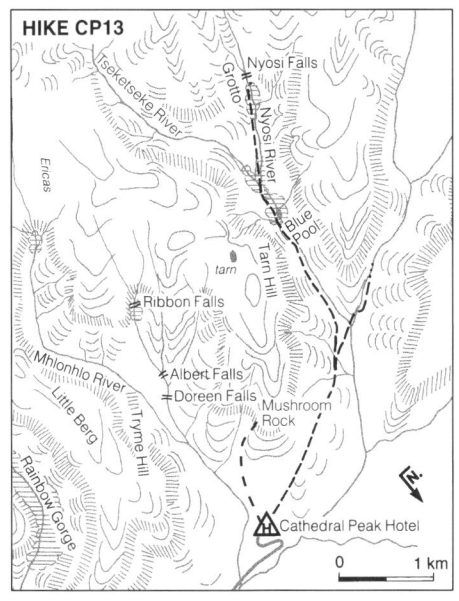

HIKE CP13

For 1.75 km the path heads upstream, but not very steeply overall. Here you reach a most delightful pool, in an hour or less from the start. There's not much point in doing this walk in any but swimming weather, for swimming is the sole point of it.

If you've liked the trip so far, you can cross the stream to go up the Nyosi Valley opposite the pool, for about 1.5 km to the falls and the overhang called The Grotto. It's a fun trip although the path is indistinct (suitable for those who don't need paths to have fun). Return either the same way, or climb out from Blue Pool, up the north-facing slope to reach the Tarn Hill path. It's a steep 1-km climb, but then you have a nice walk back along the Little Berg and down past Mushroom Rock. Savour the huge views and sky.

TWO PASSES   HIKE CP14

Route: Up Mlambonja Pass, south along the Escarpment to Windy Gap, and down Organ Pipes Pass
Distance: 38 km, starting at the hotel and ending at the top of Mike's Pass
Duration: 3 or 4 days
Grade: Extreme
General: This is one of the most popular summit hikes in the Drakensberg, but it's not easy. That is to say it's a slog. But what views!

Although the route I describe is the one commonly done, I prefer to do it the other way round: drive to the top of Mike's Pass, climb up the shorter Organ Pipes Pass route, then slip-slide down long and steep Mlambonja Pass and end at the hotel. You can start and end at the hotel by going via Tryme Hill up the Camel Pass, which meets Organ Pipes Pass after a traverse from under Castle Buttress into the Organ Pipes gully.

If you start off up Mlambonja then I suggest taking two days up for a four-day trip. However, by reversing the trip you can do the round-trip in just three as the up trip can be cut by driving up Mike's Pass – but then you either have to have a driver take the car down, or come back up to fetch it later yourself. And don't forget to carry your keys. Decisions, decisions.

Refer to the Mlambonja Pass hike description (CP2) for the first part of this route. The hike up the pass is 12.5 hard km, and it will take a full day, or two very full half days. Your only real decision here is: one or two. From Twins Cave you have to head across the saddle and traverse up under the lip of the Escarpment to reach the summit, and then proceed south just over the lip.

When doing a high-level traverse it's often easier to follow the valleys on the Lesotho side of the watershed than repeatedly to climb the lateral ridges. Do this by assessing the lie of the land. Although maps show paths here it's pretty much a case of keeping the big cliffs on your left and following your instincts.

On this hike, presuming you've taken two days to reach the summit, I would strongly urge you to hug the Escarpment, only taking short cuts to avoid unnecessary double trips like the out hike onto the promontory of Mlambonja Buttress (although it is a fantastic viewpoint). The whole section round the top of Xeni Pass, the convoluted, crinkled rim along Elephant, Plume and Cockade then looking down onto the Pyramid and Column peaks, is to my mind one of the highlights of the Drakensberg.

Instead of trying your best to scoot over to Windy Gap, linger round these parts for it may be some time, years, decades, before you come back to see it again.

Cleft Peak is a bit of a monster, reaching the northern side about 7.5 km from the summit of Mlambonja Pass. What you want to do (I think) is to traverse around it on the Lesotho side for about 3 km: from the top of Tseketseke Pass you can go either over the unnamed high point (3 202 m) rising up to the south, or around it to the right. Once around or over Cleft Peak there is a bit of a mish-mash of paths that cut down diagonally towards and then around the back of Castle Buttress, to the Kakoatsan River and then slightly up to Windy Gap directly behind the summit of Organ Pipes Pass. Just walk up the river towards the Escarpment edge and choose your camp site.

Ndumeni Dome (3 206 m) Cave might look enticing on a map, but I'd give it a miss unless conditions insisted.

There are two reasons. First, you have quite a slog up rocky ground, following indistinct cairns up the left-hand side of the dome, to the top of a gully. The first cave is just over on the left-hand side of the gully, and the second a little further down. Second, these are pretty small caves and alright for one or even two people, but others would have to sleep down a low tunnel. But Ndumeni means 'the place of thunderstorms' so, who knows, those tunnels might become your best option.

From Windy Gap, you head over the Escarpment and steeply down for 250 m, the fluted Organ Pipes rearing up ahead and on your right. At a point where the path levels off, there is a choice: either you traverse off around to the left under Castle Buttress for 750 m and down the knife-edge ridge of the Camel, or you carry on down the knife-edge ridge under the Organ Pipes. They both involve some scrambling along rocky ridges, the difference being that the Camel route takes you directly down to the hotel via Tarn or Tryme hills, while the Organ Pipes route takes you past the old lookout to the top of Mike's Pass.

The old lookout is a small timber hut 4.5 km down the ridge, at the bottom of the pass. It was indeed a lookout when the whole area below was under pine (hard to imagine now), but it can be hired as overnight accommodation. From the lookout an unofficial but well-used short cut heads off down the spur to the left, making directly for the point where the jeep track continuation of Mike's Pass meets the Contour Path jeep track. The official route heads down to the right, to The Nek, then back left along the jeep track for 3.5 km to the head of Mike's Pass continuation track.

I don't know about you, but after tackling the pass the extra 'official' 5 km seems like a lot to ask. From the Contour Path junction it's still 3 km to the gate and car park at the top of Mike's Pass (Arendsig). As the pass itself is over 5 km, you will want to avoid having to walk that too: therefore leaving a car safely parked at Arendsig is a high priority.

cathedral peak 101

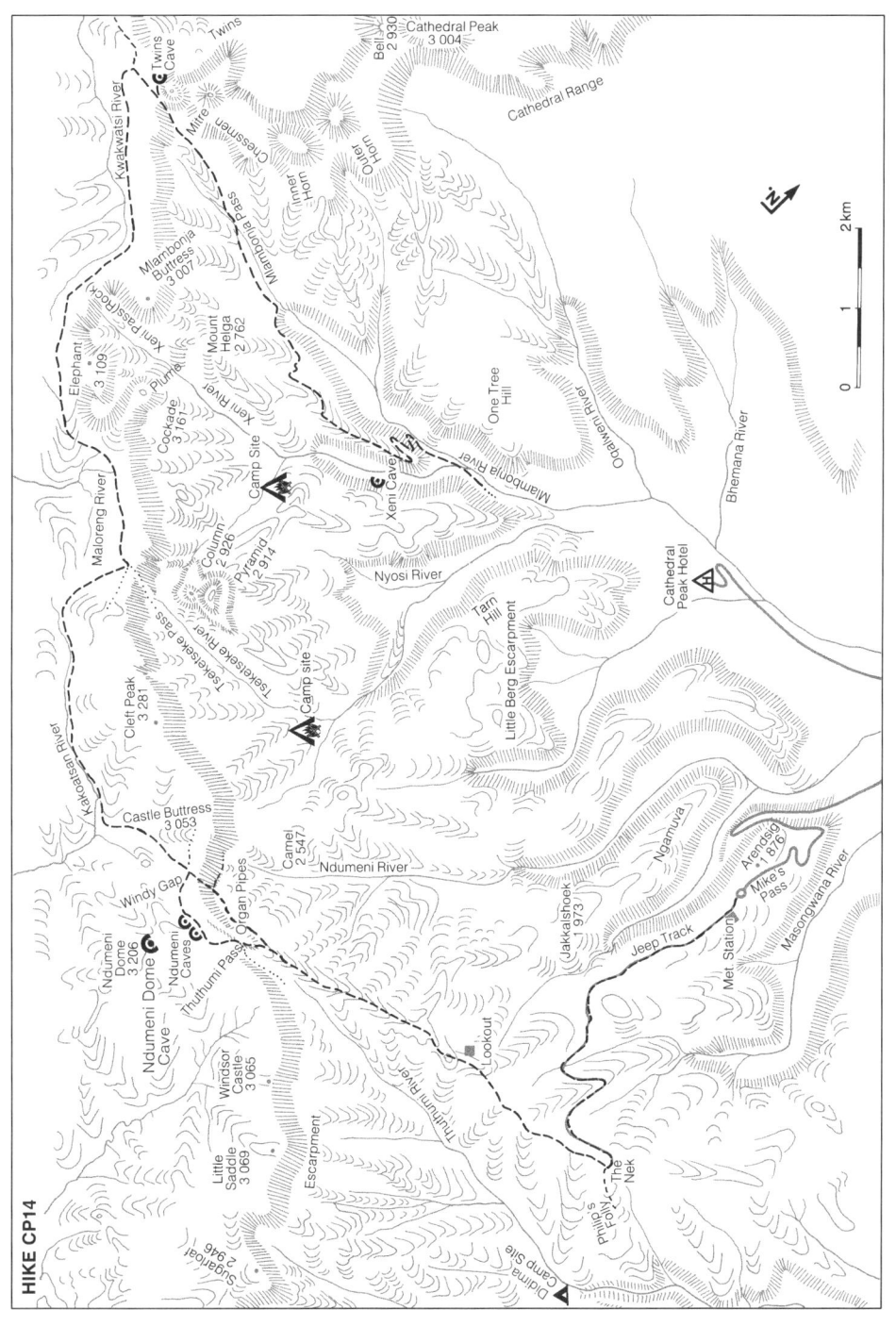

102 Cathedral Peak

CONTOUR PATH: CATHEDRAL PEAK TO DIDIMA VALLEY   HIKE CP15

Route: From the beginning of the Contour Path below Cathedral Peak summit, to the camp site above Didima Gorge
Distance: 35 km
Duration: 2 days
Grade: Severe
General: This is probably the longest way you could find to get between these two points, Cathedral Peak and Didima, or on to Monk's Cowl station (see hike MC9). So why would you do it? Because it's there, is the only answer I can give to anyone who asks. And I'm one of the people trying to champion a continuous contour path from Royal Natal National Park to Bushman's Nek. If a four-day outing in the Berg is your aim, rather than just getting from one place to another, then this would be about the very best you could find. Go for it.

The shortest and easiest route between Cathedral Peak and Didima (see hike CP9) or Monk's Cowl (links up with hike MC9) would be to follow the eMhlawazini River upstream to its very beginning on Ndanjane Ridge, near Hhlathikulu Nek, and then under the Amphlett and down to Monk's Cowl. This is just 30 km starting at Brotherton store site, and makes a great – if less interesting and varied – two-day hike.

Take a map of the area and highlight the Contour Path with a magic marker. You'll notice just how convoluted the route is, going as it has to around every crinkle, wiggle and lump of the landscape. And this area is extremely crinkly, wiggly and lumpy. Consider Cathedral Peak Hotel to be the centre of a wheel, and the Contour Path to be the rim (well, only half a rim really). From the beginning of the Contour Path in the north to where it reaches the Tryme Hill/Camel junction is 28 km. But you could walk to the base of the Camel from the hotel in just 4, albeit steep, km.

Anyway, let's presume you've decided you'd like to hike the Contour Path, maybe even set the challenge of linking up all the bits as far as you can from Mnweni to Sani Pass – now there's an honourable challenge for any hiker.

There's no real secret to this, other than that at one point it seems to disappear entirely and you have to scramble up a grassy gully at one of the Nyosi's tributaries and the bank is so eroded. But that's just how it goes.

From where the Contour Path begins to where the Mlambonja Pass route joins it (hike CP2) is a pretty straightforward 7-km walk. From there it's 4 km to the base of the main pass. This is straightforward but certainly not straight. A further 2 km around Mount Helga brings you to a side junction to the left, going to Xeni Cave, and 1.5 km cutting back towards the Berg brings you to Xeni Pass.

The next 2 km are not nice, as this is where the path plays disappearing acts and at one point I lost it entirely. Somehow I found it by doing a 30-m scramble up insanely steep grass, but I suspect I was really off-route and therefore have decided not to say exactly where, and hope you fare better. On the map it's a lovely, wide path. Once past this tricky section the path suddenly re-appears, as if by magic, and then it's another 5 km to the Tseketseke camp site and hut (see hike CP12). This would make it one long day. Either make camp at the Xeni River 5 km further back, or start up the Mlambonja Pass route (hike CP2) to cut off about 7 km to make it a 19-km day. From the camp site at Tseketseke you start off up a steep, eroded grassy bank and into a side gully, but once you are there the going is easy for most of the rest of day two. The views are wonderful and the jeep track really easy walking. After 9.5 km you come to the continuation of Mike's Pass, and it's a further 3.5 up-and-down km to The Nek. The jeep track ends here and now you have to descend the steep Philip's Folly (Philip van der Riet, perhaps). It's a fairly taxing and winding 2.5-km descent down a rocky, protea-dotted series of spurs to the upper Didima Valley and our next overnight stop. The Little Saddle, Sphinx and Didima Dome are the luminaries in the crown of the Escarpment above. You might meet Basotho traders in the valley, casually scaling slippery Thlanyaku Pass in their gumboots.

Note: The new EKZNW Didima Hotel is scheduled to open some time early in 2003. The park authority says new hiking routes will be opened for its own guests, but no information on them was available when this guide was being compiled. It's likely that a major emphasis will be on guided trails, in the Rainbow Gorge, Mike's Pass and Didima Gorge areas which lie close to the new hotel. Of particular interest will be guided walks to Bushman rock art sites. Some of the very best in the Drakensberg are to be found here, but you won't find them by yourself. There are guides to lead you, which is good for conservation and for the local economy.

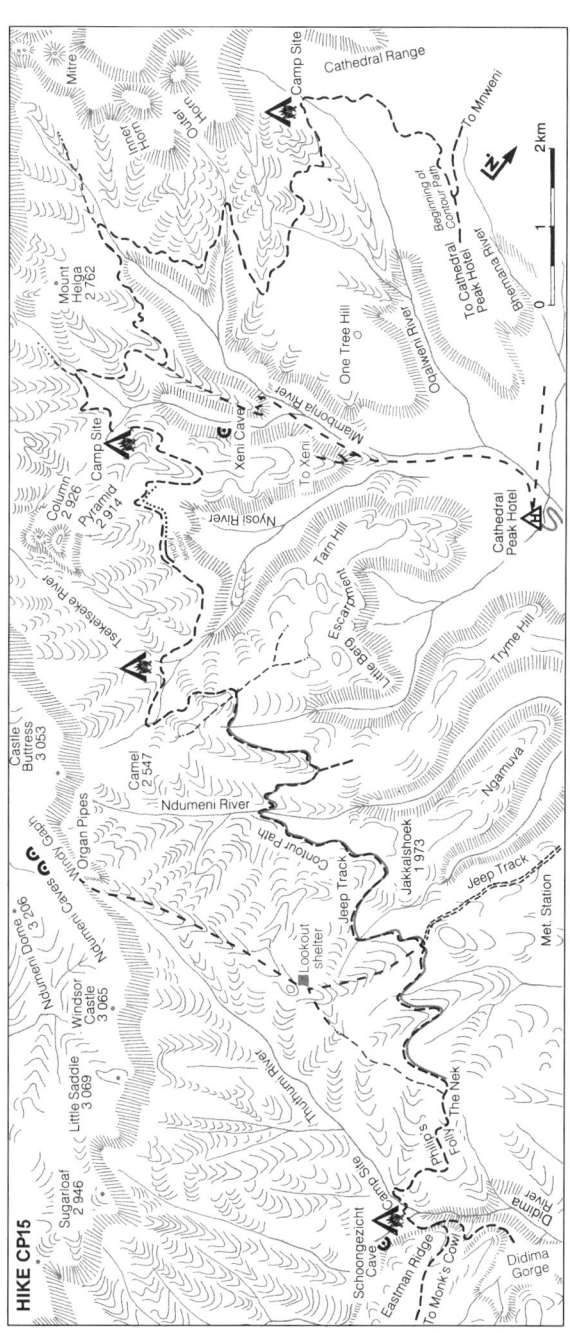

monk's cowl/nkosana

No matter where you stand on the Escarpment between the Amphitheatre's Eastern Buttress and Giant's Castle, Cathkin Peak always seems to push its way out and demand attention. When the Voortrekkers moved out of the area following annexation of Natal by the British, Scottish settler David Gray moved in and established the first permanent farm which he called Cathkin, after his home town of Cathkin Braes. And from there the peak was named. However, the Zulu name for Cathkin Peak, Mdedelelo, is far more appropriate, as it means 'make room for him' or, more specifically, 'the bully' because it's a big chunky mountain that stands proud of the main escarpment and therefore is seen to be boastful, or a 'bully', standing over everyone else. In the days before uKhahlamba-Drakensberg Park was established Mdedelelo was also the name of the forest reserve and wilderness area that stretched from the northern border of Injisuthi Reserve to the southern bank of Didima (Ndedema) Gorge.

Despite its prominence, both the small bump of Champagne Castle behind the cliff line of the Escarpment and Monk's Cowl in the dark gap between the two, are higher: Champagne Castle, at 3 248 m, is often held to be the second highest peak of the Drakensberg, but by modern reckoning it is only number three (after Mafadi and Injisuthi Dome). The route up to Champagne Castle is, in climbing terms, a doddle, but hikers know it as the exhausting Gray's Pass which was first done in 1861. It was done officially as a route by the formidable Stocker brothers only in 1888.

In 1888 the Stockers (members of the British Alpine Club, one a priest) attempted Cathkin Peak by the south gully and got to within 150 metres of the top before being turned back by a blank face. Only in 1912 was the wall scaled, by George Amphlett, Father Kelly of Bloemfontein and four others. Today much harder routes have been climbed, including the one on which George

Thompson fell, broke an ankle, then finished the climb. The story of the climbing of the 'little chief', Nkosana, is much more breathtaking. This 'little chief' is the Monk's Cowl, and it hides between Cathkin and Champagne, a dark brooding presence like a character out of *The Name of the Rose*. Or a giant dragon's fang. The 'standard route' was established in 1942 by Hans Wongschowski and party, who spoke of its 'cold, fascinating beauty'.

Of this occasion Pearse writes in *Barrier of Spears*: 'As they approached Champagne Castle Hotel in their car, a devastating storm broke over them. Trees were uprooted, the front of the car was lifted bodily into the air by a tremendous gust of wind. A nearby house collapsed like a pack of cards. It was almost as if the guardian spirits of uKhahlamba were making a last desperate effort to protect the inviolability of the virgin peak.'

Oom Hendrik Maartens, who owned the hotel in those days, flatly refused to believe such a peak could – ever – be climbed. He secretly sent a nephew up Champagne Castle to see if the cairn the party claimed to have built was there – and it was.

But the 1938 attempt by Dick Barry and Colin Gerbhardt is the one of legend. Barry was called 'the tiger' by his generation, so we need say no more of his credentials. In 1938 he was only 22 when he and Gerbhardt set off from Cathkin Park Hotel. They started the climb up the north gully in intermittent rain, mist and shine, forging a route up the north-west face: D-grade grass and rubble ledges gave way to E-grade faces. Finally E became F, and as Gerbhardt was easing up to Barry on a narrow belay stance two-thirds of the way up the peak, right next to the crux traverse pitch, his handhold pulled out and down he went. When their rope pulled taut Barry too was yanked off (he was too impatient a climber to worry about fixing belay points, and so over-confident in his own abilities he never dreamed of not completing any climb). They plummeted and tumbled about a hundred metres and, although otherwise uninjured, Barry lay unconscious for two hours.

Now they were stuck on an inaccessible ledge in shorts and socks (for that's how they climbed), their tackies safe with their food and water bottles, rain gear, extra rope, pitons and a camera in a rucksack up on their last belay ledge. The short story is that a probably concussed Barry, while looking for an easy way down to the right (Gerbhardt said he knew there wasn't one), fell to his death. In 1952 Des Watkins and Gillian Bettle found Barry's rucksack at the point from which he fell – then Watkins fell, and although Bettle held the rope Watkins suffered several fractured ribs and they had to abandon the climb. Barry's Route yielded only in 1962, the leader Malcolm Moor taking three and a half hours to do the four-metre crux section. It is seldom repeated, other than by parties going off route by following bits of abseil rope left by other parties that have gone astray.

There have been more climbing accidents on Monk's Cowl than probably any other peak in the country. Even nowadays in the MCSA journal you can read the occasional harrowing account of someone who has tried, and mostly failed. My mountaineering partner for some years, Clive Ward, took a tumble. He was trying a new aided line on Barry's Route, having fixed his etriers (a short rope-ladder) in a crack where an old bit of frayed rope hung from a piton, when the whole section of wall fell away. He went flying, holding on to a double-bed size flake which, he said later, he thought would become his tombstone. Near Cathkin Park, where the summit of the Cowl is just visible, lies a block of sandstone with a brass plaque with Barry's name on it and the words 'who gave his life to the mountains he loved'. And, I must say, when my time is up I hope I will be in the Drakensberg, or at least have my ashes scattered there. At the base of Gray's Pass is a spot marked on old maps as Keith Bush Hut. The hut is now gone (demolished in line with the old wilderness guidelines), but it marks a spot close to where Keith Bush fell when his abseil sling broke. He and his two companions had just completed the first successful ascent of the north face.

The first people we know of to have inhabited the valleys round the base of Mdedelelo were Bushmen, then the amaZizi, who were scattered during the reigns of terror in the early 1820s. A decade later the Voortrekkers arrived and established some farms, but they moved on when the British Empire started muscling in. The first British settler in the Champagne Valley was David Gray in 1858 who, as has been noted, farmed Cathkin. Then, as the Dire Straits song 'Telegraph Road' goes, came the woodcutters and hunters: Nelson at Cathkin, Van Greuning at Injisuthi, Kruger at Makuruman, as well as various recluses and runaways. One of them was 'Old Man' Hodgson who lived with his dogs in a mud hut in the Injisuthi Valley (the name means 'well-fed dogs') and sold the Zulu busts he modelled in clay to hotel guests. He had been an officer in the British Army.

In 1907 an etymologist named Dr Haviland set off from Couch and de Bath's store (now White Mountain Inn) at Ntabanlope, midway between Giant's and Champagne castles, on his bicycle. The good doctor was never seen again, but his bicycle was found a decade later in a cave about 10 kilometres away. In 1942 a skeleton with 40 golden sovereigns in what remained of a pocket was found by hikers on the slopes of Cathkin Peak. The good doctor, perhaps? And of course there has to be an Irishman in our story. In this case two brothers McCormick who were banished from Ireland for being Sinn Feiners. They lived in a cave above the kwaNdema Stream and lived the life of 'bush rangers' – that is, cattle rustlers.

The story is still told in the kraals of the valleys around here of a battle between a Zulu regiment and Bushman cattle thieves. Apparently the little hunters were trapped on a high slope somewhere above the Nkosana River. There are no passes here, so near the summit they made an extraordinary last stand. They lay on their backs, put their feet into leather thongs tied round their bow staves, and using both hands to pull the strings let fly bursts of poisoned arrows almost vertically upwards which then rained down on the pursuers. The Zulu detail were so terrified of the poisoned barbs they retreated, and in the ensuing darkness the Bushmen found a way over into Lesotho and a short-lived freedom.

To my mind the queerest bit of history involves a 'gold' rush in the upper Nkosana Valley. In the 1920s a local farmer broke the news that he'd found cinnabar (red mercuric oxide from which mercury is derived) in the Berg. For several months the upper Nkosana Valley, where the purplish-red layers of the Red beds are exposed, rang with the sound of men and picks. And today you can still see the scars of the paths they wore and the holes they dug. But it was a foolish hoax. Today Champagne Valley is the most highly developed area of the Drakensberg, because the Sterkspruit/Mpofana Valley is so easily travelled. The first hotel was Cathkin Park. It was started by W Carter Robinson in 1929 as a hostel (it was he who stocked the local rivers with brown trout and pushed to have Monk's Cowl forest reserve proclaimed). It was taken over by Otto Zunckel in 1935, and run by his two sons Udo and Gerald. While under the management of Gerald's nephew Anton (now at Bushman's Nek Hotel) it was absorbed by the Drakensberg Sun. Next came Oom Hendrik Maartens who had catered for a few mountain club July camps and became enamoured with the new craze of tourism. In 1940 he bought the farm Woestyn and erected the first buildings which were to become Champagne Castle Hotel. In 1943 he sold to J van Heynigen, whom we will meet later on the Contour Path from Cathedral.

In 1940 Captain HC Whelan bought the farm Heartsease and built El Mirador Hotel. Then came David Gray, grandson of the original David Gray in the area, who turned the farmstead on his property The Nest into the one which perhaps best of all retains the charms of the family hotels of yesteryear. In 1954 the then news editor of the *Natal Daily News*, RW Tungay, bought Dragon Peaks farm and turned it into a caravan park resort. He and his son John had a dream, and today the hills ring with the sound of music from the Drakensberg Boys' Choir, the school started on land next door.

Newer comers in the valley are Mountain Splendour Caravan and Camping Park on the other side of the road to Dragon Peaks, the Champagne Sports Resort part-owned by tennis ace Kevin Curren, and then in the Mtoti Valley over to the north, on Bell Park Dam, the more classy weekend-getaway style Cayley Lodge, near Arthur's Seat (good paragliding take-off site) and very basic Kelvin Grove Camp Site. For backpackers and hikers the preferred place to stay is my old mate Ed Salomon's place, Inkosana Lodge and Trekking. It's informal and caters for couples or groups, bed and breakfast or full board. Ed is the local magistrate when needs be, but he's also an experienced mountaineer from Monk's Cowl to the Himalayas.

FERN FOREST — HIKE MC1

Route: Drakensberg Sun chalets up the iNkwakwa Stream into the Fern Forest
Distance: 6 km
Duration: 2 hours
Grade: Easy
General: There's some confusion as to which piece of indigenous bush is the 'fern forest'. Slingsby's map marks it as being one and the same as kwaNdema Forest, but Pearse's older map shows it as Forthlo Forest, more to the east and much closer to Cathkin Park. As mentioned in the introduction, Cathkin Park was the first hotel in the Champagne Valley, so it is sad to see the buildings crumbling now. What's heartening is that the Working for Water programme has got stuck into the dense wattle infestation around here. Whenever you walk these areas, take your hat off to the men and women of Working for Water, the biggest public project ever undertaken in this country and one that is already reaping rich environmental rewards.

The Drakensberg Sun welcomes hikers and will let you have a copy of their map for nothing (they calculate, wisely, that they'll see you in the bar afterwards). Rather than getting too hung up about the map disagreements, simply make sure that you follow the green markers from the end of the chalets.

This walk gives you the time to notice every little flower and fern. It really is a lovely and very easy walk through delightful forest to the base of the Little Berg, with birds abounding in the lower stretches (robins and other typically small forest species).

The route basically follows the stream which flows into the dam at the bottom of the hotel gardens, going upstream. It first climbs up the open ground below to the north of the hotel, then crosses the stream and enters the forest, turning round at a small waterfall. To reach it you might have to duck under some fallen trees, using stones in the river bed and minding out for spiders' webs. The return path crosses the river a few times before rejoining the outward path when nearing the hotel.

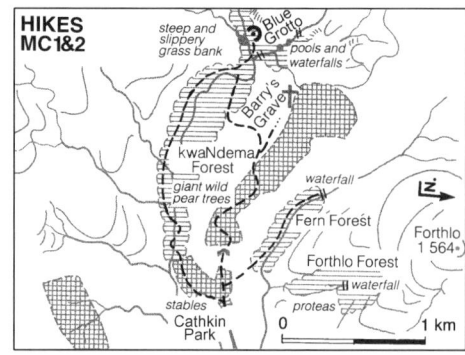

BARRY'S GRAVE AND GROTTO HIKE MC2

Route: From the Drakensberg Sun Hotel up the kwaNdema Valley back through the kwaNdema Forest, taking a detour to the grave of Dick Barry
Distance: 7.5 km
Duration: 2½ hours
Grade: Easy to moderate
General: The Grotto part of the hike will be of interest to anyone who likes to take a plunge in a natural forest pool. The forest should enthrall keen bird-watchers as I found robins, shrikes, flycatchers, batises and the occasional chat to be far more visible than in other places; but I do walk alone and quietly. For mountaineers, Dick Barry's grave is more of a shrine than merely a place of interest. If you don't know his history, you should read up about the man and his final route in *Barrier of Spears* before you set out.

Starting from the chalets below the hotel dam, take the track above old Cathkin Park following the red markers. Right at the outset, however, you should choose whether you want to hike up or come down the forested valley. I'd suggest going up the right-hand path, taking a spur up the protea grassland for about 2 km. There used to be lots of cattle paths crisscrossing the main hiking path which could get you lost. However, this is less the case now that the hotel controls a large tract of land up to the Little Berg cliff line. Around here a path leads off to the left, crosses a stream shaded by indigenous bush and leads to Barry's grave, which is surrounded by a low stone wall. The grave is a simple sandstone boulder with a brass plaque attached. It reads:

Richard Vincent Meriman
BARRY
who gave his life to the mountains he loved
MONK'S COWL
Jan. 29th, 1938
Aged 22 years
*I will lift up mine eyes unto the hills
from whence cometh my help.*

Standing here you can just see the tip of the Cowl, or Nkosana, that spiteful little chief of mountains who is reluctant to offer hospitality or to share his secrets. To continue our walk we must return along the same detour path back up onto the Little Berg (although another path comes diagonally out of the forest). Our path does a wide arc to the left around a natural bowl, with the path undulating for just over 1 km to re-enter the forest. Once inside the forest you come to a deep overhang next to a waterfall and large pool, the Blue Grotto. It is possible – though not recommended in wet weather – to explore the river above the Grotto where you'll find more falls and hanging pools. The walk from here back to the hotel is just 3 km, and will take an hour; you might get your feet wet as it is not always clear exactly where the path goes, or whether to cross the river or not. But you can't get lost, so continue downstream while keeping to the right-hand bank. I was impressed by some stout mountain wild pear trees (*Olinia emarginata*), hung with heavy limbs of monkey rope (*Secamone*).

It's a pretty damp place and these and the other forest trees are also heavily hung with old man's beard (*Usnea* lichen), spongy mosses, colourful fungi and spiders' webs. There are some dense patches of ferns, as well as large tree ferns (*Alsophila dregei*). As you walk small birds and butterflies dart in and out of the tubes of murky sunlight.

Near the end of the walk the path goes over the river to the left bank, below the hotel dam and back to the head of the Cathkin Park track. And it's probably time for a cold beer in the hotel pub by now.

STEILBERG AND VAN DAMM'S CASCADE — HIKE MC3

Route: A round-trip from the Drakensberg Sun Hotel via the Grotto and Steilberg
Distance: 10 km
Duration: 3 to 4 hours
Grade: Moderate to strenuous
General: This is an interesting walk because, although the hotel's map says 'a good path leads around the Grotto and kwaNdema Forest to the Cascades', I found them only by getting lost and floundering through chest-high bracken for a good half hour. Once again it's the scale of the Drakensberg that is so confusing: things here are bigger than you imagine. You can do this hike in either direction. But I recommend going up the Steilberg, if only to avoid getting lost in the bush and forest below. Getting back is always easier because most of the time you know the direction in which you need to go.

For starters, let's clear up one thing: 'steilberg' means steep hill, so you know this is going to be more than a breezy stroll. The path starts up the road behind the hotel, in other words up towards and then above and past the Bergview Chalets (nice if you stay there, but to me it seems a pity they were ever allowed to be built where they are, so deep into the foothills). Here the secret is to follow the hotel's yellow markers, first for about 1 km across flattish ground, then up a steep hill for about 400 m, then another 1.5 km across less steep grassland (with trees on your right) onto the spur of Steilberg.

Just 3 km from the start, on the lower spur of the Steilberg, a contour-type path branches off to the left and, although this seems at the time like the better option, it goes to Monk's Cowl conservation office so we don't want to go there (not now anyway). We have to carry on up, up, up. Another 1 km up the steep spur (we were warned!), another path looking like a contour path heads off to the right, below the Little Berg cliff line. You can take this path to reach the bottom of Van Damm's Cascade after 1.75 km (the main falls are between the two steps of the Little Berg, but above the main line of cliffs).

Carrying on along this path for another 1.5 km will take you to the bottom of Jacob's Ladder, a major path leading down a steep slope and through the Little Berg cliff line on the left of a prominent spur. Alternatively, sticking to the spur and carrying on up will take you to the top of the cascade on a circuitous route, a further 2.5 km. But then you either have to go back the way you came, or else continue along a fairly confusing route to reach the top of Jacob's Ladder and then descend to reach the bottom of the falls, 4.5 km from the top. A really great walk, but a tough and long one.

Although not marked on Slingsby's map, there is a quick route that will take you from the bottom of Van Damm's Cascade back to the hotel via the Grotto and kwaNdema Forest. Backtrack along the lower cascade path for 300 m to the next (or previous, if you came this way) stream heading for Steilberg.

A path will be found heading off down this stream's right-hand bank for 750 m to reach the kwaNdema Stream at the Grotto. Now just follow the path down the river's right-hand bank till you near the hotel, where it crosses the stream and you're almost home. I'd love to know who Van Damm was, but so far I've not been able to find out anything about him.

STABLE CAVE — HIKE MC4

Route: From either Monk's Cowl station or the Drakensberg Sun up the Steilberg to Stable Cave and back
Distance: 20 km return
Duration: 8 to 9 hours or 2 days
Grade: Strenuous
General: There is more than one way of getting to Stable Cave. In fact there are about four. The hike described here is the easiest and it also gives the opportunity to get into the mountains on a real overnight trip away from the hustle of cars and tourists. For variation a return trip via Jacob's Ladder should be considered, because it doesn't add any significant mileage and instead offers not only variety but the chance to visit both Van Damm's Cascade and the Grotto. Remember, if you plan to overnight in the cave you have to book it and pay R20 per person a night.

From the hotel (follow the yellow markers), head up the Steilberg path. Or, from the EKZNW station, head down to the Sterkspruit/Mpofana Falls (1.2 km) then climb up the Little Berg on the other side, crossing two streams below kwaHlathikulu, and continue upwards all the way around onto Steilberg to join the hotel path midway up the Little Berg scarp.

From the Monk's Cowl/Sterkspruit path bear right to reach the Drakensberg Sun path after just 100 m, then turn left to climb the rest of the way up the Little Berg scarp. No sooner have you done that than you have to descend into the valley with Van Damm's Cascade flowing down. This is the beginning of the up-down-up-down section to the top of Jacob's Ladder, and then it's still another 1 km up the side of the Little Berg to reach the plateau at a T-junction. Here you look down into the Valley of Pools (Nkwazi) ahead and to your right, and the eMhlawazini Valley to the left of that.

Just to your left the high point on the Little Berg is Verkykerskop (2 050 m), on the northern slope of which lies our cave. Turn left and for just 100 m proceed slightly uphill, to a point below the steep, stepped path that comes down from Hlathikulu Nek (an important landmark junction of the Contour Path). This path is in effect a side continuation of the Contour Path, making its way to the Valley of Pools. But we don't go up; instead we sneak off to the left here on a path that takes us along a side stream for about 400 m, climbing just 40 m, to the large cave in a small side valley.

If you were to head back along the main path for 2 km, along a narrow spur of the Little Berg with the cliffs to your right, you'd pass Anton's

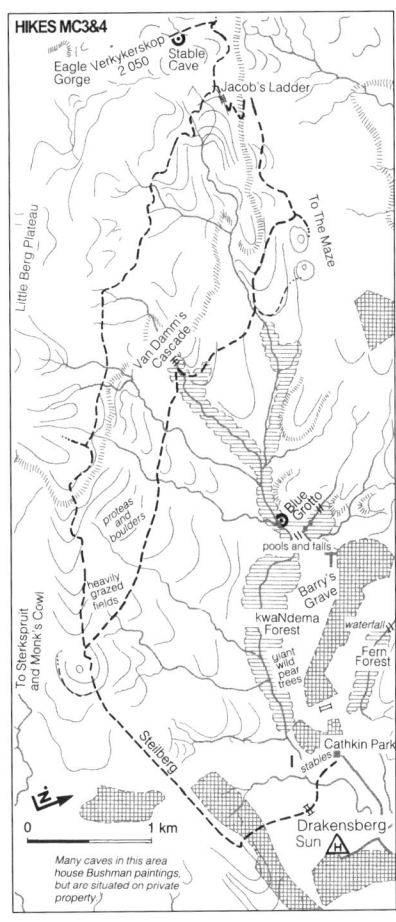

Cave, discovered by and named after Anton Zunckel when he was a boy. It's not one of the official EKZNW overnighting caves, but good to know about in the event of a storm.

THE SPHINX AND CRYSTAL FALLS — HIKE MC5

Route: Monk's Cowl EKZNW parking area to the first level of the Little Berg
Distance: 6 km
Duration: 2½ hours
Grade: Easy
General: What does 'easy' mean, exactly, when hiking in the Berg? The fact that this walk is short

in distance does not mean it's a walk round Zoo Lake. You will sweat, and it will seem a whole lot further than it really is, but that's mountains for you – they make you work for their pleasures. But this area, even the drive up the valley and past Champagne Castle Hotel (look out for the potholes) on the way to the EKZNW station, reveals breathtaking scenes of Mdedelelo and the Dragon's Back. Once on top of The Sphinx, if the weather plays along, you'll return home with photos that show you were among true warriors with their up-pointing spears.

Start off from the EKZNW car park, heading past and up behind the office diagonally to the left (south-east), following the Sterkspruit/Mpofana upstream. About 500 m from the office there is a direction sign where you head off to the left. After another 500 m you come to a T-junction where you must head to the right and up some steep zigzagging steps where you should keep strictly to the path to avoid erosion. You might find the local inhabitants selling walking sticks here. This is a heavily used path and so highly susceptible to degradation. Try not to step on the wooden erosion barriers, but over them, as continual tramping destroys them.

A fence at the top of the zigzags channels people on the right track. There are some kraals above the right-hand side of the path. Here the path heads around to the right (south and west), as it makes its way onto the lower section of The Sphinx – the obvious headland. Where you cross the second tributary of the Mpofana you'll find Crystal Falls in a small shady cove; but this is barely 2 km from the start and so hardly even qualifies as a hike. For children, however, this would be a good place for a rest before tackling The Sphinx.

The path first contours right under the large, pitted, head-shaped sandstone bulge and then loops and zigzags through the sandstone band, weathered into interesting shapes and colours. At the top of The Sphinx – completed in a few easy finger strokes on my keyboard but a steep 1-km pull up onto the Little Berg – slip off your pack and enjoy the views among the rocks and silver-leafed protea bushes.

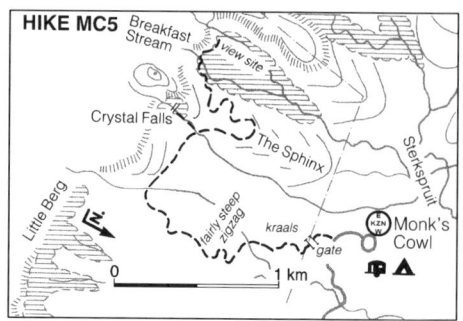

HIKE MC5

Here the path swings to the right and you reach Breakfast Stream just a short stroll from the top of The Sphinx. If this is as far as you plan to go, then you'll have plenty of time to walk around and find great angles for photographs, using the proteas or other plants as foreground detail. For inspiration, try to find a copy of Malcolm Pearse's *Camera in Quathlamba* to see what can be done with a well composed picture in the Little Berg (maybe even consider using black-and-white film and contrasting light of early morning or afternoon when the main peaks are backlit, for some dramatic shots).

CLOTHING TIPS

- Start replacing all your old T-shirts with modern hiking garments made from wicking materials.
- Cotton absorbs moisture, which can lead to extreme cold, discomfort and hypothermia.

ZULU CAVE HIKE MC6

Route: From Monk's Cowl station up to the Contour Path, past Hlathikulu Nek and down the eMhlawazini Valley
Distance: 24 km
Duration: 10-hour round-trip (2 days)
Grade: Strenuous
General: This was a well-known and often used cave in the golden days of Berg exploration, but in the past few decades has been very much overlooked as it is on a cul-de-sac. Perhaps now that it has been declared one of only a few official overnighting caves in the Monk's Cowl region (remember to book it), hikers will rediscover its charms. I have not been able to establish the specific origin of the name, although there is no lack of Zulu people in the area.

Sign the mountain register at the gate, pay your money, then head past the office and to your left (signposted) and through a gate. Carry on to the top of The Sphinx (hike MC5). From the top of The Sphinx the path heads directly towards Cathkin Peak, heading slightly uphill through tall montane grassland. Once you reach this section of path you'll find (at any rate I do) that your legs want to stretch out and you want to get closer to the big peaks as soon as possible. About 2.5 km from Breakfast Stream, with Wonder Valley falling away to your right, you reach the Contour Path at Blind Man's Corner (don't ask me, I can only guess). Turn right here (left will take you either down into Wonder Valley and the Wonder Valley Cave, or further on to Injisuthi) along what to my mind is the loveliest section of the Contour Path, as it offers really easy walking while you hug the Cathkin Ridge and all its peaks on your left.

For 2.5 km you wind in and out of delightfully wooded stream gullies, some with pools, one with a small waterfall, to Hlathikulu Nek at the base of the Amphlett. The peak was named after George Amphlett, an early member of both the Mountain Club and even more select Alpine Club. He was typical of the climbers of his time, in that he was a pillar of society – general manager of Standard Bank – and was quiet and unassuming,

according to Reg Pearse. He was among the party that made the first ascent of Cathkin Peak (3 149 m) in 1912, and had this subsidiary peak (2 620 m) named after him to commemorate that and all his many other firsts in the Berg.

At the Nek, continue to the left along the main Contour Path for 1.5 km to the junction where a path to the left up the upper eMhlawazini Valley to Keith Bush Camp (named after the ill-fated climber who fell to his death here in 1955 while abseiling off the north face of Cathkin Peak) joins the lower section of Gray's Pass (hike MC9) that heads up 'behind' Cathkin Ridge (on the northern side).

Here a lesser path turns off to the right, while the Contour Path heads downhill to cross the eMhlawazini on its way round Intunja and on to Didima (hike MC11). We must take this path to the right, along a spur that is pushed out between two branches of the eMhlawazini. It is easy to lose the path, but what we are trying to do is head down the spur to where the two streams meet just 1.75 km from the Contour Path, then cross over to the left-hand bank of the eMhlawazini.

Continue downstream for just over 1 km, crossing one larger then one smaller side stream, as the path heads uphill and away from the river which hereabouts is flanked by fairly

114 monk's cowl/nkosana

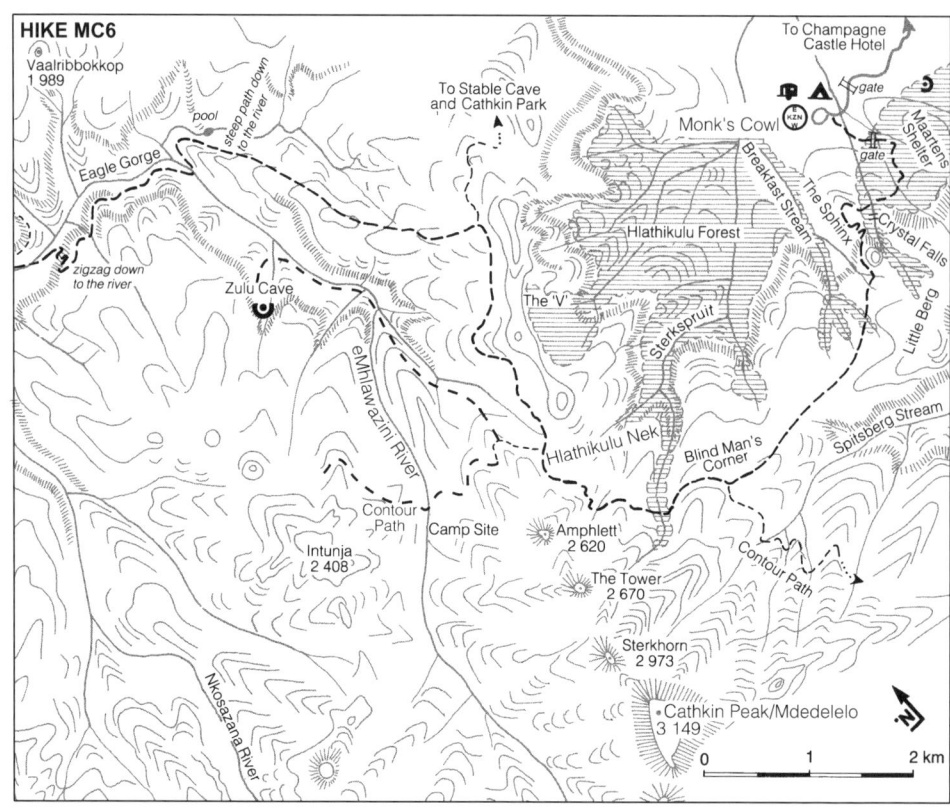

dense bush. Now the path veers to the left around a bulge, leading you up a side valley and towards the Little Berg plateau. After 500 m up this side gully you come to the cave right in the stream course, one of several grand shelters in the area which will comfortably sleep a large group, of up to 12. While I understand the social conditions that require large hiking groups, I thank fate that I've never had to be part of one. To walk in these amazing hills, and experience the wild valleys like the eMhlawazini as part of a noisy 'crocodile' is contrary to the quiet, inner time that hiking is supposed to give you. Any more than 6 people and I stay at home.

MONK'S COWL CAVE — HIKE MC7

Route: From Monk's Cowl conservation station, via the Contour Path to Cowl's Fork, and then up the ravine to the base of Monk's Cowl
Distance: 28 km round-trip
Duration: 12 hours (2 days)
Grade: Extreme

monk's cowl/nkosana 115

General: Why this cave should be one of only four set aside for hikers to overnight in, in the most popular area of the Drakensberg, beats me, but so it is. Really only a refuge for climbers, it is situated at the base of the cliffs in the gully between Cathkin Peak and the Cowl. For a really thrilling outing, you could combine this hike with a descent of Cathkin Gully on the far, northern side to Keith Bush Camp and back via the Contour Path. Monk's Ravine is an ominous thing – dark, cold and iced up in winter. But I guess that's not reason enough not to try it!

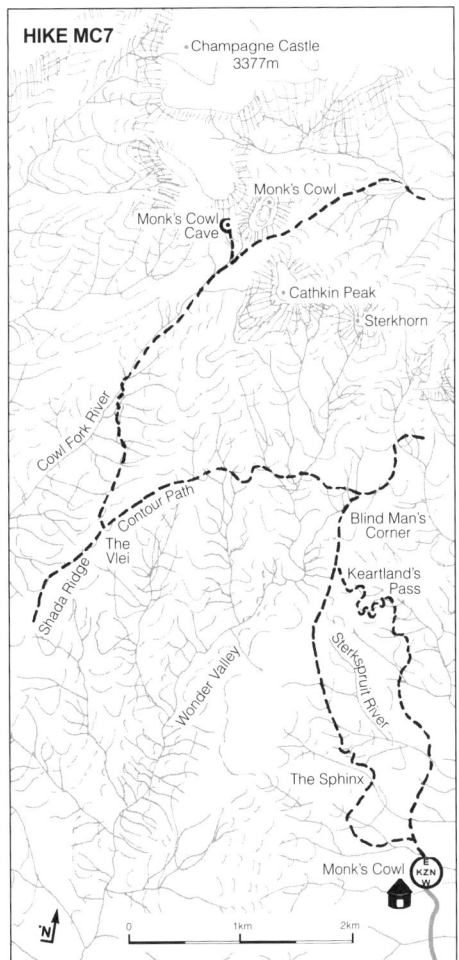

HIKE MC7

Start off from the conservation station up The Sphinx to the Contour Path at Blind Man's Corner (hikes MC5 and 6), 6 km from the camp site and parking area. Turn left to follow the Contour Path for 4 km in and out of the gullies round the base of Cathkin Peak. Where the path appears to head off along Shadow Ridge and away from Cathkin, keep right to pass through an eland fence that runs along the sharp ridge here. Head on the contour back towards the mountains and into Monk's Fork ravine 2 km from the fence.

This is 11 km from the start and you should consider camping here to make this a three- or four-day outing: the climb up the ravine to the cave will take about 3 hours; unless you've made an early start and it's good weather, you're going to be doing a 'Godbold' (Brian Godbold, who led the first ascent of Cleft Peak Frontal, had a penchant for night-time hiking epics). Also, unless ice climbing is your forte, I suggest you plan this trip for summer when the days are long and the south-facing ravine is not coffin-cold.

The route winds all the way up the right-hand side of Monk's Fork Stream, gaining some 900 m to the base of the basalt cliffs. If ever a more frightening and exhilarating prospect confronted you, I'd hate to know where. The cave is located at the base of the south-east face of the Cowl looking out over the Cowl Fork gully to the left and the cliffs of Champagne Castle to the right.

LENS TIPS

The camera lenses I carry have:
- *a 20 mm*
- *a 28–80 mm*
- *an 80–200 mm focal length*

VALLEY OF POOLS — HIKE MC8

Route: Starting either at Monk's Cowl station or Drakensberg Sun, past Stable and Anton's caves and down into the Nkwazi River Valley
Distance: 32 km return trip
Duration: 12 to 14 hours (2 to 4 days)
Grade: Strenuous
General: This hike can be done from either Cathedral or Monk's Cowl, as the Nkwazi is a tributary of the eMhlawazini that converges at Solar Cliffs, on the Cathedral side of Didima Gorge. The hike described here does not go all the way to Solar Cliffs, but you could make it a one-way 25-km hike from Monk's Cowl to Cathedral (a little like reversing the Contour Path route). Either way, you're in for a secluded, glorious time.

The first section of this route takes you to Stable Cave (hike MC5), 10 km from the start. But since this is the toughest section, and will take you between 4 and 5 hours (6 if you're camping out in the Valley of Pools and are carrying a heavy load, or are a slow walker), I would recommend that you spend your first night here (just remember to book the cave if this is your plan).

From Stable Cave return down the grassy spur to the top of Jacob's Ladder and keep on going north, along the narrow plateau. Falling away to your right are the forested valleys of the Mtoti River basin, while to your left the land drops into the eMhlawazini Valley, and beyond that the spiny scales of the Dragon's Back are in view. After 500 m a path heads off to the left across Vaalribbokkop (grey rhebuck hill) and down Hospital Spruit. Continue on along the narrowing ridge with cliffs on your right for another 2.5 km (past Anton's Cave after 2 km) a four-way junction, climbing about 50 m in the section around Anton's Cave. This cave is right on the path but since it has rock paintings you may not use it other than in an emergency.

The path to the left goes down a grassy spur to find its way to Hospital Spruit; the path to the right heads for the old Upper Tugela Location and rural KwaZulu-Natal along a broad grass arm of the Little Berg.

We continue along the middle path, heading into the wooded valley that lies just over the grassy lip a few hundred metres to the north-east (effectively straight ahead).

From this point it's about 7 km to Solar Cliffs, but that is a long way away. For the first 2 km from the four-way junction the path heads down through healthy protea veld above the Nkwazi River. It then enters the denser riverine

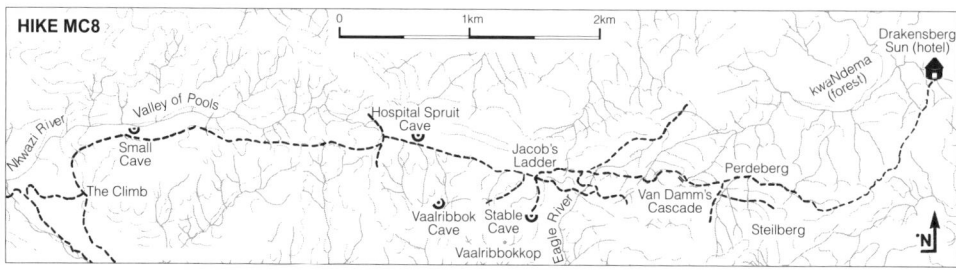

HIKE MC8

bush, crossing seven side streams by the time you've walked 2.8 km down the valley below.

There is no specific end point to the hike, and you will have to decide for yourself where to put down your load and make your temporary home in the wilderness. You might meet people from over the hill ahead which is called eSikhaleni Senyoka.

> **MEAL TIPS**
>
> Short hike food:
> - bread, Butro and cheese
> - Provitas and spread
> - pastas and sauces
> - coffee

CHAMPAGNE CASTLE VIA GRAY'S PASS — HIKE MC9

Route: From Monk's Cowl station via the Contour Path and Keith Bush Camp to the summit
Distance: 38 km return
Duration: 10 to 12 hours each way (or 2 or 3 days)
Grade: Strenuous
General: The first known ascent of the pass was by David Gray and Major Grantham, who was doing a military survey of Natal in 1861 (and of Champagne Castle as well). However the first recorded (official) ascent was by the Stocker brothers, the first real alpinists of the Berg, in 1888. The first map of the mountains by real mountaineers was made by the Stocker brothers – an astonishing feat of exploration of what were then wild, savage, remote and near-inaccessible places. What few hikers nowadays probably realise is that they have Colonel AW Durnford and the 75th Regiment of the British Army to thank for the state of the passes. Following the Langalibalele 'rebellion' (read more about it in the Giant's Castle section, page 152), they spent six months blowing up the access to many of the best passes in the Berg in an attempt to stop them being used by the local people. It is written that they camped on David Gray's farm and attempted to 'destroy' Gray's Pass. They couldn't have been very good at it, since these passes are still today used by hikers, Basotho traders, dagga smugglers and cattle rustlers. This pass is mostly a long walk, with some exposed traversing under the cliffs of Champagne Castle (maybe this is where the original pass was destroyed).

From Monk's Cowl station, follow the routes up The Sphinx (MC6) and towards Zulu Cave (MC7) to Hlathikulu Nek: from the conservation office the path goes zigzagging steeply up the sandstone 'head' directly behind the station, and is known as The Sphinx, for nearly 3 km. Once on top of this landmark it's an easy 2.5-km walk up sloping grassland of the Little Berg plateau to reach the Contour Path at Blind Man's Corner at the base of Cathkin Peak/Mdedelelo. Turn right here, winding in and out of shady stream gullies for 2.5 km to Hlathikulu Nek. This is a T-junction where you must turn left to keep the Amphlett (a continuation of Cathkin Ridge) on your left. For 1.5 km the path winds around two spurs of the Amphlett, to reach a four-way crossing on the Contour Path.

Straight ahead will take you down to cross the upper reaches of the eMhlawazini River on your way to Didima and Cathedral Peak (hike MC11); the lesser path to the right goes to Zulu Cave (MC6); but you must turn left here to follow the

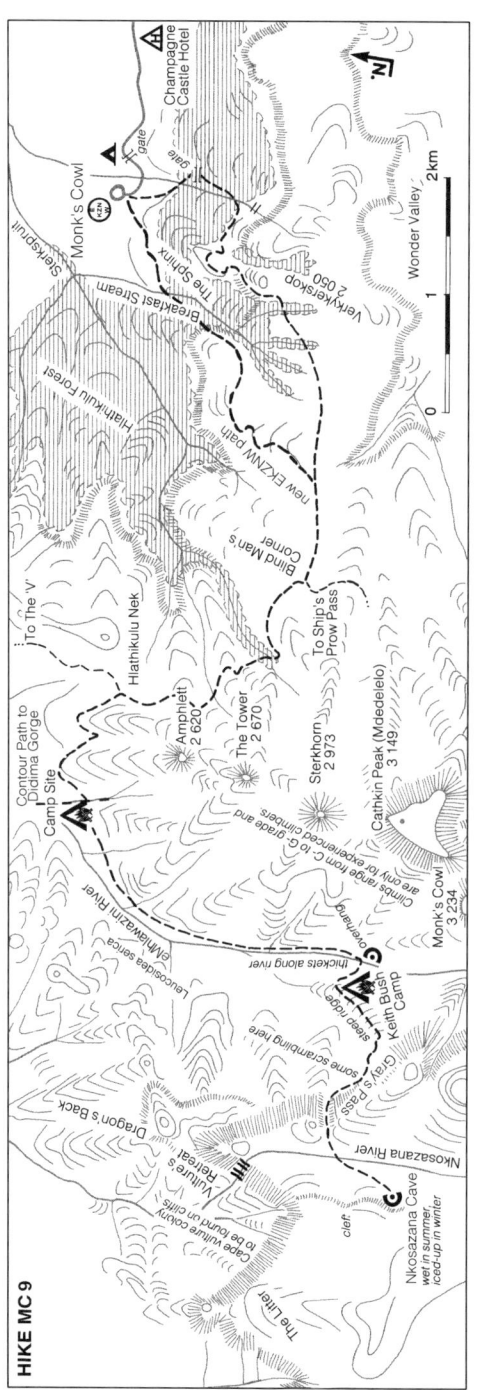

left-hand bank of the eMhlawazini for 3 km to Keith Bush Camp. The path up this section starts off easy enough, but soon begins to climb somewhat more steeply and then crosses to the right-hand side of the river just below Keith Bush Camp. There used to be a hut here but it was removed in the 1970s in keeping with the policy of having no man-made structures in wilderness areas. There also used to be a nice cave on the left-hand side of the river which hikers used when the hut went, but the roof has collapsed and it is now of little use.

On the level ground where the hut used to stand there is now a grove of *intshishi* or ouhout bushes, and among them spikes of wild dagga (*Leonotis leonurus*): the leaves will not give you upliftment if smoked even though they were once used as a poor substitute for tobacco. These days BB and Horseshoe are far better substitutes. In late summer the plants shimmer with a dazzling display of brilliant orange minarets, up to 3 m high. In the late afternoon, when the cloud shrouding Monk's Cowl has dissipated in the cool evening air, the sun casts a warm copper glow onto the peak that otherwise stands secretly plotting in its dark recess. Most hikers use this spot as an overnight camp, as it's a good 12 km from the start, with a climb from 1 480 m at the start to 2 350 m here – more than enough for one day for most hikers.

Gray's Pass begins just above the camp, keeping to the crest of a ridge rather than the stream gully on your right (the government 1:50 000 map shows the path going up the gully). This slope is highly susceptible to erosion, so take care not to leave the main, oft repaired path. After about 1 km of steady climbing you reach the main cliff base, and you'll need a long breather here. The path swings to the right to traverse under the cliffs, while continuing to climb – albeit much less steeply – for 1.5 km. This is a spectacular section, although very exposed in places, and possibly wet; at one point you have to do a short scramble up, which can be strenuous with a loaded pack. Watch out along here for baboons, which forage about the slopes, as well as pretty blue bell-like heads of *Wahlenbergia undulata* that grow in the damper places. This is a common flower of the zone between the summit and the Contour Path and is one of 10 species of *Wahlenbergia* found in the Berg. Before going into battle Zulu warriors would wash their bodies with a magic potion made from the pounded, boiled roots. This species acts as a protective charm, while a potion made from *Wahlenbergia grandiflora* makes you invisible to your foe (or, if you are a herd boy who has lost cattle, to an angry father). Another curious species is *Wahlenbergia zeyheri*: curious because the genus was named after a colleague of the great taxonomist Karl Linné (Carolus Linneaus in Latin), Professor Georg Wahlenberg of Uppsala University in Sweden, while this species is named after the German collector Carl Zeyher who visited South Africa in the 1820s.

On nearing the last few hundred metres of the summit the path veers to the left up a gully that separates the top of the Dragon's Back from Champagne Castle, which rises in three steps to its highest point 2.5 km to the south (left). The gully is littered with large rocks and the path winds back and forth across it. You will now be looking across the Nkosazana River Valley, if you can see at all through the mist that often gathers here. To find Nkosazana Cave, cross the river (which can be a boggy experience in summer) and head a few hundred metres upstream. The cave is located in a low rock band, about 150 m from the river and is marked by cairns (and, less welcoming, other people's waste after a long weekend). But, be warned, it is not a generous cave: in fact it's awful most of the time, and wet, even in winter, and sleeps four, sometimes only two people comfortably in wet conditions.

From the cave you can walk down the Nkosazana River (after the Zulu name for Monk's Cowl – Nkosana, the 'little chief', 'heir' or 'prince') for about 1 km, where the river makes shallow pools as it flows over rocky terraces and then plunges over the Escarpment.

It falls in several dramatic leaps down a giant's staircase, named Vulture's Retreat because a colony of Cape vultures nests on the cliffs to the left of the waterfall. In winter the falls ice up and stand in great white columns, or hang as giant icicles. Counter-poised against the flaking basalt scales of the Dragon's Back, Nkosana is one of the finest spectacles of the High Drakensberg and seen only by those people who hike to the summit (or Air Force helicopter pilots who train here and have to land their choppers next to the falls – sorry vultures, our national security is at stake!).

It's a short, 2.5 km stroll up the Nkosazana Valley to the highest point in the area, Champagne Castle (3 248 m), one of many 'peaks' that at one time or another were thought to be the highest along the watershed; it is still sometimes claimed in pubs and around braais to be the highest (actually only number three on the list). I put 'peaks' in inverted commas for few high points on the Berg can really be classified as peaks. One current-day mountaineer has coined the term 'kulus' for the high points of the watershed, taken from the Zulu word for 'big'. I have included a table of the 50 highest kulus of the Drakensberg at the end of the book (page 228). The return route re-traces the ascent via Gray's Pass. You can make it a circular trip by reversing the more strenuous but also more spectacular Ship's Prow Pass, hike MC10.

If Ship's Prow Pass was in a less popular area of the Drakensberg it would hardly ever be used – it is certainly among my least favourite. It's a long walk to get to the base, and it tops out at a very high point. And then there was that other 'little incident...'.

CHAMPAGNE CASTLE VIA SHIP'S PROW PASS   HIKE MC10

Route: From Monk's Cowl EKZNW station, via the Contour Path to the south, then up the Ship's Prow/Del'mhlwazini River through Ship's Prow Pass
Distance: 42 km return
Duration: 12 to 14 hours each way (or a 3-day return trip)
Grade: Extreme
General: This alternate route up or down Champagne Castle is to my mind one of the toughest in the Berg, but is used more often than many easier ones because it is one of only two ways to the top of the most visited areas of the Drakensberg. On the other hand, if you're fit and can heft a backpack with ease, and are blessed with good weather, this also happens to be one of the most breathtaking routes to the summit. The 'prow' may look like just a little triangle on your hiking map, but it is a sharp, massive bow of rock that juts out of the Escarpment, cutting the clouds like a gargantuan ship cleaving the waves.

But the seas this ship steers can be stormy indeed. On Old Year's Day 1980, two young Free State men and a lady friend from Pretoria decided to go hiking for five days in the Berg. Their intended route in the mountain register was to 'walk up Cathkin Peak' which, in retrospect, showed they had little idea where they were going. On 2 January there was a tremendous storm which washed away roads all over the foothills. They must have been caught on the summit, somewhere behind Champagne Castle (another party saw them on New Year's night in Nkosazana Cave), and anyone who has been caught in such a storm knows how terrifying they are. By the 10th they had not returned home and a helicopter rescue team was called in. After a long search (given their pathetic route description in the mountain register) their remains were found in Ship's Prow Pass. At first it was thought they had been caught in their tent camped next to the stream, but later the search-and-rescue leader Dr Sherman Ripley concluded they had been washed downstream while trying to cross the raging torrent that these streams become after a storm. Ripley called the boulder stream 'a torrential grinding machine' and, when the bodies and equipment were found, they were indeed ground to pulp.

Don't let this put you off Ship's Prow particularly, because it could have happened in many similar places. Every river in the Berg becomes dangerous when flooded, and this is by no means the only recorded death in flooded rivers in the Drakensberg. Take heed of the moral of the story and exercise great care with storms and their consequences (including lightning, which has also killed its fair share of people).

From the conservation office follow the route up The Sphinx (see hike MC6) for 5.5 km to the Contour Path. This section should take about three and a half hours, because the first part up the inscrutable Sphinx is pretty tough for its mere 2-km haul. From there the path gently climbs up a grassy plateau towards Cathkin Peak, with the full sweep of peaks from Champagne Castle to the Amphlett in view. When you reach the contour at Blind Man's Corner, you must turn left.

From here you have a 10-km walk along the Contour Path. However, in spite of its being extraordinarily beautiful and as dramatic a stretch of hiking as you'll do anywhere in the world, it is also energy sapping and you'll be

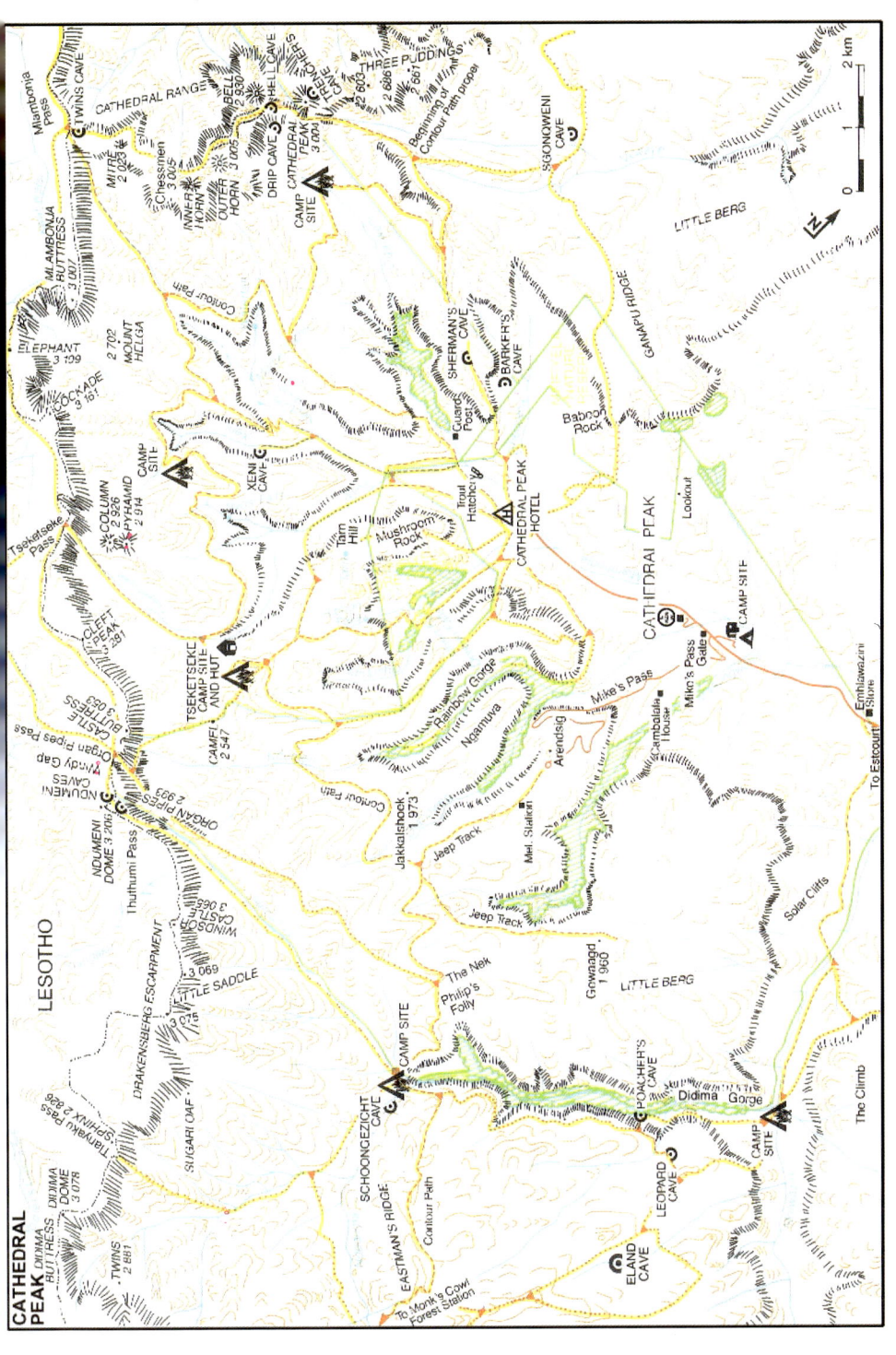

OPPOSITE: An aerial view of the Ndumeni Valley, wherein hides Rainbow Gorge.
ABOVE: Cathedral Peak Hotel may have the finest location in the universe. The Inner and Outer Horns and Bell prod the sky on the right. The Mlambonja, or hungry dog, River flows through.
LEFT: Rainbow Gorge, but you have to go there to see the magic.

ABOVE: From high up in the Tseketseke Pass, looking towards the fearsome Column, whereon hangs the incredible tale of George Thompson, and beyond to the Pyramid.

LEFT: Two therianthropes, or mystical half-human, half-animal visionary creatures that typify the Bushman trance-induced art of the Drakensberg. These figures can be seen in Eland Cave.

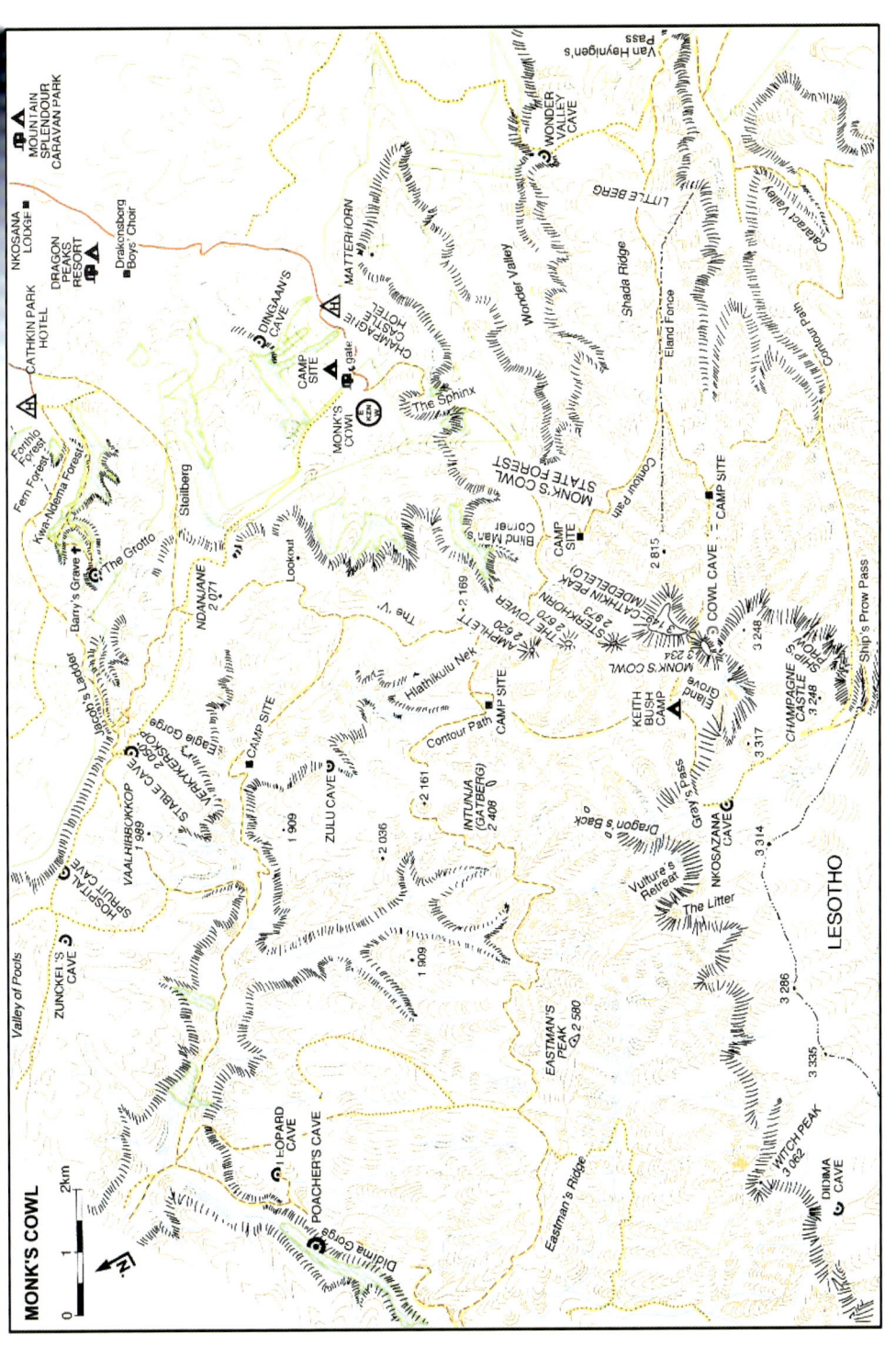

OPPOSITE: Mdedelelo (Cathkin Peak), the bully, lords over the tranquil scene of Dragon's Peak Resort.

ABOVE: Vultures' Retreat. In a nook where the Dragon's Back meets the Champagne Castle massif, close to the top of Gray's Pass.

LEFT: The simple monument to Dick Barry, 'Tiger' to a generation of rock climbers. From here the tip of Monk's Cowl is just visible.

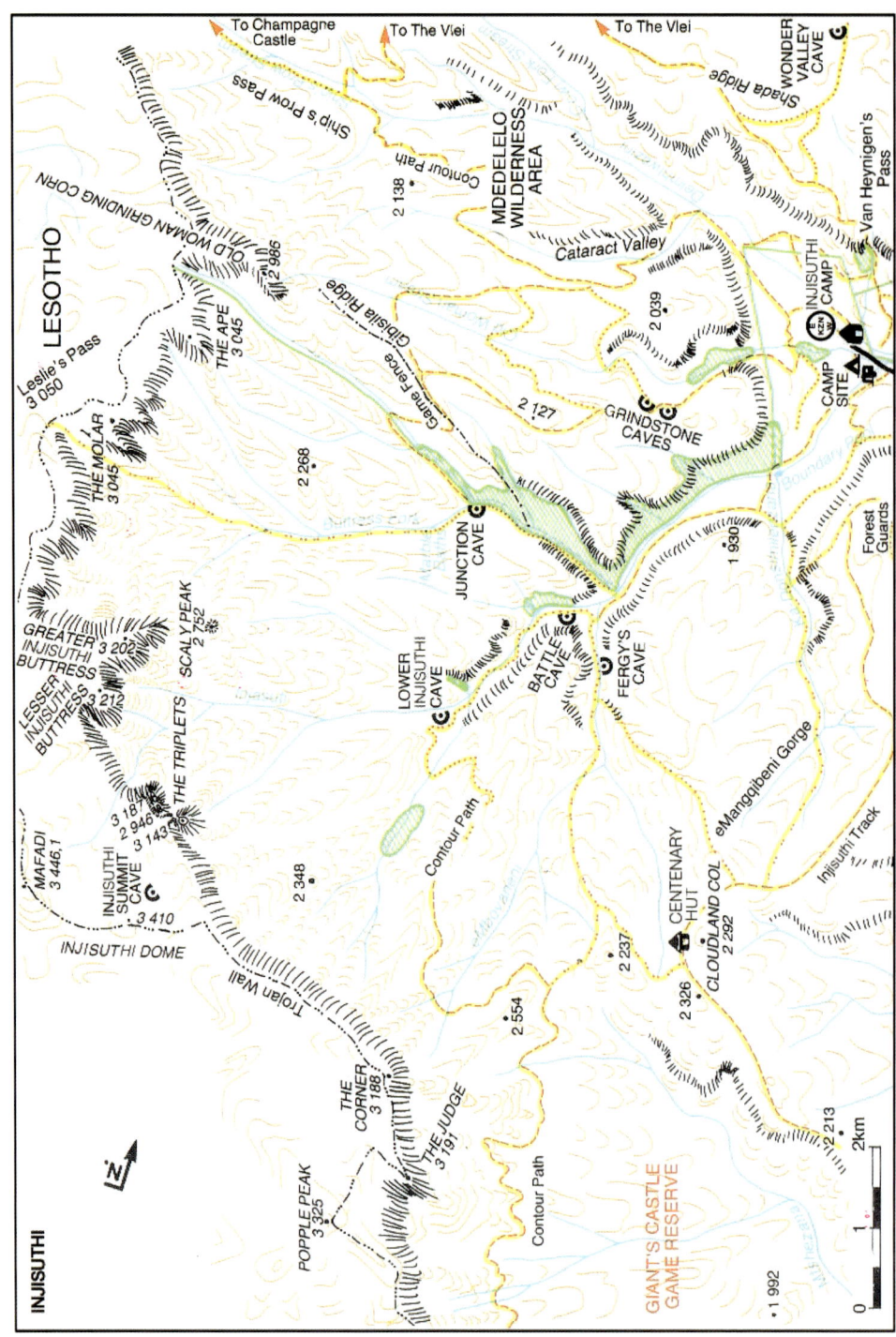

monk's cowl/nkosana

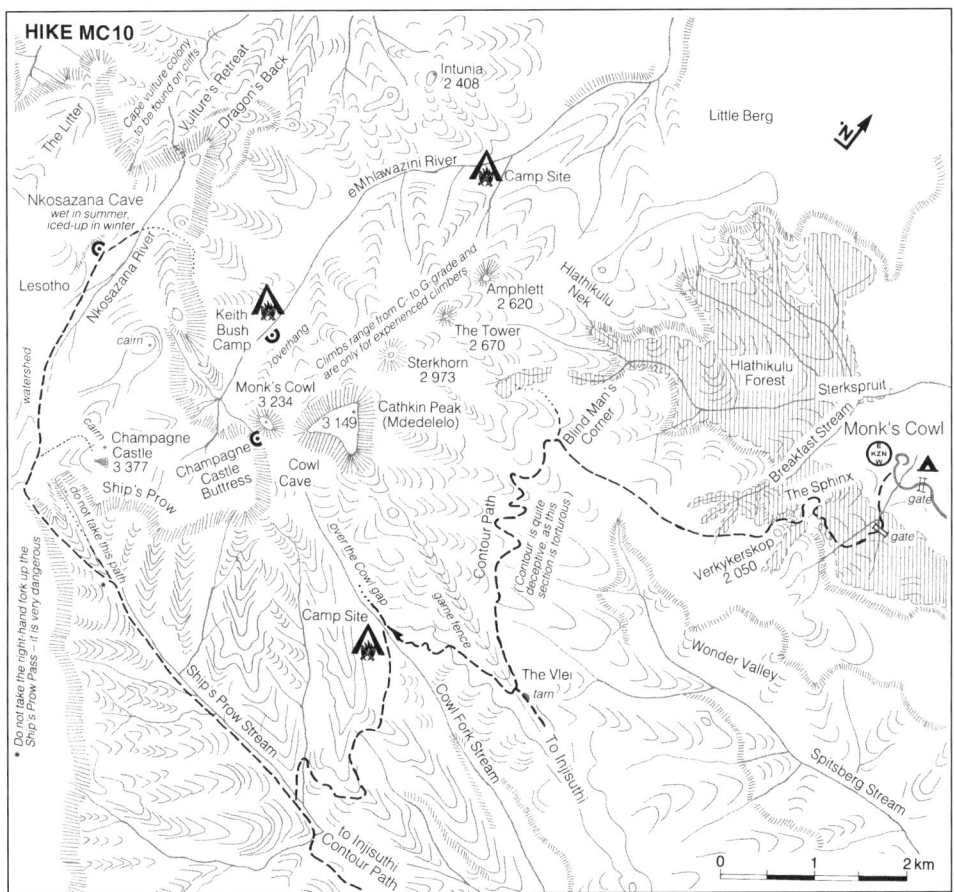

glad to reach Ship's Prow fork at the end of a solid day's walking of 15.5 km from the start. As you walk along the Contour Path the direction changes as often as the slope (which, in places such as the head of Wonder Valley or where you have to cross over the long spur coming down from Monk's Cowl 2 km from the Monk's Fork camp site, is not on the contour at all) and new windows open on views looking up to the grand ramparts on one side and down to deep wooded valleys on the other.

A cartographic note of interest to hikers using this route is that the point reached 4 km after turning left along the Contour Path is not a second junction known as Blind Man's Corner, as it would appear to be on Slingsby's map, but is in fact called The Vlei. At this point you should be able to see a tarn about 200 m down the Little Berg plateau, along a path that leads down to Injisuthi and Wonder Valley Cave (described in the next chapter, page 138). Also, a short distance ahead along the Contour Path is a fence designed to keep the small herds of eland which live in the Injisuthi area from wandering off down the Champagne Valley road to one of the hotels or to the Thokozisa tourist centre.

You should aim to overnight where the Contour Path reaches Ship's Prow Stream (where this river meets Cowl Form Stream, it becomes the Del'mhlwazini River, a northern tributary of the Injisuthi River). The pass itself is 4.5 km long, and then a little further to reach the point where you plan to stop. The first 3 km are not steep, as passes go, gaining 700 m along this section as you follow the stream's left-hand bank. Finally the stream splits around the Ship's Prow and you have to choose one of the forks: the left-hand one is easier but longer than the right-hand one. However, take great care as you decide as the right-hand approach is a boulder-strewn gully which in flash storms can become a bowling alley. If it looks even remotely as if heavy rain is on the way, take the left-hand fork. The top-most section of the right-hand fork consists of treacherous scree and vertical rock, so before trying it you should be confident of your mountaineering skills.

The reason for this pass's difficulty becomes clearer as you attempt to board the giant boat's prow – it's just so high. In fact, it stands proud at 3 300 m and as such is the highest pass of the entire Drakensberg. From the Contour Path at 1 950 m you have to climb a whopping 1 350 m to gain the summit.

And then you have to walk either behind Champagne Castle and over into the Nkosazana Valley to the right (north) to a camp site, or down to a valley to the south in Lesotho. Nkosazana Cave is reached 3 km down the Nkosazana Valley, 100 m up from the left-hand bank of the river, going downstream (check the previous hike, Gray's Pass, for more details). The easiest way down is via Gray's Pass, although Leslie's Pass 6 km in a straight line to the south will bring you down to Injisuthi camp via Junction Cave.

CONTOUR PATH: MONK'S COWL TO UPPER DIDIMA VALLEY   HIKE MC11

Route: From Monk's Cowl conservation office via The Sphinx to the Contour Path, and thereon generally northwards all along to the upper Didima Gorge in the Cathedral area
Distance: 27 km
Duration: 10 to 12 hours (2 days)
Grade: Strenuous to severe
General: This could be a there-and-back hike but most hikers would consider it a one-way hike between Monk's Cowl and Cathedral Peak. From upper Didima it's a half-day hike down to the Didima/eMhlawazini junction, past Solar Cliffs to the Cathedral camp site, but the route all the way to the northern end of the contour path is much longer (as described in hike CP6 in the previous chapter, page 90). I would rate this as the most rewarding multi-day route along the Contour Path, although transport between the two ends would have to be organised. Just bear in mind that the path at the upper end of the eMhlawazini River has become overgrown in places and this makes progress tedious.

Most hikers choose to stay at Inkosana Lodge and Trekking a way down the valley from the conservation office. However, if distance from the start and tradition are your concerns then look no further than the quaint old Champagne Castle Hotel. Is golf your game? Champagne Sports Resort. Want to impress your partner with chocolates-on-the-pillow elegance? Then Cayley Lodge will be your base (and boy will they feed you up for the hike). For the muesli and instant noodles brigade, see you at the EKZNW camp site. You can make inquiries and book through the Central Drakensberg Tourism office at the Thokozisa tourism centre at the four-way intersection on the way from Winterton. And don't forget the Saturday night *opskop* there to send you off into the wilderness.

But eventually you find yourself signing the mountain register at the park gate, and paying your entrance fee. Take the steep path that winds up the large sandstone prominence called The Sphinx – the main path to the top of the Little Berg. It's a tough first haul but leads to a delightful plateau dotted with silver-leafed proteas, and then a sloping grassy spur to the Contour Path, which is reached 5.5 km from the start. For first-time hikers the views of Cathkin, Champagne Castle, Sterkhorn, Amphlett and Turret rising up ahead and getting ever closer can be overwhelming; try not to hyperventilate.

At Blind Man's Corner turn right to head north along the Contour Path for a delightful 2.5 km, where you weave in and out of about six stream gullies, the mountains rearing up to your left, as you make your way to Hlathikulu Nek where a lesser path turns off to the right. There must be hundreds of 'hlathikulus' in KZN (the word means 'big forest'): this 'hlathikulu' is down the ridge to the east. Our route carries on to the left, looping around two spurs at the base of the Amphlett for 1.5 km till you are standing looking down to the eMhlawazini River 600 m below.

The path to the left goes up to Keith Bush Camp at the base of Gray's Pass (MC9), while that to the right goes to Zulu Cave (MC6). The way to Didima and the last refuge of the Bushmen in the Drakensberg lies ahead, down to the river, which involves a couple of big loop-backs. This point is 10 km from the start and, though not yet halfway to the camping area at the upper Didima River, it's often a midway stopping point. Be ready to bushwhack: this path is pretty much neglected by park authorities and could become overgrown.

Directly in front of you is Intunja, the 'eye of the Needle', or in Afrikaans the less-inspired Gatberg. It's only 2 km in a direct line to the other side of this pointed, holy peak, but to go around it – which we must – will take us on a winding 4.5-km loop around the mountain and over a low nek. When you reach the first main stream on the 'other' side, a line directly through the summit is the one to your crossing point of the eMhlawazini. A little over 1 km further the path climbs over the last scale of the Dragon's Back and then cuts sharply back down to a river, the Nkosazana. This is the alternative stop, 17 km from the start. This section has become heavily overgrown and hikers can find it hard going.

The Nkosazana is a small tributary of the eMhlawazini, but there's nothing small about the huge cutaway of its gorge, where it tumbles over the Vulture's Retreat on its way down from Champagne Castle. I like to think of this water as the mountain bubbly that flows, a never-ending miracle, from the Champagne mountains. On the way round Intunja you will have experienced something of the waywardness of the Contour Path. For the next 7 km it does more of the same, looping round innumerable streams to round the Litter and then slowly gain altitude as the path takes you parallel to Eastman's Ridge (named after 'Grandpa' Eastman who first climbed the high pimple on it – 2 580 m – at the Mountain Club's July camp in 1935).

Finally, on a spur opposite a lesser pimple on Eastman's Ridge (2 408 m) where a path leads off to the right down a long peninsula, or isthmus, of the Little Berg, you will have reached the high point of the hike – at 2 150 metres. The large bowl-shaped valley in front of you (the Mmesini), and the one beyond that, leads down to Didima Gorge. The Contour Path continues to the left, to maintain its general course along the base of Eastman's Ridge, but now keeping on the contour instead of the usual upping and downing, but mostly upping, since the start of this hike.

At the head of the Mmesini a path leads to the left, into the Eastman's Peak Fork Stream. It's a go-nowhere route but an interesting 8.5-km detour into this seldom-visited side valley of the Didima that will bring you around, eventually, to our end point. If you don't have time or the energy then just carry on along the right-hand side of Eastman's Ridge for another 2 km, while the path loops around a little obstacle and then proceeds down between two small grassy spurs for another 2 km to the edge of Didima Gorge.

First-time hikers in this area might want to brace themselves for the awesome sight – you have reached a very special place. The area around you, described in a 5-km arc to your right, is the world's greatest outdoor art gallery. In a few dozen caves and small overhangs are thousands of paintings executed in polychrome pigments, in the finest detail, by Bushman shamans, over thousands of years. They tell us all we know about the Bushmen, their lives and their supernatural beliefs. One man, Harold Pager, spent several years in this valley, recording every single image in a mammoth publication called *Ndedema*. It's hard to find a copy, but if ever you do you should take the time to study it.

Funny thing is, unless you know exactly where to look, the chances are you'll never locate even one of these caves on your own. That's a good thing, not only because it's against the law to visit rock art sites without a guide, but it helps to protect them – the point of the law in the first place. Sadly this has not always been the case and many, indeed most, of the rock art bequeathed us by those magical artists has been cruelly vandalised or completely destroyed. Once you understand the nature of the rock paintings, you realise that would be like breaking the stained glass windows in a mediaeval church.

The gorge drops away over the sandstone lip of the Little Berg to a wooded, boulder-choked chasm. Didima can be translated to something like 'sound of thunder' and it's an appropriate name for this place where the river tumbles and roars through the gorge. It's also a fine name for the two highest points on the Escarpment, Didima Dome (3 078 m) and Didima Buttress (3 150 m), as the name can also imply 'the place of thunder', or a place where storms are born. Some of the highest points in South Africa lie on the high ground some kilometres behind Witch Peak (3 062 m) to the south of Didima Buttress. They lie on the watershed and are unnamed, but four of them are over 3 300 m high.

But, taking our gaze away from such lofty things and getting back to the much more earthy business of finishing our hike, turn left at this intersection on the rim of Didima Gorge to cross the river after another 500 m. There is plenty of flat ground to set up your tent and absorb the sublime, deafening silence. When I dream of camping in the Drakensberg, it is of this place. There are three caves in the area that you can book. The closest to this spot is Schoongezicht, about 500 m up the valley on the left-hand side, on the lower slope of Eastman's Ridge and facing due west towards the top of Organ Pipes Pass (it is a small shelter, sleeping only four and to be avoided in wet conditions).

The second is Leopard Cave. Take the path along the upper rim of Didima Gorge for 5 km to where it turns off to the left through the cliff band to the bottom of the gorge: turn right here to cross a side valley and stream and then climb up to the edge of a grassy plateau where you'll find a large shelter. Reach Poacher's Cave, also large, by carrying on along the main path to the bottom of Didima Gorge, then heading back up the left-hand bank of the river for just over 1 km. The cave is in the cliffs looking down to the river.

The quickest way of reaching Cathedral is a one-day hike from the upper Didima camp site, down Didima Gorge to the eMhlawazini junction, then down the eMhlawazini past Solar Cliffs to Cathedral (Mlambonja) valley road. These hikes are described in the previous chapter.

monk's cowl/nkosana 133

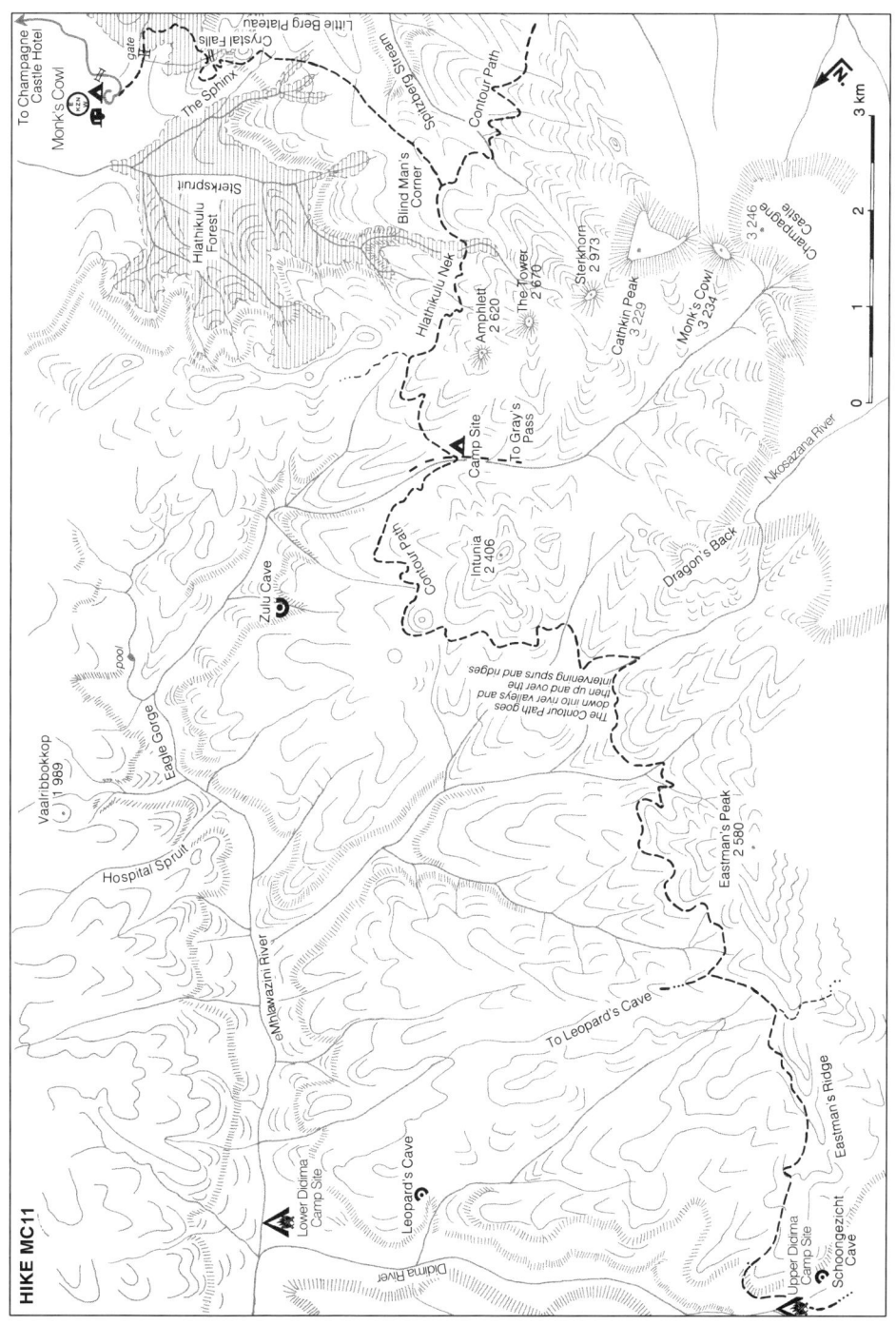

injisuthi

It's amazing sometimes, how wrong things can seem to be for so long, and how suddenly they can then come right. For years and years conservationists and mountaineers bemoaned the fragmented land control of the Drakensberg and its subsequent lack of an overall conservation plan: 'efforts have been made in the past (to consolidate the area under one authority) but it has been a story of half-hearted measures and government procrastination', wrote one author. Then it seemed that one day, overnight, we had a new government, and then we had uKhahlamba-Drakensberg Park stretching for some 300 kilometres from Royal Natal National Park to Bushman's Nek. And now, not only that, but this park is a World Heritage Site and the core of a transfrontier 'peace park'.

One of the prime pieces of the Berg that for many years lay in private hands was a small chalet resort called Solitude, close to a yellowwood forest on the southern bank of the Injisuthi River where it tumbles out from a red-shouldered gorge. In 1838 Voortrekker leader Gerrit Maritz made a laager next to what they called the Klein (little) Thukela towards Estcourt, and they would almost certainly have explored up the valley whose Zulu name, Injisuthi, 'the well fed dog', suggests it was a rich hunting area. However, the uppermost reaches of the valley were among the last areas of the Drakensberg to be explored by mountaineers, and it was only at the MCSA's 1937 July camp that some of the peaks of the area were climbed and named. The most outstanding of them is the Old Woman Grinding Corn, *kwaMfasizwa ugay'amabele*, which, like Giant's Castle to the south and Cathkin Peak to the north, stands out from the Escarpment connected by a narrow nek. Thankfully the Zulu name of *kwaMfasizwa ugay'amabele* was not turned into some fanciful European image, and the translation provides a nickname so we can simply talk about the 'Old Woman'. Looking at it from the north you can imagine the scene of the old woman kneeling over her grindstone.

But you have to walk up, up the Injisuthi Valley, to the Lower Injisuthi Cave and even higher, to where the river races over large boulders where there is no path and the massive red shoulders of the Little Berg give way to the softer green slopes of the sub-Alpine belt, before you can gaze upon the great giants that guard the valley. Early descriptions spoke of the Twins, and only in 1937 after closer inspection was it realised there were in fact three great pillars of rock standing free from the main Escarpment wall. The Eastern and Western Triplets are massive towers, more vertical and fortress-like than any other in the Drakensberg. The Middle Triplet is a mere flake of basalt so barely separated from the main wall that it is hard to see until you get really close. Then you also see it is not 'mere' in any sense and that each is a huge formation.

That anyone would contemplate climbing them is a thought that will befuddle most people, but mountaineers are not like most people: I suspect one of the reasons they climb peaks like these is just to astound the lesser mortals they refer to as 'gapers' (those who stand with gaping mouths watching them). The sheer, sometimes crumbling, faces of the Triplets were first climbed in 1950 and 1951 and they remain, along with the likes of Devil's Tooth, among the longest and hardest rock routes in the Berg.

Interesting to note is that among the opening ascent parties were two stalwart climbers of that era, Lorna Pierson and Gillian Bettle. It is with nostalgic yearning that I look at the old black-and-whites of them, obviously ruddy-cheeked in the fresh mountain air, short bob cuts and clothes of the period, wholesome young women, with their virile, wholesome young men – golden girls and boys (although the men are usually pretty scruffy in comparison). Days gone, days which we who were not there can never fully grasp. When I look longingly at these photos I recall the lines of 'Prelude' by the great Lake District Romantic, Wordsworth:

> *Bliss was in that dawn to be alive,*
> *But to be young was very heaven.*

Just north of the EKZNW chalets (there is also a camp site) the route up the Little Berg is called Van Heynigen's Pass. It was named after J van Heynigen who was chief forester at Monk's Cowl in the 1930s (and proprietor of Champagne Castle Hotel from 1943, buying it from Oom Hendrik Maartens for £6 000). He hatched the idea of connecting his forest station to Cathedral Peak by constructing a contour path that would meet the tracks built by the Mike de Villiers who started the Cathedral Peak forestry research station and built Mike's Pass. Later Van Heynigen pushed his path southwards, hoping that one day the parks board would build a path north from Giant's Castle to meet his.

In the early 1970s Reg Pearse wrote that the Natal Parks Board had begun forging a path north to Injisuthi: 'When these two paths meet there will be something like 200 kilometres of well-graded pathway'. For many years there was just talk talk talk, but today you can walk from the base of Cathedral Peak pretty much all the way to Bushman's Nek on paths through the Little Berg – admittedly sometimes a bit higher and sometimes a bit lower, and sometimes you think the whole path was laid out to be an endurance course. It is true that in places it's in nearly impassable condition, such as below the Pyramid, while elsewhere it is so tortuous you wouldn't want to believe it is the best hike between two points. It is also true that from

Sani Pass to Bushman's Nek it's the Giant's Cup hiking trail (and no longer a contour path) which, for the most part, is so far from the mountains it could be called the 'toe-hills meander'. But the basic idea is there and who knows what will happen in time....

In 1980 Solitude was purchased by the state and incorporated as a satellite section of Giant's Castle Game Reserve. On maps the name was first anglicised to Injasuti, then 'corrected' to eNjesuthi, and currently is spelt Injisuthi. It's called normalisation. Accommodation is in 15 chalets, each sleeping six and fully equipped for self catering, as well as two dormitories sleeping eight each. About 200 m downstream is a caravan park and camp site, which in autumn becomes a riot of orange *Leonotis leonurus* (wild dagga) flowers. At the office there is also a small curio and food shop, stocking only the basics. The main landmark from here is Monk's Cowl, looming up between Champagne Castle and Cathkin Peak and lording it over the Injisuthi Valley. Hiking routes start from three points in the camp: the tar road across the vehicle bridge leads to Poacher's Stream, Battle Cave, Marble Baths Cave, Lower Injisuthi Cave, Fergy's Cave and Centenary Hut; starting next to chalet 4 and continuing over a wooden footbridge this route leads to Van Heynigen's Pass, the old game guard hut, Wonder Valley Cave and the Contour Path to Monk's Cowl; starting from dormitory hut unit 2 is the route to Grindstone Caves and from there to Marble Baths, Cataract Valley, Yellowwood Forest and the old kraal and dipping tank.

The only caves that can be booked for overnight stays are Lower Injisuthi, Grindstone (two) and Marble Baths. Fergy's and Junction caves have been subject to flooding and are no longer suitable for use as shelters. 'Fergy' was Sergeant I Ferguson, a policeman who in the 1940s was given the task of guarding what was a government reserve (before it was sold to a private owner in the 1960s) against poachers. He was a man who seemed to love life in the wilds and used the cave as his headquarters. Generations of hikers also enjoyed its comforts which are, alas, no more. But Lower Injisuthi Cave is to my mind far nicer and better situated anyway, and was until recently very little used by hikers. It makes a great two-day return hike giving you access to the sacred bowl at the base of the Triplets – comparable in majesty to the base of the Amphitheatre. The other place of great majesty is Battle Cave, whose significant 'battle' scene can only be viewed on a guided tour (but read the chapter on Bushman art, page 30, and see the suggested books, page 235, to understand what it is really about). There are plans to re-open Tree Fern Cave to hikers. This cave was used for horse trails starting at Hillside camp to the south-east, so inquire about this if you please.

A new hut was opened a few years ago in time for the marking of the MCSA's 100th year, but, alas, it has, like Bannerman's Hut in Giant's Castle, been heavily vandalised by Basotho poachers and cattle thieves. No matter what EKZNW does to protect the huts, some Basothos find a way to destroy and steal: thatch roofs were burnt and were replaced with tin; that was stolen and so tiles were used; windows were broken and thick bars installed; they were smashed with rocks ... and so on. Nevertheless, the conservator in charge assured me that the hut could still be used (sleeps 12). It is located at the foot of Corner Pass. The only pass giving easy access to the summit from Injisuthi camp is Leslie's, going up Buttress Fork Stream past Marble Baths.

injisuthi 137

VAN HEYNIGEN'S PASS TO VIEW SITE — HIKE IN1

Route: From the rest camp, on a double-back route up Van Heynigen's Pass to the Little Berg plateau
Distance: 8 km return trip
Duration: 3 to 3½ hours
Grade: Moderate
General: Although this hike includes a climb to the top of the Little Berg, you should have to carry only a light day pack and therefore, given the short distance, it should be a breeze. Also, getting to the top of the Little Berg is a relative thing: the top of the pass is at around 1 800 m, with an extra 100 m to reach the top of the first grassy knoll; however, from there the montane zone of the Little Berg slopes upwards towards the Escarpment, reaching around 2 300 m before you can say you're into the sub-alpine zone.

From chalet 4 head up the Del'mhlwazini River and cross it via the wooden footbridge still in sight of camp. The path continues up the right-hand bank for a little less than 2 km, but moves up that bank and veers slowly away from the river, so fill your water bottles at the start for you will not find another reliable watering point (some side streams are encountered but they will not always yield drinking water).

Where you find yourself above some disused old forest guard huts, one path heads down past them to return to the rest camp, while our path doubles back here along the base of the Little Berg cliffs for 1.6 km and then works its way into a small, forested gully that is the base of the pass. Keep left here for we have to go up the ravine, and not carry on along the path that proceeds eastwards along the base of the cliff line. Again, you might find water here, but not in dry months. It's a charming little gorge, but we have to climb steeply upwards so the charm may wear off. In places there are stone steps but in others the path is loose soil and subject to erosion. The path tops out of the ravine at an easy angle close to the stream, and from there turns away to the left to climb again quite steeply up the grassy knoll. When you get to the crest of this spur you've reached the view site.

You can return the same way or, at the base of Van Heynigen's Pass where you exit the wooded gully, turn left (east) along the path mentioned in the paragraph above that follows the base of the cliff line for just 250 m. There, instead of continuing on a path that goes eventually to Wonder Valley (outside the park), you must head off straight down the bank towards and through the riverine bush. The last part, to the river, is very steep and zigzagged. Cross the river (the Del'mhlwazini running almost parallel to the Injisuthi), but don't relax. You have to carry on for a few hundred metres more.

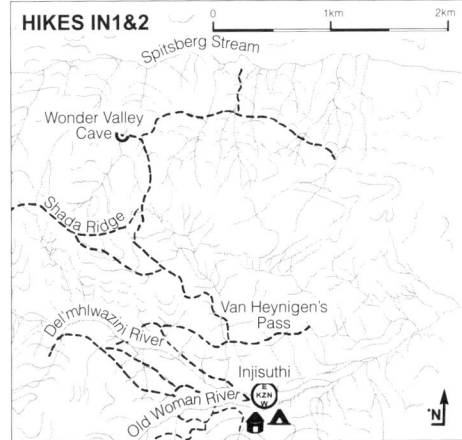

WONDER VALLEY CAVE — HIKE IN2

Route: From the rest camp up Van Heynigen's Pass to the cave overlooking Wonder Valley
Distance: 15 km return trip
Duration: 3 to 4 hours up and more than 2 hours down
Grade: Strenuous
General: Although you do not get the sense of being in the real mountains, this is the real wilderness and this is an excellent, not difficult, hike to enjoy that special excitement of overnighting in a decent Drakensberg cave (most of which, including this one, are really overhangs). Although a path goes down towards the river (Spitsberg Stream) in Wonder Valley, the valley itself lies outside the conservation area so consider the cave pretty much the end of the road. On the other hand, it also lies close to the quickest route between Injisuthi and Monk's Cowl (up Shadow Ridge), so you could use it to overnight on a longer hike.

Start as you would for hike IN1, at chalet 4, and head over the wooden footbridge (fill up with water), up the Del'mhlwazini River to above the old guard huts. Double back here along the base of the Little Berg cliffs to where the path leads you to the left into a wooded ravine. This is Van Heynigen's Pass, a pleasant if steep ascent. Once you emerge on top of the pass, you still have quite a stiff climb of about 1.5 km up Shadow Ridge before the angle of the path eases off. This happens at a junction, where we turn off to the right and the main path continues directly up the ridge in the direction of Monk's Cowl.

The path to Wonder Valley Cave starts off still on the uphill, but eases off when you reach the stream (the same one that flows down the pass ravine) 500 m from the Shadow Ridge junction. Cross the stream and carry on for another 500 m around a bulge to a second, smaller stream, where you encounter a side junction to the left (this would take you back onto Shadow Ridge). Bear right here along an easy uphill gradient that leads to flat ground covered with protea bushes. Carry on along and gently down this flattish section for about 200 m to where the path suddenly veers off to the left and goes steeply down the side of the valley to the cave (it may be a little more to the left than you expect, but the path is obvious, if eroded and rubbly). Return the same way. You make a three-day outing by going up to Wonder Valley Cave one afternoon, sleeping over, walking back down to the rest camp and up to Grindstone Caves the next day, and returning via Cataract Valley (hike IN8). I would choose this cave for an easy, romantic walk in the hills.

POACHER'S STREAM AND BOUNDARY POOL — HIKE IN3

Route: Up the Injisuthi River to Boundary Pool then up Poacher's Stream and back along the base of the Little Berg
Distance: 6.5 km
Duration: 2½ hours
Grade: Easy

General: This is the only short walk described in this chapter where all you need to carry is a water bottle, maybe something to bathe in, and possibly a tired child at the end. The pool is not a classic mountain swimming hole, being quite shallow and bouldery. But on a hot day it is good for cooling off (the much better Junction Pool below the rest camp was silted up over a decade ago so, unless a new flood has washed it clean, forget about that one). If you have a map, or as you get to know the area, you can choose a number of alternate routes for this walk. When hiking in the Berg, let boldness (but not carelessness) be your motto.

From the rest camp walk back down the main road towards the vehicle bridge (with the camp site on the other side of the river), but just before the bridge take the path to the right up the embankment. The path rejoins the river bank 1 km from the start and continues for a further kilometre to enter the main Injisuthi forest. Unfortunately our time in this wood is fleeting, before we re-emerge into sunlight to reach the stepping-stone crossing point.

Slingsby's map incorrectly shows this crossing to be before you reach the forest. (I see the new EKZNW map also shows the path not going through the forest here but on the other side of the river – when I last walked it, it crossed the river only after the forest.)

Anyway, the path crosses the Injisuthi just above Boundary Pool, formed where Poacher's Stream joins the main river. The path within the forest follows a drainage line and your boots may get very muddy. You can clean off in the fast-flowing, chilly water and then assume a low angle and bask on the grassy bank to contemplate the route back.

This is accomplished by crossing the river (if you have not already done that) and continuing up a grassy slope for about 800 m to a level platform between the sandstone cliffs and the river. The main path to Battle Cave goes to the right here, but we turn left and walk for about 300 m to cross Poacher's Stream (must have been named by Sgt Fergy after the poachers he kept encountering) and then keep left on the contour (another path turns off to the right

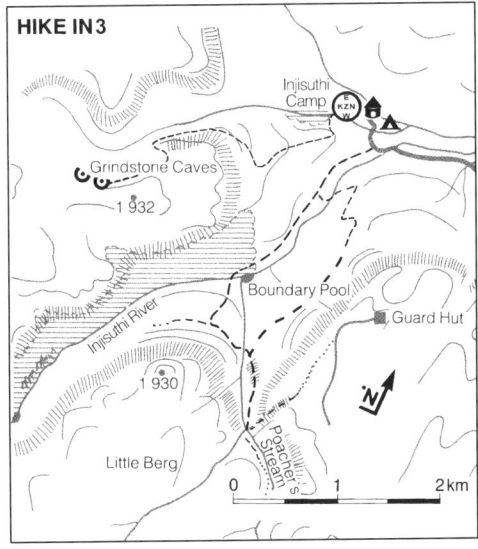

heading for the cliffs on the left-hand side of the river: this path leads up through the cliffs, comprising an interesting 4- to 5-km detour to reach the top of the Little Berg).

After an easy 1.5-km stroll along the base of the cliffs you must take the left-hand junction down the slope towards the river, and not carry on along the contour as that goes all the way to Tree Fern Cave (hike IN10). Once at the river you can choose to go upstream or downstream, the former to a crossing to rejoin the outward route and back to camp, the latter to the main road and thence back to camp. The downstream road route is a little longer. Just remember though that if it's a classic mountain pool you're after, this walk is not it.

BATTLE CAVE — HIKE IN4

Route: Up the Injisuthi Valley
Distance: 11 km return
Duration: 3 to 4 hours, plus cave tour (5 hours total)
Grade: Easy
General: You can walk this route on your own as it is also the way to Lower Injisuthi Cave for which you don't need a guide, but Battle Cave is fenced off and locked and you can see the rock art there only on a guided tour. Both times I have done this tour the guide has used a pre-recorded lecture on an old portable tape recorder that must have been handed down through several generations. I sincerely hope the quality of the tour is improved as this is an important rock art site, and a bad tour leaves a bad impression of something that could, and should, be an uplifting experience. Although this hike is guided, I'll give you directions anyway ... so that you know about it and because this is the 'gateway' to most of the Injisuthi hiking area.

Start on the main road leading out of camp and just before the vehicle bridge turn right up the embankment, then along a slope and after 1 km down into the Injisuthi Valley. Follow the path up the right-hand bank of the river for 1.5 km to where it enters a large forest, but only briefly, wends along a muddy course before exiting and crossing the Injisuthi by some stepping stones. In the rainy season you are most likely going to get your feet wet.

From the river the path heads up a grassy slope for 400 m, as if heading for the sandstone mass ahead. However, on reaching a platform level the well-maintained path turns right and for the next 1 km sails a level course to bring you back to the river bank (look out for the split boulder housing a yellowwood). Since you're heading upstream the path will naturally rise, but never require much effort. In spring and summer the path is lined with beautiful blue scilla lilies, while in late summer and autumn the bottlebrushes come into brilliant scarlet bloom. Across the river you can see the 'teeth rocks' biting out from the forest.

The path follows the Injisuthi River for a few hundred metres more, then follows the lie of the land into the eMbovaneni side valley for a distance, crosses this stream and wends its way back into the main valley to reach Battle Cave after 5.5 km. This should take about 2 hours. Interpretation of this important art site was not accurate. It is a metaphorical battle more to do with the power of magic than bows and arrows.

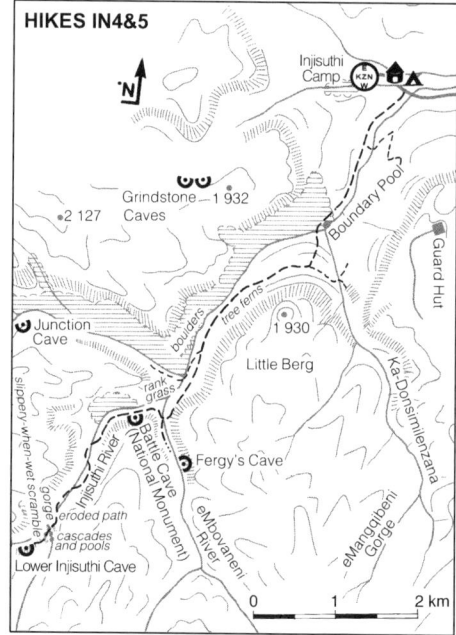

HIKES IN4&5

LOWER INJISUTHI CAVE — HIKE IN5

Route: From the rest camp up the Injisuthi Valley as far as the path goes
Distance: 17 km return
Duration: About 4 hours up and 3 hours back (2 days)
Grade: Moderate
General: It is said that photos don't lie. Maybe, but our impressions of them do. I was long seduced by photos of the Upper Injisuthi Cave but for me the reality never lived up to the dream. On the other hand, I expected very little from the lower cave, and yet it remains among my favourites. It's a very easy morning's or afternoon's walk out from the camp, and gives you access to the inner recesses of the Triplets area which, I have implied before, is one of those very special places in the Berg where you can feel the power of the dragon mountains (with Scaly Peak rising up on the right). Time your departure to include the guided walk of Battle Cave and you're two-thirds there.

The first 5.5 km of the outward walk is to Battle Cave, the previous route description. All that remains to be said about this section is how awesome the valley is: the silver ribbon of river running between the hunched, red shoulders of the Little Berg gorge, the rich green of the grasslands fading to an even more intense green of the forest on the opposite bank, the sub-Alpine grasslands ahead sweeping up to the massed ranks of dark basalt warriors – Trojan Wall and Red Wall, two Injisuthi buttresses with the Triplets at the head of this fossil army.

Having marvelled at this window into Late Stone Age culture, continue from the cave, along the fence through rank grass down to the river, which is crossed to the right-hand bank after about 650 m, once you've passed the small forest patch. There is a sandstone embankment on the left and thick bush on the right, with numerous places beside the river to stop for a break, or a dip. For the next 2 km the path crosses back and forth, four times, and it may be a little tricky at times to see exactly where it goes, but as long as you keep taking the line of least resistance you'll get back onto it.

Where the river cuts a small gorge through the sandstone band the path leads up to the left where you can look down into its rushing waters. Then it's downhill again towards the river, crossing a tributary where the rushing river has scoured out a series of Jacuzzi pools. After a short but tricky section over sloping rocks a path leads uphill to the left – don't take it unless you want to get a closer view of the Trojan Wall, or reach the Contour Path jeep track. Rather, carry on along the left-hand bank of the river, through bottlebrush and ouhout thickets to the cave. This is a comfortable overhang, with low stone walling and grass bedding provided by previous hikers for your comfort. It looks down to the river, but is partially hidden by a leafy screen.

Through a gap at the end of the overhang you can just see the tops of the Triplets, but out of sight behind them is a landmark that is even more significant. It's really just a pimple on the watershed 2 km back from the Escarpment edge but, because it rises to 3 450 m, it is the highest point on that watershed and therefore South Africa's highest 'peak'. Modern map makers seem to have pulled the name for it, Mafadi, out of a hat, but the Basothos know it as Ntheledi, 'make me slip', probably the name of the river that rises as tributaries north and south of the peak. The way to locate the Upper Injisuthi Cave is first to realise it's quite high up, and well south of the Triplets.

In fact it looks out over the northern end of the Trojan Wall, from the ridge that rises up to the south from the Triplets (the main ridge leading up to Injisuthi Dome), 500 m in from the Escarpment edge and just under 2 km from the nek of the Eastern Triplet. If you are overnighting in Lower Injisuthi Cave you'll have time to explore up the valley. There's no path, but it's easy to boulder hop up the river bed – unless a storm is brewing. Then you'd do best to stay put and fire up another brew (remember the Ship's Prow Pass incident in the previous chapter, page 120).

GRINDSTONE CAVES   HIKE IN6

Route: From the rest camp up Old Woman Stream and then climb Gibisila Ridge to the caves
Distance: 6 km return
Duration: 2 to 3 hours up, 2 hours return
Grade: Moderate
General: As a half-day outing this is a short but steep trip to these interesting caves in a narrow valley below the Little Berg plateau. To make a day outing you can return via Cataract Valley to make it a 13-km round-trip, taking about 5 hours, or 6 if you're a slow walker. There are also other routes you could take, including round-trips via the Contour Path to north or south.

The walk starts next to dormitory unit number 2 and crosses the Del'mhlwazini Stream via the footbridge. Along the first 500 m you have to cross the stream once more (to the right-hand bank), going through a small wood. Where the path crosses the river a third time, head up towards Gibisila Ridge (you can't miss it as it'll be staring you in the face). The lower slopes are covered in tall grass, with large boulders and shrubs, mainly protea trees. Do not take a path that turns off to the left, as it goes nowhere, but carry on up the ridge for a few hundred metres, where the path veers over to the right-hand side of the ridge and continues climbing up above the Old Woman Stream.

About 2.5 km from the start the path takes a turn for the worse, i.e. it heads steeply up to the left away from the river, then zigzags back to the right and continues ascending for another 500 m until you reach the first cave. It's one of the biggest in the area, and comfortably sleeps about 12 people. The second cave, about 50 m further on, is smaller and seldom used. Staring down the valley, between the stunted protea bushes, is Monk's Cowl which makes a lovely sight when caught, as if in some devious act, by the golden dawn light.

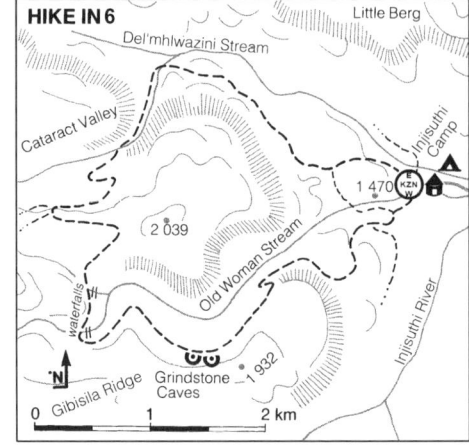

The main cave gets its name from the old grindstones found there, two of which you can still see (probably the only reason they're still there is that they're too large and heavy to fit into a backpack!). They were probably brought here by tribespeople from lower down the valley fleeing one or other impi before, during or immediately after (or all three) the reign of Shaka. If you think you live in tough times, just try to imagine life in the 1820s. If the Zulu impis didn't rape you and pillage your kraal, then the cannibals would likely take their pound of flesh.

The way back home via Cataract Valley is to carry on past the second cave, keeping to the contour, rounding a spur to reach the river after 1.2 km. Cross the Old Woman Stream just below the cliff line, head up the opposite bank, and climb out the other side of the gorge, heading up steeply to the Little Berg summit. At a nek, where a pimple rises up to your right, the route veers left for 500 m to reach the Contour Path about 3.5 km from the caves. Turn right here, away from the Contour Path and down the slope to your right, zigzagging down the Little Berg again to enter Cataract Valley.

The path heads towards the river and crosses it a number of times (as many as you need) for several hundred metres before taking you to the left-hand, right-sloping side of the valley, zigzagging through the steepest part, and to the confluence of the Del'mhlwazini Stream, where you cross Cataract Stream and head down the right-hand side of the valley, away from the Del'mhlwazini back to camp, 2 km from the confluence. The path does seem to exit the valley to the right, but 1 km above the rest camp it goes back down towards the river, home and mortgage bonds.

GRINDSTONE CAVES AND MARBLE BATHS — HIKE IN7

Route: From the rest camp to Grindstone Caves (overnight stop) then up to the Contour Path, heading generally to the south to the Injisuthi Valley and back to the rest camp
Distance: 19 km
Duration: 1½ to 2 hours to the caves, and 6 hours return (2 days)
Grade: Strenuous
General: This is a great two-day hike, which can be increased to three days by linking it to Wonder Valley Cave (hike IN2); if you do that, I'd recommend you spend the first night at Wonder Valley or your second day will be an epic. There's no other sensible way between the two caves except via the rest camp, so just accept it and enjoy a cold drink on your way through.

At Grindstone Caves (hike IN6) take the path up between the two caves to climb Old Woman Valley and on to Gibisila Ridge, which is a pleat in the skirt of the Old Woman Grinding Corn. After 1 km of steady uphill work the path splits around the ridge (a T-junction). From there the path heads up the inner, right-hand flank of first the Injisuthi and then of a northern tributary below the Old Woman. After a further 3 km of climbing, gaining about 250 m along this stretch, you finally reach the Contour Path, where you take a breather and then turn left (south-east).

Very soon you start your descent flight, down an eland fence. Eland are indeed plentiful in this area, and you'd be unlucky not to see them between here and Junction Cave. There's a gap in the fence after 500 m, where the path veers sharp right to descend a long, steep valley going

144 injisuthi

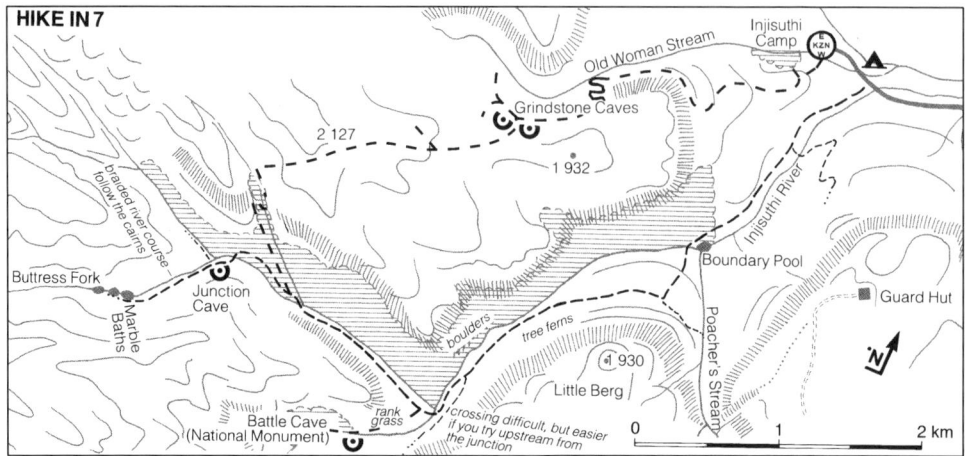

upstream. The stream is unnamed on the maps but I refer to it as Junction Stream as it meets Buttress Stream at Junction Cave. The path crosses the stream and heads down the right-hand bank. This is still the official Contour Path, hard as it may seem in some places.

It's not shown on Slingsby's map but, soon after you cross a side tributary from the right, a path heads off around the spur to the right and makes its way into Buttress Fork Valley, reaching this stream at Marble Baths. When I did this hike it was mid-winter and snow had fallen, giving the Escarpment a silver lining in the morning light. Nevertheless, the day was warm and when we reached the baths – a polished chute through the soft, cream-coloured rock – the brave among us stripped down and took a plunge. In summer the chute makes a wonderful 'bum slide'. As you look up this valley The Molar (3 045 m) bites into the sky. This, by the way, is the base of Leslie's Pass (hike IN11).

From Marble Baths go down the right-hand bank, which takes you past Junction Cave after 750 m. Although it was popular in days past as a shelter, the cave is close to the river and its roof has partly collapsed and flooding has made it unusable. Where the streams converge and the forest begins, the path seems to go all over the place, crossing the river here and there, then finding its way onto the steep, heavily eroded right-hand bank for the last 1.2 km to the confluence with the Injisuthi. The first part of this section is pleasant, along the forest edge of the left-hand bank, but the latter section decidedly uncomfortable, crumbling in places.

Cross the Injisuthi where you come to it (with luck the stepping stones will not be covered) and join the Battle Cave/Lower Injisuthi Cave path. From here on it's an easy 5-km walk along a good, wide, well-maintained path.

CLOTHING TIPS

- Always pack for possible extreme conditions.
- Don't skimp on the inner-most and outer-most layers.
- Layer your clothing: a Polartec T-shirt, a long-sleeved collared shirt, a rain-jacket or wind-breaker and down jacket.
- Take a beanie and balaclava. You never know when you might need them.
- Only underwear needs washing.

CONTOUR PATH TO MONK'S COWL — HIKE IN8

Route: From Injisuthi rest camp to the Contour Path via Grindstone Caves, passing the Old Woman, Ship's Prow, Champagne Castle and Cathkin Peak and down at Blind Man's Corner...
Distance: 19 km
Duration: 8 to 9 hours (2 days)
Grade: Strenuous (2 days), severe (1 day)
General: There are two ways to do the Contour Path between Injisuthi and Monk's Cowl: the first past Grindstone Caves (or via Junction Cave) and up Old Woman Stream to the path, and the second up Van Heynigen's Pass and Shadow Ridge. The former is the 'real' Contour Path route as it takes in the whole Contour Path between the two EKZNW camps (27.5 km). I have chosen to describe the 'lesser' route, which might seem to contradict my earlier championing of a continuous contour route from one end of the Berg to the other. The thing is, unless you are doing the Contour Path as a personal challenge, you'd never choose it as the best hiking route between the two points, as for much of the way it goes nowhere – it expends a lot of your energy just in and out of the complex ridges of the sub-Alpine zone. Also, Van Heynigen's Pass was built by that good forester precisely as his contour path route between Monk's Cowl (where he was based) and Injisuthi.

This hike starts as for Grindstone Caves (hike IN6), going up the spur behind and to the left of the office as you face the Escarpment. It starts off gently for 500 m until you reach the base of this spur, and the next 2 km are quite taxing when carrying a full pack. The caves are large and among the nicest in the Berg.

From the caves there are three routes to the Contour Path: the easiest is to keep pretty much to the level you are on, proceeding into the Old Woman Valley and crossing the stream after about 1 km. From there wend your way out of the valley to your right and cross the opposite ridge before gaining the Contour Path at the point where you gaze down into secretive Cataract Valley. This will cut out nearly half the distance of the 'official' route.

If you are determined to take the Contour Path, gain the crest of Gibisila Ridge which comes down from the Old Woman. Head upwards and after 1 km the path splits, the main route contouring to the right into the Old Woman Valley and running more or less parallel to but a few hundred metres higher than the previous short cut route. (I have to admit it seems pretty pointless going 4.5 km up the ridge to cross the Old Woman Stream and then having to descend 250 m over about 3.5 km to get to where the short cut from the caves meets the Contour Path, but there it is.) These variations are clearly marked on the old Slingsby map as well as the EKZNW maps number 2 (Cathedral Peak) and number 3 (Giant's Castle).

On the main contour path, from the point where the upper of the two variations meets it, you descend steeply for about 1 km towards Cataract Valley, in a downstream direction. Then the path turns sharp left to take a gentle downhill course upstream to cross the river about 2 km further on.

For the next 3.5 km the Contour Path climbs over three consecutively lesser ridges around the Old Woman and into Ship's Prow Stream gully, with the Prow jutting into the sky on your left and the great bulk of Champagne Castle dead ahead. The path crosses a small tributary,

146 injisuthi

HIKE IN8

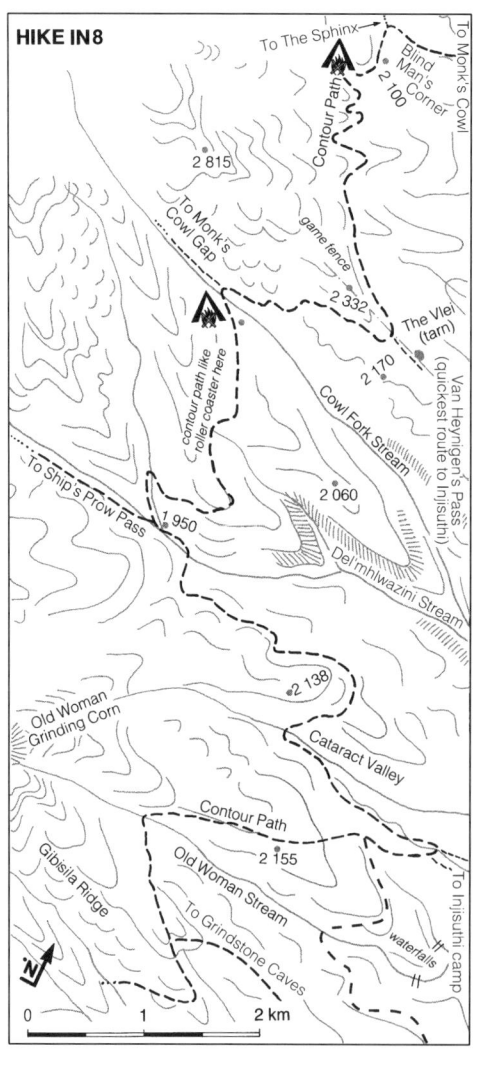

loops around a long spur to the right and 4 km further reaches Cowl Fork. There is a path up the gully and over to Keith Bush Camp but the Contour Path veers right once more and climbs gently for 2 km onto the crest of Shadow Ridge.

A right turn here (which used to be known as The Vlei) will take you to Van Heynigen's Pass and Wonder Valley Cave. But we bear left and keep on the contour for another 4 km, cruising along the way, to reach Blind Man's Corner. This is among the most spectacular scenic routes in the Berg, where every twist and turn of the path brings new aspects of the great peaks of the Monk's Cowl area.

As to how this spot got its name, I've never found a reference but would guess it was some old codger telling his hiking chum 'you can't miss the corner, even a blind man could find it, mate'. George Thompson did when he fell and broke his ankle while attempting to scale Cathkin Peak. Still groggy with concussion he led the climb to the summit, but for once this 'never say die' climber sent his companions to seek help. They roused Van Heynigen who reached the corner at dawn on Christmas Day. There was Thompson, shuffling home on hands and knees. So keep your spirits up (and turn right here to head down to The Sphinx and Monk's Cowl station).

A grassy slope leads to The Sphinx, and then winds steeply down to Monk's Cowl, passing through a gate and crossing a stream a few times on the final 1.5-km section.

CONTOUR PATH: CENTENARY TO BANNERMAN HUT — HIKE IN9

Route: From the rest camp past Fergy's Cave to the Contour Path and on to Bannerman Hut
Distance: 17 km
Duration: 6 to 7 hours (1 or 2 days)
Grade: Moderate (2 days), strenuous (1 day)
General: Much confusion surrounds the existence or not of the Centenary Hut, located close to

where the Fergy's Cave path meets the Contour Path at The Gap, the base of The Corner. When I phoned the Injisuthi office I was told it had been vandalised and was closed to hikers. However, I'm a persistent chap and phoned the chief conservator who confirmed that it is regularly vandalised and had even been burned down at one stage, but hikers could still stay there. It's located 10 km from Injisuthi camp and could make a good first night stopover on a hike to Giant's Castle.

From the hutted camp take the main road towards the vehicle bridge, then just before the bridge turn right up the embankment, over and down into the Injisuthi Valley (the route to Battle Cave and Marble Baths). Continue into the forest on the right-hand side of the Injisuthi River, and exit to cross at the stepping stones (you'll have to take off your boots when the river is high). This is just over 2 km from camp. The path climbs a grassy slope below the Little Berg cliffs and then turns right to run parallel to the river up the left-hand bank for another pleasant 2 km. Where a path turns off to the right to Marble Baths, carry on along the Battle Cave path on the left-hand bank for another 500 m to a junction up a side gully.

Where the main Battle Cave route crosses the stream to head back towards the Injisuthi, cross the stream but then turn immediately left to head up the right-hand bank of this stream gully. The once famous Fergy's Cave is found 500 m up this small valley on the left-hand side of the stream, but it is not shown on the new EKZNW hiking maps as it is no longer available to hikers. About 1.2 km further up this valley it splits in two around a bulge of the Little Berg, where we have to cross a side tributary from the right and climb that 'bulge' going steeply up for roughly 1 km. Then it eases off and 2.3 km later comes to a side junction to the left. The path to the left goes to the Injisuthi/Giant's Castle jeep track at Cloudland Col (or nek). Centenary Hut, however, is reached by keeping right just 250 m further on. If you plan to overnight here check on the state of the hut before you depart.

The hut is located roughly 50 m below and 250 m short of the Contour Path. I know that if I had any authority in EKZNW I would relocate ranger outposts to be near the hiking huts so they could control the obviously uncontrollable vandalism to these huts, which must cause a constant headache for the conservators and a drain on the park's coffers. But until I get that job I'll just have to keep on nagging in hope. You reach the well-maintained Contour Path where a prominent spur leads up to The Corner, a narrow wedge jutting out from the Escarpment. For the first 4 km the path is easy going, although there is a bit of a sustained ascent up the Mtshezana Stream inside the actual 'corner' (Corner Pass goes up here). Then you traverse under The Judge and Popple Peak, at 3 331 m one of the 'kulus' of the area. Several tributaries feed the Mtshezana directly below Popple Peak, and at the main one the Contour Path devolves from a wide track to an ill-defined path as it negotiates its way through these stream beds for over 1 km.

With just over 2 km to go to Bannerman Hut, located a little way up Bannerman Pass above the Contour Path (you can't miss its new imitation red tile roof), the route reverts to a higher form. (Unfortunately, the presence of a field ranger's post close by has not prevented this hut from being continuously vandalised – either it's not close enough, or it's not used regularly enough.)

Once at Bannerman you have a number of choices: continue southwards along the Contour Path for 4.5 km then turn left at The Tarn (more like a large seepage area) down Bannerman Path for 6.5 km to Giant's rest camp; take the 18-km slog along the contour to Giant's Hut beyond the base of Giant's Castle Pass at the foot of Giant's Castle Peak (3 315 m), where it stands next to a tarn; or you could climb Bannerman as it is one of the easiest pass routes to the summit: though maps show the upper reaches as being 'rock', it is really just strewn with boulders – and cattle skeletons where rustlers have sacrificed their stolen goods to make a quick escape. Most of the upper reaches are virtually paved steps.

TREE FERN CAVE   HIKE IN10

Route: Injisuthi rest camp eastwards along the outermost Little Berg Escarpment to a cave above the Sholoti Valley
Distance: 16 km return hike
Duration: 4 hours there and 3 return
Grade: Moderate to strenuous
General: This is a new hiking route in the area, for, while the paths have existed for a long time, Tree Fern Cave has been closed to hikers for over 20 years – although it was used during most of that time as an overnight shelter for horse trailists from Hillside Camp, which is a satellite conservation post and camp site of Giant's Castle close to White Mountain Inn. Because this cave was closed to hikers when the EKZNW maps were drawn up, neither it nor the path there is shown. However, with the closure of Fergy's and Junction caves it was felt another hiking cave was needed and this one was earmarked. It will apparently be signposted one of these days from Injisuthi. You will find it clearly marked on Slingsby's map though.

Take the road out of camp and cross the vehicle bridge over the Injisuthi. The road does a sharp double-back to the left and just about 2 km from camp a path (shown on the EKZNW map as a circular route to/from Boundary Pool) heads up the left-hand side of the river for 800 m. Then it turns sharp left away from the river and zigzags up towards the Little Berg cliffs.

At the base of the cliffs you come to the Poacher's Stream path, where you turn left with

injisuthi 149

HIKE IN10

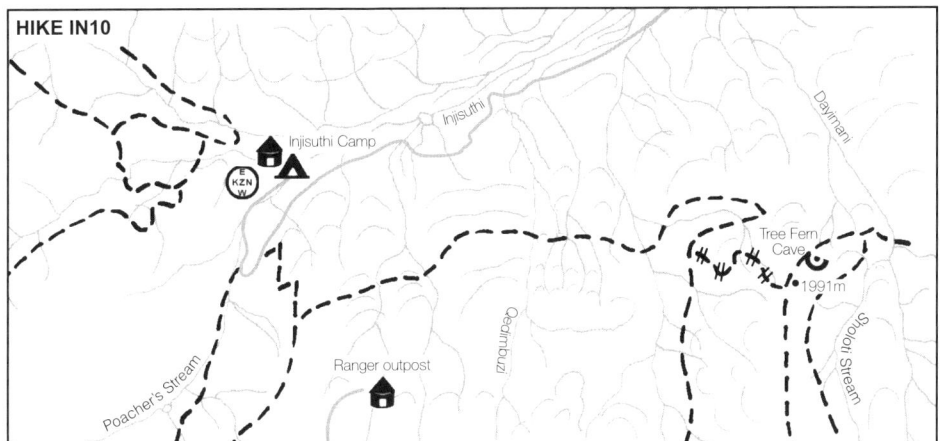

the cliffs on your right. After 1.5 km from the junction you pass a large sandstone boulder on your left called the Block Rock. Approximately 250 m past that there is an intersection that is closed off, so carry on straight, past the wood above the path on your right.

The path crosses a few small stream gullies before crossing the Qedimbuzi Stream 2 km along this 'contour path'. After crossing a few minor gullies for one kilometre, you cross the Dayimani Stream.

The path does a big loop up a side gully (keep to the right to avoid two restricted paths to the left) to begin its assault of the Little Berg. At the point where you find yourself some 80 m above the Dayimani crossing point, a minor path continues up that gully, but our path begins a steep, zigzagging 1-km climb up the broken ground to the left. Then you come to a T-junction with a path that leads up to Pimple Hill to the right and to Tree Fern Cave to the left. Turn left. You will reach the cave after 700 m, dropping down the last few hundred metres to where you look down a steep slope into the Sholoti River Valley. There is a prominent krans 200 to 250 m left of the cave.

Of interest to anyone who has both the older Slingsby and the new EKZNW maps: the latter shows the Sholoti to be a higher tributary of the Dayimani, and the Dayimani flowing below the cave, whereas Slingsby shows the Dayimani to be the stream crossed before the path begins its ascent of the Little Berg. The stream is unnamed on the newer map. I tend to go with Slingsby here because the stream in question is a large one and is unlikely not to have a name when the much smaller one crossed before it, the Qedimbuzi, does.

LESLIE'S PASS   HIKE IN11

Route: From the rest camp to Marble Baths, then up Buttress Fork to the summit
Distance: 14.5 km one way
Duration: About 7 to 8 hours
Grade: Extreme

150 injisuthi

General: The pass was named after Leslie, the son of Roden Symons who became the second warden of Giant's Castle Game Reserve in 1906. Leslie's is the only viable pass in the Injisuthi area: Ship's Prow tops out 6.5 km to the north-west, and Bannerman about 13 km to the south-east (there is Corner Pass before that but it's not used by hikers). That alone is one reason why Leslie's is fairly well used, even though there is nothing much of interest where it tops out. But it does give access to the upper Injisuthi area, including the Upper Injisuthi Cave and Mafadi Peak, the highest point in South Africa at 3 450 m (Slingsby has it as 3 446 m).

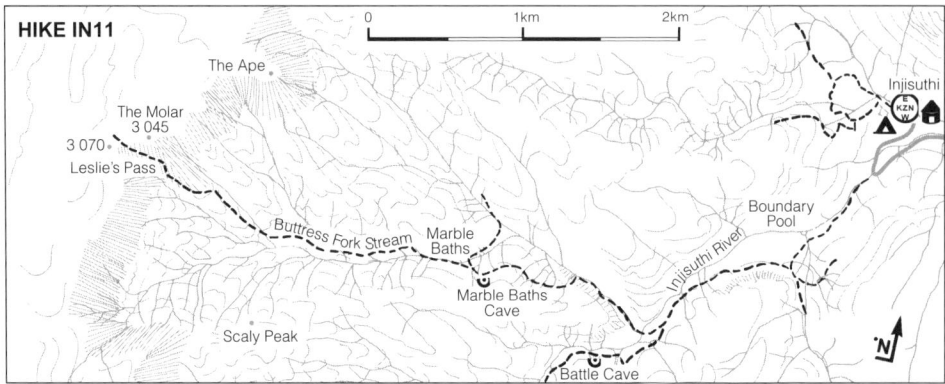

HIKE IN11

Take the route out of camp (starting down the road) towards Battle Cave and the Injisuthi Valley, past Boundary Pool. Around 4.75 km from camp you turn right off the main Battle Cave/Lower Injisuthi Cave path to cross the Injisuthi and head up the left-hand side of Buttress Fork Stream. After 1.3 km this path turns sharply left to ascend the sometimes awkward slope, before levelling off and returning to the river at Marble Baths, 3 km from the turnoff to Injisuthi. Just before you reach the baths you'll pass Marble Baths Cave on your left. This is 8.5 km from the start, so you can see you'll need an early start to get up the pass in one day.

Looking up Buttress Fork Valley, you should be able to see The Molar sticking up above the Little Berg slopes on the right. The river is named after Injisuthi Buttress because its main tributary rises on the watershed above it. For the first 2.5 km the pass keeps to the left-hand bank of the stream. It then crosses the stream between two side streams on the right and for 1 km along and 300 m up proceeds up the main spur leading directly to The Molar. This is a very steep and tough section, but not more so than several dozen other passes.

Then it eases off for a short section to cross into and over the gully on the left, and more or less heads up that gully to the top, veering off at one point away to the left up the open slope before coming back into the gully next to The Molar. The last 600 m of the pass steepens considerably once again and you're going to have to call on deep reserves to keep going. There is little shelter at the rocky top of the pass, and you'll have to descend to the stream to pitch a tent on the level bank.

There are any number of shorter walks from the rest camp, such as to the yellowwood forest (about a 6-km, 2-hour round-trip of the Del'mhlwazini/Cowl Fork Stream), past the two old guard huts, or up one of the other rivers – the Old Woman Stream or Injisuthi River, or down the Injisuthi for just over 1 km to Junction Pool (where the Del'mhlwazini meets the Injisuthi), but as they are so short and easy, they hardly need any more description than that given on the maps. The reason for dropping these shorter hiking descriptions from the old version of this book is that Injisuthi is really about hiking more than strolling; I prefer to give hikers access to some new, exciting routes such as Leslie's Pass, Tree Fern Cave and the Contour Path towards Giant's Castle.

If you'd like to do a short walk, particularly families with small children (older children like to be driven!) but you're unsure of directions, buy a walking-route brochure at the office.

Because of all the stream junctions in the area, and the dense riverine growth in places, the hardest part of these walks is often just getting on to the right path at the start. Don't be afraid in persisting to get the description exactly right. Failing that, just point your nose in the right direction and you will get there just as well (other than meeting the occasional dead-end in impenetrable bush or reeds, which I tend to do more than sometimes). If you do only one shortish walk here, then choose the guided walk to Battle Cave, which gives you a sense of the area's varied habitats, great views of some of the higher peaks and access to one of the Berg's special rock art sites.

MOUNTAIN SAFETY TIPS

- Have some idea of emergency procedure.
- Sign the mountain register and give all pertinent information: number in the party, planned route, tent colour.
- This can mean life or death when rescuers are risking their lives – voluntarily it should be noted – to save yours.
- Have an escape route and a plan for splitting up to go for help.
- Make clear time and place arrangements for meeting up again.
- The Berg is a big place and you can get lost there without even trying.
- Do not change the plan agreed on unless you find yourself in a life-threatening situation.
- If you do have to leave a rendezvous area, try to make marks that will be visible to the rescue party.
- A cellphone should be considered essential emergency equipment (and not an accessory) on the summit.
- Have a good working torch.
- Carry a compass, map and first-aid kit.
- Wear bright clothing.
- Choose tent and backpack for their conspicuousness.
- A GPS and marine-type flares – to be used only in life-threatening situations – are your next line of defence.
- Have clothing and equipment to deal with the worst possible weather as you do not know what awaits you in the Berg.
- The mountain gods watch and they like to punish foolish people who underestimate their powers.

giant's castle

Giant's Castle Peak (3 315 m) has at various times been considered the second, third, fourth, even fifth highest peak in South Africa. It is certainly one of the highest and made more impressive by standing proud on a 4-km-long knife-edge that forms a hinge for the entire Drakensberg. As such it is possibly the most obvious reference point of all. In fact it is only the 12th highest peak, or 'kulu', depending on how you define 'peak'. If by 'peak' we mean completely free-standing, then Giant's could be argued to be the highest one in South Africa, but only the 12th highest point. Semantics: it's high enough when you climb it.

The name Giant's Castle was originally given to what we now call Garden Castle way to the south, by the 'insatiable' Captain AF Gardiner, Royal Navy (and you should read more about him in the last chapter, page 193). However, by the time the first map was made of the area, that name had been transferred to its present-day location (people say now because the ridge resembles a giant lying down, but I believe that's idle nonsense. As with Cathedral, it just got mixed up on early rough maps; it was a little known area then and very hard to map, with each person giving new names on each new map). The Zulu name for the ridge is either Bhulihawu, the 'shield thrasher', or Phosihawu, the 'shield flinger'. These poetic images refer to the storms which brew around its mighty precipices and are then flung out over the foothills like the shield of a supernatural impi. Zulu people will not point a straight finger at the mountain, lest it unleash its terrible forces – they use a crooked one. It would be appropriate if one of these more evocative and apt names came back into use because it simply does not resemble a castle.

The first we know about the area is from scant records about commandos chasing Bushmen into the passes of the area. Tragically ironic is that the last Bushman known to have lived – and died – in the Drakensberg was shot by such a commando just two decades prior to the declaration of the reserve. There's a faint chance they could have found some sort of sanctuary there ... then again it's unlikely, given prevailing attitudes and how animals were treated by the early game wardens. It was only as late as the mid-20th century that Bushman culture was widely accepted as being of immense value and its passing seen as a great loss.

It was a brave and tenacious party of adventurers that set out from the *Dargle* in February 1864 to explore the Giant's Castle area, still sheltering Bushmen who would have been antagonistic and armed with poisoned arrows. We know from the diary of surveyor Augustus Bovill that they located the Giant's Pass, climbed it and the Giant itself, and descended by another pass, almost certainly the Hlathimba, on their 10-day exploration.

In 1873 the independent-minded amaHlubi chief Langalibalele (who had already had run-ins with Zulu King Mpande and British administrator Sir Theophilus Shepstone), in the wake of the Zulu Wars, refused to acknowledge British gun and marriage laws (he had 80 wives) and started plotting open revolt. As the Colony of Natal felt seriously threatened all available troops were called up: British Army forces, six volunteer regiments and a 'native' contingent. The plan was to encircle Langalibalele and prevent him escaping up the Bushman's River Pass into Lesotho, with as little fuss and loss of life as possible. However the poor maps available caused a complete botch-up of the plan and finally a full-scale engagement occurred.

Oh, the blunders. In the ensuing mêlée led by Major AW Durnford, five of his men were killed. They are remembered in the peaks Erskine, Bond, Potterill, Kambule and Katana. There is also Carbineer Point, as well as Mount Durnford and the route that is now Langalibalele Pass. Of course the recalcitrant chief was eventually brought to book, but this small incident had widespread repercussions in the colony. One of them was that JE Fannin was commissioned to map the passes of that area properly, while Durnford (now colonel) and the 75th Regiment were sent out to blow up the final approaches. Many years later, warden Roden Symons, while he was out looking for the mysteriously vanished hiker Rev Bates, found numerous skeletons in the pass as evidence of the 'smoke on the pass', as the Langalibalele rebellion was called at the time.

Then there was silence, until in November 1903 Sydney Barnes (the first of three Barneses to fill the post of warden here) came trundling up the Bushman's River Valley in an ox wagon, and set up camp in a cave close to the larger cut-away which had once been a major refuge for Bushmen, and set about proclaiming his new kingdom as the domain of wild animals and wild mountains. 'No man could have lived a lonelier and more isolated life,' muses Reg Pearse, but at least he was being paid. I reckon it was Eden. The purpose of Giant's Castle Game Reserve was to protect the dwindling herds of eland: the spur coming down from Giant's South Ridge is called Mpofana, the 'place of eland', and you are very likely to see them still there.

But what of the other animals? In 1915 Philip Barnes took over (Symons having moved on to Hluhluwe). Predators killed 'royal game' so they were to be eliminated. Over 32 years Barnes shot 600 jackals, but I'm relieved to report that those wily creatures live on all over the Berg. Others weren't so lucky: leopards, serval and caracal were all shot on sight and, although the two smaller species survive in unknown number, leopards have not been seen for many years. In 1918 a hunting party set out to make 'one last determined effort to eradicate the menace' of wild dogs that took refuge in Lesotho. A pack of 17, as well as one spotted hyena, were wiped out and they've not been seen since (Nkenthsane, or 'wild dog hill', commemorates the event). How modern conservators must shudder. We're pretty sure which mountaineers first set foot on top of Giant's Castle Peak; surveyors have so often made the first ascent of peaks here and earlier in the Cape Mountains. It's a strenuous enough effort to climb the pass, and few hikers would care to undertake the final arduous climb from the head of the pass through the rock bands to the highest point on the ridge. But who would look to the massed walls all around the head of the pass and scheme of finding a way up them? Rock climbers, of course.

Directly below the main peak, a gully runs right down the east face (directly behind Giant's Hut). This was the next route to be tackled (by JM Sweeney and party in 1941), and, as long as it's not winter ice-choked, it does not require a rope. In 1954 Martin Winter allowed his eyes to wander up the south-east ridge and his mind to wonder about the South Peak (The Gable). That was the first rock route forged up the mountain. Six years later Des Watkins took a more audacious line up the South Face. The *pièce de résistance* of routes must be the one led by Transvaaler Ted Scholes in 1950 up the North Face, directly up the 'castle'. It was a grand year for the confident but reticent climber, notching up not only this one but the first Devil's Tooth ascent in August and in December the Eastern Injisuthi Triplet. Three finer, harder routes would be difficult to find.

Today the reserve is best known for its superb rest camp and restaurant (more suited to the pockets of foreign tourists than hikers, it must be said), and the Main Caves Bushman rock art museum which was initiated by warden Bill Barnes in the 1960s. But birders and photographers vie for a chance to book a day at the famous lammergeier hide, where, in winter, carcasses are set out. First always to the spoils are the crows, followed closely by white-necked ravens. Then the smaller hawks swoop in: rock kestrels maybe, definitely a jackal buzzard or two and the occasional lanner falcon. Then it's the Cape vultures which follow the mess line to the hide, dropping in like huge transport aircraft with pendulous undercarriages let down. Finally, those golden and charcoal lords of the mountain skies appear, tentatively, to see what cooks at the ossiary. On a good day, their alter egos, the black eagles, might deign to honour the lowlanders with a surprise visit. There is no budget accommodation at Giant's Castle, but you can park at a picnic site (where ravens have a penchant for pecking rubber windscreen seals) and hike out from there.

MAIN CAVES — HIKE GC1

Route: From the rest camp into the Two Dassie Stream Forest and up to the caves
Distance: 3 km return
Duration: 1 hour walking and 1 hour cave tour
Grade: Easy
General: This is such an easy walk that an extended return-trip is advised, past Durnford's Camp

and then along the River Walk. But, if you do only one walk at Giant's Castle, this has to be it. The Bushman paintings in the two shelters may be faded and vandalised in part, but they do constitute one of the most varied of all rock art sites in the Drakensberg, and they are by far the easiest to reach. A raised wooden walkway has been constructed to keep visitors a little way away from the rock surfaces. Tours are all guided and take place most of the day on the hour from the cave fence gate (you must first pay at reception).

This walk is signposted all the way from the main camp so a hike description is hardly required. You walk along the road out at the mountain end of camp, then along a wide, partly cemented path down past the boulders that mark Durnford's Camp to the wooden footbridge over Two Dassie Stream.

Then the path takes you some way into the forest and seemingly away from the rock band where the caves are situated ... but don't panic: this is the new route designed to give you a more interesting and varied walk, as well as to enhance your experience by leading you in one way and out the next so that you don't encounter other bothersome and noisy groups on their way in to this sacred site.

After a short walk into the forest you have to head across a second footbridge and then climb up the fairly steep path to the right back to the caves. They were obviously visited and even used by the 75th Regiment, among whom there were bold marksmen who used various paintings for target practice (you almost wish a ricochet would have hit one of them). During the 1960s warden Bill Barnes commissioned the current museum display of lifelike hunter-gatherers going about their daily business in a section of the south-facing cave alongside an area with paintings. One old codger – the 'old man of the cave' – would have been the leader of the group and their shaman, for he is engaged in creating a painted image on the cave wall. If you'd like to learn more about the Drakensberg Bushmen, as well as see artefacts including the things found in Eland Cave near Didima that were previously displayed here, you should visit the Pietermaritzburg Museum. These images have lost their rich polychrome pigments in most instances, yet their number and variety are perhaps unmatched in the Drakensberg.

FOREST AND RIVER WALK — HIKE GC2

Route: From the rest camp along the Main Caves path into the forest, and return along the left-hand bank of the Bushman's River and up to the picnic site
Distance: Minimum of 5 km
Duration: Minimum of 1½ hours
Grade: Easy
General: There is no fixed distance or duration to this walk, since the path up Two Dassie Stream goes all the way up to the Contour Path. There's a lovely swimming hole 3.5 km up the stream, if you want to make a longer outing of the walk. The forest section is short, but there is one exquisite area around the crossing that leads up to the caves and on a hot day the shade will provide a welcome respite.

156 giant's castle

Take the road out of camp towards the Main Caves and follow this, often cemented walkway across the wooden footbridge then up Two Dassie Stream into the forest. Before you reach the forest, or on your return along the same route, take some time to visit Durnford's Camp among the large boulders. The '75' you see on the dark, lichen encrusted rock was carved by the regiment's cook who was obviously bored while the troops were out blowing up the passes. Colonel Durnford had been a major in the Royal Engineers when he inherited command almost by chance during the Langalibalele rebellion. He led a small mounted force of regular soldiers, volunteer Carbineers and Basotho conscripts to the top of the Drakensberg where the main action took place. Durnford was lucky to escape, while his loyal Zulu guide and interpreter Elijah Kambule (recognised by Langalibalele's indunas or chief's commanders as 'Shepstone's man' which almost certainly avoided more extensive bloodshed) was cut down by assegais as the vastly outnumbered British force fled the scene of engagement. Durnford was stabbed twice but barged his way through the chanting throng on his horse Chieftain.

Also unlucky was trooper Robert Erskine, whose loose saddle pitched him into a group of blood-thirsty warriors. Next was Edwin Bond, shot through the head. Then the Basotho, Katana, was dropped from his horse as he tried to ford a stream. Charles Potterill's horse was stabbed and killed under him and, as Potterill raced away, he was pursued by three impis. In hand-to-hand combat Potterill shot one with his drawn pistol as the tribesman planted his spear in the white man's body. The other two Zulus were soon upon him. Had Captain Allison, who was a Carbineer or colonial volunteer, been able to lead his force of 500 mounted and armed Basotho loyalists up the non-existent Champagne Castle Pass to join Durnford's, things would have turned out very differently.

There is a plaque bolted to the rock which briefly commemorates the action. Cast your eyes up the mountains along Langalibalele Ridge and they are led right into the pass where all this took place. To the left from there is first the cross marking the Carbineer's grave, then the points of Erskine, Bond, Mount Durnford, Kambule, Carbineers Point and finally Katana where Long Wall forms a vast blank face right up to Giant's Castle Pass.

Continue across the wooden footbridge and up Two Dassie Stream into the forest. Where a path leads up to the caves above the stream to the right, carry on in the forest up the river as far as you please. That may be as far as the pool, a further 2.5 km. The path may be overgrown with rank grass but it is nevertheless a pleasant walk.

On your return along the same path, take the River Walk path from the wooden footbridge where the main path leads back up to camp.

This follows the left-hand bank of the Bushman's River below the rest camp, crossing

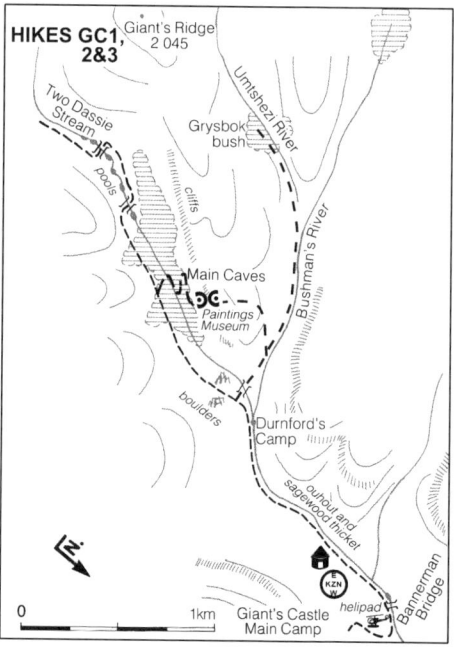

twice via wooden bridges. If your wrist is subtle and you enjoy the challenge of wild river trout, then you can try casting here. (You can get a permit either at the camp or at some of the hotels in the area.) The river is lined with quite dense mountain sage (*Buddleja*) and ouhout (*leucosidea*) bush, and you could get fairly close in winter to eland that browse the leaves of the mountain sage. Cross a bridge where the path from Bannerman Ridge reaches the river and go steeply up to the picnic site, and then right along the tar road back to camp.

GRYSBOK BUSH — HIKE GC3

Route: From the rest camp past Durnford's Camp and up the Bushman's River in the direction of Langalibalele Pass
Distance: 7 km return trip
Duration: 2½ hours
Grade: Easy
General: As with all the walks in the area of the rest camp this is a signposted route so you really shouldn't get lost. It leads into the largest forest patch in this area, which is a good place to sit quietly and watch out for bushbuck, one of the most handsome of all antelope, with their dark saddle stripes and white dots along the belly. They are shy and rather beautiful, and to see one is a true gift of the forest. I once lay still and watched a handsome ram (*nyoni*) browsing for some minutes before it wandered off. They eat mainly fallen wild fruits, shoots and roots. In *Stories from the Karkloof Hills* by Charles Scott-Shaw there's an insightful short story about the *nyoni*, 'Hunting Old Greybeard'.

From the rest camp take the path towards the Main Caves and cross Two Dassie Stream just above its confluence with the Bushman's River. Climb slightly towards the promontory where the caves are situated, along a cemented path. But, where the outward-bound path from the caves joins the Bushman's River, keep right to follow the left-hand river bank.

About 500 m onward a path leads off to the left towards Giant's Ridge, but our path carries on along the river. Another 500 m onwards the path splits around Middle Ridge where the Umtshezi River comes in from the left to meet the Bushman's. You can follow the path to the left for a short way up the Umtshezi River, or keep to the right further up the main valley. This path leads eventually up Langalibalele Ridge above Grysbok Bush.

MEAL TIPS

Long hike food:
- Breakfast is coffee, tea or hot chocolate (depending on my mood and the weather) with instant flavoured oats.
- Lunch is biltong strips and chocolate.
- Sundowners comprise whisky and Provitas with pork pâté and cheese.
- Supper is Chinese two-minute noodles with chopped salami.
- A final cup of coffee or hot chocolate.
- Whisky as a nightcap.

158 giant's castle

MEANDER HUT HIKE GC4

Route: From the picnic site
Distance: 11 km
Duration: 2 hours each way
Grade: Moderate
General: The route described here is the main hiking path to the least used of the hiking huts in the park, which overlooks the wonderfully green and lush Meander Stream valley. A shorter route is along the management track that starts at the staff quarters a way up the road past the picnic site and warden's house and goes up to the Lammergeier hide at Red Hill. But to keep the park officials happy we'll stick to the official route....

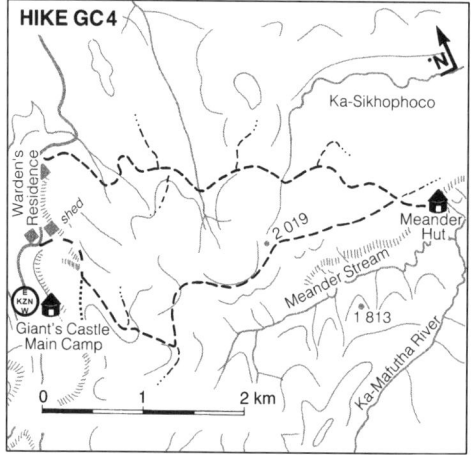

Park at the picnic spot, or walk the 500 m from the rest camp down the tar road. Take the path up the hill behind the warden's residence past an iron shed. The house was started in 1903 by the first warden Sydney Barnes who came up by ox wagon as far as the present Witteberg entrance gate and who for most of his tenure lived in a cave near where the rest camp was built. It was only much later made into the lovely home it is now. The three Barneses who had a hand in building the place all happened to be wardens of the park.

The path climbs up the side of a grass-covered and rocky ridge with lots of scattered bush. Paths branch off, first one to the right after some 750 m, then another to the left 500 m further where the angle of the ground has eased off. Carrying on straight the path goes downhill for only a short distance to reach a T-junction where you stand looking down over Meander Stream.

Turn right here and follow the top of the steep-sided valley, going down, up and down but never strenuously so, for 3 km to a four-way junction where this path meets a jeep track. Turn right here and the hut, which sleeps only four people, is reached just 100 m or so down the path. It is perched above the river and looks out across the stream that well earns its name, sweeping up the Little Berg to the Giant's Ridge.

You can return the same way, or retrace your route to the four-way intersection just a few hundred metres behind the hut and carry on straight instead of turning left to follow the line of the valley.

After 1 km you come to a jeep track where you turn left at the T-junction. The track crosses a stream and 1 km further on, all the while pretty much on the flat, a path to The Lakes view site turns off to the right (a 5-km round-trip), but we keep to the track for another 3 km, going gently downhill all the way to the main park road near the staff quarters. Optional detour: you're still about 2 km from the camp, so turn left and gently roll into camp, where the beers are always cold.

GIANT'S HUT
HIKE GC5

Route: From the rest camp, below the Main Caves and up Giant's Ridge to the hut on the Contour Path
Distance: 11 km one way
Duration: 5 hours
Grade: Moderate to strenuous
General: The grading of hikes is always a little problematical, because there are several highly variable factors, like the weather, your fitness and the weight of your pack. Few hikes of 10 km or less can truly be called hard, unless they are up one of the passes. But even then the hike up Langalibalele Pass can hardly be equated with Giant's Pass. So is the walk up to Giant's Hut moderate or strenuous? I'm not sure, but I'd say it depends on how fast you walk it. Take it slowly and the effort seems undemanding; push yourself and your body starts talking.

There is more than one way to the hut and, presuming you are overnighting there, it's advised that you return by one of the five or six other options (Two Dassie or Oribi Ridge, Two Dassie Stream, Giant's Ridge, Middle Ridge, Langalibalele Ridge and Bannerman Ridge). That is why only a one-way trip is described here. The hut sleeps eight and is equipped with bunks, mattresses, tables, benches, and a flush toilet, and has running water. It is usually in good condition, unlike the other two on the Contour Path that are regularly vandalised by Basotho poachers or cattle thieves. Check up on the condition of the hut before you set out.

The route up Giant's Ridge is not the shortest way to the hut, but is probably the easiest. The quickest way is up Two Dassie Stream and then up the steep ridge between its two upper tributaries. However, even though I have walked it and found it completely passable, I see on the map that this path is shown to peter out up the stream somewhere.

From the rest camp take the path towards the Main Caves and cross the wooden footbridge a little way past Durnford's Camp. Turn right (it's signposted) to Langalibalele and Giant's ridges and pass beneath the caves. There is a junction after 700 m where the two main paths split, our route going to the left to begin its long climb up the Little Berg. The path starts off along the right-hand slope of the ridge, where it is lightly wooded, and passes a small overhang. A steep but short zigzag on a good path follows this, before it edges along the ridge slope for a further 1.5 km until the crest of the ridge is attained.

And here I have a major gripe with whoever maintains these paths: if the park authorities wonder why hikers make so many alternate paths, it's because this so-called hiking path and many others in the Drakensberg are not wide enough to walk on, unless you have only one leg (or you walk like a horse, placing each foot exactly in front of the other and not to the side as we two-legged, upright primates do). When you're tired after a long hike and just want to free-wheel along the home stretch, you find yourself stumbling and tripping over your own feet, and cursing.

Baboons can often be seen scuffling along the ridge looking for something to eat, and they will eat just about anything. It's easy to overlook baboons and see them only as a nuisance. But just stop and observe for a short time if you get the chance. You might be amazed at how fascinating these creatures are. How else but by foraging can they survive from the driest bush of

160 giant's castle

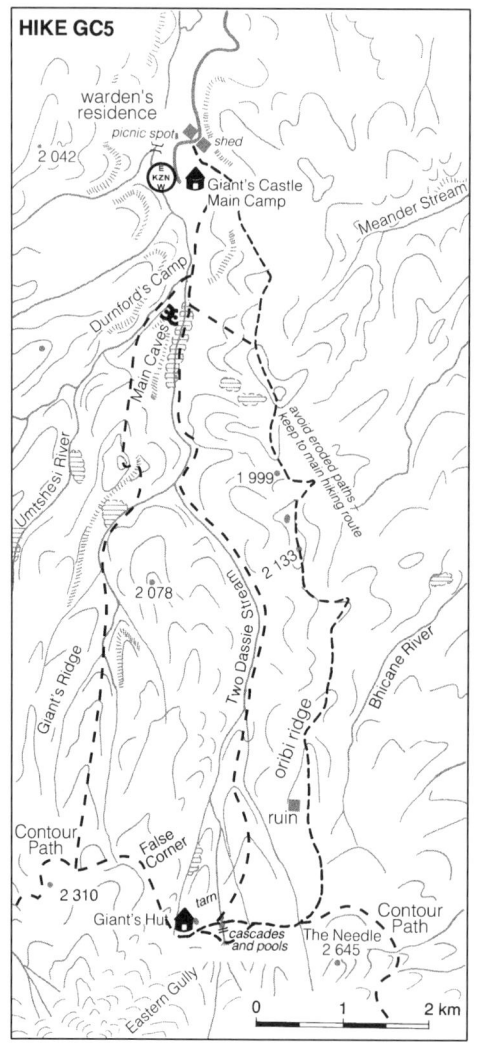

HIKE GC5

the Kalahari to the highest mountains of the Drakensberg and everywhere in between? Higher up the ridge you are likely to see small herds of eland, maybe a ridge or two distant, and grey rhebuck that everywhere are common but not plentiful.

Raptors are often sighted, partly because of the bird hide in the area, and lammergeiers now regularly patrol the skies along the high ridges and peaks. Less regularly seen are bald ibises which, like the lammergeiers, are an endangered species. They sometimes alight on the Little Berg grasslands to feed, but are extremely shy and you'll need binoculars to see them properly.

On reaching the Contour Path (you can't miss it, because it's signposted and at a major T-junction) turn left and it's still another 2 km round False Corner (the spur leading up to Giant's Castle Peak) to the stone and thatch hut. It's situated next to a largish tarn where, if you're unobtrusive, you might see rhebuck, mountain reedbuck, eland and even shy oribi come to drink at dawn or dusk. With stealth you could get some good photographs. The massive walls of Giant's Ridge rise up behind the hut like ramparts of a ... giant's castle.

Sit looking at them in the still of morning or evening and think of a Sweeney, Winter, Watkins or Scholes sitting right where you are, planning their bold routes directly up these sheer faces and plan yours.

BANNERMAN HUT   HIKE GC6

Route: From the picnic site across the Bushman's River and up Bannerman Ridge and north along the Contour Path to the hut
Distance: 11.5 km one way
Duration: 5 hours
Grade: Moderate to strenuous
General: The hut is similar in design to Giant's Hut, except that the grass roof was burnt,

replaced with a corrugated iron roof that was subsequently stolen, and now with what looks like red tiles but is in fact metal sheeting that will hopefully not be a target for thieves. It is book-ended by two of the Berg's 'kulus', or big ones – Giant's Castle to the south and Popple Peak to the north, both over 3 300 metres. If you start early you could reach the hut by late morning and be in Bannerman Cave on the summit by late afternoon. Obviously the later you start the more you'll be hiking in the heat of the day on the open Little Berg, unless it's raining, or snowing, or just cloudy (you can expect these conditions for most of the year).

The picnic site is found just beyond a large oak tree, 500 m up the road from the rest camp reception. There is ample parking around the tree, but unfortunately the ravens here have taken to pecking at rubber windscreen wipers and windscreen seals. You can fill your water bottles at the tap on the left. At the far end of the mowed grass area you find a cemented path leading steeply down to cross the river at a wooden bridge. Across the bridge head upstream for about 200 m, cross a stream and go up the well-defined and signposted path, past a lone African holly tree (*Ilex mitis*). The path is cemented on the steeper sections past the first low rock band.

Once you reach the Little Berg Plateau, in the form of Bannerman Ridge, the condition of the path deteriorates and it is often badly eroded, causing ugly scars. I don't know the solution to this erosion, but one needs to be found. There are two problems: one is the nature of the soil in some areas where it is easily compacted and quickly eroded (and then there are areas where the soil is intact and the path not eroded at all); the other is that the paths are really made for horse patrols and are too narrow for people, causing hikers to walk on either side.

The 4 km up to the Contour Path is not too taxing, unless you walk as if you are being pursued by angry beasts, and then a 4-km uphill jog with a heavy pack is obviously going to take its toll. The last wild dogs were killed here nearly a century ago, the last Bushman before that, and leopards haven't been seen for many decades, so relax.

What you are more likely to see is the 'long legged marking eagle' or secretary bird strutting the rank grass in search of beetles, locusts, lizards, mice, frogs, snakes, eggs and even nestlings. I sometimes wonder how terrestrial birds such as francolins and quails survive at

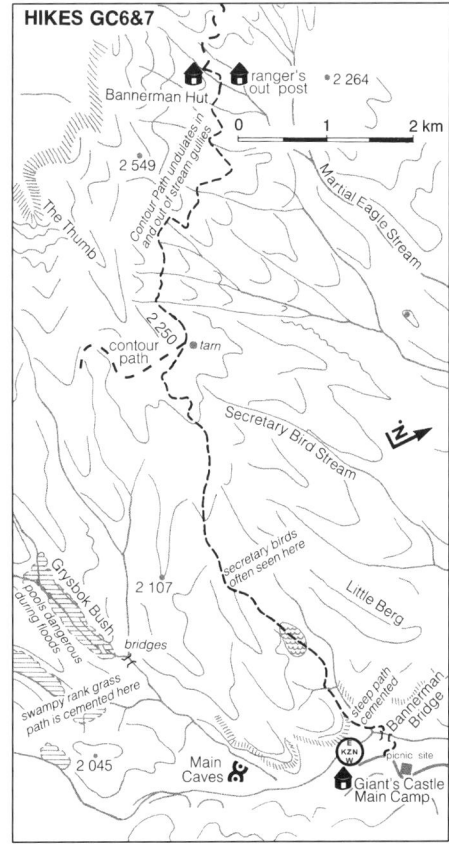

all, what with predation and veld fires. The common name of *Sagittarius serpentarius* (the snake hunter) comes from its Arabic name *saqr-et-tair*, or hunting bird. The English name was derived from the French corruption *secrétaire*.

Approaching the Contour Path you pass a vlei on your right, marked on the map as a tarn. The lilies and reeds growing there definitely suggest a vlei, but maybe it once was a tarn (shallow lake).

Turn right here and amble for 4.5 km past The Thumb and Bannerman Face to the hut, located a little way above the Contour Path in the sub-Alpine zone where a large community of *Protea dracomontana* begins. Despite being close to a field ranger post, this hut is quite frequently vandalised by Basothos and then repaired, so don't blame the park for the state in which you find it. It requires virtual continuous repair.

TWO HUTS VIA CONTOUR PATH — HIKE GC7

Route: Circular route from Giant's rest camp, via Giant's and Bannerman huts
Distance: 40.5 km
Duration: 4, 7 and 4 hours, over 3 days
Grade: Strenuous
General: There is no right, or better, way to do this hike since the routes up Bannerman and Giant's ridges are so similar. Even though the ridge walks up to the huts gain 490 m and 450 m respectively, the walk between the two huts is more taxing because of all the upping and downing you have to do. There's precious little that's flat about this Contour Path. The walks up to and down from the two huts are really quite short and take only half a day's hiking each; the walk between is longer. If you've not hiked here previously, it's a majestic feeling standing beneath the great peaks with their overwhelming sense of history. Remember to book the huts.

From the rest camp walk towards Main Caves, cross the footbridge over Two Dassie Stream and walk below the caves for a short way up the Bushman's River (all signposted). Where the path splits, right to Langalibalele and left to Giant's, go left up the Little Berg. This ridge takes you all the way to the Contour Path midway between Giant's Castle Pass and Giant's Castle Peak. Turn left to round the main spur coming down from the peak, walking just 2 km on to the hut. It's situated next to a scenic tarn which provides excellent photographs.

The next day head back to the intersection with the Giant's Ridge Pass. Now is a good time to take a careful look at your map to estimate what lies ahead. You will know, for example, that what at first appears to be an easy walk between the intersection and the hut is not level at all. The Contour Path always ascends and descends when rounding spurs, and descends and then ascends at river or gully crossings: it's the natural thing to do. Between the hut and this intersection, although you seem to be rounding only one major spur, you have also crossed six gullies which all add to the upping and downing. Now look at the path ahead: I count 44 stream crossings (not all will have water all year), and as many ridges. That's how many times you'll be shifting gear, and then some more because there are more pleats to the landscape than there are side streams.

In some instances you gain or lose only a few metres, while at other places the difference is as much as 60 or 70 m – look carefully at the contour intervals. At least this path is good and mostly wide: imagine the early hikers who had no paths to follow, and that should cheer you.

The intersections at Giant's, Langalibalele and Bannerman ridges are marked by cairns and signposts (every few years they seem to reproduce new ones which keep crumbling). Bannerman Hut is located a short distance up (to the left) of the path, on a knoll where Bannerman Pass begins.

On the third day you have to backtrack for 5 km to a vlei where the Bannerman Ridge path branches off to the left. There's always a chance to see antelope, large birds, even jackals here, so keep alert, as well as for wild flowers that are apparent everywhere in all seasons but winter.

The very last part of this hike always seems the cruellest. For kilometres before the end you can see the rest camp up ahead as you follow more of a drainage line than a stream (which gets slushy in summer). Then, instead of the path crossing the Bushman's River and taking you straight to the bar, you have to head downstream, away from the camp, slog up the steep path to the picnic site, and only then make a sharp right to coast home. I curse the route maker every time I climb that steep cement path to the picnic site.

And no, I don't know who Bannerman was but I suspect he may have been associated with Colonel Durnford and the 75th Regiment – the notorious pass blowers.

LOTHENI VIA CONTOUR PATH — HIKE GC8

Route: From Giant's Hut, along the base of Giant's Castle on the Contour Path to Sheba's Breasts and down the Little Berg to Lotheni camp
Distance: 31 km
Duration: 10 to 12 hours, 2 days
Grade: Severe
General: The grading for this hike is given not so much for the climb up to Giant's Hut, nor even for the overall distance, as for the impressive 5-km descent to Lotheni camp site. You could walk from Lotheni to Giant's, if your heart can handle the look of that climb. Although Giant's Hut is a convenient place to break the hike, it still leaves a hard 20-km hike the next day so it's advised that you break on the flat ground somewhere near the eChibini tarns (17 km), which are outside the game reserve area so it's safe to camp. It's a hard choice I know, but it's yours.

To reach Giant's Hut proceed past Durnford's Camp towards the Main Caves, cross Two Dassie Stream via the footbridge and head below the caves into the Bushman's River Valley. Follow the signposts up the side of Giant's Ridge and eventually crest the ridge and reach the Contour Path 2 km shy of the hut.

From Giant's Hut continue eastwards along the Contour Path. Follow the base of Giant's Castle past South Ridge, loop around The Needle, climb gently passing the Oribi Ridge junction, and then traverse below The Gable. Directly below The Gable, 5 km from the hut, you'll pass a side junction to the left that leads to Highmoor, a very pleasant but distant satellite camp of Giant's Castle that has a camp site and trout dam.

The path rises briefly from this junction but soon levels off for nearly 2 km and finally descends gently between the end of Giant's Castle and a small koppie that heralds your

164 giant's castle

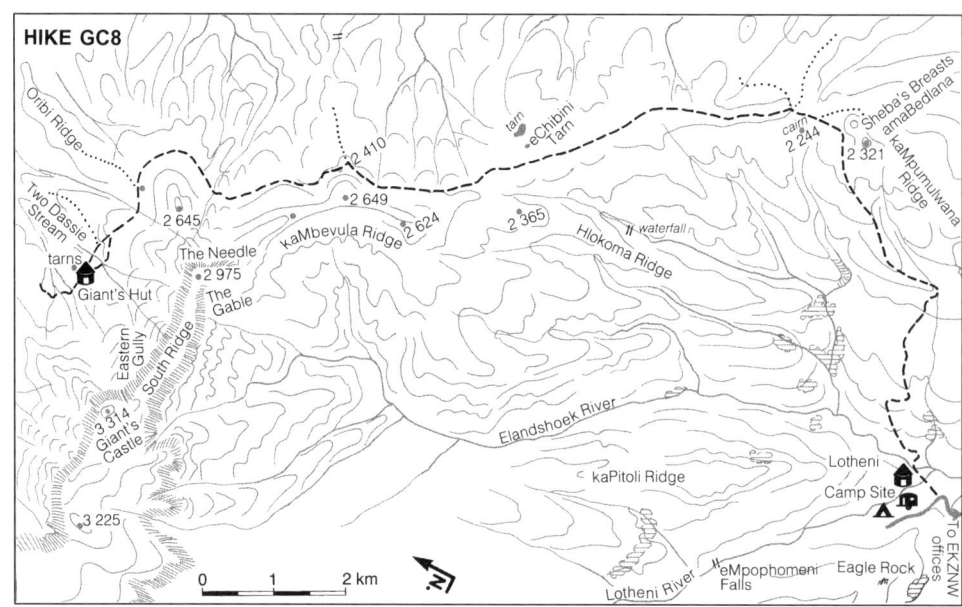

arrival at the tarns. If you do decide to camp here then head off to the left to the top of one of many gullies to find water.

From the eChibini area you gaze down into the lovely Lotheni Valley, although 'magnificent' might be a better word to describe the Drakensberg's major landforms and biggest rivers. To the south myriad streams leap and tumble down towards Lotheni, with patches of brilliant green forest hiding in the narrowest gorges. Beyond them is Hlokoma Ridge, and beyond that kaPitoli and only then, some 6 km distant, the actual Lotheni River.

From the tarns the path rolls easily for 3.5 km, losing height very slowly, to Sheba's Breasts (in Zulu just 'the breasts' – amaBedlana). It's easy to see where their Zulu name comes from, but why they should be Sheba's I can only guess. As you approach Sheba's Breasts two paths marked by a large cairn lead off pretty much to nowhere: the faithful of the southern Berg will at once recognise this as the old Mkhomazi Wilderness Area, the largest and least trampled area of the entire Drakensberg. It's there, for the intrepid among hikers, to discover as it should be – wide, wild open spaces and no-one to hold your hand.

But we must heft our packs and head for another of the less-visited camps. Rounding the south-eastern bulges the path heads out onto a spur where you feel it shouldn't; you'd rather keep well over to the right on the less daunting profile of kaMpumulwana Ridge. But we must stick to the path. Lotheni camp site lies directly ahead but it's 5 km away and about 700 m up. The first 2 km are the killer, losing 300 m down the sharp nose of this ridge. Then it eases off substantially along a grassy apron almost devoid of any intrusions such as boulder outcrops or trees, before taking a 'landing approach' type of lead down the last slope of the Little Berg to cross first a tributary and then the main Lotheni and eventually you reach the camp road. The camp site is about 500 m to the right and the office and chalets 1.5 km to the left. There are also some lovely, lonely cottages for hire.

BANNERMAN PASS — HIKE GC9

Route: From Bannerman Hut to Bannerman Cave
Distance: 9 km return
Duration: 6 hours
Grade: Severe
General: From the hut this is an easy day hike, even though the pass itself is steep. It's one of the easiest Berg passes, but some maps would have you believe it's much harder than it is. There is an obvious path all the way up, and the gradient is never too steep. There is one cave high up in the pass, and a second on the summit, but over a ridge in a valley to the south.

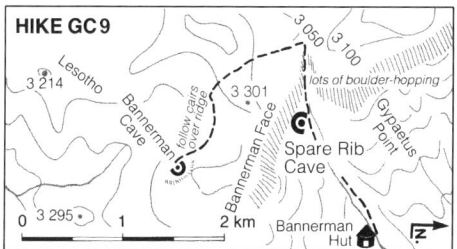

From Bannerman Hut you start up the right-hand side of the stream which flows down the pass (a tributary of Martial Eagle Stream). The path is easy to follow as it picks its way through the somewhat broken terrain round the bottom of the pass, crossing the stream a few times. There are lots of waist-high proteas and this area is particularly rich in wild flowers. From here you should be able to discern that the pass has two sections – a lower approach slope and the very steep gully through which it funnels between the main escarpment cliffs. A large boulder more or less marks the divide.

The path soon starts its zigzagging course, which it maintains all the way to the top. The whole gully is rock-choked, but small cairns mark the entire route: all you have to do is follow them. Even when you seem to lose the path, you can just scramble up the boulders and soon you'll pick it up again. It really is that obvious.

At the base of the cliff line, Spare Rib Cave is located over on the left-hand side of the gully. The traverse across is sloping and a little tricky, and I can't see why anyone would want to use this cave other than as an emergency shelter, but there it is, looking into and down the pass. The pass tops out in a narrow cleft, with the broad expanse of Bannerman Face curving around to the left. You can traverse out to the right into a heavily grazed bowl which is the head of the Sanqebethu River, or you can scramble up the ridge to your left.

To get to Bannerman Cave you have to climb over the high ridge on the southern side of the pass, heading to the left around the highest point, but keeping as close to due south as you can. Once over the ridge you're in Lesotho. Head down the left-hand side of this bowl-shaped valley, across the top of the left-most stream gully. You will need to descend just over 100 m for the next 1 km to locate the large shelter, which faces due west (into Lesotho).

The head of Langalibalele Pass is situated just 1.5 km to the south and is reached either by heading on down the valley you're in on the left-hand side to round a side ridge, then curve round to the left up another stream, or from the cave contour round the bluff you're on (east) and then drop down to the right into the next valley (south). Easy Langalibalele Pass is used by all manner of scavengers, so you are advised not to camp in sight or in view of the head of the pass.

LANGALIBALELE PASS — HIKE GC10

Route: From the rest camp up Langalibalele Ridge to the Contour path, and then to the left up one branch of the Bushman's River
Distance: 9 km one way
Duration: 5 to 6 hours
Grade: Severe to extreme
General: This grading might appear to make this pass tougher than Bannerman but that's only because of the different starting points. You could quite easily walk from the rest camp up this pass and back in a day, with a light day pack.

From the rest camp take the Main Caves path down to cross Two Dassie Stream, then head right below the main caves on the marked Giant's/Langalibalele route. Where the Giant's Ridge path heads off to the left up a knoll, keep right up the main Bushman's River Valley, and head for Grysbok Bush. The path follows the course of the river for a little over 1.5 km, where it splits into side gorges first to the left (the Mtshezi – don't take this path) then to the right.

The path crosses the Bushman's River and then proceeds, not up the river any more but climbing the nose of the ridge, to the right above Grysbok Bush. It's an unrelenting 2-km climb, with the steepest section right in the middle and then easing off towards the Contour Path.

You will almost certainly want to stop here to catch your breath and gird your loins for the final assault. Again the path begins up the spur, following it as it curves round to the left, and then actually contours for a few hundred metres to the river. The Bushman's, or Mtshezi (both this branch and the one coming down Giant's Pass gully are accorded equal status as the source of the Bushman's), is then crossed and from there to the summit the path follows the ramp-like, more flattened left-hand side of the gully.

This is still a well used route over the Drakensberg and you are advised not to camp near the head of this pass or down the Langalibalele Valley in Lesotho, as thievery has

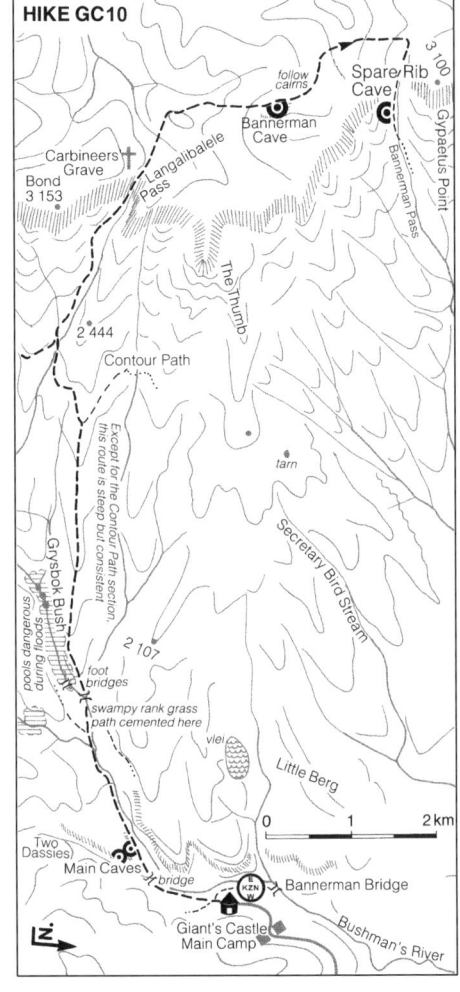

occurred. Either head up to Bannerman Cave (turn sharply up the valley to the right and near the top take a diagonal course up and across to the left – the cave is about 1 km to the left and 100 m higher than the top of this valley), head down, or traverse south along the Escarpment. You could do a round-trip up this pass and down Bannerman, overnighting in Bannerman Cave or Hut. The more attractive round-trip is why a one-way distance only is given.

GIANT'S PASS   HIKE GC11

Route: From the rest camp, up Giant's Ridge to the Contour Path, right for 2 km and up the pass to the nek separating Giant's Castle from the main Drakensberg
Distance: 14 km
Duration: About 7 hours
Grade: Extreme
General: This is not anyone's favourite route to the top of the Berg, but it does get you to the top of one of the most scenic areas, and once on top the walking southwards is superb and very easy for two or three full days if you avoid the main peaks. The lower section of the pass, though, is a complete enigma, the middle section totally confusing, and the upper section steep, rocky and not easy to follow. It might have been with this route in mind that James Thurber wrote the lines: 'The way is long and getting longer. The road goes uphill all the way, and even further. I wish you luck, you'll need it.'

The route from the rest camp up Giant's Ridge to the Contour Path has already been fully described in hike GC5, so I'll not repeat that part here; if you're going up the pass, this section will not be your concern, especially since you are directed all the way.

Once you reach the Contour Path you must turn right and proceed for exactly 2 km (though how you measure this I'm not sure): the path first ascends for about 80 m in altitude, turns right and crosses a stream, then continues around two prominent spurs and crosses two obvious streams. Once there (the fourth stream from where you joined the Contour Path), the pass path hives off up the spur to your left.

However, most hikers seem to carry on along the contour for almost another 1 km, around two more spurs to reach the main Bushman's River gorge and head up that. Consequently, this lower section is a maze of paths, some leading somewhere but most giving you plenty of options for finding your own route.

The official path (the one indicated on the EKZNW map number 3) carries on up the spur described and slowly works its way round to the right, over the ridge and into the depression on the other side. From there it takes a jagged course up to the right, working its way along the rocky slope below the massive, unnamed face and huge flake at the western hinge of the Castle. Slingsby's map shows the path going all the way up the Bushman's River's left-hand bank. But you can't, because it's so heavily eroded in places the bank has washed away and you'll find yourself grovelling up rubble banks while looking for the route.

Just as you approach the base of the cliffs along the official route, about 200 m shy of the main gully, you will pass the small shelter of Giant's Cave, which can be used if you have no other

168 giant's castle

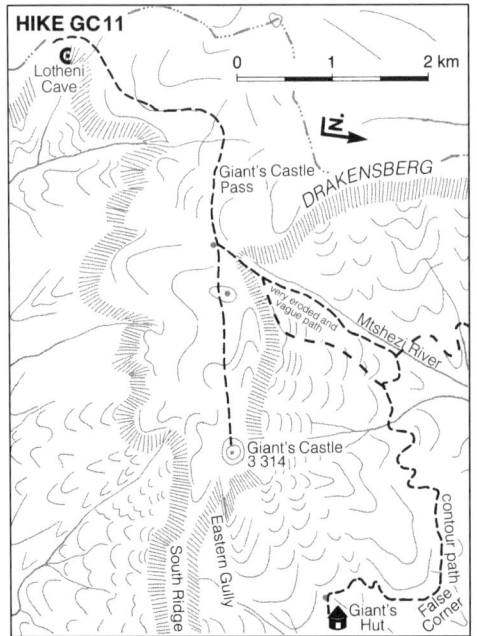

looking in the sky above the cliffs and you could very well see these huge, falcon-shaped birds soaring on the updraughts. Ahead of you lies the bowl of the upper Lotheni Valley, with the Tent, the Hawk and then Redi Peak as obvious landmarks, like sentinels guarding the ramparts of an ancient and gigantic castle that is the Escarpment.

There is level ground directly below, but it gets swampy in summer and brittle with hoarfrost in winter. Water is obtainable either over a small lip further down the slope or several hundred metres along a bridle path to the right. For me, this is one of the spots in the Drakensberg where the voices of nature seem to sing their most vaunted praise songs.

There is a good network of paths in Giant's Castle Reserve and in adjoining areas of the park, and this book cannot describe them all. All you need to walk to the less visited places including World's View and Wildebeest Plateau, The Lakes and Oribi Ridge is a good map. You should be able to buy a copy of the EKZNW hiking map number 3 at the shop, but they do run out of stock from time to time.

shelter (there is none on top). There is also a usable shelter a little higher up on the right-hand side of the main gully at the cliff base.

Once you reach the main cliffs, you should pick up a more prominent path that is marked by small cairns. If you can't, then make your way over to the right-hand side of the gully and work your way upwards: there is a path here so you should find it if you stay alert.

I constantly repair cairns that have crumbled or are ambiguous (I think of it as my particular hiking mission; call me the cairn man if ou will), and you can do that too, to make them stand out. This is not only to make it safer for those who follow, but also to ensure we all stick to the correct path and don't go making new ones all over the place.

The top of this pass, when you finally get there, makes it all worth while. You top out among a pile of boulders, where on each side rise the massed, dark walls of the Escarpment. Lammergeiers are very common so keep

You can also start at the lesser known Highmoor or Hillside camp sites to take less trodden paths into the Little Berg, in order to discover its secret valleys bursting with small forests, waterfalls and resplendent pools. Some people consider Highmoor to be the best secret of the Drakensberg.

The EKZNW maps are superb in this respect, showing very clearly the state of the paths and the nature of the landforms.

Private hiking guide and honorary ranger Dave Sclanders has a permit to take hikers into secret valleys and caves of the Little Berg, and to sleep in unmarked caves in the Giant's and Injisuthi areas. He also knows of Bushman painting sites – and other secrets of the Berg – that no-one else does. Refer to 'Useful contacts' (page 232) for his details.

mkhomazi

The Drakensberg used to be a jigsaw of land ownership until the U-D Park was declared several years ago under EKZNW (when the old Natal Parks Board and KwaZulu Nature Conservation departments amalgamated). Wilderness areas fell away within the park, although the two old game reserves, Giant's Castle and Royal Natal, have (for historical reasons not fully clear to us mere walkers) been retained as management entities within the new park. South of Giant's Castle, most of the entire southern half of the Berg fell into either the Mkhomazi or Mzimkhulu wilderness areas, studded within which, like raisins in a Christmas cake, were some small reserves such as Loteni (Lotheni), Kamberg, Highmoor and Vergelegen. Both their conservation status and management policies were different from those of the wilderness areas because the reserves existed before these were proclaimed in the early 1970s.

In the second edition of *Drakensberg Walks* I changed the names of Mkhomazi and Mzimkhulu to Cobham and Garden Castle respectively, but that caused confusion. Because they fall under more conservation offices than just two, I've chosen to retain the very widely accepted geographical descriptions and the names of the two major rivers of the respective regions. There is no 'right' name for them (although it's true that now Cobham and Garden Castle are the two larger, main KZN offices of the two areas).

The EKZNW offices serving this area are at Lotheni, Kamberg (from where it is not practical to access the main Drakensberg – but it has its attractions as we shall see), Vergelegen and Mkhomazi, which used to be a forest station. This area is better known by fly-fishermen than by hikers, as the Mooi, Lotheni and Mkhomazi rivers (as well as the Pholela to the south) are stocked with trout. The Mkhomazi area is the least-visited area of the Berg where there are EKZNW offices and rest camps. In many ways this is a pity, since it is a place of big rivers, caves galore and numerous easy summit passes. The reason it is less visited than all the other areas is because the Escarpment or high Berg is far from the various rest camps. Kamberg in particular, which lies due east of Giant's Castle, has seven trout-filled dams on the Mooi River, and the rest camp is jealously guarded as the domain of fishermen. Some new bungalows have been built, and there is a camp site. But what should attract other visitors is the Bushman Rock Art Interpretive Centre from where walking tours are conducted to Games Pass Shelter, arguably the most important rock art site in South Africa. It was there that the art of the Bushmen was first seriously studied, in the 1920s. It was from the panel dubbed the Rosetta Stone that the connection between the art and the supernatural was first discerned. A high quality film which puts the cave and its paintings into a universal perspective is shown before each tour (there is a reasonable charge for the full tour package – see hike MK2, page 175).

The cave is easily reached in one hour along a very well-constructed path. There are several distinct panels, starting with some faded scenes, then the Rosetta Stone, and finally the main attraction which is a section a few metres across where numerous polychrome eland seem to walk right across the rock wall. You should not miss it.

Lotheni rest camp is also used mainly by trout fishermen, but it has a nice hutted camp and a camp site from which the popular peaks of Redi, the Hawk and the Tent are reached. Lotheni Pass itself is neither easy nor convenient (it's a slog up past Ash Cave), but Hlathimba and Mlahlangubo passes to the south are much easier. The latter two are accessed from Vergelegen camp. Vergelegen is in fact the most popular starting point for hikers as it gives access to many of the easier passes, as well as to Thaba Ntlenyana, at 3 482 m the highest point in southern Africa. Unfortunately one of the two chalets burned down, and the other is the home of the officer in charge, so rudimentary camping facilities only are provided. There are plans to upgrade the camp and the hiking paths around Vergelegen, but, as the officer told me, other financial concerns take priority at the moment. The two most direct routes to this peak (really a high point about four kilometres inland on the kaNtuba Ridge) are Nhlangeni and kaNtuba but, as both are long and hard, Mkhomazi Pass is the one most often taken. It's also a long haul up from Vergelegen, but as it was originally intended to be the road route up to Lesotho before the construction of Sani Pass, it's easy going.

The other passes that give hikers reasonable access to the summit are (from north to south) eNtubeni, Hlathimba (all of its three branches), Mlahlangubo and Phinong, which is the main dagga smuggling route down from Lesotho and should be avoided. It is not often recognised that this section of the Berg includes many of its highest 'kulus', some of which are well known. Redi Peak (3 314 m) is a favourite one for summit hikers to bag and often the aim of hiking parties. To the south are two 'kulus' one seldom hears of, but Mohlesi (3 301 m) and kaNtuba (3 355 m) stand out among giants.

A small and inexperienced party set out from Lotheni one sunny Friday in July, under the leadership of medical student David Harrison. They were bound for Lotheni Cave, up the already snow-filled and never very pleasant kaMashilenga Pass, and a hike they will never forget. That was the weekend of the 'big snow' of 1988. Harrison, his sister and two friends were not equipped for snow (they had no tent and only one had proper boots), and even before they reached the summit they were wading through deep drifts. That they reached the top at all is an indication of either their tenacity or their foolhardiness. They never found the cave; in fact snow covered everything and they couldn't recognise any feature at all. Near tragedies led to amazing escapes, first over the lip of the Escarpment (down sheer cliffs, using the snow as a cushion as they leapt over precipices and down ice falls), and then into a tiny shelter that finally saved their lives (but not all their digits from frostbite). For three days helicopter rescuers searched for them, finally locating Harrison, who had left the other three to go for help, in the maze of Little Berg ridges and valleys where they had gone off course. It's a harrowing story, and well worth locating a copy of Reg Pearse's book *The Dragon's Wrath* (later published under the name of his co-author James Byrom), for the full account. Another favourite of mine in this book is the story of how the crippled photographer Gunter Stein finally conquered the Amphitheatre, and so very nearly died doing it.

Sani Pass was originally a mule route over the mountains until, in 1955, David Alexander and friends began constructing a road for their Land Rovers, so they could trade between Himeville and Mokhotlong. So the Mokhotlong Mountain Transport Company (MMT) was created, and the pass which it made famous. Over the years Cruisers, Hiluxes and others joined the Land Rover, and the pass was continuously upgraded. A simple inn was built at the top of the pass to give shelter to travellers. Some years ago it came into the hands of Jonathan Aldous whose family had run the Himeville Arms for many years, and it has since been expanded – but the spirit remains the same at 'southern Africa's highest pub'. MMT was sold and moved to Underberg, where it became Sani Pass Tours (as it is still known). There are now plans afoot to tar the pass. This idea is greatly favoured by the Lesotho 4x4 minibus taximen and other traders who ply the pass in their heavily laden bakkies. But the thought shocks mountaineers and the owners of Sani Top Lodge as well as the three or four tour companies that ferry sight-seers up the pass every day of the year that it is not closed by snow or rockfalls. A fair compromise between these two opposing interest groups might be to upgrade the pass but keep the surface gravel. A tarred road through the heart of the Drakensberg World Heritage Site does seem to me to be a travesty – but then I don't have to make my living up and down it as a taxi-driver.

The old Giant's Cup Motors, which used to be the base for MMT, is now Sani Lodge backpackers' lodge and tea garden. The ruins you see at the bottom of the pass are those of Ridgeway's Store, which did not survive the building of a 4x4 route into Lesotho. The main establishment in the upper Mkhomozana Valley is the wall-enclosed Sani Pass Hotel which does not encourage hikers or day visitors, and is more of a golfing resort and conference centre. There is another small guesthouse on a farm in the valley, although I have not visited it. If you plan to visit Sani Top Lodge, and you should not miss this mountain highlight, you can take advantage of the two-night package offered by Himeville Arms and the lodge, including a 4x4 trip up the pass. If you time it right you could get snowed in for several days (the statistics say late July is the most likely time for this). Just take good boots.

172 mkhomazi

There are skis at the lodge, which look as if they were bought as a job lot from the *Dromedaris*. Following a land swap whereby EKZNW gained the farm Duart Castle, the old Mkhomazi Trail has ceased to be; the huts at Surprise, Kerry, Bundoran and Glenora are ruins, and a valley that was once pristine wilderness now rings with the busy sounds of people, cattle and minibuses.

CONTOUR PATH: LOTHENI TO SANI PASS — HIKE MK1

Route: Lotheni camp site to Sani Pass
Distance: 58 km
Duration: 4 or 5 days
Grade: Extreme
General: The Contour Path is not continuous across the Mkhomazi area, at times descending to below the Little Berg and at one point climbing to the top of the main Escarpment and traversing it for about 3 km. However, for hikers looking for a real challenge, this is it. You can also extend the hike by two days by starting at Giant's rest camp and heading for Giant's Hut for the first night (see hike GC5).

Day 1 (12 km): From the Lotheni hutted site at 1 500 m head up the left-hand bank of the Ngodwini River, below Eagle Rock on your right and past the waterfall in a side stream on the left 4 km from camp. A little over 4 km, where you ascend two steepish ridges, brings you to the Contour Path at 2 350 m, near a tarn.

At this point you are standing directly below massive Redi Peak (3 314 m). This pass should not be attempted by hikers. Turn left here. After 2 km you will come to Buttress Pass or The Passage running up a spur between two minor stream gullies. Another 1 km brings you to the eMbaxeni Stream which is the suggested camping spot.

An alternative route starts at Lotheni camp site and follows the left-hand bank of that river up to the Contour Path, past Yellowwood Cave (see hike MK5, page 186). This extends the hike by 5 km. It meets the Contour Path at the base of kaMashilenga Pass which is therefore often used as the route to the summit, but it is not recommended at all as it is steep and eroded and involves tricky scrambling.

Day 2 (7 km): This is a shortish day because of having to climb Hlathimba Pass which you want to do as fun and not torture. From the camp site continue on the contour for a little over 1 km and then descend to the Hlathimba River. Here you round the Buttress, a narrow headland which terminates in the Fingers. You have a straightforward climb up a grassy slope taking the left stream gully (two other possible routes go up to the right, branching again after 500 m), and by doing this you'll be following many historic ascents (including the one done by the Carbineers under Major Durnford). It's one of the Berg's two or three easiest ascents and takes you past the small but dry Hlathimba Cave.

Head south along the top of the Drakensberg, round the back of Duart Castle across an almost level valley where the walking is easy. Lynx Cave is found 1.5 km south, one buttress past Duart Castle, just over the lip of the Escarpment (it faces north into a minor gully). It's a fairly decent cave and well sheltered in bad weather (and it comfortably sleeps six) but can be difficult to

mkhomazi 173

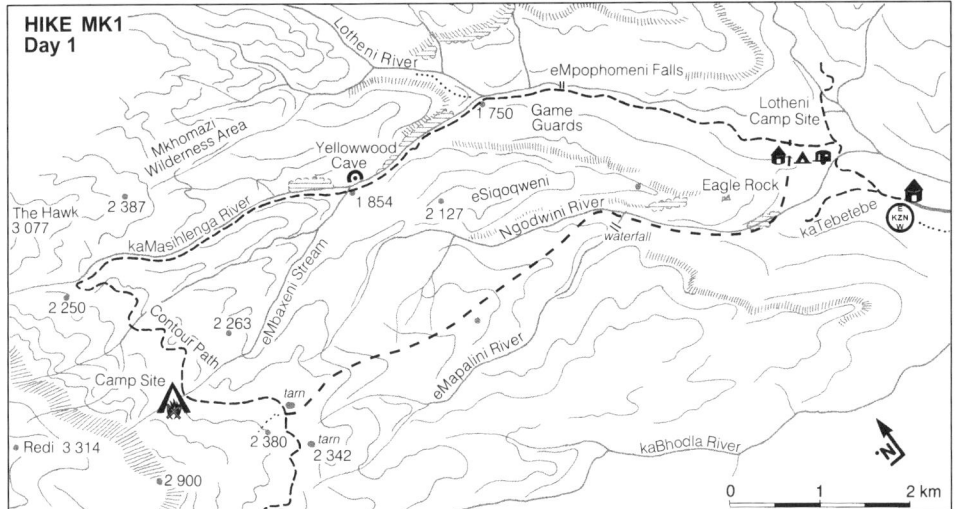

locate and often is wet in summer. A better option in this case is the cave near the top of Hlathimba Pass. This cave will be found 40 m from the summit, and slightly above on the left.

Day 3 (19 km): After an easy day comes this long one. From Lynx Cave continue south for just over 1 km to the head of Mlahlangubo Pass, an easy grassy descent on the south side of the main Mlahlangubo omkhulu Stream. It reaches the Contour Path after 1.5 km, but from this point on the path is (to be kind) vague and you will have to keep your senses to stay on it.

You begin by ascending a grassy spur for about 750 m, then angle back towards the Escarpment. For the next 2 km the path dips in and out of numerous stream gullies, generally descending to the base of Ngaqamadola Pass up the Mlahlangubo omhoane Stream. Round two spurs 1.5 km further on and you come to an alternative ascent route, starting up the ridge.

For the next 5 km the path takes you on a wide, convoluted loop under The Saddle, crossing so many streams you lose count. These all flow down to the Mkhomazi whose head is on the north side of the prominent triangular Nhlangeni Peak (3 068 m). The last 2 km to the Mkhomazi River goes steeply down a prominent ridge. You could break here if you plan to do the last 25-km section in two days. Otherwise take courage and head away from the Escarpment for 4 km, along the spur running out from Nhlangeni Peak and crossing a stream gully. Do not take the path down the Mkhomazi River, as it's a 15-km journey to Vergelegen EKZNW office which has no accommodation.

After 4 km the path turns sharply round a spur to head back towards the Escarpment and the Nhlangeni River is reached another 1 km on. This is the recommended stop, where the Nhlangeni Pass heads up the valley for 5 km.

Day 4 (20 km): Contour for 2 km and you come to a muddy spring on a side stream that issues sulfurous water (there is a path here down into the Mkhomazi Valley). The path meanders around kaNtuba Ridge, across two small gullies and then descends to the kaNtuba River. It crosses the river and heads up a grassy slope on the other side for just over 1 km. Look out for the turn to the left or you might find yourself climbing Manguan Pass.

About 1 km after the turnoff you come to what appears to be a T-junction, where you must turn right and so not descend the spur, but contour for a short way and then descend to the Ntshintshini River (one of many spellings for the ouhout bush).

Cross the river and for the next 2.5 km loop along the base of Mqatsheni to reach the crest of Burnera Ridge. One path goes down the ridge for nearly 20 km, while the Contour Path continues around to the right into the Mqatsheni Valley. This is a possible camp site for a 5-day trip.

The next 4 km winds in and out of several stream gullies to cut across the large Phinong cutback, passing under The Pillars at 1.5 km. This brings you to the crest of the Koko Tabagi Ridge extending down from the jutting out Phinong Peak.

Once you round this ridge you will be looking into the Mkhomazana (little Mkhomazi) Valley, at least as impressive as the Mkhomazi and maybe more so because of the impossible Sani Pass road that winds up it. From the ridge it is 6 km to the road, winding under the Twelve Apostles. This section is in shade most of the time. You will descend about 250 m along the course, and reach the pass 2.5 km above the police post. It's a further 10 km from there to the Sani Lodge backpackers' place and you will have to arrange transport down.

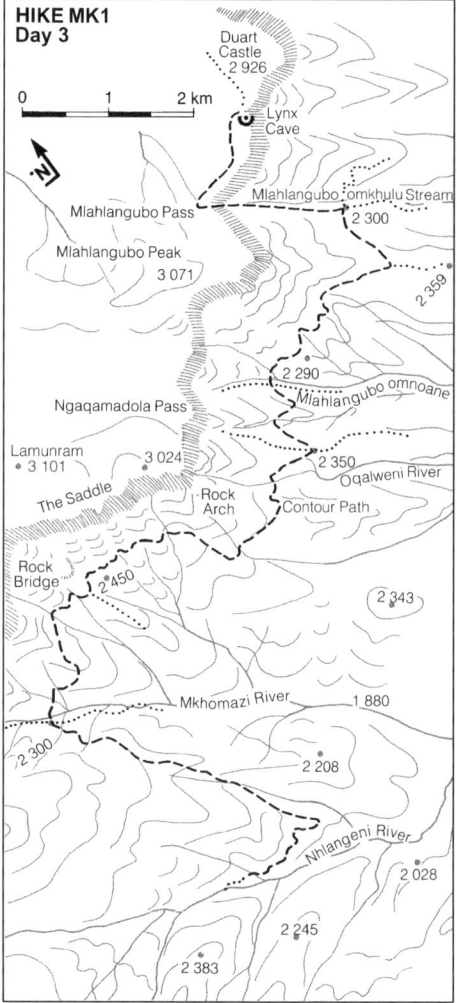

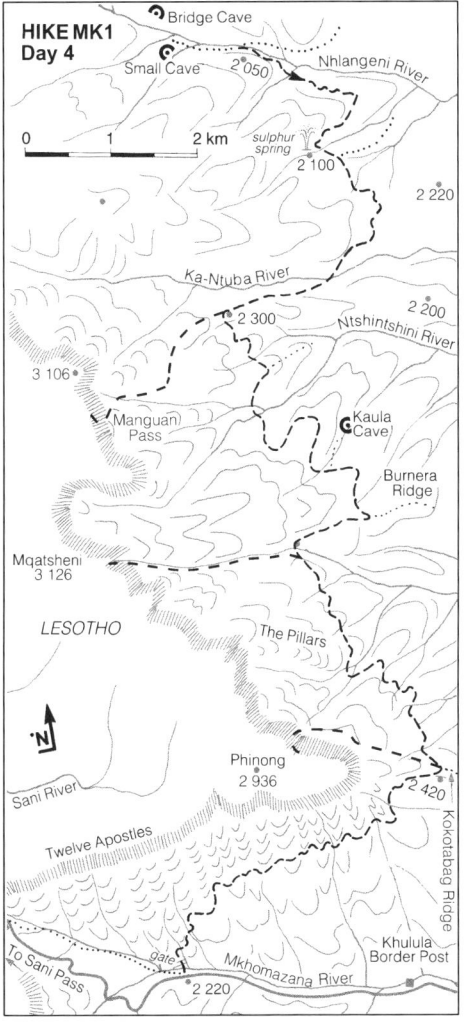

PACKING TIPS

- Packing usually stymies most people, even regulars.
- I follow a simple rule: clothes in the bottom compartment, all the rest in the top.
- Compress your sleeping bag at the bottom of the top bit.
- The large side pockets hold the stove and gas cylinders.
- The smaller pockets take things like head torch, penknife, cutlery, batteries and snacks – for easy access.
- All my food is pre-packed into packets and plastic containers.
- I use containers and plastic bottles of all sizes for different things: film canisters for sauces, spices, and sugar.
- Peanut butter jars do for hot chocolate, coffee and the like.
- Ice-cream tubs work for bulk.
- I always pack a small sample bottle of dish-washing liquid and a washing sponge.
- A small chopping board and serrated knife go too – people laugh on day one: by the end everyone's using them.

GAME PASS SHELTER — HIKE MK2

Route: Kamberg rest camp to Little Berg Cave
Distance: 6 km return
Duration: About 3 hours
Grade: Easy
General: There are other short walks in the Kamberg reserve, which lies on the delightful Mooi River, past Giant's Castle on the Nottingham Road/Bulwer gravel road, but other than this rock

176 mkhomazi

art experience it's a place for fly-fishers. At the time of writing in 2002 an interpretive centre had just been completed and I was one of the first people to see the excellent audio-visual show on the Bushmen and their spiritual art heritage. This show and the guided tour cost R40 in 2002, but will no doubt increase over the years. It is worth every cent. There is no better way or place to see rock art, and this experience far exceeds that at the Giant's Main Caves (hike GC1, page 154). Accommodation is in small bungalows.

The path is well laid out, wide and regularly maintained, so is acceptable for just about anyone who can walk and climb stairs – it's only 3 km to the shelter but you still have to climb to near the top of the Little Berg.

The path does get steep towards the end at the cliff line. Although the main eland frieze is the most impressive feature, the Rosetta Stone panel has even greater significance, as is clearly explained by Professor David Lewis-Williams in the video which forms part of the tour.

I was told by my guide it was named after a person called Rosetta, but that's a rural myth. It's a semantic pun on the more famous Rosetta Stone of ancient Egypt that was the key to unlocking the secret hieroglyphic texts. So it was with this Rosetta Stone and Bushman art.

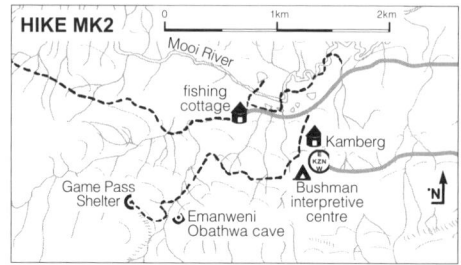

HIKE MK2

CAMERA TIPS

- Use Fuji Velvia or Provia films for slides.
- Fuji and Agfa have good 100–200 ASA negative film.
- Good pics need a tripod.

CYPRESS CAVE AND SINCLAIR'S SHELTER — HIKE MK3

Route: Mkhomazi EKZNW office to Cypress Cave
Distance: 8 km return
Duration: 2 hours out and 1½ return, or 2 days
Grade: Easy
General: This is a fine way to experience a night or two in a cave without a major slog first. The shelter comfortably sleeps up to six and is close to the Nzinga River. It was an area heavily infested with wattles but for some years the Working for Water people have been busy and over time should eradicate them. You might also see some ruins along the way, evidence that this area was once extensively farmed. This hike is suitable for children of just about any age.

There is no accommodation at Mkhomazi (there is a picnic site at the turnoff at Nzinga Falls), and only two hiking trails lead out from it. One heads north to Cypress and Sinclair's caves, and the other is a new one to McKenzie's Caves. Head out on the north-bound path and loop

ABOVE: Looking across the Old Woman Stream Valley, the Old, snow-dusted Woman Grinding Corn is on the extreme left and Monk's Cowl and Cathkin Peak on the right.
RIGHT: Winter can be an extreme time to be caught on the Drakensberg summit, but in the Little Berg (at Grindstone Caves), it can be sublime.

TOP: A frigid July morning breaks in Wonder Valley Cave.
ABOVE: 10-cm-high everlastings are typical of the summit vegetation.
RIGHT: Hiking across the Little Berg plateau from Injisuthi to Giant's Castle – after a snowstorm, warm winter sun.

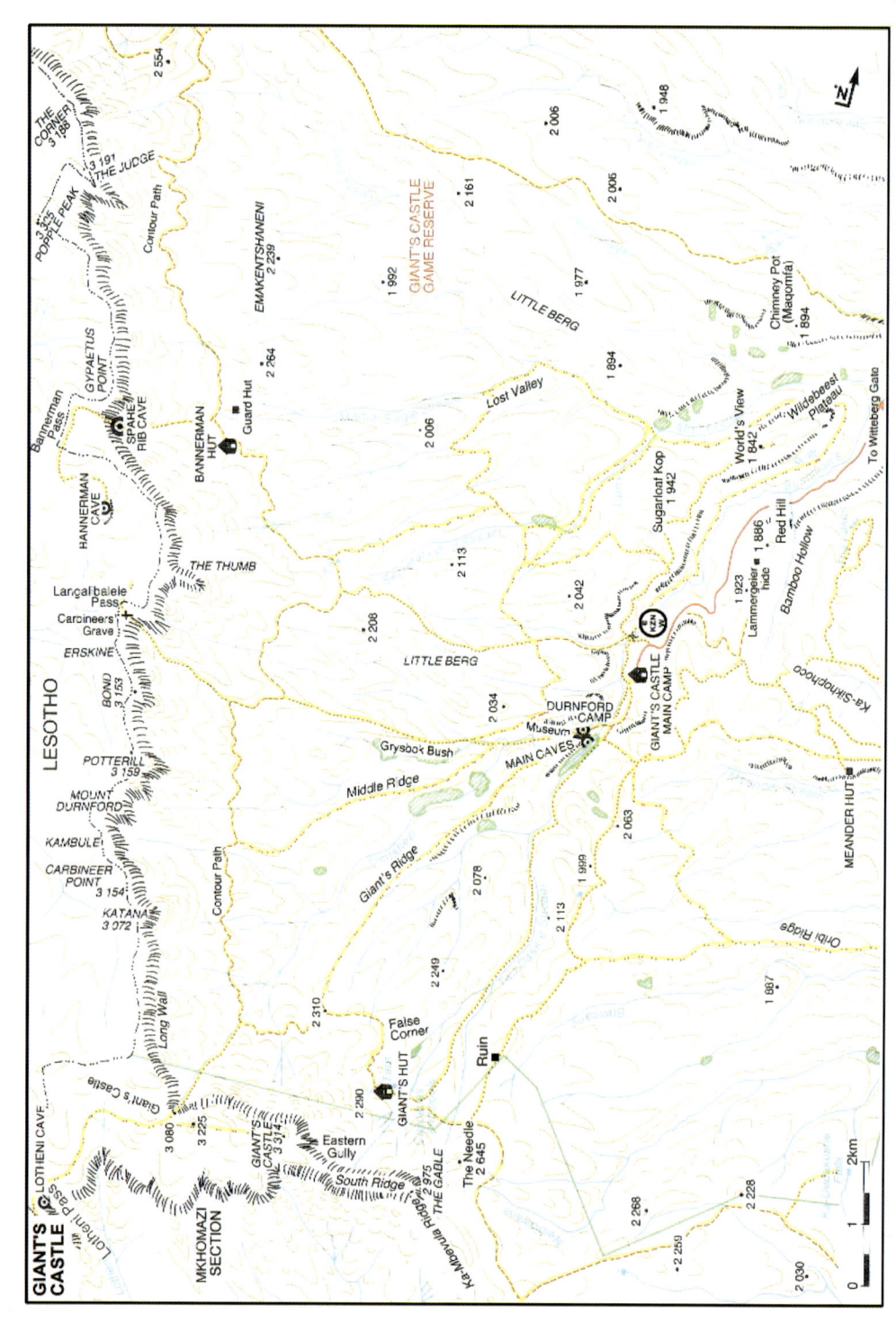

ABOVE: The small tarn in front of Giant's Hut, on the Contour Path directly below the massive 'castle', is a favourite drinking spot of antelope including grey rhebuck, mountain reedbuck, eland and oribi.

LEFT: A few of the hundreds of small flowerheads on an everlasting bush, each the size of a small coin. These plants are otherwise known as *Helichrysums*, or sun flowers in Greek, for obvious reason. Although Latin was the language of choice for early taxonomists, they retained any earlier Greek names.

LEFT: Heading for Redi Peak, one of the 'kulus' of the Southern Berg.
TOP: The ice fall at the top of Lotheni Pass is a favourite winter ice-climbing venue.
ABOVE: Setting up camp near the top of Ka-Masihlenga Pass.

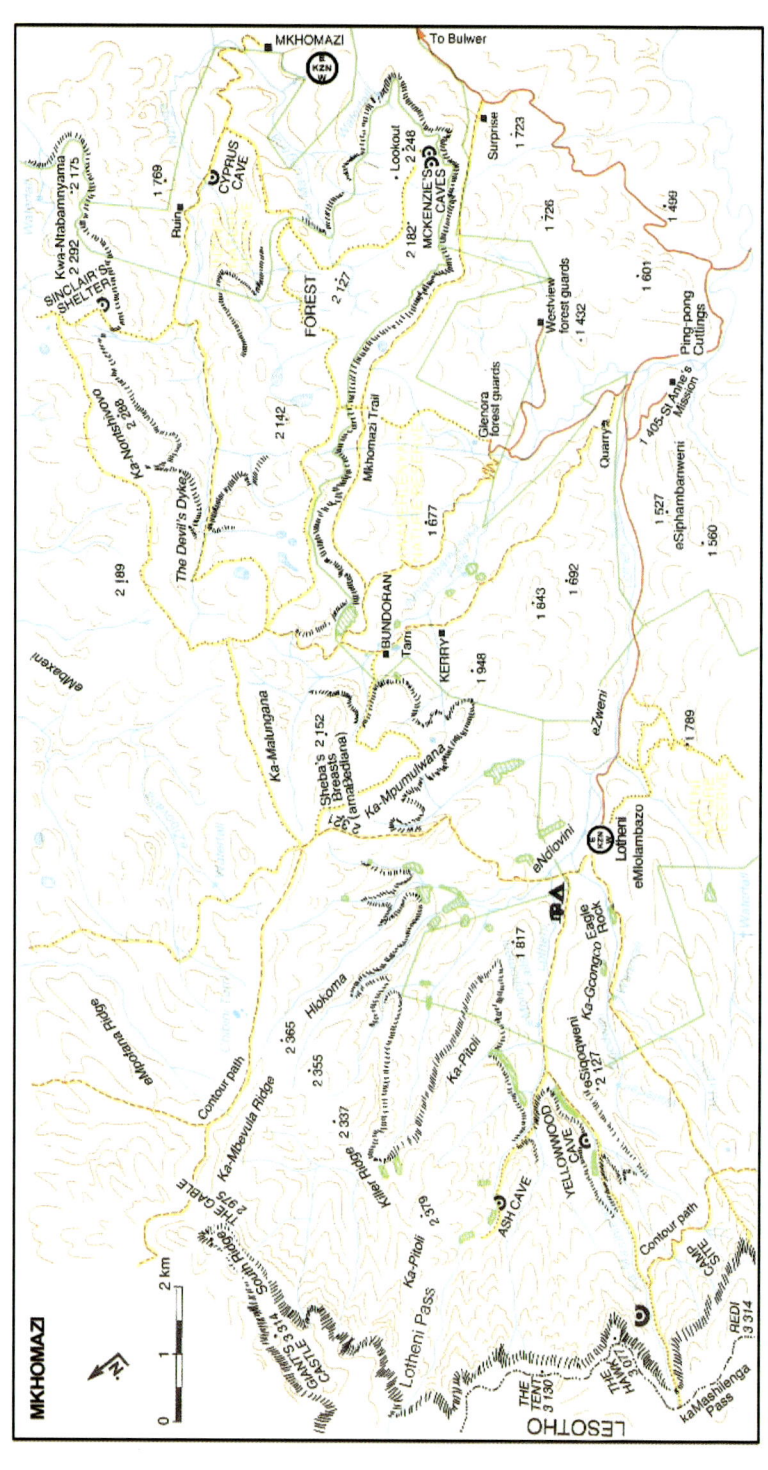

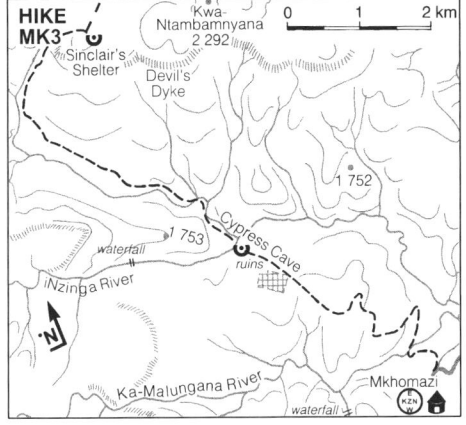

around to the left to the Nzinga River. Cross the river and for the next 2 km zigzag in wide loops up the first step of the Little Berg, which in this area is 20 to 30 km from the High Berg.

The gradient lessens off and the path passes first a side junction to the right and then a four-way crossing, both of which are closed to hikers. About 500 m further along a level plateau a path leads off to the left to lose itself in the Little Berg maze. Keep right and descend gently for 1.2 km to the cave, looking down to the confluence of the two main tributaries of the Nzinga. From Cypress Cave cross the stream and head to the right around the nose of a spur to follow the left-hand bank of the Nzinga River for about 800 m to a crossing. Cross the river and carry on up the opposite slope for a little over 2 km, heading slowly away from the river. The path then forks, left down to the river and right up towards the Devil's Dyke to the north.

You have to climb right to the top of the Devil's Dyke, heading up a stream gully and then a corner in the 'dyke' wall. The shelter is located in the sloping back (north) side of this wall, looking directly down a stream course.

By continuing up the Nzinga River, along the base of the Devil's Dyke, you can do a very interesting two-day hike around the large tarn area where the dyke joins the kaMalungana Ridge, returning down this ridge.

WALKING TIPS

- Follow the tracks and paths.
- Do not make short cuts.
- Short cuts cause erosion.

McKENZIE'S CAVES — HIKE MK4

Route: From Mkhomazi office to the two caves
Distance: 20 km return
Duration: About 4 hours out and 3 return, or 2 days
Grade: Moderate
General: The old route to the caves used to start off along the Cypress Cave path and then take a wide loop around to the west. There is a new, more direct and signposted path to the two large caves on Makungana Mountain, 1.5 km to the south-east of the lookout tower and repeater mast. The preferred of the two caves is about 250 m from a small stream. Together the caves can sleep more people than you'd want to go walking with (I hope!). Mkhomazi will be out of the way for most people, except those living in the southern Midlands. The road from Giant's Castle (north–south) to Mkhomazi is not too bad but the stretch from there through Lower Lotheni to Himeville and Underberg is worthy of the Tanzanian backwaters.

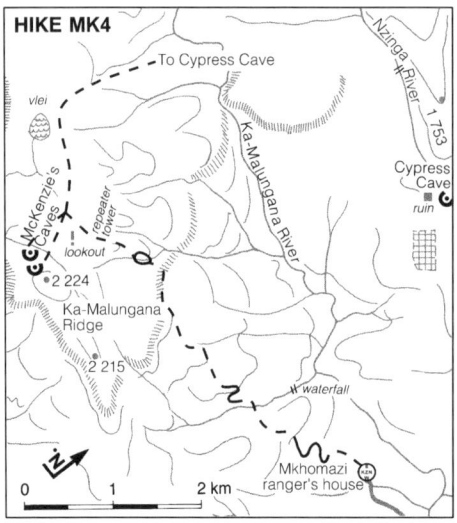

From the EKZNW office (where the routes are signposted) head steeply up a grassy slope onto a ridge above a stream, for 2 km. An old trail goes straight on but the new hiking path heads to the right into the stream valley and ascends steeply up the Little Berg, past a waterfall.

The path reaches a more or less level terrace and continues on between the two prominent points of Makungana 'mountain' (really the high end points of Ka-Malungana Ridge which can be followed all the way to the base of Giant's Castle).

The path passes between the two minor bumps at the edge of the Little Berg, then heads on to pass between two larger ones 1 km further along this flattish terrace. It skirts around the slightly lower one on the left (the one on the right has the towers) and descends a few hundred metres to the first cave. Find the second cave after 200 m, directly west of the first, in the direction in which the caves face. There is no water at either, and the second is further from the stream found at the base of the two high points on the ridge.

YELLOWWOOD CAVE   HIKE MK5

Route: From the Lotheni camp site up the Lotheni and kaMashilenga valleys
Distance: 14 km return
Duration: 3 hours each way
Grade: Strenuous
General: This cave sleeps only four people comfortably, is located in a narrow gorge and is therefore very cold in winter. It is probably the most popular stopover en route to the summit, as it is found on the kaMashilenga Pass route. However, don't be fooled by appearances: this path is not recommended as it involves some tricky negotiating through large boulders and rank vegetation (consider wearing leggings or long pants).

From Lotheni camp site follow the path up the left-hand bank of the river for 5 km, past the eMpophomeni Falls. About 1 km past the falls the path splits around the imposing Little Berg headland and our path then follows the left-hand bank of the left-hand fork (kaMashilenga). The route up the Lotheni to the right, the old path to Ash Cave, is now closed. A forest stretch lines the south-facing right-hand bank of the stream, and Yellowwood Cave is reached just short of 2 km from the previous fork, at a break in the forest and on the left-hand side (not the right, as shown on Slingsby's map) of the valley.

To ascend the pass, if you insist on taking this route, cross the first tributary almost immediately after leaving the cave and the ill-defined path that sticks to the left-hand bank of the river all the way to the summit. It's 6 km to the top of the pass, reaching the start of the Contour Path in this region after a steep 3.5-km scramble. You can camp here as an alternative to using Yellowwood Cave, but you'll struggle to find place to pitch a tent (try a little bit lower down on the opposite side of the stream where there's a level spot for just one tent, sheltered by *intshishi* bushes). It's 10.5 km from the camp site and 2.5 km to the top from this point.

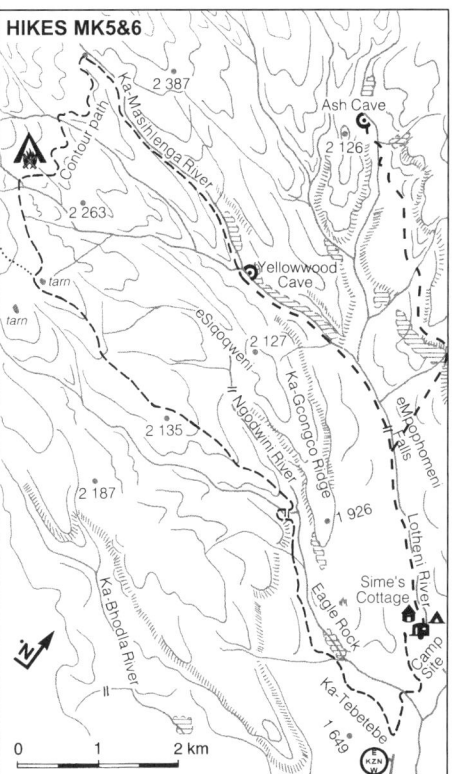

SNAKE-BITE TIPS

- People react differently to snake bites.
- If signs of poisoning begin to show, immobilise the victim.
- Treat the patient symptomatically – and don't over-react.
- Cutting and sucking the wound is of no use.
- A tourniquet damages tissue.

ASH CAVE — HIKE MK6

Route: From the Lotheni camp site, up the Lotheni River to the cave
Distance: 15 km return
Duration: 4 hours out and 3 return
Grade: Moderate
General: While the previous cave is best in summer, I'd choose this one in winter as it is warmer, although it is exposed to wind, so not good in a storm. Once at the cave, however, there is nowhere else to go and the passes up to Lotheni are not hiking routes. So this is ideally suited to an overnight trip or some time out.

From Lotheni camp site take the path up the left-hand bank of the Lotheni River to the eMpophomeni Falls, 3 km up. Although you can continue along this course to Yellowwood Cave, the path further up the Lotheni is now closed.

Therefore cross the river and ascend the slope opposite to gain the Eagle Trail near a forest patch on the next level up.

On reaching the higher level, contour round to the left (north-east) above the Lotheni Valley for 3 km. The cave is situated on the south side of the river, about 100 m up a steep slope and so is really nice in good weather but will be exposed to the onslaughts of bad.

Don't be tempted by old (Slingsby's) maps to try to reach Ash Cave via the Yellowwood Cave route, as that trail over from the ka-Mashilenga Valley really does not 'go' now.

HLATHIMBA PASS AND REDI PEAK — HIKE MK7

Route: From the Lotheni hutted camp up the Ngodwini Stream to the Contour Path, then south to Hlathimba Pass and up to the summit to bag a 'kulu'
Distance: 19 km one way
Duration: Two days (about 12 hours' walking)
Grade: Extreme
General: This is one of the easiest and nicest routes to the summit and gives the chance to ascend one of the Berg's 'kulus' (see page 228). A one-way-only description is given, because you can make a round-trip by taking either Buttress Pass (The Passage) or the less favoured but more direct kaMashilenga Pass down to Lotheni. The return trip can be made in three days, but rather allocate four if you're not familiar with the Berg, or have not hiked to the summit before.

From the hutted camp bear left to take the first path to follow the left-hand side of the Ngodwini Stream, around the side Mapalini (formerly eMpatini) Valley with its waterfall. At this point the path leaves the Ngodwini Valley and heads steeply up the spur between the two streams for 1.5 km to reach the top of the first Little Berg 'step'. You pass a high point to your left and continue gently up for 1.5 km when you have to ascend the second 'step' to reach the Contour Path at a tarn, about 9 km from camp.

It would certainly make a nice camp site and it will do if you're taking two days to the summit, but it's still way too early to think about that if you're headed for the pass. Turn left here and traverse for 2 km around the base of Redi Peak to where The Buttress Pass, also known as The Passage, ascends this buttress – and don't forget the location as this is the recommended descent, from out along the jutting-out buttress south of Redi Peak and not directly down the front of the peak to the tarn, as that requires a rope down one 10-m section.

As you continue along the contour for 500 m a path comes up (or goes down) kaZwelele Ridge. Pass this and another 500 m on you cross the eMbaxeni Stream which is followed by a short ascent (just to test you). Then it continues contouring around to the right for a further 2.5 km to reach the Hlathimba River, which you should cross.

At this point you might realise there are two passes here: one directly up in front of you, in other words up the left-most tributary, and another up the cutback on the right. In fact this cutback route also splits about 250 m further up, but you should attempt these routes only if you know the area well as they are steeper and you could end up under a waterfall if you take the wrong gully.

Stick to the direct left-most tributary and from this point it's an easy grassy climb up the left-hand side of the stream as it is only 1.5 km and about 500 m in altitude: piffling for the Drakensberg. However, once at the top of the pass, if you're not planning to stop over in

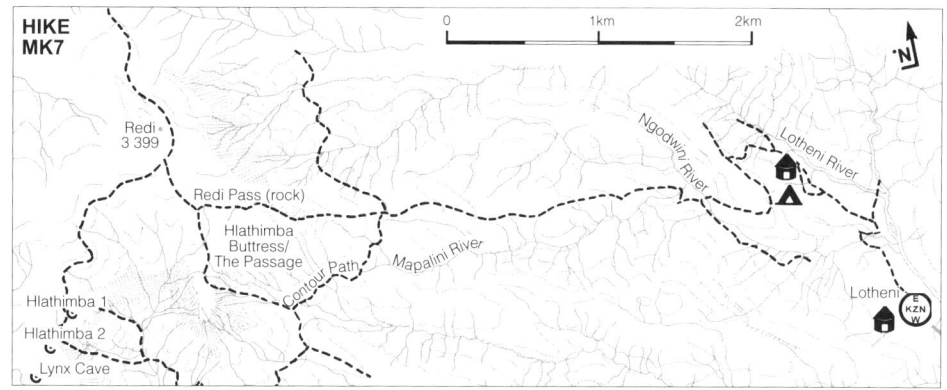

Hlathimba Cave (situated just short of the top of the pass and up to your left) you're still 3.5 km and 500 m short of Redi.

When heading for the summit of Redi do not try to follow the edge of the Escarpment, unless you really want to appreciate the views along the edge (and they are stupendous, with The Buttress creating a deep corner), but take the most direct route following the lie of the land up the high ground in a north-westerly direction. Remember, if returning via The Buttress route, when you have dropped down the first 300 m, do not take the more logical seeming contour to the left, but keep right to walk out onto The Buttress to reach the descent route. Alternatively from the top of Redi head west (the angle of the Escarpment here) for 2.5 km to the head of kaMashilenga Pass.

Don't make the mistake of thinking the Escarpment runs in a north–south direction (it is more north-west–south-east) which could throw your sense of direction. Hlathimba was the first pass well known to white colonists, easy as it is, and featured in early incidents.

NGAQAMADOLA PASSES — HIKE MK8

Route: A possible circular route from Vergelegen hut (the old bungalow now the home of the officer in charge) up Inkangala (iNkangala) Ridge to the summit and down the Mlahlangubo omhoane Stream, or the other way round
Distance: 26-km circular route
Duration: About 7 hours up and 5 down
Grade: Severe to extreme
General: There are actually two parallel passes running up either side of a ridge, one following the main Mlahlangubo omhoane Stream and the other starting on the crest of a ridge south of a southerly tributary (you have to look at the map for this to make sense) and then into this tributary's gully. The easier-than-most passes grading is given because the round-trip is very straightforward and short for a summit hike and experienced hikers will find it surprisingly accommodating. However, not many hikers these days visit Vergelegen, so if you're looking for solitude even on main holidays, this could be your place.

From the Umkomaas homestead take the unmarked path to the left, miss the first left turn (Mkhomazi Pass) and take the second after 100 m to the path leading up Plumpudding Hill and Inkangala Ridge (all unmarked). It starts climbing the Little Berg, rising 350 m over the first 1 km. Then it levels off over the next 1 km to the base of Plumpudding where it rears up again. Here, and 500 m further, paths turn off to the right (north-west) to the Mlahlangubo Valley.

Carry on straight up the zigzags to reach Plumpudding at 2 124 m, and thereafter you have an easier 3 km before the path starts climbing again. The ridge narrows and there are still two obvious steps to surmount before you reach the Contour Path, although in this area it's not the walking highway of further north.

The pass continues straight up the ridge, steeply but never with difficulty. It slowly sidles over to the right-hand slope and makes for the stream. From halfway up the pass it follows the left-hand stream bank all the way to the summit.

On your left is an unnamed high point of 3 006 m, and beyond that Ngaqamadola Peak (3 166 m) and Ridge, and between, the southern Saddle: not nearly as impressive as the one in the Cathedral/Mnweni area, but a saddle nonetheless. Before lies a delightful unnamed valley leading inland to the most wonderful of all valleys on top of the Berg, a side valley of the Mohlesi which Slingsby calls the Boja-ba-tsotse. By following this valley in a generally south-south-west direction to a gorge-like confluence with the Mohlesi where you turn upstream to the left, you can skirt all the impeding high ridge of the Escarpment until you reach kaNtuba Ridge and its extension Thaba Ntlenyana. Hop over the low point on this ridge and it's a short, downhill walk to Sani Top.

When you reach the top of the pass the ground slopes away to your right towards the head of the valley. Just 500 m down, where it levels off but still several hundred metres short of the stream course, you reach the northern arm of Ngaqamadola Pass. The descent is down the right-hand bank of the Mlahlangubo omhoane Stream to the Contour Path. You can continue all the way down this valley to a fork 4.5 km downstream, and then take either fork back to Vergelegen, or you can head south along the Contour Path, around a spur, over a stream, to the crest of Inkangala Ridge and down that.

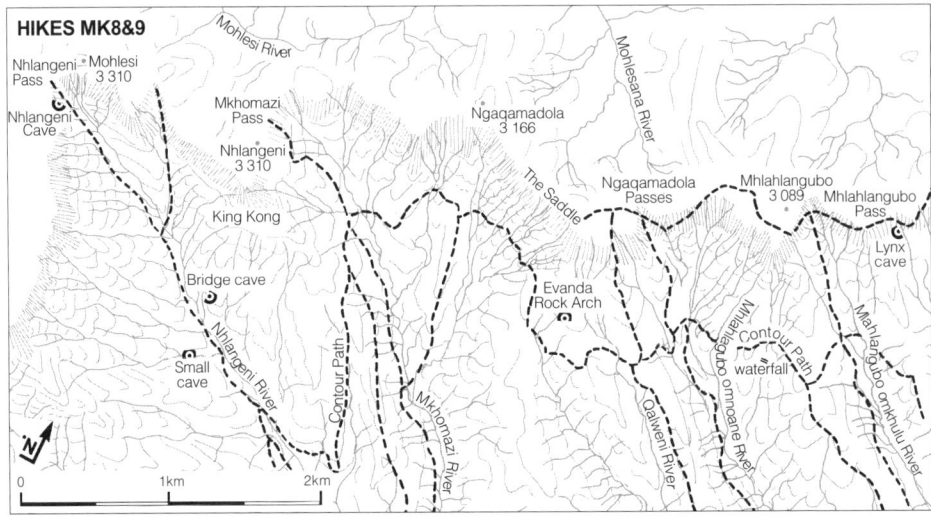

MKHOMAZI–NHLANGENI PASS HIKE MK9

Route: From Vergelegen up the Mkhomazi River to its source; an alternative route from halfway up the Nhlangeni cutback
Distance: 17 km (and 20 km) one way
Duration: 10 to 12 hours (2 days)
Grade: Extreme
General: The route up the Mkhomazi was the first one proposed as a possible road link to Lesotho, which correctly implies that it is an easy one to walk. However, it is a very long route and really should be broken at Bird's Nest Cave. The Mkhomazi and Nhlangeni passes are separated by the brutish juggernaut of Nhlangeni Peak that sticks out from the Escarpment like the peak of a gargantuan triangular cap.

Take the path left from the old Umkomaas farm house (now the home of the officer in charge) – the road makes a sharp loop – and first left up the right-hand side of the Mkhomazi Valley. After 1.5 km cross a side stream near the main river, but continue up the right-hand bank. The path goes along the side of a steep ridge and works its way above the river, crossing several streams.

After 5 km the path descends the ridge to cross the Mkhomazi, then heads straight up the slope opposite, zigzagging for a short way. About 50 m above the river the path splits around kaNtuba Ridge, the more prominent path branching off right to continue up the left-hand side of the main valley for another 4 km.

Now deep into the maze of Little Berg gorges, there is a confluence of the Mkhomazi and Nhlangeni rivers. The path keeps left to follow the Nhlangeni and a little way further the Nhlangeni Pass route turns left to climb up the ridge above the Mkhomazi Pass path. Follow the left-hand bank of the Mkhomazi for 1.5 km along the Ngcingweni Forest to where the path crosses the river. Bird's Nest Cave is on your left just, and really just, past the crossing point, within spitting distance of the river. This is a most convenient overnight stop on the route.

From the cave cross the river and follow a short, but very sharp ascent up Ngcingweni Ridge starting at the top end of the forest and working up and over the crest of the ridge, to the northern side and along the north-sloping base – now back in the Mkhomazi Valley. Follow this valley all the way to the summit, although 2 km after rounding Ngcingweni Ridge the path does work its way away from the main river and through some side gullies for about 1.3 km before re-uniting with the Mkhomazi.

Around this section do not take a path down to the river to cross it and head up a steep embankment on the north-western side of the river, but keep to the left-hand side of the main valley. A little over 5 km after leaving the Nhlangeni Valley you finally reach the Contour Path, which is rather vague at this point.

For the first part of the ascent the path sticks to the left-hand bank of the main river. However, it then veers sharp left up a small ridge for about 100 vertical metres, before contouring under the rock bands to regain the source of the Mkhomazi, which is then followed right to the summit. You top out on the north side of Nhlangeni Peak, with a lesser high point on your right. Ahead of you is the wonderful, extensive Mohlesi Valley which acts as a highway between Giant's Castle and kaNtuba–Thaba Ntlenyana (with Sani Pass over the kaNtuba Ridge). The Basotho call this pass the Mohlesi, as the river rises on the north-eastern slope of Thaba Ntlenyana, runs east almost to the Escarpment edge and then veers north then north-west at the head of the pass. (Slingsby shows the Mohlesi Pass as a north fork of the Nhlangeni Pass, but that is really no pass at all and better avoided.)

A climb to the summit of Nhlangeni Peak (or Pinnacle as it is more commonly known) will be rewarded by grand views of the mountains left and right, as well as the free-standing tower of King Kong directly ahead. The Ngaqamadola passes are reached about 5 km to the north, over or around the Ngaqamadola Ridge, while Nhlangeni Pass is located in the furthest cut-back a full 3 km south-south-east.

Sani Pass

It is possible to walk this pass up the Mkhomazana River, but that would be a little pointless since there is a road all the way up to Sani Top; the pass is named, as many are, for the river that rises over the watershed in Lesotho. The Sani Valley is the main trading route of the region, heading inland to Mokhotlong. It takes about two to three hours to drive the 50-odd km there, through some of the most spectacular countryside in Lesotho. From Mokhotlong you can now drive on a tar road all the way to Maseru (but be warned that in winter it becomes covered with ice and can be treacherous).

In 1946 the entrepid veteran of the war in Italy David Alexander organised a pony trip up the steep bridle path to Sani Top. He became convinced he could build a jeep track up the pass (having driven them up similar mule tracks in the Appenines). He did, and also started the Mokhotlong Mountain Transport Company (MMT) which really opened up the area. The company was later sold to Michael Clarke and is now the Sani Pass Tours company which ferries tourists rather than trade goods. Two of the colourful characters of pre-road days were the immigrant traders Waring and Lamont. They both grew rich but Lamont ended up living and dying in a hovel at the present-day police post. Alexander then got the idea of building a traveller's inn at the summit to replace the rather primitive Lesotho government rest hut. He convinced the barman at the Underberg Hotel, Jimmy James, to build first the Pack Horse Inn at Mokhotlong, and then Sani Top Chalet – the highest hotel and pub in southern Africa, and likely all of Africa.

MMT was based in Himeville, whose famous watering hole and inn, the Himeville Arms, was run for many years by the Aldous family. Jonathan Aldous sold the Himeville Arms some years ago and is now proprietor of Sani Top Chalet, thinking nothing of commuting up and down the pass. If you are wise take advantage of his hospitality. If luck is with you, you could be trapped there for weeks in a big snowstorm.

Sani Pass Tours, as well as two other tour companies, runs daily trips up the pass and you can enquire about the weekend package offered by the Himeville Arms and Sani Top.

From all the camp sites and EKZNW stations there are numerous shorter walks than the ones described here. If you'd like to do shorter walks, I'd suggest you choose Lotheni as there are easy walks for children including Jacob's Ladder, a series of five plunges into what I'd say is the best mountain pool in the world. There is Eagle Rock and the longer Eagle Educational Trail up above the Lotheni River. But Vergelegen, Kamberg and Mkhomazi all have a network of marked and unmarked paths that could keep you busy for a lifetime.

For instance, at Kamberg everyone does the Games Pass Shelter guided walk, and tootles round the trout dams (there's supposedly a wheelchair trail). But few people know about the slightly further Christmas Cave which has fine Bushman paintings (you have to go with a guide though, and they have to be cajoled). From the Vergelegen picnic spot, there's a short walk up to the east to the summit of the Pyramid.

mzimkhulu

Ask any farmer in the Mzimkhulu area what the major issue here is and he or she will say stock theft. It's an old 'custom' invented by the Bushmen when white settlers moved into their hunting grounds, and later adopted by the Basotho as their national sport. But, whereas the Bushmen had just cause, the modern Basotho cattle and horse thieves are brazen criminals pillaging the rich pickings of a foreign country. The two points to the south of Sani Pass are the major landmark of the southern Drakensberg: Hodgson's Peaks are named after a farmer who, in 1862, joined a posse to follow Bushman cattle thieves into the mountains. While chasing a mounted Bushman along the summit near Mzimkhulu Pass, Thomas Hodgson was severely wounded in the thigh. He died the following day and is buried somewhere up there. Robert Speirs, who was among the commando, was lost without horse or food for about two weeks after the incident. He spent some time in a cave, which must still have been used by Bushmen after this because scenes depicting the incident were painted on the walls. It was named Speirs' Cave and hikers who are persistent will locate it along the Mzimkhulu Pass route.

Three decades earlier the formation, 'a remarkable mountain' with a singularly indented outline was named Giant's Cup by explorer Captain AF Gardiner. He was an ex-navy officer who took zealously to mission work after his wife died. He was instrumental in founding Durban by establishing a mission station at Berea (so-called because according to the Bible 'Berea had noble men') above Port Natal. From there he set off to find a wagon route over the Drakensberg. In 1835, with Dick King in his party, he investigated all the main valleys from Sani to Bushman's Nek but eventually abandoned the high ground and made for Port St Johns. Along the way he was 'quite startled at the appearance of a rugged mountain, which I have named Giant's Castle' because of its resemblence to Edinburgh Castle. Somehow that name got transferred to a higher peak way to the north, and Gardiner's 'Giant's Castle' is now known as Garden Castle. But, long, long before either Hodgson or Gardiner, in fact even long before the Dutch settled at the Cape, these mountains had been identified by white people.

In 1593 the Portuguese ship *Santo Alberto* was bound for home from Cochin, with a rich cargo. It was wrecked on the Wild Coast and some 300 survivors set off on foot for Lourenço Marques (Maputo). It was January and the many swollen rivers forced them to take a wide, inland route north. In May they were around the lower Lotheni Valley where they reported seeing towering above them to the west, a great range of snow-covered hills. To the south of Giant's Cup/Hodgson's Peaks, about midway between Sani Pass and Bushman's Nek, a horn-shaped pinnacle (The Rhino) stands free of the main Escarpment.

In previous times Bushman's Nek must have been an amazing sight, with flights of massive bearded vultures (lammergeiers) gliding the high peaks in aerial splendour. The local name for the area, and the triple summits of the final 'book-end' peak of the range, is Thaba Ntsu – the 'mountain of the lammergeier'. English speakers called them the Devil's Knuckles. One of only two lammergeier eggs ever to be collected was recovered here in 1883 so we can assume up to that stage the birds still nested in this area. They eat mainly bone marrow and, where farming has replaced large, wild herds of antelope near their mountain habitat, they rely on pastoral societies whose dead sheep and cattle provide food. In southern Africa only Lesotho provides these conditions.

Accommodation in this area which provides direct access for hikers into the mountains is found at the base of Sani Pass (see previous chapter), a hotel, caravan park and EKZNW camp site at Garden Castle, and a hotel and caravan park at Bushman's Nek (the EKZNW station at Bushman's Nek has only a picnic site and trail hut). Prices and the ambience at Garden Castle Hotel will not suit most hikers (it's neither outsider-friendly nor particularly good value for money), even though it is one of the old resorts favoured for decades by mountaineers. My favourite in the region is Bushman's Nek, which, even though it has become largely a time-share resort, still welcomes hikers and has built self-catering units specially for the likes of you and me. It's been completely refurbished and a great attraction is Zunckels Restaurant and Bar, run by master chef, raconteur and legend-in-his-own-lifetime, Anton Zunckel. There is ample accommodation at farms and in guesthouses, many of which offer fly-fishing as an attraction.

The gateway to this area is Underberg, and a trip would be incomplete without a detour into Tom Wimber's White Cottage Books store. It specialises in Africana and good quality second-hand books. The owner is another Drakensberg legend and, if you can leave the store unladen, you're either broke or not a book lover.

Although some of the finest rock art caves in the region are to be found in the Cobham area they are now closed to the public. You can however take guided walks from Garden Castle and Bushman's Nek to various cave sites. It is my policy not to reveal the location of any other rock art sites, but rather to point hikers towards those caves that can be visited only with a registered guide. This policy is endorsed by EKZNW, who have included on their new maps only those caves designated for overnight accommodation. Sehlaba Thebe Park lies below Thaba Ntsu, but is in Lesotho. There is a so-called lodge there (it used to be the prime minister's private retreat), which can be booked by hikers. Otherwise the many caves round the rim of the park are open to all. As with Mkhomazi, discussed in the previous chapter, all hikes described here are long and concentrate on reaching either caves on the Little Berg or the summit via some of the many passes in the area. From each of the three accommodation points, however, there are numerous shorter walks and these are described in EKZNW booklets available at the different conservation offices. The two hotels also have their own preferred walks, as well as guides and guided outings almost daily. If there isn't one the duty manager will organise one for you if you give him or her sufficient warning.

From Cobham (Pholela), a recommended short walk is northwards to the Ngenwa Valley and Gxalingenwa Forest. Gxalingenwa forest was one of many refuges for people in the times of the Difaqane but it also has the meaning of a secret or dangerous place like the woods of old Europe with witches and wolves. At Garden Castle it is a tradition to do the Mashai Pass climb every Thursday, I believe, and this really should be done with the guide if it's your first time in the area because it is not straightforward. Lives have been put in peril and even lost by people going off route in poor weather. Also, the route is not up the Rhino Pass as many people think, assuming the name of the dominant peak is synonymous with the pass of that name. Other good hikes are to The Monk and Sleeping Beauty Cave (8 km return), Hidden Valley (18 km return) and Three Pools and Bushman's Rock (9 km return).

GIANT'S CUP TRAIL HIKE MZ1

Route: Sani Pass to Bushman's Nek
Distance: 60.3 km
Duration: 5 days
Grade: Strenuous (in total distance)
General: The only thing that's changed on this hike in the years since the last edition of *Drakensberg Walks* is that there is no longer a National Hiking Way organisation and the trail is now run by EKZNW. It still keeps to the Little Berg area and even beyond, in places where the Drakensberg is only a distant view. Only at Garden Castle (Swiman Hut) do you get close to the main range, and then briefly before it swings away to Bushman's Nek EKZNW office. This route was taken before the days of the uKhahlamba-Drakensberg Park when the Hiking Way board had to struggle to get access rights to the many and varied land parcels for the trail to traverse. I believe that EKZNW should look to re-routing the trail along the Contour Path level to give hikers a real mountain experience. And, if they don't want to bring such large, organised numbers too close to the High Berg, then they should consider upgrading the Contour Path south from Pholela to Bushman's Nek as a wilderness trail, linking the various caves.

While not everyone enjoys such organised and controlled hiking conditions, (until such time as the authorities come round to my way of thinking) this trail can be considered the southern-most extension of the Contour Path. The hot showers at some of the huts are worth the effort.

mzimkhulu

Accommodation on this hike is more comfortable than many similar former NHW trails, with multiple rooms, decent mattresses, firewood and even wood stoves and hot showers at some (Pholela, Swiman). Transport must be arranged between the start on Sani Pass and the end at Bushman's Nek EKZNW camp. It is no longer safe (or even practical) to park your car on the pass where the trail begins, and this needs to be addressed by the trail authorities.

Day 1 (13.3 km): The start of the trail is marked about 5 km above Sani Pass Hotel, on the left, but you'll miss it if you're looking at the road, where you should be, or the pass itself, which you can't help gawking at. Most parties skip this day because of transport or parking difficulties, which is a pity as I regard it as the best part of the trail, if the shortest. After an easy 2.5-km stroll along an almost level grassland platform, you'll find the path climbs for several hundred metres, contours again and then descends to the Gxalingenwa Stream. The steepish slope down to Ngenwa Pool is scattered with protea bushes. It's a great place to swim and, even if the main pool is occupied, just wander upstream and you'll find many more, connected by cascades. There is a log bridge you have to cross. It's also a good lunch spot, but if the weather's miserable continue up the opposite side to a rock shelter.

From this shelter the path undulates around Ndlovini Hill and then down to Trout Beck Stream. Follow the river all the way down to Cobham EKZNW camp, every now and again passing through a game fence and finally taking a suspension bridge across the Pholela River to the trail hut (the old stone farmhouse). Even though it's in the middle of the rest camp this is the nicest hut and has the luxury of hot showers.

Day 2 (9 km): A short walk from Cobham to Mzimkhuluwana allows you an exploration of the surrounding countryside, valleys and Little Berg spurs, or simply to laze around the pool downriver from Mzimkhulwana Hut. From the hut the path climbs up quite steeply to Tortoise Rock, where the gradient eases off as you make your way past Bathplug Cave (it's a short detour up to the cave where the water disappears through a hole in the floor). From there it's a long but gentle descent to Mzimkulwana.

Day 3 (12.2 km): Cross the short suspension bridge below the hut and then climb quite steeply up Little Bamboo Mountain, named after the indigenous grass *Arundinaria tessellata* which grows here. Below the mountain, in a grassy plateau, is Crane Tarn where rare wattled cranes might be seen in late summer or autumn. Pieces of petrified wood can be seen along the shale outcrops; enjoy them but don't remove any as you'll just jettison them later when your pack starts to drag, and that will confound geologists and spoil everything for other hikers in the Berg.

From the tarn area the path begins its long descent to Killcrankie Stream and Boulder Pool (there's a large boulder in it). The sometimes loose path passes through a large community of tall *Protea subvestita* bushes, with everlastings and other wild flowers which attract butterflies and lady bugs by the score. The pool is a little short of midway, but a great place to swim and linger, maybe for lunch. After this the route enters farmland, past kraals and houses, and follows the Garden Castle road for 1 km to the Mzimkhulu River. Just past the river the path turns off to the left, over a farm fence, and then for some inexplicable reason goes right over a hill instead of around it. The path then crosses a weir and comes to Winterhoek camp, with its thatched bungalows shaded by oak trees.

mzimkhulu 197

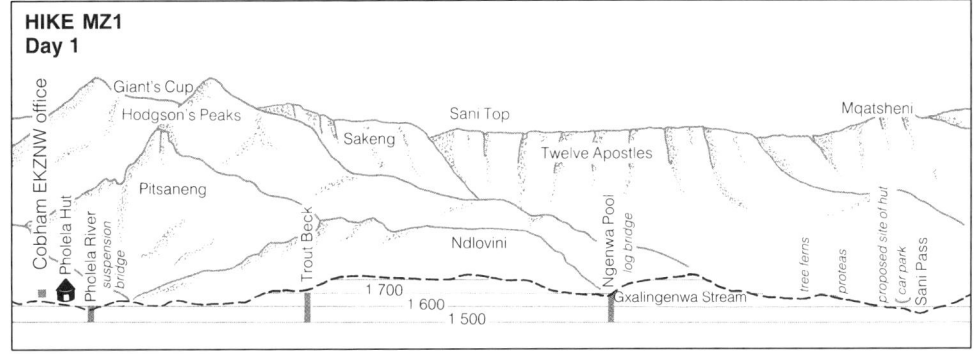

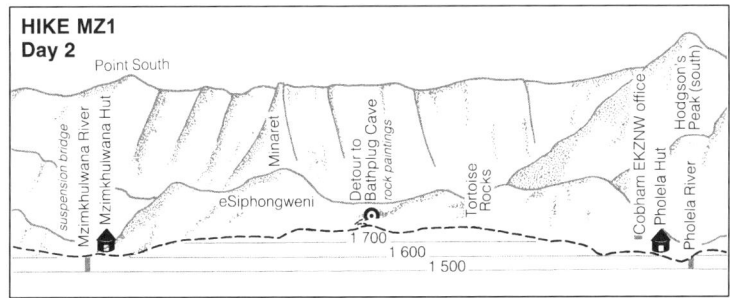

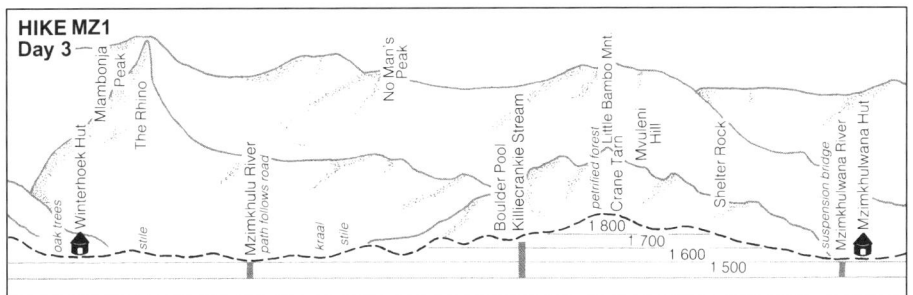

Day 4 (12.8 km): Winterhoek to Swiman Hut at Garden Castle camp typifies the southern Berg: rank grassland in all directions is broken only occasionally by an outcrop of rock or a lone protea bush that's survived the seasonal bush fires. In spring and summer the veld is alive with wild flowers including orange and crimson watsonias (which are best in the season after a fire), yellow and mauve asters and yellow, cerise and white everlastings. By Drakensberg hiking standards, the first part of this section up Black Eagle Pass on the lower slopes of Garden Castle is a mere warm up. However, on this hike it is the most challenging section on the second longest day. You are very likely to see jackal buzzards here as well as black eagles as they nest in the vicinity.

Ahead of you from the top of the pass level grassland stretches to the base of the Escarpment, with The Rhino dead ahead. To your right and below lie the valleys of Mzimkhulu and Mlambonja with the famous

198 mzimkhulu

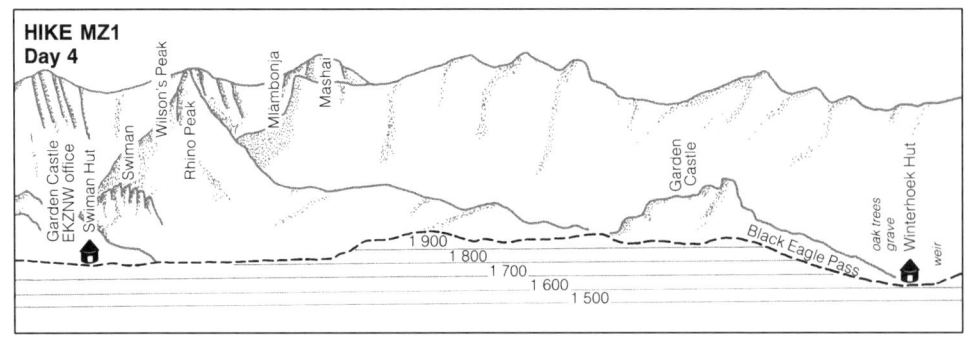

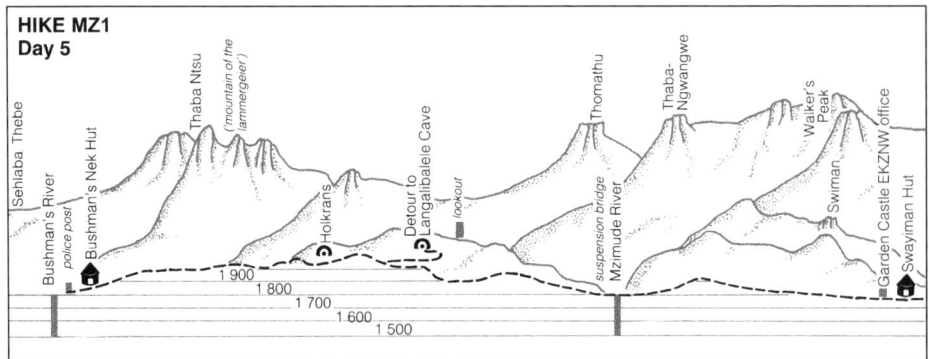

trout-fishing resort on Lake Naverone; to your left is the collywobbling course of the Mzimude with its serpentine meanders and ox-bow lakes. It's a lovely place to sit and stare, but there's precious little water so be sure to carry enough for the day's conditions (two litres if it's hot).

Swiman Hut is located close to Garden Castle rest camp and, although it's situated in a most scenic spot below the castellations of Swiman and The Monk, with The Rhino nudging the sky to the north, the hut itself looks like a low-cost suburban *pondok*. Pity.

Day 5 (13 km): The path begins gently up to Bucquay's Nek and then down to cross the Mzimude via a suspension bridge. From there it threads its way upwards through rocky steps to Langalibalele Cave, a short distance off to the left after crossing a stream. The cave faces northwards (in the direction you've come) and is located in a low rock band. It's much larger than it seems, the entrance being partially blocked by a collapsed roof 'beam'. There are some faded paintings on a very exposed slab on the outside of the cave.

This is the usual lunch stop, as it's the last water source on the hike, just over halfway and, well, a lekker spot. To the right of the cave, facing outwards, you might see kestrels, lanner falcons, jackal buzzards and maybe Cape vultures thermalling on the ridge edge of the Little Berg.

From the cave it's a short climb to a level valley where the lookout can be seen on the hill to the left; look out for grey rhebuck here, but they'll take flight as soon as they hear you. The path round exits this valley and then descends first a little steeply and then more gently to Bushman's Nek police post and rest camp. The trail hut is located off the path to the right, about 1 km before the end of the trail.

GXALINGENWA RIVER TRAIL HIKE MZ2

Route: From Sani Pass up Gxalingenwa River
Distance: 3.5 km return
Duration: 1 to 1½ hours
Grade: Easy
General: This is an easy walk for guests at the hotel or backpackers from the lodge who want to enjoy a saunter into the foothills. The rivers, forests and caves of the Little Berg are a rambler's delight; this walk has all three and is short enough for even non-hikers to get a taste of what the mountains offer. A longer walk can be taken along the Giant's Cup Trail Path, crossing the river above the forest and heading over into the Cobham area. The beautiful indigenous forest was once a hiding place, and its name also means 'the place where you should not go'. At one point there is a waterfall with a deep pool at its base, one of several that are great for swimming.

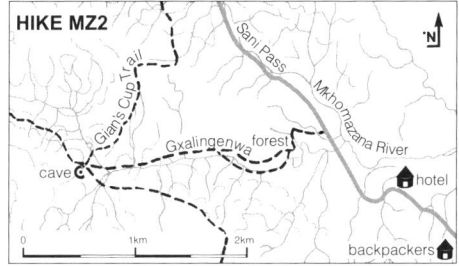

The walk starts just above the culvert opposite the hotel golf course. You can see an old dipping tank nearby, which was used until in 1958 a hotel replaced farming. The valley here is overgrown in places with exotic trees and brambles, but in time this should be cleared out by the Working for Water project.

The first of many river crossings (eight in total) is 500 m from the start, through an overgrowth of wattle and bramble. There is also *intshishi* bush along the river and this should re-establish itself when the wattle is cleared. In summer you might need to go a little further upstream to cross at a rocky area.

The second crossing is about 250 m further up, through very tussocky *Merxmuellera* grass. This is a stout grass used to make brooms. But it's an invader species that is very low in nutrition and indicates badly overgrazed land. Another 300 m

through better but obviously grazed grassland you cross the river a third time, where sedges and *ncema* grasses occur. Now the path continues above the river on the left-hand side through thick grassland where you should look out for the many wild flowers that occur, for example watsonias, gladioluses, digitaria and senecio whose yellow cluster-heads are deadly to horses and humans alike.

Where the trail forks keep to the lower path to cross the river onto the cooler south-facing bank. Note the more woody, fynbos vegetation on this cooler and damper slope, including tree ferns and proteas, *Buddleja* and mountain sage. After a brief climb the path descends through a glade to the forest, and Gxalingenwa Cave can be seen up to the left.

The path takes you only a short way into this yellowwood or temperate Afro-montane forest, typical of all those found in the Berg. If you'd like to know a little more about the trees, get hold of the EKZNW trail brochure: some trees have their national tree identification numbers marked so can be read up about later (or before if you're the organised type).

Return to the glade and take the path across the river at the big rock below an African holly tree, then up to the cave. A stream flows over the cave in summer, and small animals as well as hikers use the shelter on occasion. There are some very faded painted images, so faded that they will be disappointing if you've planned the walk solely to see cave paintings. From the cave continue back down to the river and the start. This 'Gxalingenwa Cave' is not to be confused with another of the same name some 8 km further upriver. The route there is not straightforward and shouldn't be attempted without a good map.

NGENWA RIVER ROUND-TRIP — HIKE MZ3

Route: From Cobham a circular trip via Gxalingenwa and Emerald streams
Distance: 24 km
Duration: 12 hours (2 days)
Grade: Strenuous
General: Although you could do this hike on a good summer's day, it is one heck of a challenge and should rather be considered an overnight hike. Alternatively, you could choose either route out and do that as a linear, there-and-back hike either up Emerald Stream or backtracking the hiking trail path to Ngenwa Pool. Gxalingenwa Cave is a designated overnight place so make that your target if you plan this as a 2-day outing. You can get a trail brochure at the Cobham office, which sells books and curios. Remember, you must book the hut if you want to sleep there.

Starting at Cobham go upriver and cross the suspension bridge, backtracking along the Giant's Cup Trail path (if you walk backwards you'll be able to see the trail markers). You follow this for about 2 km up the tinkling Trout Beck, to below a rock band then veer right up a side stream, climbing up around the base of Ndlovini Hill until the path levels off and then descends to Ngenwa Pool on the Gxalingenwa Stream. Strip off, have a swim and then enjoy lunch because the hard work is ahead.

The trail path crosses the river via a log bridge, but our trail turns left up the left-hand bank of the river for 4 km to Baboon Rock. Two paths, about 200 m apart, branch off to the left around Baboon Rock and away from the river. You should stick to the main valley for another 1.5 km. The main path crosses the river and heads up towards the Giant's Cup and Masubasuba Pass.

However, to reach the cave you should not cross here, but continue for another 150 m to a

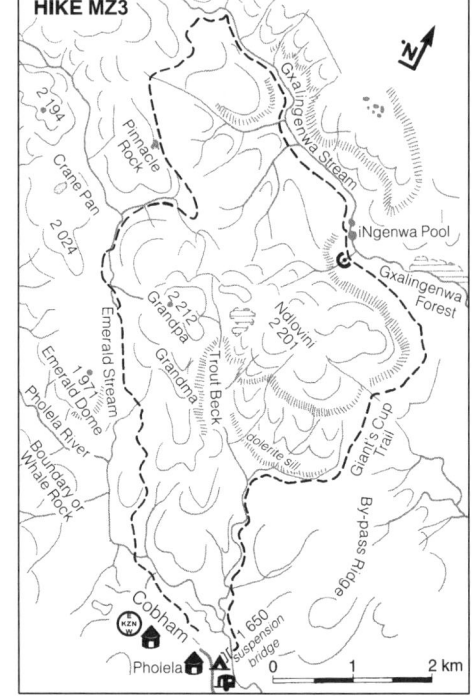

ABOVE: In winter the summit plateau can be a somewhat bleak place. However, in summer it is a riot of flowers. Sometimes it's just the flame-like heads of kniphofias around a typical spring area which makes walking a sloshy affair. In other places it can be carpets as far as you can see.

RIGHT: Not all Berg lovers are hikers: at places such as Lotheni and Kamberg still-water trout are the prize. At others, mainly Cobham and southwards, wild, wily, white-water fish offer a greater challenge.

ABOVE: Perhaps the most important of all Bushman paintings anywhere – the Rosetta Stone panel in Games Pass Shelter. This frieze conclusively linked Bushman art to a mystical, spiritual belief system and not just pictures of slain animals and funny people. This and other paintings are explained during a tour of the shelter.
RIGHT: A summer watsonia: diamonds in a green grass sea.
OPPOSITE: Jacob's Ladder Falls near Lotheni camp.

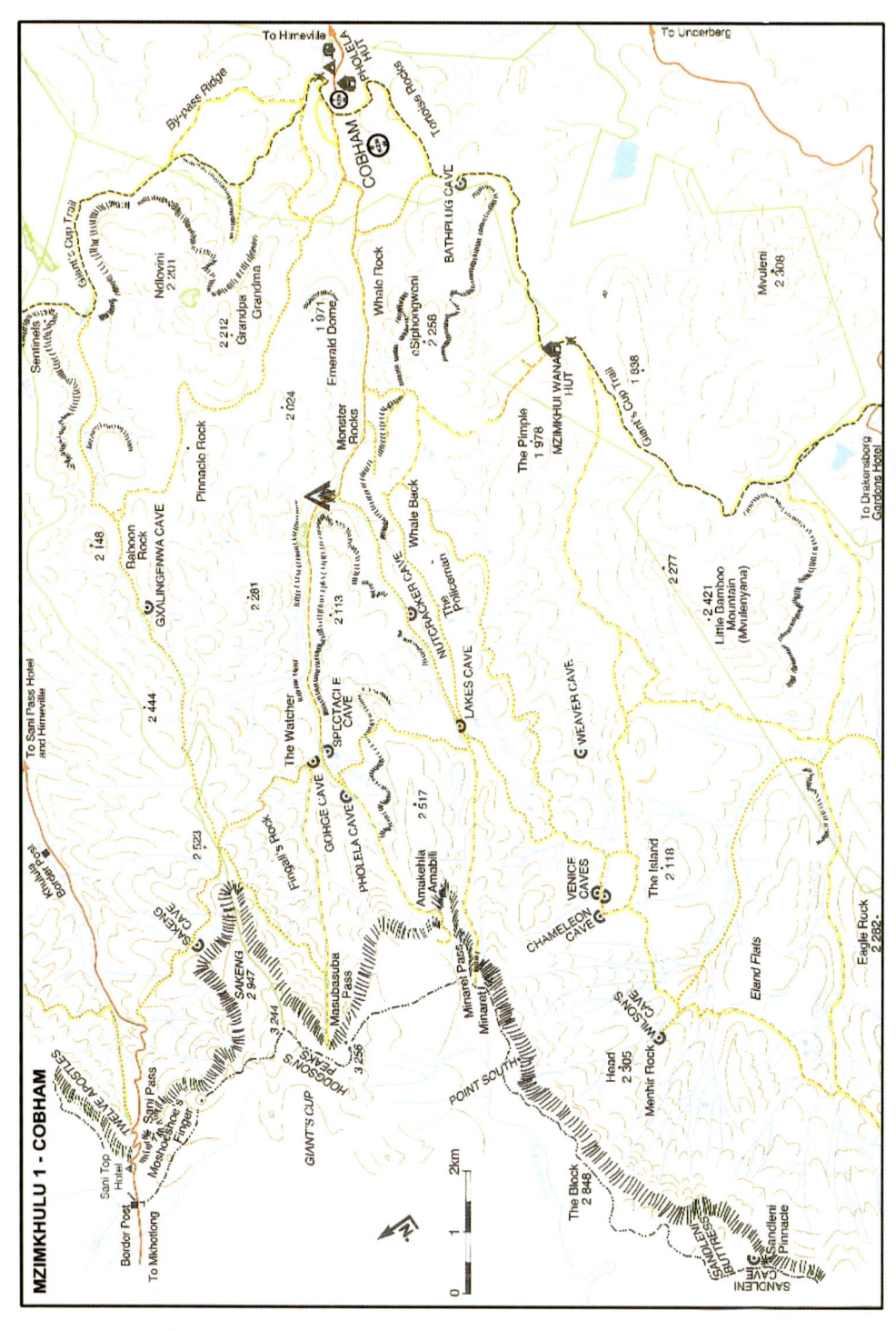

ABOVE: Looking north from Giant's Castle along a snow-sprinkled Lesotho plateau. The block-shaped mountain in the far, centre, distance is Cathkin Peak.

RIGHT: You can reach the summit of Rhino Peak via Mashai Pass, but some people prefer to climb the vertical face and then abseil down.

OVERLEAF: Eland roam the Lake District, above Cobham camp. The Drakensberg herd of some 1 500 animals is the largest in southern Africa, if not on the continent.

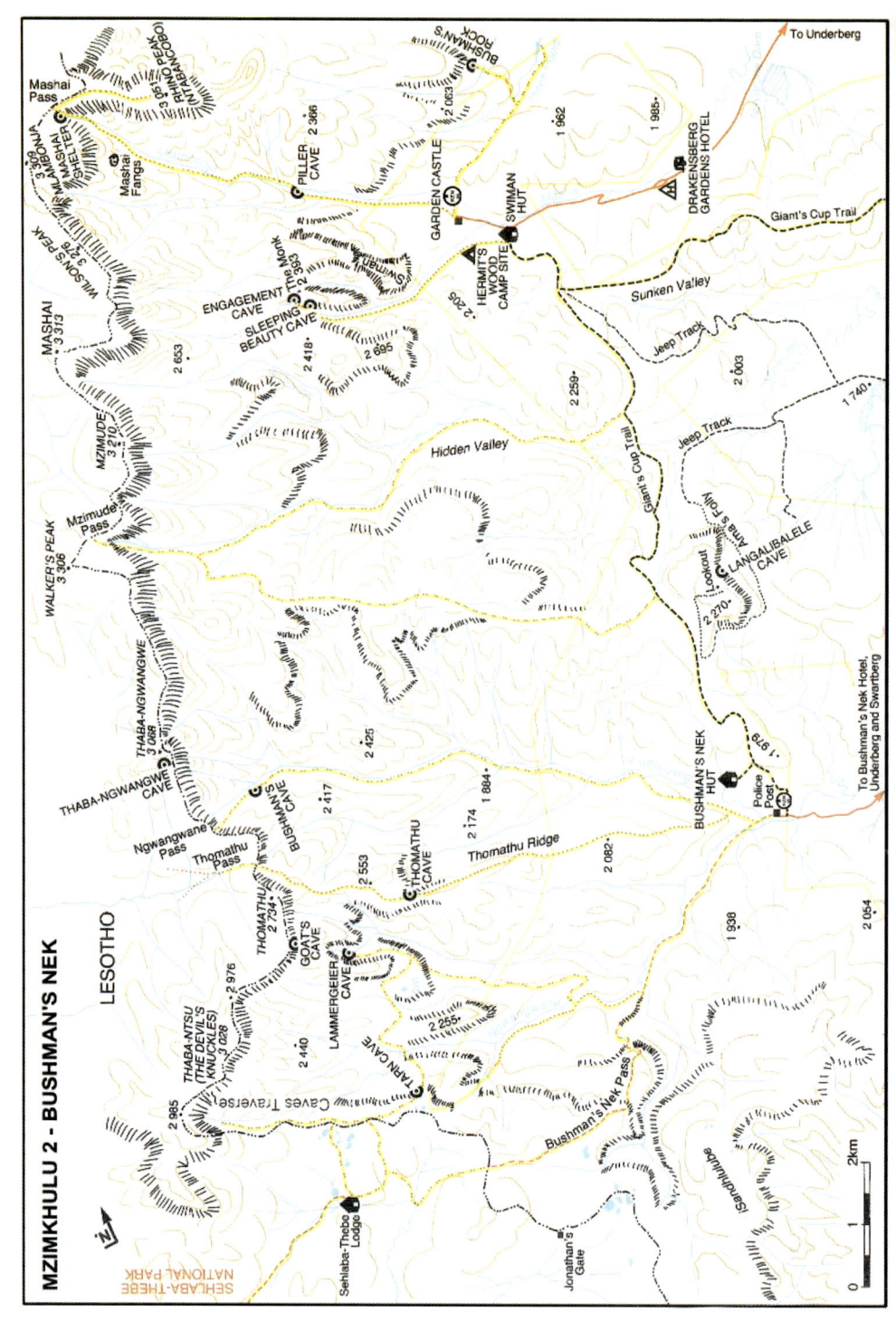

side stream up to the left. You will find the large cave is situated just 200 m up this side valley.

On day two go back down the river to Baboon Rock and take the turnoff to the right on an undulating traverse below this formation and Pinnacle Rock which finally, after nearly 3 km, curves sharply round to the right to follow a rivulet to Emerald Stream. Once you are headed down towards Cobham you cross the river twice before it sticks to the right-hand bank for the last 2.5 km. Here you should turn right and head back down to the river, cross it and then follow the right-hand bank downstream for the last 1.5 km to Cobham camp site and trail hut: where the path forks, the easier route is right, away from the river.

PHOLELA CAVE AND AMAKEHLA PASS — HIKE MZ4

Route: From Cobham up the Pholela River to the cave, then up the pass to the head of a southerly tributary
Distance: 17.5 km one way
Duration: About 9 hours (2 days)
Grade: Extreme (strenuous to the cave)
General: Most first-time summiters in this area head straight up the Pholela River to its head in the bowl of the Giant's Cup and up Masubasuba Pass. However, this route is in a shocking state and should be avoided. By far the better route is up Amakehla Pass, following the southerly tributary. The route at the top of the pass poses no technical difficulties, but it does wind through rock bands and will give vertigo sufferers something to cling on to.

From Cobham head up the Pholela Valley, with the Giant's Cup looming dead ahead, to reach the river after 1 km. Thereafter the path follows the left-hand bank for about 1 km before taking the direct course where the river loops away to the right. You regain the river after another 1.5 km and follow it for 3 km below the Little Berg formation of the Whale Back, on your left – a number of paths lead up the Whale Back.

At the confluence of the iNhlabeni, cross this tributary (the path to the left goes up to Lakes Cave and eventually Minaret Pass), and continue round a headland following the course of the Pholela. After 1 km you cross the river, then cross it again three times in succession a few hundred metres on.

Back on the left-hand bank, continue up the valley for 3 km to where three gorge-like valleys meet. Gorge Cave, the smallest of the area, is reached up the northerly, right-hand valley; much larger Spectacle Cave up the southerly, left-hand stream; and Pholela Cave up the middle, that is, straight on. However, the Pholela River actually turns sharp right here up the northerly of the three gorges. That route will take you up Masubasuba Pass. Pholela Cave is 700 m ahead after crossing the side stream leading to Spectacle Cave, but it's on the right-hand side of the valley.

Amakehla Pass continues up the left-hand side of the stream, for 2 km, into a huge bowl at the base of the mountain wall. Where you reach the base of the near-vertical cliffs, the path leaves the stream gully and goes up the slope to the left, making its way around the twin spires of Amakehla Amabili (meaning 'the fingers'), winding its way along and up a very steep slope, finally finding its way up a secluded gully on the southern side of the 'amabilis'.

Another pass just to the south of this, going more directly up the ridge to the south from Lakes Cave, is Minaret Pass, used by dagga smugglers. However, this one is even steeper and more sinuous than Amakehla. Both lead into the upper Pitsaneng Valley. This large river can be followed to a curved horseshoe bend near the top of Stones Pass, 5.5 km to the south-south-west.

You can return via either Giant's Cup or Masubasuba Pass, past Gorge Cave and down the Pholela, if you don't mind trailing through knee-deep erosion gullies.

GEAR TIPS

- When I started hiking I had a miniature brass pressure cooker. Now I use a Pocket Rocket stove with re-usable high-pressure MSR cylinders.
- The smaller gas stoves with re-usable high-pressure cylinders are the best option.
- Then I had a canvas and leather Bergen's backpack, a bulky old army sleeping bag, a close-cell 'gaper pad' (a thin blue roll-up 'mattress') and no tent.
- I now have a two-person Sunseeker and three-person Cadac dome tent, which I prefer though my Kestrel A-frame still does duty in the high mountains.
- The excellent 75-litre Sunseeker backpack is no longer available – pity.
- The Backpacker Boulder or similar 75–80 litre model is a good Berg size pack.

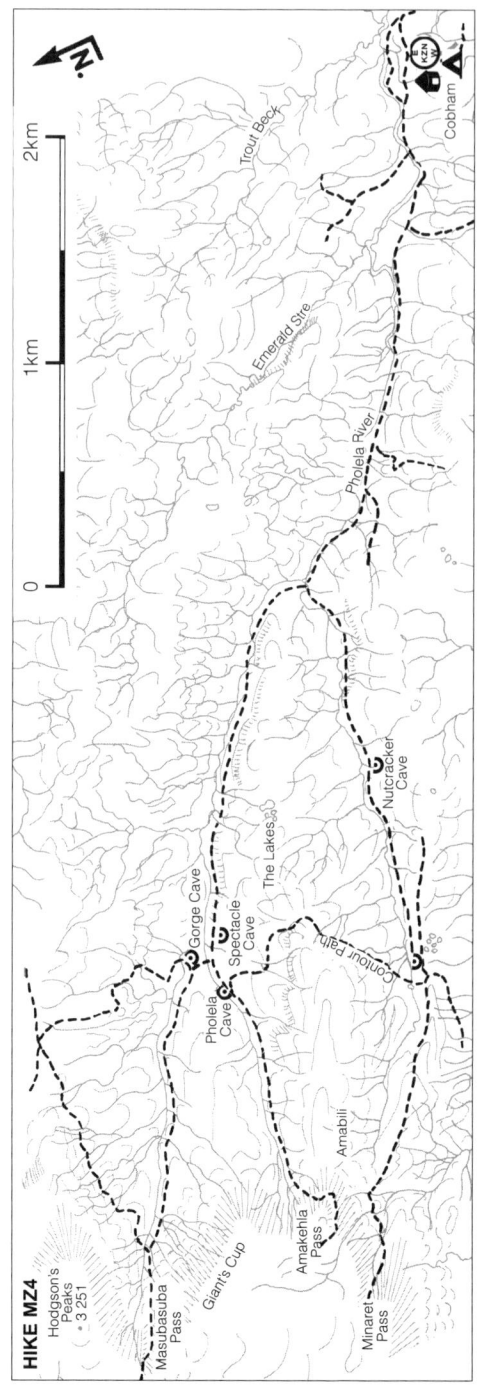

THE HIKE OF MANY CAVES   HIKE MZ5

Route: There is no one prescribed route from Cobham, as any nine caves in the Little Berg can be used in any direction and any order
Distance: Variable, from 8 to about 14 km
Duration: Up to 5 hours
Grade: Moderate
General: There are nine caves in the upper Little Berg area of Cobham, around the Contour Path level. You can plan a multi-day hike using all, some or any of these shelters. I will describe just one option that includes what I think is the best of them, and makes the most logical three-day route going up the Pholela River to Pholela, along the Contour Path to Venice Caves, and back along the Whale Back. By linking Pholela (or one of the other nearby caves), Lakes and Venice caves, or even Nutcracker and Weaver, you could make this a really pleasant and easy three- or four-day hike. There is no correct route, so you should plan your hike using either Slingsby's or the new EKZNW hiking map.

Start up Pholela River as for the Amakehla Pass/Giant's Cup hike (previous hike) for 8.5 km. One option is to fork to the left to follow the left-hand bank of the iNhlabeni Stream and carry on for 2.5 km to Nutcracker Cave, and then a further 2.5 km to Lakes Caves and the 'lakes' just beyond that near the Contour Path. The longer route will take you over the iNhlabeni and a further 5 km (with three more river crossings), to the intersection of three gorges. Three great caves are located within half a square kilometre so if you don't like the first one.... Cross the first stream, turn right and cross the second to swing to the east (it feels like the north) away from the Berg, then carry on up the most right-hand valley – the main Pholela tributary – for 250 m to the smallest overnight shelter in the area, Gorge Cave; carry on straight ahead for 800 m to find Pholela Cave on the right-hand bank; turn left for just 150 m to find Spectacle Cave straddling the small side gorge.

Whichever cave you choose, you have to make your way to Pholela Cave, where you turn sharp back to the left and away from the main Berg's Pitsaneng headland to follow the Contour Path around the Little Berg, for 3 km, with some good hamstring stretching as you ascend in the middle, to the Minaret Pass intersection. Turn left here and after less than 100 m there's yet another intersection, at a group of tarns (the 'lakes'). Lakes Cave is found some 650 m to the left from here; straight on takes you along the Whale Back in the direction of Siphongweni Rock; turning right takes you through the Lake District for 2 km.

At the next intersection turn right and head down to the Mzimkhulwana River, 1 km away. You should not cross the river but head up the right-hand bank for about 800 m to the two smallish Venice Caves, found opposite one another on either side of the stream. The much larger Chameleon Cave is reached by veering up to the left just past the caves, climbing out of the valley and contouring round for about 700 m. It faces south-east and looks down into the Mlahlangubo Valley and, especially in winter, is the best option of the three.

While you can book Weaver Cave, I suggest you don't as very few people have ever found it. Instead, make your way down along the Mzimkhulwana Valley to the hiking trail hut, which can be booked by non-trailists. Continue past Venice Caves and then down the river for another 2.6 km to a side gorge with a largish stream; the cave is situated 200 m up this side valley on the left.

Alternatively, contour back onto the Whale Back along a very winding but easy 9-km path.

On reaching the plateau, with Siphongweni Rock just over 2 km away on your right, turn left for 500 m to find a path on the edge of the Little Berg leading down to the Pholela River path, then head downstream for 6.5 km to the camp.

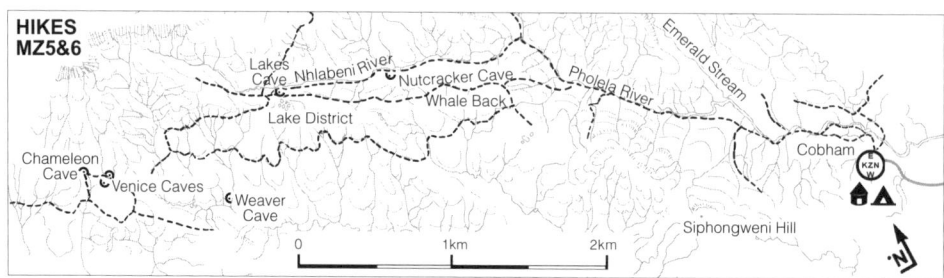

THE LAKE DISTRICT — HIKE MZ6

Route: Linear or circular route from Cobham to the top of the Little Berg
Distance: 14 km one way
Duration: 6 hours up and 4 down
Grade: Strenuous
General: This is a shortened version of the previous hike and is designed to be an overnight hike to the Lakes Cave. There will be ample time to explore the area above the caves in the morning, before heading back down. Remember to book the cave or you'll get into trouble with the law.

From Cobham follow the left-hand bank of the Pholela River (you reach the river only after the first kilometre).

Continue to follow the left-hand bank past the big boulder called Whale Rock (there are some badly defaced Bushman paintings low down) and continue with the steep cliffs of Siphongweni Rock and the Whale Back on your left. The path continues upriver for 7.5 km, where you'll see Nutcracker Cave about 40 m above you on the left. From there it's another 2 km to Lakes Cave, climbing about 170 m vertically, so some effort will be needed to get to the day's end.

The cave is your overnight shelter. It's a large cave that's well worth the stipend. About 300 m past the cave you come to the Contour Path and the heart of the 'lake district' which is extremely picturesque, as the name suggests. The main Berg here has no outstanding peaks, but four passes lead off the Contour Path which itself is worth exploring.

To vary the route take an alternative return journey, making your way from the cave up to the Contour Path intersection, where you turn sharp left along the top of the short-grassed Whale Back towards the pinnacle of Siphongweni Rock.

As you approach the rock keep to the left-hand side of the Whale Back until, 2 km short of the end of this Little Berg feature, you take a zigzagging path down to your left to the Pholela River and follow it back to camp where you can re-live your hike.

MZIMKHULU PASS   HIKE MZ7

Route: From Castle View Farm
Distance: 15 km
Duration: About 7 hours
Grade: Extreme
General: There are in fact three options to take up the upper Mzimkhulu Valley, the usual route starting off up the Mzimkhulu and then taking a more southerly ridge route around a headland to link up with the top of Verkyker Pass. It's a steep but fairly easy route. Thomas Hodgson is believed to be buried just a few kilometres to the north-west from the top of these passes. If you can locate Speirs' Cave (the guy who got left behind after Hodgson died and had to do an epic walk-out) it's well worth visiting as there are some beautiful antelope renderings as well as a scene from the Hodgson incident.
   The start is from the farm Castle View, owned by Dr John Hamilton who allows hikers access by arrangement (see 'Useful contacts', page 231).

Once you've got the farm key drive past the hotel to the EKZNW office to pay your fees and sign the mountain register.
   Return to the farm, about 500 m past the store on your left, where you can park under some trees near sheds and the farmhouse. A stipend to the caretaker has become customary.
   There are also the routes to Wilson's Cave and Stones Passes, on which you'll be unlucky not to see eland, grey rhebuck, oribi or mountain reedbuck. Great Bushman paintings can be seen in the area by serious mountaineers but they are difficult to find.
   A path winds down through the farm to the Mzimkhulu. Where you cross the river turn right up the right-hand bank for 7 km through the Little Berg gorge.
   Cross at a tributary from the right, then soon after cross again to the left-hand bank. After 1.5 km cross again to the right and Fun Cave is 250 m further on, up to your right (Verkyker Cave is a little further on, on the left-hand side of the river). Fun Cave is the one most often used by hikers going up the Berg to the north of The Rhino.
   It is situated right at the base of Mzimkhulu Pass, where the valley is crowded by the looming basalt folds of the mighty mountains. It's a large and nicely comfortable cave, which could be homed in on to break the trip into an overnight trip.
   Scramble to the right above the river for about 400 m, onto the ridge which ends as the big knoll in which Fun Cave is situated.
   This ridge separates the Verkyker and Mzimkhulu passes. In fact Mzimkhulu Pass consists of three routes, which reach the Escarpment up fairly obvious cutbacks: the northerly route is set back the deepest and therefore has the lesser angle and is possible; the middle route involves some technical scrambling (which is not recommended for the

214 mzimkhulu

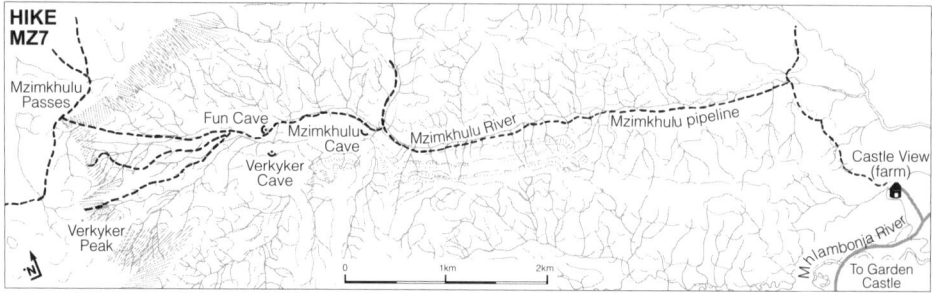

faint-hearted); and the southerly one is the one used by stock thieves – it's the 'official' route – so can be done, but be careful.

The south Mzimkhulu Pass route keeps to the crest of the ridge, then begins to traverse right on the north side of the block-like headland and follows the south aspect of the Mzimkhulu south gully, in and out of several side gullies, and finally into the gully for the last, easy 'grass step' section.

To meet up with Verkyker Pass, traverse to the left and up around the headland. There is no definite path, and it is a longer but even easier route to the top.

SLEEPING BEAUTY CAVE — HIKE MZ8

Route: From Garden Castle camp up The Monk to the cave
Distance: 8 km return
Duration: 2 hours up and 2 down
Grade: Strenuous
General: Since the Bushman Caves route was closed to hikers not taking a guided tour, this has become one of the favourite shorter hikes from the camp site. However, it is more than a little steep, gaining nearly 400 m in altitude over just 4 km, mostly in the last 1.5 km. On the other hand, it gives the opportunity to camp out in a cave just a short way from base, and so for groups with teenagers it is suitable. (I wouldn't, however, recommend taking younger children as the route really is quite hard.)

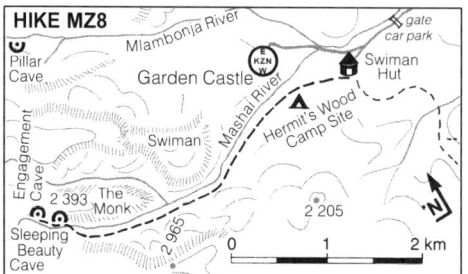

If you are not camping at the EKZNW camp you can park at the entrance gate, pay an entry fee and sign the mountain register. If you plan to overnight you'll also have to book and pay for the cave accommodation.

Follow the road to the camp site, and carry on up the right-hand side of the Mashai River. There's a small forest on the other (right-hand) side of the river. About 1 km past the camp site the valley narrows as it enters the sandstone portals of the Little Berg, but the path itself remains user-friendly for some way yet, even though you have started to ascend by now.

Up on your right are the castellations of Swiman and further up The Monk, while dead ahead looms the 3 313-m bulk of Mashai Peak (the name is taken from the Collins sketch of the Berg, see page 220). Although there is a Mashai Pass in the vicinity, it does not go up anywhere near here, or indeed anywhere near Mashai Peak, which stands as the headwall of the river up which we progress. From here the path tends to become rank with *Hyparrhenia* and *Danthonia* grasses, as well as that scratchy, most widespread plant on earth, bracken (*Pteridium aquilinium*).

Once you feel you are getting really high up in the Little Berg, the path crosses the river and makes its way ever higher to Sleeping Beauty Cave, above the river on the right. Some 700 m on, over a knoll, you come to Engagement Cave which must have some previous romantic tie, but I don't know for sure. The only return is to backtrack along the same route.

MASHAI PASS AND RHINO PEAK — HIKE MZ9

Route: Garden Castle EKZNW office, up the Mlambonja Valley to the summit 'hinge', if I can call it that, of Rhino Peak
Distance: 15 km return, with a 4-km extension
Duration: 10 hours for the full trip, 8 to the top of the pass only
Grade: Extreme
General: This route should really be called Mlambonja Pass, as it follows the river of that name; although that might confuse it with the pass of the same name in the Cathedral area. The peak after which this pass is named, Mashai, as well as the small shelter near the summit, actually stands 4 km away to the south-east. If you're staying at Garden Castle Hotel (a tad expensive for hikers I dare say, if one of the old holiday favourites) then reserve Thursday for a virtually compulsory guided trip up Mashai Pass and the Rhino.

Pay your entry fee and do not for a moment contemplate not filling in the mountain register: many hikers have been caught high up Mashai Pass in failing weather. The lucky ones find Mashai Cave and squeeze in for a long night. Some have to be rescued by the good people of the Mountain Club Search and Rescue Team. Once a misguided person who tried to find his own way down The Rhino in wet, icy conditions did so in a body bag.

If conditions are poor, be they mist, rain or ice, then do not attempt the Rhino traverse – nor if you cannot handle exposure – because it is a tricky 2-km trek out onto the free-standing peak. On the other hand, it's hard to resist the magnetic urge to conquer a peak such as this.

From the office head to the right around the grassy rump up the Mlambonja (hungry dog) Valley, reaching the river after 1.3 km. About 2.2 km further up, the path crosses the river for the first of numerous times, just below Pillar Cave (on the left-hand bank). This is hardly worth using as it is a mere 2.7 km from the start.

The path closely follows the river, ascending a little more seriously now, round two bends to another crossing at about 2 200 m altitude. The next 2 km, up the left-hand bank, can be considered the 'ramp' stage of the pass, going up to

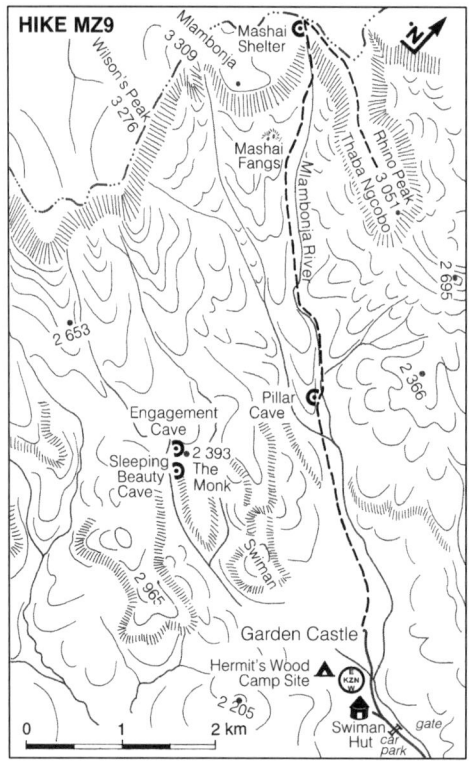

2 500 m where the gully is flanked by the main crags of the Escarpment. From here up the path is stony and eroded for the final 1 km and 400 m ascent. Mashai Cave is a small shelter found up on the left-hand side of Mashai Pass, close to where it tops out.

A brief last rise brings you to a level platform on which you must head sharp right (due north) to make your way onto the Rhino's snout. Make for the crest of the ridge, and once there you have just over 1 km to go. It is recommended that, unless you are a mountaineer, you do not proceed all the way to the summit of the peak (150 m higher) as it does get tricky near the top, and the exposure is considerable. This traverse will take about an hour, each way, so also be careful not to push the time beyond what is safe. Return the same way, and do not, under any circumstance, try to take an 'easy' way down. The only shorter route down involves at least two pitches of abseiling.

The Rhino (3 051 m) is the only significant free-standing peak south of Giant's Castle. From its shape, the name is obvious (I fancy it is a black rhino, for the narrow 'snout', stubby horn and foul temper). I've seldom met anyone who's made it up in good weather. In fact, I've met people who've attempted its well-trodden if stony course numerous times only to get blown back, or snowed on, or pelted with hail.

The peak is known as Thaba Ngcobo to the Zulus. Ngcobo was a local sub-chief who chased a stock-killing leopard into the mountains here. One version of the story has him slaying the leopard with his spear and returning home a hero, while another has him and the leopard both dying in mortal, hand-to-claw combat.

If you wish to visit the Bushman rock art in the area, there is an easy 3-km walk, with a 1-km detour to three lovely pools down a side stream (and back up again). However, you have to book a guide beforehand through the EKZNW office; enquire about the guide's fee.

BUSHMAN'S CAVE AND PASS — HIKE MZ10

Route: Bushman's Nek police post up the Bushman's River to the cave and Ngwangwane Pass
Distance: 10 km one way
Duration: About 5 hours; shorter if you do only the river or cave section
Grade: Severe

General: While this is the most direct route to the summit, reaching the watershed at the base of the block-shaped Thaba Ngwangwe, 'mountain of the pied starlings', and the Bushman's River walk is up one of the loveliest valleys in the Drakensberg, the pass itself is becoming badly eroded and you need to climb a steep grassy ridge to avoid worsening it.

Because of this it makes a better down than up route, and if you want to do a round summit hike then you might consider taking the ridge route above the river on the left. This path is well used by cattle thieves and other mounted parties, so is well defined but has no water until beyond Thomathu Cave where it crosses the head of a stream.

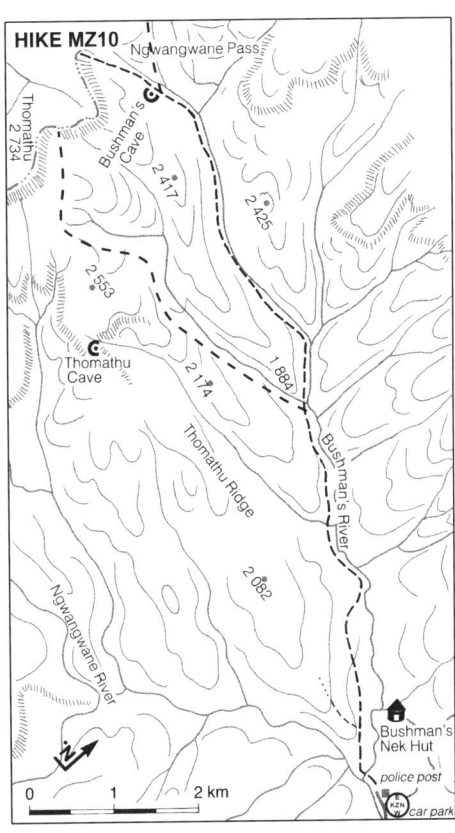

Park at the EKZNW office, where you pay your dues and fill in the mountain register. Die-hard hikers do the round-trip up and down the Escarpment in one day, but I think it really is a two-day trip, or three if you continue to Sehlaba Thebe Park in Lesotho. If you intend to do that then you must sign out at the police post (and don't forget your passport).

There's a picnic site immediately opposite the police gate, near a small fall and pool. You have to cross the river where the northerly Bushman's joins the larger, southerly Ngwangwe, using a small island with a wild willow. From there you have to head to the right of Thomathu Ridge, or else you'll find yourself up the Ngwangwe Valley en route to Sehlaba Thebe. After 500 m the Thomathu Ridge path goes up the crest of the spur to the left.

Do not be tempted to make for the river, but keep to the wide jeep track (no longer used) for 2.5 km, along which it reverts to a path, and reaches the river. Cross a side stream and then continue for another 1.5 km up where the Little Berg creates a gorge to another side-stream crossing. For the next 1.2 km the path sticks close to the river, and along this stretch – if you thought there were some nice pools before – there are some 'benchmark' swimming holes that could detain you indefinitely.

For 3.5 km the path continues steeply (500 m in all) up the river's left-hand bank, to reach Bushman's Cave a little over 5 km and 2 hours from the start. It's a nice large cave but is often used by Basotho travellers (traders, dagga smugglers, cattle thieves ... some make the trip just to buy tobacco).

From the cave cross over to the right-hand side of the river and climb the grassy spur between the two stream gullies to the saddle below Ngwangwe Peak (3 068 m). It tops out at only 2 500 m, a mere 200 m higher than the cave and, together with its twin Thomathu Peak (2 734 m), must be regarded as the easiest of all true Berg passes.

As suggested, make the return trip via Thomathu Pass (or even better, vice versa), 1.5 km south-east at the base of Thomathu. Near the head of the pass is the famous Bushman's Gate rock arch, which rivals the Cedarberg's Wolfberg Arch as a spectacular natural wonder. It really should be visited and photographed. However, Goat's Herd Summit Cave a little beyond this to the south-east, which was once a favourite camping site for hikers, has been trashed by army anti-stock theft patrols and should be avoided. Shame, SANDF!

Thomathu Pass starts in the saddle on the northern slope of Thomathu Peak, and contours out along the ridge to the right for over 1 km, then descends the nose for another kilometre, before dropping steeply down the right-hand spur to Thomathu Cave. The path is well used by horses and cattle, and therefore easy to follow, as the cave is easy to find.

SEHLABA THEBE CAVES TRAVERSE — HIKE MZ11

Route: From Bushman's Nek police post up Bushman's Nek Pass to Sehlaba Thebe Park, and from there joining the caves that lie more or less at the top of the Little Berg all the way from there to Thaba Ngwangwe.
Distance: 32 km
Duration: 2 or 3 days
Grade: Strenuous to severe
General: Like so much in the southern Berg, there is no specific route, other than that up Bushman's Nek Pass. This is a great wilderness area, with numerous caves to choose from. The walk described here links the best ones, but you are unlikely to use more than two of them, depending on your route and speed. I would also suggest extending your stay at Sehlaha Thebe (meaning 'shield' in Sesotho) as this enormous shield is an extensive Alpine meadow full of natural rock features, caves and old stone kraals. There is also the lodge (which looks more like a specification-built suburban house than a mountain lodge) which you can stay in.

Get your passport stamped at the police post, cross the Bushman's River at the wild willow, and a little further on cross to the south, left-hand bank of the Ngwangwe. The path follows the river for close on 3.5 km, then turns up the Little Berg on your left along a none too steep but badly eroded bridle path. The path zigzags up through boulders, where it was blasted many years ago in an attempt to stop Bushman cattle thieves. It certainly has had no impact on Basotho stock thieves. On reaching the actual nek there is a series of tarns and a wide plateau stretching to your left (south-west). There are pools to swim in along the way, as well as in the many tarns. Just make sure not to disturb the dainty, white and very rare water lilies, *Aponogeton ranunculiflorus*, otherwise known as the 'crown jewels of Sehlaba Thebe'. They were discovered in 1970 by a visiting British botanist, and do not occur anywhere else.

Black eagles and lammergeiers patrol the skies, secretary birds strut the grass meadows, yellow-billed and black ducks bob on the tarns, and little Drakensberg siskins swarm over the grasslands in large flocks, growing fat on the seed heads. From the plateau, head for the north-eastern corner of the shield, past a large tarn, where you'll find the very large Tarn Cave just over the lip, facing directly towards the three peaks of Thaba Ntsu (Devil's Knuckles).

From here you have to find your own way north by contouring around the front of the mountain, five prominent spurs and two river valleys to reach Lammergeier Cave in a narrow side gully directly 2.5 km due east of Tarn Cave and only 100 m lower in altitude.

This part of the trip is a great navigational test, requiring accurate map-reading (remember my friend Adrian's dictum that everything in the Drakensberg is 'Very Big'), or the use of a GPS; the new EKZNW maps have a GPS grid, which makes locating your position a whole lot easier.

To reach Thomathu Cave head just west of true north for 1.5 km, down the stream gully, cross the river head over the steep grassy slope on the other side, pass the head of another gully on your right and you'll find the cave just over the ridge looking down into the next valley, at about 2 300 m altitude. The cave is just on the north side of the Thomathu Ridge path so one strategy is to keep more left than you need to until you find the ridge path, then head down to find the cave (it's 500 m down from there that the path meets a definite water course below a high point on the ridge).

Bushman's Cave is next. Contour around to the north-east, around the head of the first valley, around a long spur, back into and around the next valley, and over a nek into the Bushman's River Valley. Once close to the river you'll pick up the Ngwangwe Pass path, where you must turn upstream for nearly 2 km to reach the cave. The return to the police post and EKZNW office is 10 km downstream, passing the best pools you're likely to see in a long time. It's a good path all the way down, but don't try to take a short cut to keep close to the river on the

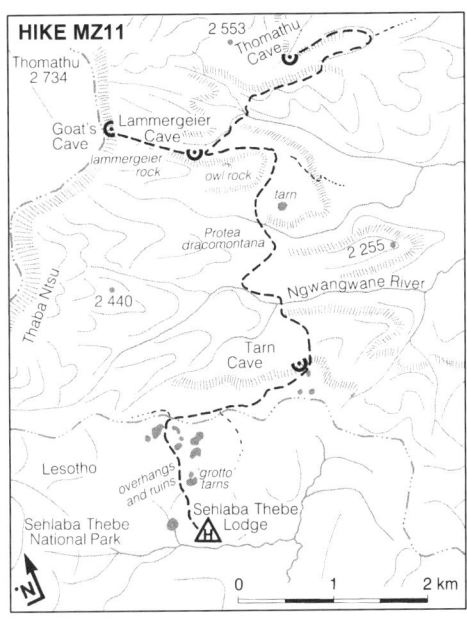

last 2 km (from where you see the gum trees), as there's no way through the rank vegetation.

And so ends our Drakensberg adventure, which for me started 15 years ago when I set out to research my first book on the Berg. I have now walked all the way along the bottom and top of the range, but it will be many years before I can say I've walked a decent majority of the paths in between.

For the section detailing all the passes (which I believe has never been done before), I relied heavily on the knowledge of two Berg stalwarts, Midlands farmer Greig Stewart and Underberg vet Tod Collins. Tod kindly allowed me to use his own sketch map of the southern Berg (pages 220 to 221), while the side views of the northern range (pages 224 to 227) were taken from the endpapers of the book *Mountain Splendour* by Reg Pearse (Howard Timmins, 1978). The artwork was done by Muriel Zonneveld of Estcourt, a lifelong friend of the Pearses'. Reg's son Malcolm owns the copyright to this work and has kindly allowed me to use it in this book.

the hiking passes

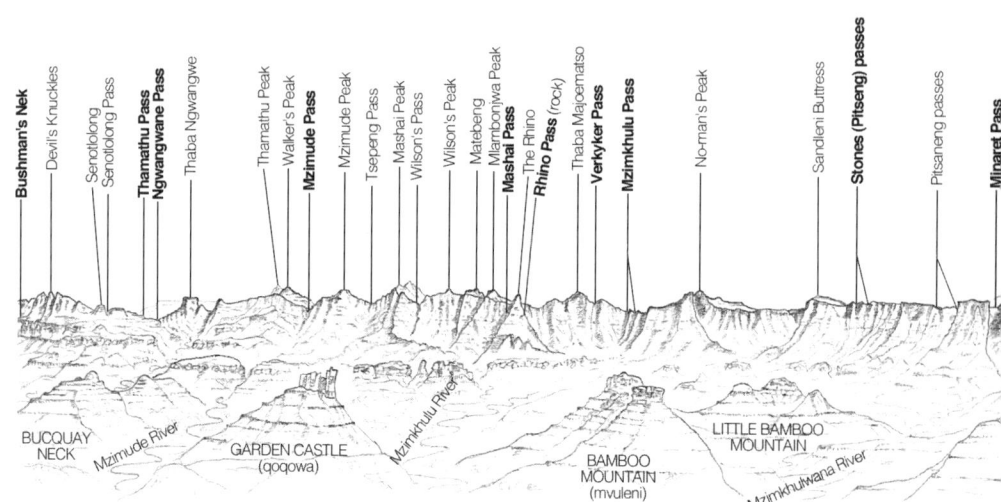

There are around 60 passes along the Drakensberg, ranging from the easiest Chain Ladder ascent to rock routes such as Injisuthi or Lotheni passes. Others are feasible, but require scrambling of even easy rock routes that, while used by mountaineers, are not recommended for hikers (Xeni, Corner, Redi). Then there are the passes that have more than just one option, such as Organ Pipes (Camel, Thuthumi), Jarding/Jarateng, and Mzimkhulu/Verkyker. This list includes only those technical routes that are sometimes used by hikers, but they must be considered as risky to hikers. They are marked by an asterisk*.

Bushman's Nek (2 360 m): Not really a pass at all, as it tops out onto the high Little Berg plateau known as Sehlaba thebe (the shield), and not the main Escarpment. Like the other two passes in the area it is highly eroded in places and the cause of many parallel scars. This seems to be the result of heavy horse traffic in all cases – one reason why some conservators wish to see their use banned in sensitive areas. Remember your passport, as Sehlaba Thebe is in Lesotho and you have to go through the police post.

Thamathu Pass (2 500 m): Another heavily over-used route that was mostly trashed by South African stock theft troops, as was the once popular Goat's Herd Cave near the summit. Lammergeier Cave lower down the valley, where it flattens out, is perhaps a wiser option as a place to overnight. On the other hand, it tops out into the delightful Thamathu or Senotlolong Valley near the spectacular rock arch known as Basotho Gate.

Ngwangwane Pass (2 500 m): Also known as Bushman's Pass as the river of that name rises here. It's an easy route to the summit but is heavily over-used and really should be closed, even though it is such an attractive one. It is also a logical route all the way up the Bushman's River to the southerly base of the huge, fortress-like Thaba Nwgangwe. The pools along the river are classics.

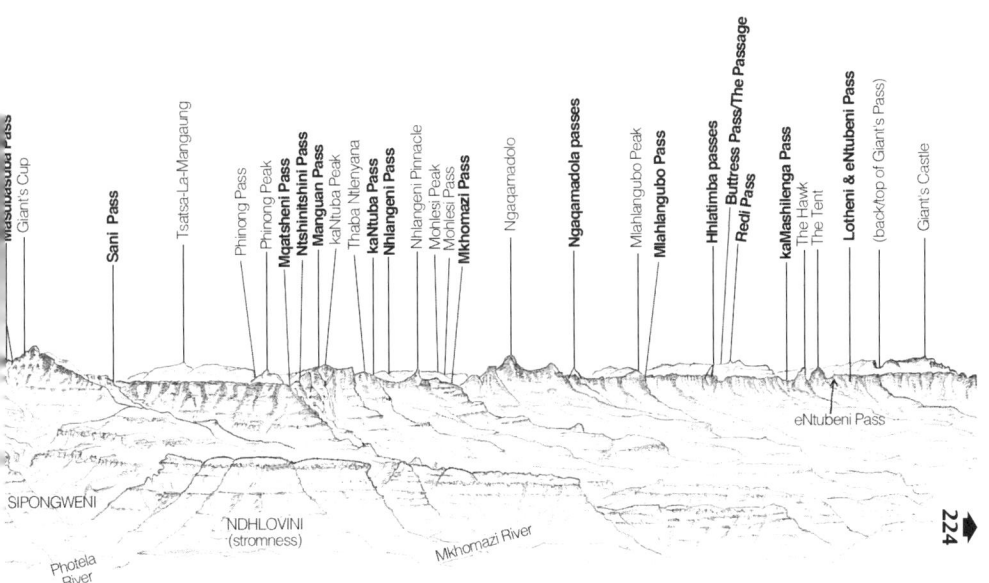

Mzimude Pass (3 050 m): There are two approaches to this pass, one from Swiman/Garden Castle and the other Bushman's Nek/Langalibalele Cave. The two branches meet at the base of the Escarpment, but soon branch out into many heads. This is because the route is used by cattle rustlers and cattle do not always keep to one path when they're being chased – for slaughter, judging from the skeletons. There are two excellent caves on the north slope just 50 m from the top of the most direct route.

Mashai Pass (2 900 m): Every Thursday guests at Garden Castle Hotel are entreated to take a hike up this pass, a tradition that goes back some 50 years. It's a steep and stony but well used pass (naturally), crisscrossing the Mlambonja River, and is a bit eroded in some places higher up. It seems to be inexplicably windy and storms are frequent, but there is a small shelter very near the top, on the left, to save wretched souls caught out in a storm. The route onto The Rhino is in fact a 4-km return trip that should be attempted only by those with a head for serious exposure.

Rhino Pass (3 000 m)*: This is a tricky route and used only by fanatical 'pass baggers'. One gully is iced up for at least half the year, while the other receives sun all winter. Still, it is a rather technical route while the much easier, shorter and more sensible one up to The Rhino is via Mashai Pass.

Verkyker Pass (3 000 m): Accessed from Fun Cave, and in fact very similar to the previous route in ease. It tops out slightly higher than the Mzimkhulu south route and a little way to the south, round a big headland. The top part is steep, but just keep to the north (right-hand) side of the gully.

Mzimkhulu Pass (2 800 m): One of the most pleasant of Berg passes, and an easy route up from Fun Cave. The start is from Giant's View Farm. What may be confusing is that there are three possible heads to the pass, but keep your wits and try to head straight up.

Stones (Pitseng) passes (2 800 m): The Slingsby map shows only one path, but there are in fact two, both easy grass scrambles and well used by Basotho stock thieves. Wilson's Cave is located well above (north-east) the easy, direct route up from Giant's View Farm (see Mzimkhulu chapter on using this route, page 213). From the top it is only 2 km south along the Escarpment to Sandleni Cave which looks out onto the Sandleni Pinnacle and Eland Flats below.

Minaret Pass (2 850 m)*: Unlike Amakehla Pass, this is a long and difficult route that must be kept open by Basotho travellers as the path is, amazingly, fairly well worn. It starts at Lakes Cave and heads up the ridge to the south (the left-hand side) of the cave. This is most surprising as the summit is a steep, narrow gully with a large chockstone blocking it, and it has to be negotiated with some nerve. I would not recommend it but it can be done: I suspect that among the Basotho smugglers are some potentially fine mountaineers.

Amakehla Pass (2 900 m): The most direct and easiest route up from Pholela (or Spectacle) Cave, the first part is straightforward up the stream. The final approach is a trifle sinuous up a slope to the left (south) of the gully and requires some nerve. Increasing use, though, is causing erosion.

Masubasuba Pass (3 050 m): There are several heads to this pass which summits right into the Giant's Cup. It should really be called the Pholela Pass from the South African side. The best route up is from Pholela Cave, climbing directly to the top of the steep ridge north-east of the cave (i.e. above it) and then taking an easy traverse back to the Pholela River path. The route via Fingall's Rock is more scenic but a lot longer and more arduous. The top of the route is very steep and paths are very heavily eroded: new paths are developing all over the place and the pass should rather be avoided altogether.

Sani Pass (2 850 m): I suppose you could hike it, even though the last 7 km from the police post is a heavy-going trudge. Spectacular driving though (4x4 recommended), with a lovely pub at the top – even soft beds and hot meals.

Mqatsheni Pass (3 010 m)*: Follows the Burnera Ridge for about 15 km up from the wilderness leadership school, contours to the left (south) side of the ridge to the Mqatsheni River, then follows a side gully to the south up to the summit. This final section involves lots of scrambling and requires a strong nerve. Not recommended for casual hikers.

Ntshinitshini Pass (3 100 m): A difficult pass to find and to do. Follows into the cutback at the head of the Ntshintshini River and keeps to the main, right-hand gully of the headwaters, north of the main cutback. This pass foils most parties.

Manguan Pass (3 000 m): Branches off kaNtuba Pass at the river, follows a ridge most of the way up the Escarpment but then contours and climbs to the south side of that ridge and zigzags to the top of a shallow saddle (the route up the grassy ridge just north of the path that zigzags up through the rock bands is in fact easier).

kaNtuba Pass (3 250 m): A long and devious route from Bird's Nest Cave that thwarts most parties. It's long, it's steep and chances are you'll get lost as it meanders its way through the Little Berg from the Nhlangeni Valley, up a side gully and a ridge to the sulphur springs, and then down into the kaNtuba Valley. And then it's still a long way to the top in the sharp cutback at the head of this river. However, it does bring you out into a beautiful Alpine valley at the headwaters of the Sehonghong River (sometimes identified incorrectly as the Boja-bo-totse). kaNtuba Ridge reaches a high point of 3 401 m and lies just south of and very close to Thaba Ntlenyana, the highest point in southern Africa (3 482 m).

Nhlangeni Pass (3 200 m): From Bird's Nest Cave this pass goes all the way up the left-hand side of the Nhlangeni River. It's even longer than Mkhomazi and a rougher route, but it does summit on the south side of where the Thaba Ntlenyana (kaNtuba) ridge joins the Escarpment, in the beautiful Mohlesi Valley (to my mind the best valley of the entire watershed area). Mohlesi Pass, shown on Slingsby's map as a northerly fork of this pass, should not be classified as a route.

Mkhomazi Pass (2 850 m): This is an easy pass to hike – in fact before Sani was built it was mooted as a road route into Lesotho. Its only drawback for hikers is that it's a long way from Vergelegen camp. Best to break the trip at lovely Bird's Nest Cave, on the Nhlangeni River, before the route hops over the Little Berg at the top end of Ngcingweni Forest into the Mkhomazi Valley. About 1 km from the summit the path zigs to the left and then zags back to the Mkhomazi headwaters 500 m from the top. The Basotho call this the Mohlesi Pass as the Mohlesi Stream rises right behind it, runs east towards the Escarpment, turns sharp north just near the head of this pass and then makes a huge north-west curve inland.

Ngaqamadola Pass (2 800 m): Most paths from Vergelegen lead directly up towards the twin Ngaqamadolo passes. They go up either side of the narrower, northernmost of two very sharp spurs (the south spur leads up to Ngaqamadola Peak, 3 006 m). They are both fairly easy grassy routes into the cutbacks.

Mlahlangubo Pass (2 900 m): An easy pass from Vergelegen camp. Go north-east to Rooibessiebos camp site and climb steeply up the Little Berg to a vague Contour Path. Head east around Mlahlangubo Peak, cross two streams still on the general contour, then head up a grassy ridge on the south side of the main Mlahlangubo Stream.

Hlathimba Pass (2 820 m): The route takes the south end of the Lotheni Contour Path all the way to the summit. It was often used in historic times, and thought to be some other pass (as in the Langalibalele rebellion, when this confusion indirectly led to the bloodshed). There are in fact two passes, separated by a large spur-like buttress. Both go up fairly obvious, grassy cutbacks well south of the deep gully behind Hlathimba Buttress (which can be indentified by the amazing waterfall, which freezes in winter). The southernmost is the easier, popular route but both have medium size caves near the summit. The last three passes described should be considered better alternatives to kaMashilenga Pass.

Buttress Pass/The Passage (2 950 m): Very straightforward, hence the alternativee name. It starts on the Contour Path 2 km south of Redi Pass and goes up a grassy ridge onto Hlathimba Buttress, a spectacular headland leading south-east off Redi Peak.

Redi Pass (2 900 m)*: A direct route from Lotheni up to the Contour Path via the waterfall on the Ngodwini Stream path, and straight up the front slope of Redi Peak. Near the top it is correctly marked as a rock route, but this really involves only a short scramble section where packs need to be hauled up a 10-m section.

kaMashilenga Pass (3 140 m): This is the most direct route from Lotheni rest camp to the summit, most hikers making for Lotheni Cave about 5 km north of the head of the pass. In both cases this is a pity for the pass is a miserable, awkward scramble up from Yellowwood Cave, and Lotheni Cave is nothing to rave about.

Lotheni and eNtubeni Pass (2 880 m)*: Although both are shown on the Slingsby map, and seem like nice routes to the very desirable Hawk/Tent/Redi area just south of Giant's Castle, they both involve some technical scrambling up rock faces and should be avoided by hikers. In winter they offer superb technical ice climbing. Lotheni, the northerly one, is the more difficult. Either way, it's a long slog from Lotheni rest camp via Ash Cave.

Giant's Pass (3 080 m): A tough, rocky and steep ascent, but it gets you to the top of one of the Berg's most scenic sections. A 15-km slog up from the rest camp, via Giant's Ridge. The official route starts on the Contour Path 2 km east of the gully up a ridge and traverses right under the cliffs (past a cave) and into the gully at the top. However, most hikers attempt to go straight up the left-hand bank of the river. This route is hard to follow and is very badly eroded. About halfway up the path disappears into a maze of erosion gullies.

Jarding (Jarateng) passes (3 030 m, average of three): Not properly shown on the hiking maps, and little known to most hikers. There are in fact three passes here. The named pass summits on the south side of Mount Durnford. However, there are two much easier routes, one that goes up between Durnford and Potterill and the other between Kambule and Carbineer points. This southernmost route is the easiest of the three. The problem with the Jarateng route is that the lower end is overgrown and boulder-strewn. In all three cases you should keep to the grass on the left-hand (when ascending), or the south, side. These passes are best remembered as possible escape routes off the summit.

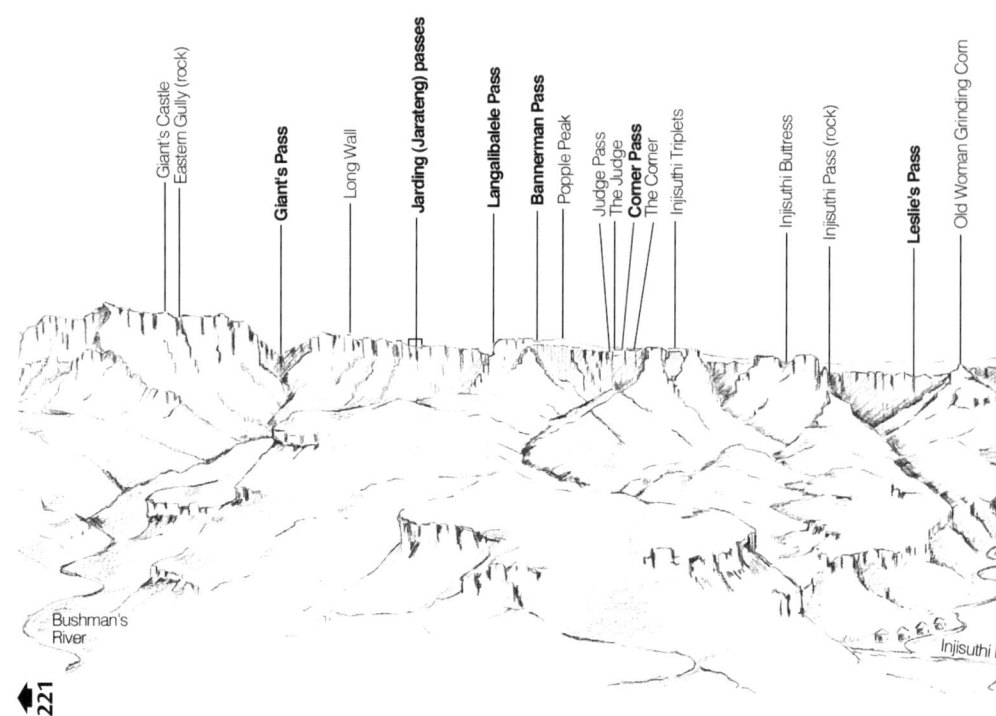

Langalibalele Pass (2 950 m): This has to be the easiest proper pass of the entire Berg, notwithstanding the Chain Ladder approach. Named after a Zulu chief who used it in evading British troops during a brief rebellion, it's more of a ramp than a gully. There's plenty of traffic up and down this route, so avoid sleeping anywhere near the head of the pass. It's well signposted from Giant's Camp, but used more by poachers, smugglers and cattle thieves than hikers.

Bannerman Pass (3 050 m): I consider this one of the easiest Berg passes, starting off from Bannerman's Hut on the Contour Path. The path is pretty good all the way up, even where the gully is rock-choked you can pick your way past the cairns (and cattle skeletons). Bannerman Cave is found a few kilometres over the summit ridge to the south.

Corner Pass (3 188 m): Little known to anyone but ardent mountaineers, it is a fairly straightforward route to the summit from Fergy's Cave (no longer used). It starts on the Contour Path (the Injisuthi jeep track) at The Gap, a few kilometres south of Centenary Hut. The route goes up the 'open book' gully on the south side of The Corner. It does involve one short scramble round a boulder in the gully, but it is not technically difficult.

Leslie's Pass (3 050 m): Not often used by hikers, but the only route to the top in the entire Injisuthi area. It is not difficult, just very long from the EKZNW rest camp. Most people overnight in Junction Cave before tackling the Buttress Fork Stream. Where the stream splits into many side streams at the base of The Ape, the pass goes up the central ridge and then left at the cliff line into the cutback.

Ship's Prow Pass (3 300 m): This is the 'other' pass serving Monk's Cowl/Champagne Valley and it's one of the toughest of the popular hiking ascents (matched by Mlambonja), both in steepness and the summit altitude. Two ascent/descent gullies are located on either side of the Prow, and the south one is the easier, recommended route

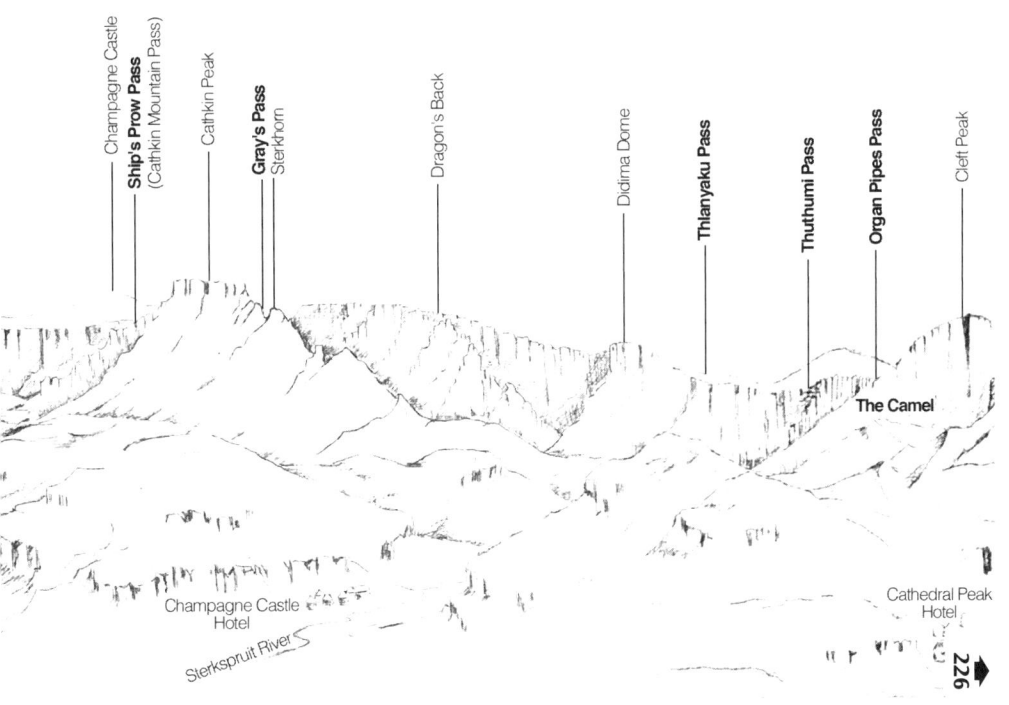

while the north one is very bouldery. The latter is dangerous during flash-flood conditions and best avoided then.

Gray's Pass (3 050 m): Probably the most used pass in the Berg after the Chain Ladders, being the route up from Monk's Cowl. But it's a long walk and most parties camp at the base at Keith Bush Camp (small cave). Nkosazana Cave opposite-left of the summit point is a dark, wet hole. But it's a good access to Vulture's Retreat and Champagne Castle. The valley gets badly polluted at holiday times. You should make a round trip down Ship's Prow Pass.

Thlanyaku Pass (2 750 m): Unlucky for some indeed – this pass seems to be an ideal route to access the amazing valley of Yoddler's Cascades (great place for a romantic weekend), especially since it summits at the lowest point on the Escarpment for miles and miles. However, the final approach (turning right halfway up the Didima Buttress Stream, behind Eastman's Ridge) is loose and stony. It follows a ridge route and not the stream gully and traverses right under the cliff line. Not for people with exposure problems.

Thuthumi Pass (3 100 m): An easy pass, topping out in a gully just below the two small Lower Ndumeni Caves. The path is used by the Basotho, but starts a long way from any direct line, at the top of Didima Gorge, and goes up the Thuthumi Stream gully (with the Organ Pipes Ridge on your right).

Organ Pipes Pass (2 990 m): Starts from the top of Mike's Pass and goes via the jeep track/Contour Path. The new route goes directly up past the Old Lookout hut and the knife-edge ridge. Spectacular but steep. A good path all the way (with cairns through the rocky ridge section). An alternative is **The Camel** (2 990 m) which starts from Cathedral Peak Hotel (Mushroom Rock or Tryme Hill) and joins Organ Pipes near the top.

Tseketseke Pass (3 010 m)*: Seldom used, but can be done. Starts at the hut on the Contour Path below the Pyramid and Column peaks and goes up the left-hand bank of Tseketseke Stream; the top-most part is steep and daunting.

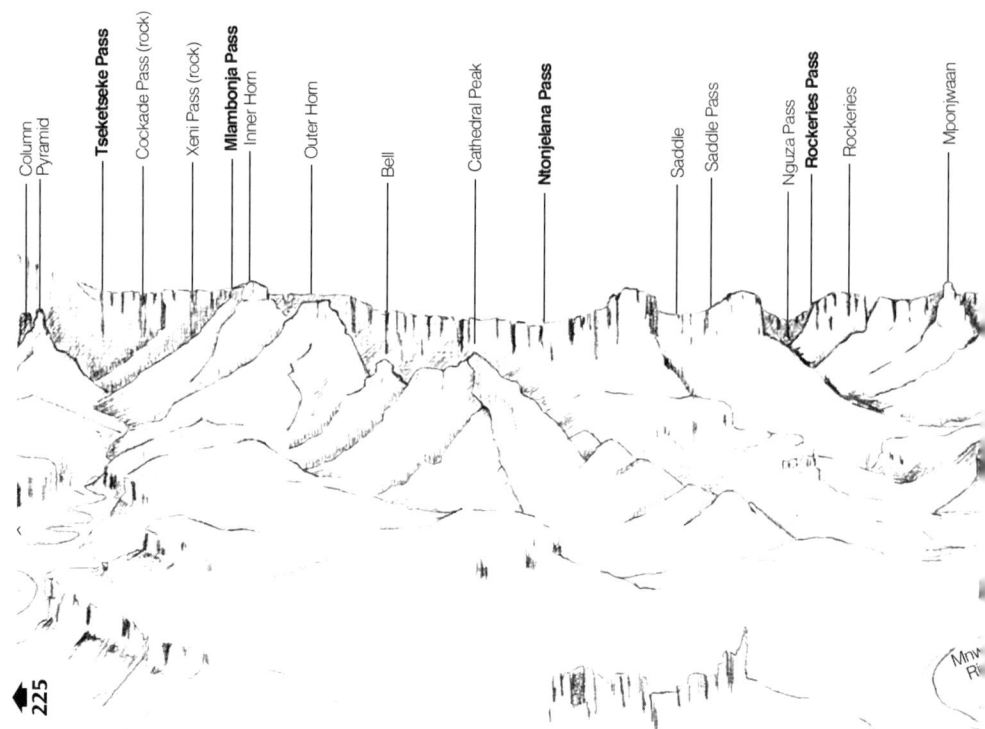

Mlambonja Pass (2 900 m): A very tough walk for one day from the hotel, with an eroded approach and very steep grassy top section, but a nice cave in the gully between the Twins and Escarpment. There's no water in the cave but a drip nearby. Otherwise it's a schlep up and over into Kwakwatsi Valley. Hikers on the way up usually break the hike by camping among the boulders at the base of the pass. Like a few other passes, this one is heavily used only because it is the most direct way up from a popular area, otherwise it would likely fall into disuse. The 'summit' cave is also a hop over the saddle and traverse under the buttress away from the real summit.

Ntonjelana Pass (2 850 m): Locals say this is a tough one, but mainly because it is long, starts 'nowhere' (from Makhela's Kraal at the base of Rockeries Pass) and goes 'nowhere' (a saddle 2 km north of Mlambonja Pass) – which sounds great to me.

Rockeries Pass (2 920 m): The easiest pass of the Mnweni area, relative to the Mnweni's toughness, goes up behind the Rockeries and is the preferred way up for a round trip. One short, difficult section is where the stream comes down from the Nguza Pass (technical) on the left. The only usable shelter is Scaly Cave.

Mnweni Pass (2 910 m): A long, tough, steep, but not technical pass. One usually has to overnight at Shepherd's Cave at the bottom of the pass proper, which ascends the awesome Mnweni Cutback or Five Star Cave on the Mbundini

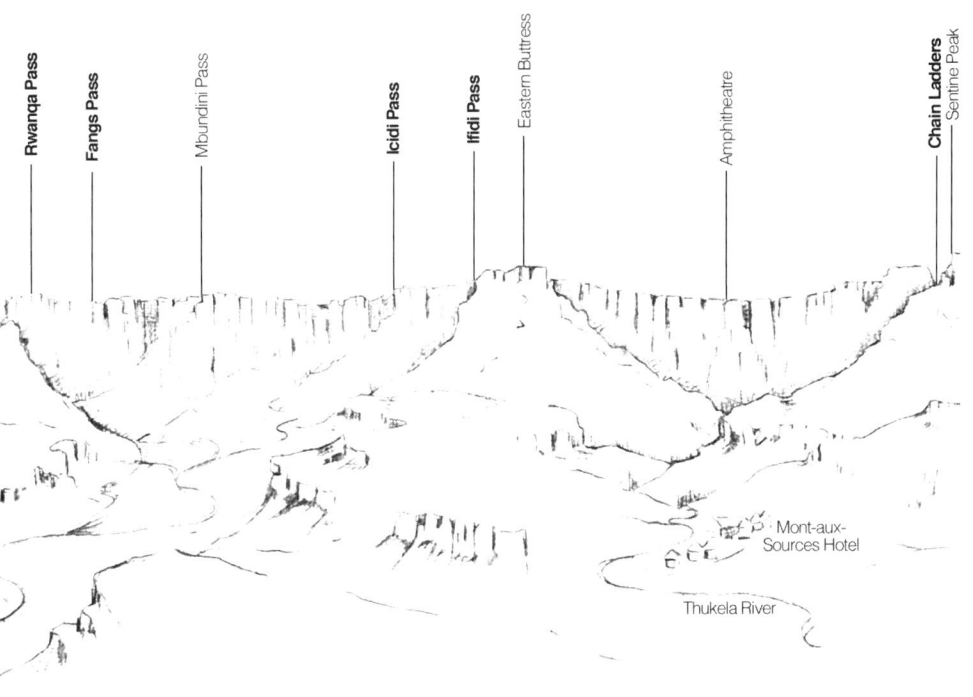

River side of the confluence, but these are often used by locals or the Basotho so a better option may be to camp among the bushes at the confluence of the Mnweni and Mbundini rivers if the caves are not to your liking.

Rwanqa Pass (2 950 m): A very steep and laborious route, traversing on steep grass; not to be recommended to any but the most ardent adventurers. Starts from Shepherd's Cave.

Fangs Pass (3 000 m): Ascends from Shepherd's Cave up the gully to the north of Mnweni Pass, is used by dagga smugglers and is a very scenic way to the top.

Icidi Pass (3 100 m): Very long and remote, with the top section steep and boulder-choked. It has a fork near the top, one prong holding a stream, so could be dangerous to impassable after rain, the other iced up in winter (requires technical equipment).

Ifidi Pass (3 000 m): Seldom done as the summit is rocky and it's one of the longest walks in the Berg. Much easier to go down from Ifidi 'cave' overhang than up. Start at the Mnweni visitors' centre, which is seldom used. The final approach is rocky.

Chain Ladders (tops out at 2 990 m): From Witzieshoek/Sentinel car park to top of Amphitheatre. A 'walk in the park' as far as Berg passes go. Duration of ascent is 1 to 1½ hours.

the highest peaks/'kulus'

Since mountaineers first set foot in the Berg, the argument has raged about which is the highest peak, and the second and the third.... First to be nominated was Mont-aux-Sources, although it turns out to be only number 18 on our list (but the 26 highest point on the watershed). Prominent points in every area have had their share of the limelight: Cleft Peak, Champagne Castle, Giant's Castle, and so on. Few south of Giant's Castle were ever noticed, yet there are more 'kulus' in the south than the more fancied north. To clear up the confusion once and for all, the highest point in South Africa is a little basalt crown about 2 km back from Injisuthi Buttress, lying on the watershed with Lesotho. Modern map makers have dubbed it Mafadi, but in Lesotho it is named after the river that rises on its western flank, Ntheledi. It stands at 3 449 m. (A new official survey using sophisticated GPS methods has measured it at a metre higher but this won't appear on maps until the government printer reprints that map.)

In order to clarify this matter, the MCSA published a list of the top 50 'kulus' by Cliff Murch in the annual *Journal*, 1994. A kulu is defined as a singular point, not less than 30 minutes' walking from another kulu, so you don't count consecutive points all along the same high ridge as often occurs. In Scotland there is a popular pastime of 'bagging Munros' – peaks of over 3 000 feet (about 900 m). In South Africa the challenge is to 'catch kulus' (the word is derived from the Zulu for 'big' – *khulu*) over 3 000 m. While there are 161 distinct kulus in the Drakensberg, many are so far unnamed, being high points on ridges not visible from South Africa, or simply those points along the Escarpment that are not outstanding enough to have warranted attention, so this list (in order of height) contains only the 34 highest that have recognisable names. The 'location' column indicates whether it is FREE-standing, ON the Escarpment or INland on the Lesotho side.

NAME	HEIGHT	AREA	LOCATION
Mafadi/Ntheledi	3 450*	Injisuthi	in
Injisuthi Dome	3 410	Injisuthi	in
Champagne Castle	3 377	eMhlawazini	in
kaNtuba	3 355	Mkhomazi	in
Trojan Wall	3 343	Injisuthi	on
Pampiring	3 335	Didima	in
Thaba Tsooana	3 333	eMhlawazini	in
Lithobolong	3 225	Injisuthi	in
Popple Peak	3 325	Bushman's River (N)	in/on
Giant's Castle	3 314	Bushman's River	free
Redi	3 314	Lotheni	on
Mashai	3 313	Mzimkhulu (S)	in
Mlambonja Peak	3 309	Mzimkhulu (S)	in
Walker's Peak	3 306	Mzimkhulu (S)	in/on
Mohlesi	3 301	Mkhomazi	on

Mount Durnford	3 294	Bushman's River	on
Icidi Buttress	3 290	Mnweni	on
Mont-aux-Sources	3 282	Thukela	in
Cleft Peak	3 281	Mlambonja	on
Terateng	3 280*	Lotheni	in
Wilson's Peak	3 276	Mkhomazi (S)	on
Namahadi Peak	3 275*	Maluti	in
Litseketseke Spur	3 267	Lotheni	in
Long Wall	3 257	Bushman's River	in/on
Hodgson's Peak (S)	3 257	Mzimkhulu	in
Namahadi Ridge	3 257	Namahadi	in
Mqatsheni	3 249	Mkhomazi	in
Champagne Castle Buttress	3 248	eMhlawazini	on
Hodgson's Peak (N)	3 244	Mzimkhulu	in
Stimela Peak	3 239	Mnweni	on
Bannerman Face	3 235	Bushman's River (N)	on
Monk's Cowl	3 234	eMhlawazini	free
Black and Tan Wall	3 224	Mnweni Cutback	in/on
Lithabaneng	3 220*	Lotheni	in

OTHER WELL-KNOWN PEAKS

Sentinel	3 165	Thukela	free
Ifidi Peak	3 219	Mnweni	on
Mbundini Buttress	3 120	Mnweni	on
Mnweni Outer Buttress	3 099	Mnweni Cutback	free
Mponjwane	3 177	Ntonjelana	free
Saddle (south rise)	3 060	Ntonjelana	on
Cathedral Peak	3 004	Mponjwane Spur	free
Ndumeni Dome	3 206	Didima	in
Didima Dome	3 078	Didima	on
Didima Buttress	3 170	Didima	on
Injisuthi W Triplet	3 187	Injisuthi	free
The Tent	3 130	Lotheni	on
Rhino Peak	3 051	Mzimkhulu (S)	on/free
Thaba Ntsu/Devil's Knuckles	3 028	Mzimkhulu (S)	on
Ben Macdhui	3 001	NE Cape	n/a

The 'location' column indicates whether it is FREE-standing, ON the Escarpment or INland on the Lesotho side.
(* – newest calculated height)

helpful words

ENGLISH	ZULU	SESOTHO
Hello	Sawubona	Lumela
reply – good day	Yebo, sawubona	E, lumela
How are you?	Usaphila (s); Nisaphila (p)	O phela joang
I am well	Ngisaphila unjani wena (s)	Keea phela
	Sisaphila ninjani nini (p)	
My name is David	Igama lami ngingu David	Bitso laka ke David
What is your name?	Ubani igama lakho?	Omang bitso la hau?
I do not understand	Angizwa ukuthi uthini	Ha ke utloe
Thank you	Ngiyabonga (s); Siyabonga (p)	Keea leboha
Goodbye (go well)	Hamba kahle	Tsamaea hantle
I want to go to Mnweni	Ngifisa ukuya Mnweni	Ke batla ho tsamaea Mnweni
Where does this path go?	Iyakuphi lendlela	Tsela e e ea kae?
I am ill	Ngiyagula	Keea kula
I have none	Anginakho	Ha ke na eona
Where are you going?	Uyaphi?	O ea kae?
I am going to (Injisuthi)	Ngiya (Injisuthi)	Ke ea (Injisuthi)
What is the time?	Isikhathisini?	Nakoke mang?
Come!	Woza!	Tlo koana!
When?	Nini?	Neng?
Where?	Kuphi?	Kae?
Tomorrow	Kusasa	Hosane
Please...	Ngicela...	Nthuse...
What is the name of this place?	Kuthiwa yini igama lalendawo?	Keng bitso la tuloe?
I need (beer)	Ngidinga (utshwala)	Keea batla (joala)
I wish to buy (bread)	Ngicela (isinkwa)	Ke batla ho reka (muroko)
Here is (tobacco)	Naku (ugwayi)	Ke e (koae)
Blanket	Ingubo	Kobo
Candles	iKhandlela	Likerese
Cave	Imbobo	Hlokomela
Fire	Umbilo	Mollo
Food	Ukudla	Lijo
Home	iKhaya	Ntlo
Medicine	Umuthi	Moreana
Tea	Itiye	Teee
Water	Amanzi	Metsi

useful contacts

EKZNW
Rest camps
Royal Natal National Park	(036) 438-6412
Rugged Glen (camping and horses)	(036) 438-6422
Cathedral Peak	(036) 488-1880
Monk's Cowl	(036) 468-1103
Injisuthi	(036) 431-7848
Giant's Castle	(036) 353-3718
Vergelegen	(033) 702-0712
Lotheni	(033) 702-0540
Highmoor	(033) 263-7240
Kamberg	(033) 263-7251
Mkhomazi	(033) 263-6444
Cobham	(033) 702-0831
Garden Castle	(033) 701-1823
Bushman's Nek (sub-office of Garden Castle)	(033) 701-1823

Head office
(Queen Elizabeth Park, Pietermaritzburg)
Reservations	(033) 845-1000
General information	(033) 845-1002
Management	(033) 845-1999
Map enquiries	(033) 845-1343/1354
	www.kznwildlife.com (includes on-line bookings)

Mnweni Guides
Berg Watch – Meridy Pfotenhauer	(033) 394-4064
Mnweni Tourist Centre – Zacharia Dlamini	(072) 184-4758

Mzimkhulu Pass
Crofter's Trading Store – John Hamilton	(033) 701-1812
	(to arrange to collect the key for the Castle View hike, MZ7)

Buffalo Thorn Community Guides
c/o Monk's Cowl EKZNW office
Brighton Dlamini	(082) 216-9974
Steven Mabaso	(083) 753-2842, Private Bag X2, Winterton, 3340

Berg Free Adventures

Giant's Castle/Injisuthi area – Dave Sclanders (033) 386-5622 (tel or fax)
 bergfree@mweb.co.za, www.bergfree.co.za
Giant's Cup Trail transfers – Sandy Leask (033) 702-1228
 cameronadventures@hotmail.com

Central (northern) Drakensberg Information

Thokozisa Office (036) 488-1207, fax (036) 488-1795
 cdta@futurenet.co.za

Sani Saunter (southern Berg)

Information office, Underberg (033) 702-1902
 www.sanisaunter.com
Amafa (KZN Heritage, rock art custodians) (033) 394-6543
Mountain Club of South Africa (KZN) (031) 702-7844 or 082- 990-5877
Durban Rambler Club (031) 764-4721 or 083-544-6379
Mountain Backpackers Club – Lawrence Bates (031) 266-3970
Pietermaritzburg Ramblers Club (033) 344-2874
Midlands Hiking Club (033) 330-3763

White Cottage Books, Underberg

Tom Wimber (033) 701-2059, fax and a/h (033) 701-1050
 whitecottage@sai.co.za

RECOMMENDED PRIVATE ACCOMMODATION (NORTH TO SOUTH)

There are far more places to stay in the Berg area than could be included here. However, the following establishments are those which are known to the author and can be recommended. They all offer direct hiking access to the mountains.

Price categories are: A = R100–199, B = R200–299, C = R300–399, D = R400–499, E = >R500 a person a night sharing, applicable from February 2003. Please check if the price is for bed and breakfast only or full board.

Amphitheatre, The Cavern

The last-remaining of the true old family holiday hotels with old-fashioned prices. About to become third generation Carte family-owned, it has the feel of yesteryear and is a firm favourite.

Price category: C
(036) 438-6270, fax (036) 438-6334,
cavern@iafrica.com

Montusi

Also owned by the Carte family, this is a much more modern establishment, aimed primarily at the week-end-getaway market. It has a compendium of facilities including high-wire and trapeze, and horse-riding.

Price category: E
(036) 438-6243, fax (036) 438-6566
montusi@iafrica.com

Witzieshoek Mountain Resort
Built by a local chief in the 1930s, it is the only place fully in South Africa that is actually in, or on, the Drakensberg. Fairly simple but neat and tidy accommodation, atmospheric bar and great views to eat by. Lammergeiers are regularly fed on the property.
Price category: B
(058) 713-6361, manager (083) 500-0181

Cathedral Peak, Cathderal Peak Hotel
Still owned by the Van der Riets who built it in the 1930s, it has been greatly expanded and transformed from a stone inn into a fashionable weekend resort. Possibly has the most awesome Berg setting. Offers guided walks, horse-riding, helicopter flips and daily activities. Harry's Bar is an institution, and the hotel has its own wedding chapel.
Price category: C
(036) 488-1888, fax (036) 488-1889
reservations@cathedralpeak.co.za

EKZNW Didima Hotel
Just opened at the time of going to press: inspired architecture but poor siting, individual units strung right along and in full view of the road.
Price category: B – C, bed only
Contact EKZNW reservations

Champagne Valley, Cayley Lodge
A modern guesthouse situated on Bell Park Dam, not aimed at the hiking market but somewhere you'd want to go to impress someone (or treat yourself) after a tough hike in the mountains. Outstanding accommodation, food and service.
Price category: D
(036) 468-1222, fax (036) 468-1020
cayley@planethotels.co.za

Champagne Castle Hotel
The second oldest hotel in the valley retains much of its old-world charm and remains a family favourite. It is famously sited, like Cathedral Peak, virtually within touching distance of the great peaks. Newly renovated to modern standards, it offers hiking and horse-riding as well as other activities. Ask for a copy of the hotel's history for some fascinating reading.
Price category: C–E
(036) 468-1063, fax (036) 468-1306
champagnecastle@futurenet.co.za

Champagne Sports Resort
A luxury hotel with regular hotel rooms and time-share log cabins. The grounds sweep down to a full golf course with expansive views of the mountains beyond. Other extensive sporting facilities include tennis, squash and mountain biking.
Price category: D–E
(036) 468-1088, fax (036) 468-1072
csrres@futurenet.co.za

Drakensberg Sun
Incorporates the old Cathkin Park Hotel property, and is very hiker friendly – some of the hikes described start on the property. Standard, reliable Southern Sun style of hospitality in a Berg environment, with a high quality of service (including guided walks).
Price category: C standard, E luxury
(036) 468-1000, fax (036) 468-1224
shakitab@southernsun.com

Inkosana Lodge and Trekking
The only establishment, created and hosted by mountaineer Ed Salomons, that caters specifically for hikers and backpackers. Casual atmosphere, rooms for small or large groups and meals by arrangement.
Price category: A–B
Tel/fax (036) 468-1202
inkosana@futurenet.co.za

The Nest
The site of David Gray's farm, Berg pioneer after whom Gray's Pass is named. Another of that increasingly lonely group of 'old Berg hotels', it is perhaps a little out of walking range of the mountains but deserves its place here for its pedigree. In other words a great family hotel with affordable prices.

Price category: B–C
(036) 468-1068, fax (036) 468-1390
thenest@futurerest.co.za

Underberg, Bushman's Nek Hotel
Another of the great family hotels, although this one dates to only the 1950s. It has retained all the charms of the old Berg, has incredible views over the southernmost high peaks, great walking, horse-riding by arrangement, and prices to make you weep (with joy). Very hiker friendly, and the legend of Anton Zunckel as an extra draw card. Includes special hikers' self-catering rooms, time-share or casual bookings when available.
Price category: B
Tel/fax (031) 572-7717

Garden Castle Hotel
Another 1950s establishment, this one presides over the Garden Castle area as the other old hotels do over their respective Drakensberg domains. While not really welcoming outside hikers, it does have its own guided walks including those to nearby rock art and the famous weekly climb up Mashai Pass to The Rhino. There is also a golf course. The hotel's atmosphere is still rather old-fashioned.
Price category: C
(033) 701-1355, fax (033) 701-0070
drak@iafrica.com

Himeville Arms
Included here for convenience and for old times' sake. A great kick-off point for trips up Sani Pass, or as a place to head for down the mountains. You can enjoy great pub and weekend lunches.

Price category: B
(033) 702-1305, fax (033) 702-1302
himevillearms@futurenet.co.za

Sani Top Chalet
What can you say about the highest inn and licensed pub in Africa, other than to thank the mountain gods for Jonathan Aldous and his Sani Top inn? If you've never spent a night there, you don't fully know the Berg. You can go hiking, skiing in winter, trout fishing or pony trekking from the lodge.
Price category: A–C for overnight and 'top and bottom' packages (one night at a guesthouse below and one night at the lodge)
Tel/fax (033) 701-1064
sanipass@futurenet.co.za

Sani Valley
A backpackers' place alive with the sounds of many languages, built on the historic site of the old Mokhotlong Mountain Transport company's premises (started by David Alexander who built the pass and the lodge on the summit). Daily tours up the pass organised, and hiking routes.
Price category: A
(033) 702-0203

Sani Valley Lodge
A luxury fully-catered or self-catering log-cabin guesthouse and game park (zebra, eland, black wildebeest and others), with a large dam offering some watersports and fly fishing. You can walk, horse-ride or go on game drives.
Price category: B–D
Tel/fax (033) 702-0203 or cell (082) 572-1807

book list

I made use of my richly stocked bookcase and referred to old favourites which are listed below. Sadly quite a few of these are no longer readily available although they contain a wealth of knowledge and information. The books in the short additional list at the end of my references are those currently available from the publisher which pertain to the Drakensberg or contain general regional references that are useful.

Animals and birds
Birds of Prey of Southern Africa by Peter Steyn (David Philip, Cape Town; 1982)
Concise Guide to the Animal Tracks of Southern Africa, A by Louis Liebenberg (David Philip, Cape Town; 1992)
Mammals of the Southern African Subregion, The by Reay Smithers (University of Pretoria, Pretoria; 1983)
Roberts' Birds of Southern Africa edited by Gordon Lindsay Maclean (John Voelcker Bird Book Trust, Cape Town; 1940 to present)

General
Bushmen, The by Alf Wannenburgh, photographs by Peter Johnson and Anthony Bannister (Struik, Cape Town; 1999)
Camera in Quathlamba: Photographing the Drakensberg, A by Malcolm Pearse (Howard Timmins, Cape Town; 1980)
Cradle of Rivers: The Natal Drakensberg, A by David Dodds (Centaur, Cape Town; 1975)
Dragon's Wrath, The by Reg Pearse (Macmillan, Johannesburg; 1986)
Drakensberg of Natal, The by Doyle Liebenberg (Bulpin, Cape Town; 1972)
Guide to the Drakensberg, A by August Sycholt (Struik, Cape Town; 2002)
Indigenous Healing Plants by Margaret Roberts (Southern Book Publishers, Halfway House; 1990)
Saga of Sani Pass and Mokhotlong, The by Michael Clarke (White Cottage Books, Underberg; 2001)
Sani Pass: Riding the Dragon by David Alexander (Published by the author, Durban; 1992 and 2002)
Stories from the Karkloof Hills by Charles Scott Shaw (Shuter and Shooter, Pietermaritzburg; 1990)
Zulu by Roger and Pat de la Harpe, Barry Leitch and Sue Derwent (Struik, Cape Town; 1998)

Geography/geology
Fossil Reptiles of the South African Karoo by MA Cluver (SA Museum, Cape Town; 1978)
Geology for South African Students: An Introductory Text Book by G Hamilton and H Cooke (CNA; 1954)
Landforms in Africa: An Introduction to Geomorphology by Colin Buckle (Longman, England; 1978)

Mountaineering/hiking
Barrier of Spears: Drama of the Drakensberg by Reg Pearse (Howard Timmins, Cape Town; 1973; and Southern/Struik, Cape Town; 1989)
Complete Guide to Walks and Trails in Southern Africa, The by Jaynee Levy (Struik, Cape Town; 1989)
Journals of the Mountain Club of South Africa, The (Cape Town)
Mountains of Southern Africa by David Bristow and Clive Ward (Struik, Cape Town; 1985)
Peak to Climb, A by Jose Burman (Struik, Cape Town; 1966)

Rock art
Fragile Heritage: A Rock Art Field Guide by David Lewis-Williams and Geoffrey Blundell (Wits University Press, Johannesburg; 1998)
Images of Power: Understanding San Rock Art by David Lewis-Williams and Thomas Dowson (Struik, Cape Town; 2000)
Ndedema by Harold Pager (Akademische Druck Verlag Anstadt, Graz; 1971)
Rock Paintings of the Drakensberg, Natal and Griqualand by A Wilcox (Struik, Cape Town; 1973)

Vegetation
Account of the Plant Ecology of the Cathedral Peak Area of the Natal Drakensberg, An by Donald Killick (Botanical Survey of South Africa, Memoir 34; 1982)
Complete Field Guide to Trees of Natal, Zululand and Transkei, The by Elsa Pooley (KwaZulu-Natal Herbarium, Durban; 1993)
Field Guide to the Flora of the Natal Drakensberg, A by Donald Killick (Jonathan Ball and AD Donker, Johannesburg; 1990)
Field Guide to the Natal Drakensberg, A by Pat and David Irwin and John Ackhurst (KZN Wildlife Society, now Wessa, Durban; 1980)
Field Guide to the Wild Flowers of KwaZulu-Natal and the Eastern Region, A by Elsa Pooley (KwaZulu-Natal Herbarium, Durban; 1998)
Fynbos: South Africa's Unique Floral Kingdom by Richard Cowling and Dave Richardson, photographs by Colin Paterson-Jones (Fernwood Press, Cape Town; 1995)
Guide to the Grasses of South Africa by Frits van Oudtshoorn (Briza Publications, Pretoria; 1992)
Mountain Splendour: The Wild Flowers of the Drakensberg by Reg Pearse (Howard Timmins, Cape Town; 1978)
Trees of Natal by Eugene Moll (University of Cape Town Eco-Lab Trust, Cape Town; 1981)
Trees of Southern Africa by KC Palgrave (Struik, Cape Town; 2002)
Wild Flowers of the Natal Drakensberg by W Trauseld (Purnell, Cape Town; 1977)

If you're passing through Underberg there is a fine book shop, White Cottage Books, run by Tom Wimber, a Berg enthusiast who specialises in Africana, including books on the Drakensberg. If you'd like to contact him you'll find the details in the useful contacts list, page 232.

extra reading

Hiking Trails of South Africa by Willie and Sandra Olivier (Struik, Cape Town; 2003)
Newman's Birds of Southern Africa by Kenneth Newman (Struik, Cape Town; 2002)
Sasol Birds of South Africa by I Sinclair (Struik, Cape Town; 2002)
Snakes and Snakebites by J Marais (Struik, Cape Town; 1999)

index

Page references in italics indicate maps and photographs.

Ablutions 17, 40, 87
African holly 23, 161
Albert Falls 96, 97, 98
Alsophila dregei 21, *22*, 109
Amakehla Pass 209–210, *210*, 222
Amphitheatre
   hikes 38–62, *50*
   overview 36–38, *51*
   animals 25–29, *26*, *27*, *28*, 153–154
Anton's Cave 111, 116
Aponogeton ranunculiflorus 218
Arendsig Plateau 92, 100
Aristida grass 21
Arundinaria tessellata 196
Ash Cave 170, *186*, 187–188

Baboon Rock 90, 91, 200
baboons 159–160
backpacks 12, 210
bald ibis 160
Bannerman Cave 165, 167
Bannerman Hut 146–148, *147*,
   160–162, *161*, 162–163, 165
Bannerman Pass 148, 150, 163, 165,
   165, 224
Barker's Chalet 82, 88
Barry's Grave and Grotto 108–109,
   108, *127*
Barry's Route 105
Battle Cave 33, 136, 140, *140*, 141, 147
bearded vulture *see* lammergeier
berg adder 28
Berg cycad 21, *22*, 89
Bergview Chalets 109–110
birds 28–29, 82, 83
Bird's Nest Cave 191
Bitis arietans 28, *28*
Black Eagle Pass 197
black eagles 29
Blind Man's Corner 113, 115, 131, 146
Blue Pool and Nyosi Grotto 98–99, *99*
boots 11–12
Boundary Pool 139
Breakfast Stream 112

Buddleja salviifolia 22, *24*, 157, 199
bushbuck 26, *26*, 157
Bushman Rock Art Interpretative
   Centre 170
Bushman's Cave and Pass 216–218, *217*
Bushman's Gate rock arch 218
Bushman's Nek 194, 220
Bushman's Nek Hotel 233–234
Bushman's River 166, 167
Bushman's River Pass 153
Bushmen 30–33, 47, 106
   see also rock art
Buttress Fork Stream 150
Buttress Fork Valley 144
Buttress Pass 188, 223
Buttress Stream 144

Cambalala House 92
Cannibal Cave 38, 48, *48*, 57
Cape vultures 29, 154
Carbineer Point 153, 156
Castle Buttress 99, 100
Cataract Valley 138, 142, 143, 145
Caterpillar and Catfish Cookhouse
   37–38
caterpillar grass 23
Cathedral Peak
   hikes 82–103
   history 79–81
Cathedral Peak hike 82–83, *83*
Cathedral Peak Hotel 80–81, 87, *123*,
   233
Cathedral Peak to Didima Valley
   102–103, *103*
Cathkin Park Hotel 105, 107
Cathkin Peak 81, 104, *177*, *205*
Cavern Berg Hotel 38, 232
Cayley Lodge 107, 130, 233
cellphones 14–15
Celtis africana 23
Centenary Hut 147
Centenary to Bannerman Hut
   146–148, *147*
Chain Ladders 38–40, *39*, *51*, 227

Chameleon Cave 211
Champagne Castle 104, 119
Champagne Castle Hotel 105, 107,
   130, 233
Champagne Castle via Grays' Pass
   117–119, *118*
Champagne Castle via Ship's Prow Pass
   120, 129–130, *129*
Champagne Sports Resort 107, 130, 233
Christmas Cave 192
Cleft Peak 97, 100
climate 19–20
clothing 11, 112, 144
Cobham camp 196, *205–206*
Cobham Hike of Many Caves
   211–212, *212*
Column Peak 81, 97, 100, *124*
common spikethorn 22, *24*
Contour Path
Contour Path to Didima Valley
   102–103, *103*
Centenary to Bannerman Hut
   146–148, *147*
Contour Path to Monk's Cowl
   145–146, *146*
Lotheni to Sani Pass 172–174, *173*,
   174, *175*
Mnweni to Cathedral 76–77, *78*
Monk's Cowl to Upper Didima Valley
   130–132, *133*
to Lotheni 163–164, *164*
Two Huts hike from Giant's rest camp
   162–163
Corner Pass 136, 150, 224
Cowl Fork 146
Crystal Falls 112
Cypress Cave and Sinclair's Shelter
   176, *185*, *185*

Danthonia distica 23, 215
Dayimani Stream 149
Del'mhlwazini River 137, 142
Devil's Dyke 185
Devil's Hoek Valley 44–45, *45*, 46

Devil's Tooth 42, 154
Didima Buttress 132
Didima Dome 103, 132
Didima Gorge hike 93–95, *94*
Didima Hotel 81, 103, 233
Didima Valley
    from Cathedral Peak 102–103, *103*
    from Monk's Cowl 130–132, *133*
Doreen Falls 96, 97, 98
Dragon Peaks Farm 017
Dragon's Back 116, 119, *127*, 131
Drakensberg Boys' Choir 107
Drakensberg Inn 38
Drakensberg Sun Hotel 107, 108, 233
Durnford's Camp 156

Eagle Rock 192
Eastman's Ridge 131–132
eland 25–26, *206–207*
Eland Cave *124*, 155
El Mirador Hotel 107
eMhlawazini River 113, 117
Encephalartos ghellinckii 21, *22*, 89
Engagement Cave 215
eNtubeni Pass 170, 223
equipment 10–12
erica *24*
Ericaceae family *24*
everlasting 22, *24*, *178*, *181*

Fairy Glen 59–60, 60, *60*
Fangs Pass 72–73, *73*, 227
Fergy's Cave 136, 147
Fern Forest hike 107–108, *108*
Festuca caprina 23
Festuca costata 21, *22*
food 15–16, 117, 157
Fun Cave 213

Game Pass Shelter 31–32, 170, 175–176, *176*, *202*
Ganapu Ridge and Sherman's Cave 90–91, *90*
Garden Castle 193–194
Garden Castle Hotel 194, 234
geology 18–19
Gewaagd House 92
Giant's Castle
    hikes 154–168
    history 152–154
Giant's Castle Forest and River Walk 155–157, *156*
Giant's Castle Peak 152

Giant's Cave 167
Giant's Cup 193
Giant's Cup Trail 136, 195–198, *197*, *198*
Giant's Hut 159–160, *160*, 162–163, *163*, *181*
Giant's Pass 153, 167–168, *168*, 223
Giant's Ridge 159, 162, 163, 166
Gibisila Ridge 142, 143, 145
global positioning system (GPS) 14, 93
Goat's Herd Summit Cave 218
Gorge Cave 209, 211
GPS 14, 93
grading of hikes 12–13
Grasscutters Cave 74
Gray's Pass 104, 106, 113, 117–119, *118*, 130, 225
Greyia sutherlandii 20, *21*
grey rhebuck 26, *27*
Grindstone Caves 136, 138, 142–143, *142*, 145, *177*
    and Marble Baths 143–144, *144*
Grysbok Bush *156*, 157, 166
Gudu Bush and Falls 42–43, *43*, 62
Guernsey lily 22, *24*, 39
Gxalingenwa Cave 199, 200
Gxalingenwa Forest 195
Gxalingenwa River Trail 199–200, *199*
Gypaetus barbatus see lammergeier

Halleria lucida 43
Harpechloa flax 23
Helichrysum sp. 22, *24*, *178*, *181*
Hemachatus haemachatus 28, *28*
Heteropogon contortus 22
Highmoor 163, 168
Highveld protea 20, *21*
Hillside Camp 136, 168
Himeville Arms 171, 192, 234
Hlathikulu Nek 111, 113, 117, 131
Hlathimba Cave 189
Hlathimba Pass 153, 170, 172, 223
    and Redi Peak 188–189, *189*
Hodgson's Peaks 193
Hyparrhenia grass 215

Icidi Pass 73–74, *74*, 227
Ifidi Pass 40, *74*, 75, 227
Ilex mitis 23, 161
Injisuthi
    hikes 137–151
    overview 134–136
Injisuthi Camp 130

Injisuthi Dome 104
Inkosana Lodge and Trekking 107, 130, 233
Intunja 131
Jacob's Ladder 110, 111, 116, 192
Jacob's Ladder Falls *203*
Jarateng Pass 223
Jarding (Jarateng) passes 223
Jubilee Cave 74
Junction Cave 33, 130, 136, 144
June grass 23

KaMashilenga Pass 170, 172, *183*, 223
Kamberg 31–32, 170, 192
kaNtuba Pass 170, 190, 222
Keith Bush Camp 113, 118, 131, 146
Keith Bush Hut 106
Kelvin Grove camp site 107
klipspringer 26, *27*
Kniphofia sp. *24*, 55, *201*
Koeleria cristata 23
KwaZulu–Natal bottlebrush 20, *21*

Lake District 212–213, *212*
Lakes Cave 209, 210, 211, 212
lammergeier 9, 28, 37, 160, 154, 194
Lammergeier Cave 219
Langalibalele Cave 198
Langalibalele Pass 153, 165, 166–167, *166*, 224
Ledger's Cave 37, *53*, *55*, 67, 69
Leonotis leonurus 23, 118, 136
Leopard Cave 132
Leslie's Pass 130, 136, 144, 149–151, *150*, 224
Leucosidea sericea 21, *23*, 67, 118, 157
Lion Buttress 57–59, *58*
Little Saddle 103
Lotheni Pass *183*, 223
Lotheni rest camp 170
Lotheni to Sani Pass 172–174, *173*, *174*, *175*
Lotheni via Contour Path 163–164, *164*
Lower Injisuthi Cave 136, *140*, 141–142
Lynx Cave 172–173

McKenzie's Caves 185–186, *186*
Mafadi Peak 104, 141, 150
Mahai camp site 10, 38, 40
    hike from Rugged Glen 61–62, *62*
    hike to Gudu Falls 42–43, *43*
Main Caves hike 154–155, *156*
Makhela's Kraal 69, 70

Manguan Pass 222
maps 13–14, 16
   Amphitheatre *49*
   Cathedral Peak area *121*
   Cobham area *204*
   Drakensberg *34, 35*
   Garden Castle area *208*
   Giant's Castle area *180*
   Injisuthi area *128*
   Mhomazi area *184*
   Mnweni *54*
   Monk's Cowl area *125*
Marble Baths 87, 150
   and Grindstone Caves 143–144, *144*
Marble Baths Cave 136
Mashai Cave 215, 216
Mashai Pass 195, 221
   and Rhino Peak 215–216, *216*
Mashai Peak 215
Masongwana Gorge 92–93, *93*
Masubasuba Pass 200, 222
Maytenus heterophylla 22, *24*
Mbundini Pass 72–73
Mdedelelo 112, *126*
   see also Cathkin Peak
Meander Hut hike 158, *158*
Merxmuellera grass 199
Mike's Pass 91, 92, 99, 100, 103, 135
Minaret Pass 210, 222
Mkhomazi and Nhlangeni Pass
   190, 191–192
Mkhomazi Pass 170, 222–223
Mkhomazi Wilderness Area 164
   hikes 172–192
   overview 169–172
Mlahlangubo Pass 170, 173, 223
Mlambonja Buttress 100
Mlambonja Pass 98, 99–100, 226
   to Twins Cave 84–85, *85*
Mlambonja Valley hike 86–87, *87*
Mnweni 53
   hikes 65–78
   overview 63–65
Mnweni Baths 63
Mnweni Pass 65–67, *68*, 226–227
Mohlesi 170, 190, 191–192
monkey rope 42, 109
Monk's Cowl 102, *177*
   hikes 107–133
   history 104–107
Monk's Cowl Cave 114–115, 215
Monk's Cowl from Contour Path
   145–146, *146*

Monk's Cowl to Upper Didima Valley
   130–132, *133*
Mont-aux-Sources 36, 38–40, *39*, 51
Montusi 232
moraea lily 24
Moraea sp. 24
mountain olinia *24*, 109
mountain reedbuck 26, *26*
mountain safety 151
mountain sage 157, 199
Mountain Splendour Caravan &
   Camping Park 107
mountain wild pear 109
Mount Durnford 153
Mpofana 153
Mponjwane Cave 67, 69
Mponjwane Pinnacle *56*
Mqatsheni Pass 222
Mtshezana Stream 148
Mushroom Rock 98, 99
   and Tarn Hill 95, *96*
Mzimkhulu
   hikes 195–219
   overview 193–195
Mzimkhulu Pass 213–214, *213*, 221
Mzimude Pass 221

Nana-berry 22, *23*
Ncema grass 199
Ndumeni Dome Cave 100
Ndumeni Valley *122*
Neptune's Pool 86
Nerine sarniensis 22, *24*, 39
Ngaqamadola passes 173, 189–190,
   190, 223
Ngenwa Pool 196
Ngenwa River round-trip 200, *200*, 209
Ngodwini Stream 188
Nguza Pass 69
Ngwangwane Pass 220
Nhlangeni Pass 173, *190*, 191–192, 222
Nhlangeni Peak 173, 191, 192
Nkosana *see* Monk's Cowl
Nkosazana Cave 119, 120
Nkosazana River 131
Nkosazana Valley 119, 130
Ntonjelana Pass 70–71, *71*, 226
Ntshinitshini Pass 222
Nutcracker Cave 211, 212
Nxwaye River 90
Nyosi Grotto and Blue Pool hike
   98–99, *99*
Nzinga River 185

Old man's beard lichens 42, 109
Old Woman Grinding Corn 134,
   143, *177*
Old Woman Stream Valley 142, 143, 145
Olinia emarginata 24, 109
One Tree Hill 85, 89
Oqalweni Circuit 88–89, *89*
Oqalweni Valley walk 87–88, *88*
Orange Peel Gap 83, 89, 90
Oreotragus oreotragus 26, *27*
Organ Pipes Pass 93, 95, 97, 98,
   99–100, 225
oribi 26, *26*
Oribi Ridge 163
ouhout 21, *23*, 67, 118, 157
Ourebia ourebi 26, *26*

Pelea capreolus 26, *27*
Philip's Folly 103
Phinong Pass 170
Pholela Cave 209, 211
   and Amakehla Pass 209–210, *210*
photography 78, 112, 115, 176
Pimple Hill 149
Pinnacle (Nhlangeni Peak) 192
Plowman's Kop and Spa Pools hike
   43–44, *44*
Plumpudding Hill 190
Poa binata 23
Poacher's Cave 95, 132
Poacher's Stream and Boundary Pool
   138–139, *139*
Podocarpus falcatus 21, *23*
Podocarpus latifolius 21, *23*
Popple Peak 148, 161
Protea caffra 20, *21, 23,* 41
Protea dracomontana 22, 162
Protea nubigena 22, *24,* 46
Protea roupelliae 20, *21,* 41
proteas 20, 20–21, *21, 22,* 41
Protea savanna 20
Protea subvestita 20, 196
Pteridium aquilinum 215
puff adder 28, *28*
Pyramid Peak 81, 97, 100, 192

Qedimbuzi Stream 149

Rainbow Gorge hike 91–92, *91, 123*
red-hot poker *24,* 55, *201*
Redi Pass 223
Redi Peak 168, 170, 172, *182,*
   188–189, *189*

red oat grass 21, *22*
Redunca fulvorufula 26, *26*
Rhino Pass 221
Rhino Peak *205*, 215–216, *216*
Rhus dentata 22, *23*
Ribbon Falls 98
rinkhals 28, *28*
river lily *24*, 42
rock art 30–33, 140
  Cathedral Peak area 103
  Cobham area 194
  Eland Cave *124*, 155
  Game Pass Shelter 31–32, 170, 175–176, *176*, *202*
  Giant's Castle 154, 155
  Main Caves 154, 155
  Monk's Cowl area 132
  Rhino Peak 216
Rockeries Pass 68–69, *68*, 226
Royal Natal Hotel 37
Rugged Glen to Mahai 61–62, *62*
Rwanqa Pass 227
Rydal Mount Hotel 37

Sagewood 22, *24*
Sagittarius serpentarius 162
Sani Pass 171, 192, 222
Sani Top Chalet 171–172, 192, 234
Sani Valley 234
Sani Valley Lodge 234
Scaly Cave 69
Scaly Peak 141
Schizostylis coccinea 24, 42
Schoongezicht Cave 132
Secamone 42, 109
secretary bird 161
Sehlaba Thebe Caves traverse 218–219, *219*
Sehlaba Thebe Park 194
Senqu (Orange) River 36–37
Sgonqweni Cave 83, 90
Sheba's Breasts 164
Shepherd's Cave 67, 72
Sherman's Cave 89
  and Ganapu Ridge 90–91, *90*
Ship's Prow Pass 119, 120, 129–130, *129*, 150, 224–225
Ship's Prow Stream gully 145
Sholoti Stream 149
Sigubudu Ridge to Surprise Ridge 46–47, *47*
silver protea 20, *21*
Sinclair's Shelter hike 176, 185, *185*

sleeping bags 12
Sleeping Beauty Cave hike 214–215, *214*
snakes 27–28, *28*, 60, 187
Solar Cliffs 93, 94
Solitude Resort 134, 136
Spare Rib Cave 10, 165
Spectacle Cave 209, 211
Speirs' Cave 193, 213
Sphinx 103, 117, 120, 131, 146
spitting cobra 28, *28*
Stable Cave 110–111, *111*, 116
Steilberg and Van Damm's Cascade 109–110, *111*
Stones Passes 210, 213, 221–222
Streptocarpus 42
Surprise Ridge 46–47, *47*
  and Cannibal Cave hike 48, *48*, 57
Swiman Hut 196, 197, 198

Tarn Cave 219
Tarn Hill and Mushroom Rock 95, *96*
Tendele Hutted Camp 37
tents 10, 11, 210
Thaba Ntlenyana 170, 190, 192
Thaba Ntsu 194
The Camel Pass 95, 97, 98, 99, 100, 225
The Gable 163
The Grotto hike 60–61, *60*
The Hawk 168, 170
The Judge 148
Themeda triandra 21, *22*
The Molar 144, 150
The Nest 107, 233
The Rhino 194
The Tent 168, 170
The Thumb 162
Thlanyaku Pass 103, 225
Thomathu Cave 219
Thomathu Pass 218, 220
Thukela Falls 36
Thukela Gorge hike 40–42, *41*
Thuthumi Pass 95, 225
Trachypogon spicatus 22
Tragelaphus scriptus 26, *26*
tree fern 21, *22*, 109
Tree Fern Cave 136, 139, 148–149, *149*
tree fuchsia 43
Triplets 135, 141, 142
Tryme Hill and waterfalls hike 96–97, *96*, 98
Tseketseke Hut 97–98, *98*, 102

Tseketseke Pass 100, *124*, 225–226
tussock grass 21, *22*
Twins Cave 70, 84, 85, 99
Two Dassie Stream 156, 157, 159, 162, 163
Two Passes hike 99–100, 101

Umtshezi River 157
Underberg 194
Usnea lichen 42, 109

Vaalribbokkop 116
Valley of Pools 111, 116–117, *116*
Van Damm's Cascade 109–110, 111
Van Heynigen's Pass 135, 137, *137*, 145, 146
vegetation 20–25, *21*, *22*, *23*, *24*
Vemvaan Valley 41, 45, *45*, 46
Venice Caves 211
Vergelegen 170, 192
Verkyker Cave 213
Verkyker Pass 221
Verkykerskop 111
Vultures' Retreat 119, *127*, 131

Wahlenbergia grandiflora* 119
Wahlenbergia undulata 22, 119
Wahlenbergia zeyheri 119
Waterfall Cave 63, 64
  and Ntonjelana Pass 70–71, *71*
watsonia *202*
wattled crane 196
Weaver Cave 211
white stinkwood *23*
wild dagga *24*, 118, 136
wild pear tree 109
Wilson's Cave 213
Winterhoek camp 196
Witch Peak 132
Witzieshoek Mountain Resort 37, 232
Wonder Valley 143
Wonder Valley Cave 113, 129, 136, *137*, 138, 146, *178*

Xeni Cave 85, 86
Xeni Pass 100

Yellowwood Cave 172, 186–187, *187*
yellowwoods 21, *23*

Zulu Cave 113–114, *114*, 117, 131
Zulu etiquette 77